T·H·E
DADDY
GUIDE

Real-Life Advice and Tips from over 250 Dads and Other Experts

Kevin Nelson

CONTEMPORARY BOOKS

Library of Congress Cataloging-in-Publication Data

Nelson, Kevin, 1953–   .
       The daddy guide : real-life advice and tips from over 250 dads and other experts
A to Z / Kevin Nelson.
             p.   cm.
       Includes bibliographical references and index.
       ISBN 0-8092-2963-3
       1. Fatherhood—United States. 2. Parenting—United States. 3. Child rearing—
United States. 4. Marriage—United States. I. Title.
       HQ756.N45 1998
       649′.1—dc21   97-47047
                                                                        CIP

Cover design by Jeanette Wojtyla
Cover and interior illustration copyright © Laura Jane Coats
Interior design by Nancy Freeborn

Published by Contemporary Books
An imprint of NTC/Contemporary Publishing Group, Inc.
4255 West Touhy Avenue, Lincolnwood (Chicago), Illinois 60646-1975 U.S.A.
Printed in the United States of America
International Standard Book Number: 0-8092-2963-3

15   14   13   12   11   10   9   8   7   6   5   4   3   2   1

For my daughters, Leah and Annie,
and my father, Delmar Nelson

CONTENTS

PREFACE ix

ADVICE AND INSPIRATION 1
The Greatest Job You'll Ever Have • Coping Skills • Advice from an Elder •
Ignore the Media: You *Can* Do It

BECOMING A FATHER 12
What We Fear as Fathers • Being a Dad in a Mom's World • Another Tool for Dads: The Net •
Web Sites for Fathers and Families

BIRTH COACH 21
Why You Should Be a Birth Coach: A Nurse's View • How to Be a Great Labor Coach •
Cutting the Cord: A Man's Prerogative • What to Bring to the Hospital

CARS 30
Now That I Have a Bigger Family, Do I Need a Bigger Car? • Sports-Utes: Choice of the
Rugged, Macho Family Man • Minivans: A More Practical Alternative? • Station Wagons •
Children and Car Seats • Children and Air Bags • More Car Resources

CHILD CARE AND PRESCHOOLS 39
Men and Child Care • Use Those Analytical Skills: Questions to Ask When Assessing
Child Care • Child-Care Centers • Family Child Care • Nannies • How to Find Child Care •
Preschools

CLUBS AND OUTDOOR ACTIVITIES 52
Bicycling: A Part of Growing Up • Canoeing: A Passion for Traveling on Water •
Camping: Start Simply and Progress from There • Selling the Experience of Fishing •
Hiking: Creating a Love of Nature • Youth Organizations and Clubs •
More Activities for You and Your Child

COOKING AND FOOD 65
Fundamentals of Good Cooking • How Not to Be Intimidated in the Kitchen •
Cooking Resources • Dining Out with Baby and Other Food Topics • Cooking with
Children: Do You Dare?

DIAPERS AND OTHER MANLY CHORES 76

Changing Diapers and Other Household Issues • Diapering Tips • Housework: Doing a
Good, Clean, Fast Job • Schlepping the Baby: Problems and Solutions

DISCIPLINE 88

The Key to Discipline: Remembering Your Own Childhood • Do Babies Manipulate? •
Ten Reasons Not to Spank a Child • Tips on Handling Toddlers • The TOUGHLOVE Approach

GROWING A CHILD: WHAT FATHERS CAN DO 100

Being Involved: Good for Baby, Good for You • A Child Needs Dad in the Tender Years, Too •
Connecting with Your Child • Let Your Child Take the Lead: Techniques for Play •
Open Your Mouth and Sing • Becoming a Better Listener

HEALTHY AND SAFE BABY 113

A Thumbnail Guide to Infant Health • Immunization Guidelines • How to Get a Good
Night's Sleep • Circumcision: One Physician's View • Circumcision: Another Physician's View •
Kidproofing and Baby Products • A Safe Crib Is a Good Crib • Health Care Resources

HOUSEHOLD AND FAMILY EMERGENCIES 129

Infant CPR • Burn Prevention Measures • What to Keep in Your First-Aid Kit •
Fire Prevention Checklist • Preparing for a Disaster

JOB, CAREER, AND FAMILY 136

How to Be a Responsible Father • Working Nights and Weekends • Don't Bring It Home
with You • Real-World Strategies for Fathers Who Want to Take Time Off When Their Baby
Is Born • The Daddy Track and Other Hard Realities • Changing Jobs When You Have a Family •
Downsizing Your Lifestyle: Pluses and Minuses • Running a Small Business and Being
a New Dad • Working at Home

LIFE INSURANCE 153

Now That I Have a Child, Do I Need Life Insurance? • Term or Whole Life? • Finding the Right Agent

LOVE AND SEX 159

Maintaining Connections with Your Partner and Child • Being on the "Same Team" with
Your Spouse • Sex and the New Father • Tips on Having a Healthy Sex Life

MISCELLANY 170

Naming Your Child • Eight Reasons to Celebrate Your Child's Birth with a Cigar • Coping with
In-Laws • Raising Twins • When to Have Another Child and What to Expect If You Do

MONEY 181

How to Get Out of Debt and Stay There • Taking Care of the Nickels • Creating a Stress-Free
Family Budget • Marde's Money Advice • Finding Out Where You Stand • A Few Words
About Retirement • Teaching Kids About Money

OWNING A HOME 196

The Difference Between a House and a Home • Family and Home • Questions to Ask
Yourself Before You Buy • Home Buying Resources • Owning a Home: A Matter of Values

PETS 206
Cats and Babies • Dogs and Babies • We Have Seen the Future, and It Is Furry

READING ALOUD 213
Do the Right Thing: Read Aloud to Your Kids • Great Read-Aloud Books • Reading to Your
Kids: An Actor's Perspective • Poetry: For Men and Boys, Too • Read, Read, Read • Kid 'Zines

SAVING FOR COLLEGE 224
Saving for College: An Overview • How to Develop a Bundle for College • College
Investment Plans • More Options and Resources

SPIRITUALITY 233
Fatherhood as a Spiritual Journey • Is Faith Important in a Family? • Worshipping with
Your Family • Fishing and the Spiritual Life • Transmitting Values to Your Children

SPORTS 245
Basketball: There Are Only Barriers of the Mind • Golf: Teaching the Game for a Lifetime •
Gymnastics: Developing Coordination, Flexibility, and Self-Confidence • Hockey: Let Your
Kid Play Other Sports Too • Little League: Stay Positive and Keep the Focus on Fun •
Football: Learning to Play—and Cheerlead • Soccer: Does Your Child Enjoy Playing Without You? •
Swimming: A Gift for Life • Tennis: Playing Without Adult Responsibilities and Pressures

SUPPORTING MOM 259
Taking Care of Mom During Pregnancy • The Ultrasound Exam: Is It a Boy . . . or a Girl? •
More About the Ultrasound and How You Can Help • After the Baby Comes Home

TELEVISION 269
How to Take Control of Your TV • Living in a TV-Free Zone: One Father's Story •
Warning: Watching Sports on TV May Be Hazardous to Family Life

TOYS, PROJECTS, COMPUTERS 278
Common Sense Wisdom About Toys • Toy Safety • Toy Catalogs • Work Projects for
Father and Child • Computers and Kids • Children's Software

TRAVEL: BUSINESS AND FAMILY 290
One Dad's View: Put Those Travel Plans on Hold • Traveling with a Baby • The Grand Tour:
Traveling Overseas with a Family • Business Travel: Staying in Touch with Your Family •
More Tips When You Have to Travel on Business • Easy Travel to Distant Web Sites

VIDEO AND PHOTOGRAPHY 302
How to Shoot Great Video • Tips on Buying a Camcorder • Photography: How to Take
Great Baby Pictures • What Camera Should I Buy?

BIBLIOGRAPHY 311

INDEX 315

PREFACE

Never before have so many experts come together in one book with one purpose in mind: to give advice and counsel to new and expectant fathers. Many of the experts interviewed in this book are fathers themselves. When speaking with them, I often asked them to talk as if to a new or expectant father. So, in large part, *The Daddy Guide* consists of fathers speaking to new and expectant fathers on the multifaceted subject of fatherhood: what it means to be a father, the changes that have occurred and will occur in a new father's life, the issues each new father now faces as a family man, how to be a loving and supportive partner, and how to raise children with the respect, dignity, and love they deserve.

This is a book for fathers. But it's also a book for mothers. I suspect that many women will dip into these pages to find out what men are saying and thinking. Much of the advice in these pages applies equally well to both parents, though I describe this book as a "parenting" manual only reluctantly. *Parenting* these days is a euphemism for "mothering." When a man sees a book or magazine with *parenting* in the title (or a variation thereof), he naturally and reasonably shuns it like the plague. He knows it's not for him. He knows it's probably intended for a female audience.

The Daddy Guide is the exception: a parenting guide written for men, from the man's point of view. Fatherhood being a big subject, I took a "big tent" approach to it. Everyone (or at least everyone I could get hold of) has a say. Grandfathers, fathers, sons—the views of several generations of men are contained here. I wanted this book to speak to all dads: white dads, black dads, Hispanic dads, Asian dads, single dads, divorced dads, stay-at-home dads, working dads, conservative dads, liberal dads, Christian dads, Jewish dads, agnostic dads, teenage dads, Gen-X dads, middle-aged dads, homosexual dads, living-with-a-partner dads, and, yes, even happily married heterosexual dads. Fathers of all types are represented in this book, although there is nothing that specifically refers to any of these groups. I believe that what we have in common as fathers is larger than what separates us. When you're a dad, first and foremost, you're a dad. The rest are details.

I proudly note that some of the experts interviewed in this book are women, many of whom are moms. They, too, occupy an honored place in this book. Grandmothers, mothers, and daughters all have a say on how men can be good dads—how they can help and support their partners and love and nurture their children.

This book contains advice and wisdom from more than two hundred experts. These men and women live in every part of the United States and Canada. Some of the occupations represented in this book are financial planner, policeman, author, psychologist, rabbi, salesman, teacher, social worker, nurse, insurance agent, actor, coach, magazine editor, consultant, general building contractor, navy lieutenant, minister, student, financial director, university professor, therapist, bank examiner, physician, small business owner, principal, spiritual director, adventure writer, furniture maker, real estate broker, and stay-at-home dad.

Several of the experts interviewed in this book are internationally recognized authorities in their fields. Many of the experts (including these same authorities) have written books on the subject about which they're being interviewed; some of these books have reached the bestseller lists. Other experts, while perhaps not as well known, are highly successful in their chosen careers. Still more of the experts are fathers who have years of experience in what they're discussing. (Throughout the book, at the end of each section, I've given source notes; contact information, including web sites or E-mail addresses when available; and additional information and tips. I hope you find these useful.)

One stereotype about men is that they are less verbal than women and, hence, less willing to talk. I didn't find that to be the case. All of the experts I spoke with—men and women—gave generously of their time and considerable knowledge, and I am deeply indebted to all of them for their help. If this book has any relevance to new fathers, and I think it does, it is due to the hundreds of people who contributed to it.

More than 150 companies and organizations are cited in these pages, as are dozens and dozens of books. I made every effort to cite further resources for new and expectant fathers on the topics I covered, so that if they have more questions, they'll know where to get the answers. One caveat: phone numbers, addresses, and web sites do change. Those listed in the book are accurate to the best of my ability at the time of publication.

When you become a father, all of your life changes—every inch of it—and the subject matter of *The Daddy Guide* reflects this. Just flip to the table of contents and you'll see what I mean. In writing a book of such vast scope, I found myself touched by the life and death dramas of two of the fathers with whom I spoke. One father suffered a brain aneurysm and fell into a coma the day after I interviewed him. I learned about it the week after we spoke. At the time of his sudden, chilling collapse, he and his wife were preparing to celebrate their daughter's first birthday. As I write this, he has just emerged from his coma and is showing signs of progress. He may yet defy the odds and pull out of it. Another father whom I contacted for this book was in the middle of a different sort of family crisis: his older boy (a teenager) was suffering from leukemia, while his healthy, younger son was getting ready to undergo a bone-marrow transplant operation to save his brother's life. These two fathers contributed to this book, and my gratitude and prayers go out to them and their families.

It took me about nine months to research and write this book, but I think I can reasonably argue that I've been working on it since 1988 when my first daughter, Annie, was born. I have two daughters, Annie and Leah. We have just celebrated Annie's ninth birthday. Leah died when she was five days old from complications suffered after birth. I love being a dad. It gives me immense joy and satisfaction. However, as a father I've also experienced incredible sadness over Leah, a sadness that, in some ways, never lifts.

It takes guts to become a dad (or a mom), and sometimes it calls on reserves buried deep inside you that you're not sure you possess. I hope what happened to Leah and the story of these two fathers doesn't scare any prospective readers away. Being a father is the most rewarding thing I've ever done in my life. In fact, while writing this book, I learned I am going to become a dad again. I enjoy being a father more than anything else I do. It's a kick being with my kid. It's fun watching her grow up. I probably laugh with my daughter more than with anyone else, and so I've tried (I hope the effort isn't too visible) to pack this book with lots of humor. Dad humor, if you will. The worst kind of all.

It is my belief that while men can be found pontificating and editorializing on every issue under the sun, when it comes to communicating the love they feel for their children and partners and the love they need in their own lives, they often fall strangely silent. Partly this is due to embarrassment, I think. They have a harder time showing affection (or need) than women. Men clearly want to be judged by their deeds. I am always amused by feature articles in the newspaper about men and women of accomplishment. Invariably, if the woman has children, they are mentioned prominently in the article as a sign that indeed, *she has it all*. But children are seldom cited in an article about a man. He doesn't mention them, and the writer doesn't ask.

But we guys certainly do care about our kids, though we may show it in different ways and not talk or write about it nearly as much. *The Daddy Guide*, fittingly I think, contains more interviews with fathers than any other book I've ever seen. Fathers talk in their own voices, about their children and partners and families, and how meaningful these people are in their lives.

Fathers get knocked around a lot these days. If you believe what you read in the papers or see on TV, you might think that fathers today are incompetent, child-abusing deadbeats with a lust for battering and bloodshed. The fact is that this generation of fathers participates more actively in their children's lives than any previous generation in history. We are present in the lives of our children. *The Daddy Guide* is one small reflection of that. My goal in writing it was to recognize the often-slighted contributions of fathers, to inspire new and expectant fathers to participate in the lives of their kids, and to give them the tools to do it.

The emphasis in the book is on new and expectant fathers, but I think even veteran dads—fathers of six-year-olds and twelve-year-olds and seventeen-year-olds—can learn from this book. I have a nine-year-old daughter, and I learned a lot writing it. So much emphasis these days is put on nurturing a child when he or she is a baby, in the earliest years of life. This is certainly vital, but being a dad means being there for your child in the first year of life and the second year and the third year and the fourth year and the fifth year and all the years after that.

In the interests of inclusiveness, as well as simplicity, for the most part I used the term *partner* rather than *wife*. Jennifer and I weren't married when Leah was born, so I am hardly one to expect that all the men and women who have children (and who read this book) will be married. The essential message of this book—love your children and participate actively in their lives—applies equally well to married and unmarried couples. Most parents would agree that the ideal mate is one who pitches in and helps raise the child together—that is, a partner. Thus, the use of the term.

I want to thank three women in particular for their contributions to *The Daddy Guide*. Susan Bernard wrote *The Mommy Guide*, which served as a role model for this book. My editor, Kara Leverte, pegged me as a father who might enjoy writing a book of this kind. She was right. It was a great opportunity for me, and I thank her for it. She got me started in the right direction and provided wisdom and guidance throughout. Jennifer Kaiser, my wife *and* partner, read some sections of the book and made many helpful comments. We often discussed many of these topics over the dinner table, and her ideas and advice helped me immensely. Her love serves as a source of strength always.

Kevin Nelson

So you're about to become a father or you already are one. *Congratulations! Welcome to the club. What took you so long?*

In the movie City Slickers, *Billy Crystal, Daniel Stern, and Bruno Kirby play three lifelong friends who live in New York City. Each in the midst of his own midlife crisis, they sign on for a cattle drive in the West. They ride horses, rope cattle, and, for a time, live the life of a cowboy. There's a wonderful scene in which one day, they're all riding together and Daniel Stern's character, in a philosophical mood, asks each of them to talk about the "best day" of his life—not counting the day when their kids were born. "That's too easy," says Stern.*

The Billy Crystal character says the best day of his life was when his father took him to Yankee Stadium for the first time. Daniel Stern's character comes next. He says his best day was his wedding day when his father gave him a little wink during the ceremony. "I felt like a man. I made it," said Stern.

Bruno Kirby's character's best day was also his worst. His mom and dad were fighting. His father was cheating on his mother and, while still a young man, Bruno confronted him about it. He told his father that he and his mom didn't want him around anymore. From then on, he'd take care of the family. His father left and never came back.

Three men, three memories. Each man's memory of the best day of his life involved his father. Granted this was a movie, but my guess is that most men, if asked to recall the best day of their lives apart from the birth of their own children, would probably talk about their father, too. I know I would.

> "Kids don't pick up training because parents sit around and talk to them about values. Children watch their parents live values. Youngsters don't care about what you say, but they watch what you do."
> —General Colin Powell, father of Michael, Linda, and Annemarie

■

> "A man is a family thing. His meaning is a family meaning."
> —Writer William Saroyan, father of Lucy and Aram

The best day of my life was when I was twelve years old. I hit two home runs in a Little League All-Star Game. My father, whose eyes were failing because of a diabetic condition, saw the balls fly over the fence. He died three months after the game. He's been dead more than thirty years. I think of him every day of my life.

There is no higher calling—not president, not general, not senator—than being a father. Being a dad is a never-ending education. You're always learning what you don't know. And you never get it right entirely.

But if you're like me, nothing in your life will be as important or as meaningful to you as being a father. It's the most challenging, yet rewarding job I know. You make mistakes and you do the best you can. Most people want to "make a difference" during their life. Being a good dad is one way to make a difference.

And if you play your cards right, who knows? Maybe someday your kids will be asked about the best day of their life, and they'll talk about you.

THE GREATEST JOB YOU'LL EVER HAVE

A father is essential and irreplaceable. Both in the family and in society at large, only a father can do a father's job. These simple thoughts lie at the heart of David Blankenhorn's message. The founder and president of the Institute for American Values in New York City, Blankenhorn is the author of *Fatherless America*, an important and controversial book about what it means to be a father today. He lectures widely and talks to dads around the country about the issues they face. He is the father of Raymond, Sophia, and Alexandra.

Q: What do you enjoy most about being a father?
Blankenhorn: The first thing is that it allows me to be relaxed and silly and playful. I'm kind of a wound-up guy normally. I take a very serious approach to life. But there's this sense of playfulness when I'm with my kids. It's fun to do things that make people laugh.

Q: That's important though, isn't it? That's one of the things that a child looks for in a father.
Blankenhorn: Children tend to look to mothers for soothing and comfort. They tend to look to fathers for stimulation, playfulness, rough and tumble play. The father–child relationship tends to be more stimulating, more exciting. Fathers spend a higher proportion of their time with children in play.

Q: *You read a lot these days about what makes a good father. Is there only one way to be a dad?*

Blankenhorn: It's pretty obvious that there isn't only one way to be a good father. There's not one personality type or one kind of man. But fatherhood is a social role. There are core ingredients of fatherhood that need to be there.

Q: *Such as?*

Blankenhorn: The first is the provider–protector role. Men are pretty well hardwired for that. It's our primary job as fathers: to provide for and protect our family. The second essential role is as teacher and coach—what scholars call the task of cultural transmission. Teaching our kids what it means to be a responsible person, passing on a way of life. Not just providing for our child's physical survival, but raising a person who has character and integrity. Mothers do this, too, but we fathers bring our own set of skills to the task.

Q: *Provider, protector, teacher, coach. Are there other core ingredients of being a father?*

Blankenhorn: Nurturer. This is the day-to-day raising of the child. Making sure your children brush their teeth, dressing them warmly, reading them bedtime stories. In the past nurturing was essentially the domain of mothers. Now fathers are more involved in this area. They're more demonstrative in their feelings toward their children. More fathers today freely say "I love you" to their children, whereas their fathers may have been more emotionally restrained.

Q: *I'm glad you mentioned these other jobs that fathers do because so much emphasis these days is put on the nurturing side.*

Blankenhorn: I know. It's all about 50/50 duties in the household. Some people want to collapse everything about being a dad to: Does he change diapers? Does he get up in the middle of the night? I have two sixteen-month-old twins. I can go toe-to-toe with any father in the numbers of diapers I've changed, but it's not the main issue. It's missing the point. It's not the way you measure a father's contribution. This period in a child's life doesn't last very long. What happens after that?

Q: *A lot of fathers take great pride in their nurturing skills, though. They've become very good at it.*

Blankenhorn: Fathers can nurture, absolutely. There are fathers out there who on a scale of one to ten rate about a twelve. They're fantastic fathers. But in the nurturing arena, men typically follow the leadership of the mom. They're often coached by the mom. Mom plays the chief role in nurturing the child. In one sense, the father's special role

"I could not point to any need in childhood as strong as that for a father's protection."
—Sigmund Freud, father of Mathilde

■

"If it wasn't for my father, I think I might be in jail now, not the NBA. He always taught me to do the right thing, to never forget my roots, and to never forget that I've been fortunate."
—NBA star Shaquille O'Neal, son of Phillip Harrison

"My father saved my life. I am what I am because of him."

—Oprah Winfrey, daughter of Vernon Winfrey

■

"My dad used to tell me that you're never as good as they say you are when they say you're good, and you're never as bad as they say you are when they say you're bad. And once you understand that, you can survive all this."

—Actor George Clooney, son of Nick

is to nurture the mother. Give her a back rub, tell her she's beautiful. Your job at a deeper level is to help her. Part of the way you do that is by changing diapers and sharing in household tasks and nurturing the child. But fathers will never be as good at being moms as moms are.

Q: Fathers are not junior moms or No. 2 moms, in other words. I think that's an important message for new dads who may be struggling with how to handle all their new responsibilities.
Blankenhorn: Becoming a father is the single most transformative life experience for men. It changes them the most, with marriage possibly causing the next biggest change. Becoming a father changes how you look at yourself, how you view your parents, your relationship with your wife. It changes and deepens a man in profound ways, probably more than any other experience he has in life. After he has a baby, a man gets worried about things. He asks himself, Do I need to work harder? Should I ask for a raise? Maybe he takes care of insurance that he's been neglecting. His anxiety is about being a good provider, and this anxiety is a sign of health and maturity. Men think about whether they can create a home where their children are provided for and protected. Moms tend to focus on the nurturing. As I say, dads need to nurture the moms, and one of the ways they can support mom is to turn their attention to these other areas.

Q: Is it harder to be a good father than it used to be?
Blankenhorn: When I was researching my book I asked that same question to hundreds of dads around the country, and they said it was. These were not wimps, either. These were regular guys—blue collar guys and professionals, everybody. There were two reasons why they felt it was harder. First, the larger society does not support family life and the passing on of good values to children. Men feel like they're swimming upstream. Children watch TV, they go to movies, the neighborhood's iffy, it's not safe outside, drugs in schools—it's harder to protect your child. The second reason was that the list of attributes that defines a good father keeps getting longer and longer. I was born in 1955. The standard view of a father at that time was that he needed to be a good provider, not cheat on his wife, don't be abusive, be a good role model, and spend some time with your kids. Nowadays, there's all of that and more. A good father needs to be flexible in sharing household duties, he needs to be intimate with his partner and emotionally available to her, he needs to bond with his children. Moms are often not in the home taking care of the children as their moms were, so men must do more of the chores and more of the child raising than they used to. Much of that is very rewarding. But it makes it harder.

Q: Is it worth the effort? Is being a good dad a worthwhile endeavor?

Blankenhorn: Fatherhood is the best thing that happens to most men. Some guys get to be king or president or CEO of some big company and have their own Lear jet. Some guys are like Michael Jordan. But for most men, being a father is the most important thing they will ever do in their life. It's the biggest contribution to society they will ever make. And when they look back at the end of their life, very few guys will say, "If only I'd spent more time at my job or bought that racehorse I'd always dreamed about." Most men will look back and think about their families and they'll ask themselves, "Who was I as a son? Who was I as a husband and a father?"

Contact: The Institute for American Values is a nonprofit organization devoted to family issues. It publishes a newsletter, answers questions, and provides information for fathers and their families. Institute for American Values, 1841 Broadway, Room 211, New York, NY 10023; 212-246-3942.

COPING SKILLS

When Dr. Arthur Law became a father, he noticed that his wife started going to support groups for new mothers. He began looking around for similar groups for new fathers and, not surprisingly, found none. So Law, who's a pediatrician, took the unusual step of forming one at the hospital where he practices. For over twenty months he has conducted once-a-month chat sessions with new fathers and their babies. The babies mostly cry, eat, and sleep while their dads talk and listen. They learn about feeding their babies solid foods, how to get a good night's sleep, checking that infant car seats are safe, and other practical topics. Equally important, they realize that the problems they face are not unique to them. In talking to these men (and through his own experience with his infant son, Anthony), Law has learned some coping skills that he would like to pass on to other new fathers. They are as follows:

Reach Out. Men like to think they can do it all themselves. To ask for help or simply needing to talk to someone is to show weakness on some level—"the tough guy image," as Law says. But it may be useful to join a group like Law's (if one exists in your area) where you can be around other new fathers and their babies. Fathers do not receive the social support that mothers do. When Law is running errands with his son people say to him, "Oh, you're baby-sitting." It's very common for fathers to hear that. When a man spends time with his child, he's baby-sitting. When a woman spends time with her child, she's caring for

"Exercise is the sure cure for me. I get on my bike and push until I'm almost in pain. A good workout clears my head. It helps me realize that there's nothing that serious that could happen to us that we're not going to get through it as a family."
—Policeman Jim Taranto, father of Ariel

■

"Never lie, [my father] told me, never break your word, be always respectful of others and protective of women, and never back down if honor is at stake."
—Scientist Edward O. Wilson, son of Edward

him. Meeting and spending time with other new fathers will provide some social acceptance for what you are doing.

Get Information. Knowledge is power—in child raising and everything else. If you have a question or concern, peek into one of those books about raising children your partner is always reading. Or call your pediatrician or family physician. As Law says, "There is no such thing as a dumb question."

Be Flexible. Expect to be "sleep deprived" the first two months after a baby is born. A baby has no sleep schedule—no schedule of any kind. That's one of the things she must learn. She may have a "good night" and sleep three or four hours one night. But the next night she may keep you up all night. After about two months, she begins to develop a more regular sleeping pattern. One father in Law's group said that the two-month mark was "like coming out of a tunnel." Two months is about when the baby smiles for the first time, handing you a reward for all that hard work and missed sleep. The sleep issue is a symbol of the flexibility a man must show when he becomes a father. Children are always throwing your carefully conceived schedules out of whack.

Be Patient. Be Still More Patient. There will be times when you are alone with the baby and the baby is crying his head off for no apparent reason. You will try everything under the sun to comfort him, and nothing will work. Sometimes this happens in one of Law's meetings. For many of the men, it's their first time out with the baby without the mom around. A dad has a baby who just won't stop bawling. He wants to leave, but Law and the other men talk him into staying. Finally, the baby quiets. "Taking the baby out without Mom is a great teaching tool," says Law. And the more you do it, the more secure you will feel.

Keep Trying. The first few months of a baby's life can be discouraging for the father. Everything the baby does seems to be directed toward her mother. Law calls this the "mommy phase." Every child goes through mommy phases and daddy phases in her life, times when she seems to feel more secure with one parent over the other. These are normal stages of development that have little or nothing to do with a child's true affections. "Keep trying even if you feel left out," says Law. "Stick with it. If you don't participate the child will only get more mommy-oriented."

Ask for Some Breathing Room When You Need It. A baby will test your patience. You will get angry and upset. These are completely normal and natural emotions. Tell your partner you need some time to decompress. She'll understand. Take a walk in the cool night air for twenty minutes. Talk it out to yourself; think it through. When you come back, you'll be in a better frame of mind and ready to give it another try.

Cut Out the Clutter in Your Life. When you become a father, time becomes an even more precious commodity than it was before. You find out very quickly that you can't do it all. Your job remains important to you, but you now need to spend more time at home with your family. Not only do you need to, but you want to. This forces you to cut out some of the clutter in your life. "You find out what's important to you, and you cut out the things that aren't," says Law.

Exercise. Law is a bike rider; that's how he works out the stress. Run, bike, hike, walk, swim, play basketball, golf, go to the gym—whatever it takes. Exercise needs to be a part of your regular schedule, however tight that schedule is.

Take Some Time for Yourself (and Give Some Time to Your Partner). Exercise will help keep you sane, but you may need to do more. Call up a buddy; go have a beer. Take in a bargain matinee at the Bijou. Every parent needs breaks from the baby from time to time, including your partner. Take turns. Give her some baby-free time to see her friends or exercise or whatever she needs to do. You'll find that keeping your partner happy is one of the best coping strategies you can have.

> "Take care to have your stocking well gartered up, and your shoes well-buckled; for nothing gives a more slovenly air to a man than ill-dressed legs."
> —Lord Chesterton, advising his son Phillip on how gentlemen of the eighteenth century dressed

ADVICE FROM AN ELDER

To become a father is to take a risk. You open yourself up in ways you've never done before. You are going to take shots as a father. You are going to experience trials. You will have extraordinary joys and, at times, face extraordinary trials.

Sigmunt Lateiner knows about risk and survival. Married for nearly fifty years, a father of two sons, a grandfather, a survivor of the Holocaust, an immigrant who built a business in this country from the ground up, he offers a valuable perspective to young fathers just starting out, who may feel overwhelmed by the new pressures and responsibilities they've taken on. "I believe in hard work and being honest," Lateiner says. "You must keep believing in the future. Everybody has disappointments. You just have to bypass them and still believe in the future. You must not get discouraged."

Lateiner was born in 1923 in Podhajce, a small town in the forests of southeastern Poland. His father died of heart failure when Sigmunt was twelve. Emanuel Lateiner was a dentist and his oldest child followed him into the profession, studying at the university in Luow,

"In the really important decisions in life, others cannot help you. No matter how much they would like to. You must rely only on yourself. That is the fate of each one of us."
—Playwright Eugene O'Neill, to his son Shane

which is now part of the Republic of the Ukraine. In 1939, Germany invaded Poland and the horrors began. Four years later, the Nazis murdered his mother, brother, and sister in cold blood.

"One day you have a family and the next day you're by yourself," says Lateiner, shaking his head. For all that he has seen and done in his life, Lateiner has a very matter of fact nature. He does not dwell on the sadnesses or disappointments. "I didn't try to get too deep into the reasons why these things were occurring," he says. "It was just a fight for survival. You use your brains. But that wasn't enough all the time. You had to have luck, too."

Lateiner had luck. While standing on a street corner with other Jews in Luow, he got an urge to take off. That urge saved his life. Moments later the Gestapo arrived. They rounded up everyone on the corner and shot them. Lateiner hid and ran to avoid capture. He scavenged for food in the forest. "Like an animal, you're trying to survive," he says in describing that time. For over a year a Christian family hid him in their home in a village in the Polish countryside, and he made it through.

In Germany after the war, Lateiner met and married Caroline, and in 1949, they arrived in Jacksonville, Florida, with their six-month-old baby, Emanuel, named after Sigmunt's father. Thus begins a classic rags-to-riches immigrant's tale. He spoke Russian and Polish but no English. He had no money, no job. Though trained as a dentist in Poland, he could not practice dentistry in this country. But like many men, he was willing to do anything to support his family.

He worked in an office for ten months, and, after the family moved across country to Oakland, California, he worked six and one-half days a week pumping gas. He worked in a furniture factory and later as a driver and supervisor for a linen rental company. In 1959, he went out on his own and bought a small dry-cleaning plant on Mission and A Streets in Hayward. The business steadily grew, and, in 1973, Latco Uniform and Linen Rental Service opened a new 25,000-square-foot plant in an industrial park. It employed sixty people and represented the culmination of years of work and dreams.

The next year the plant burned to the ground. A photograph of flames shooting from the burning building appeared on the front page of the local *Argus*. But Lateiner was still a young man and in his mind there was only one thing for him to do: rebuild.

Sigmunt Lateiner's secret of success is no secret at all. It's the oldest lesson in the books: never ever give up. Sometimes a man has to take a stand in this life. Lateiner and many other men will tell you that fatherhood is as good a place as any to do it.

Now in his middle seventies, Lateiner sold his business and retired after heart bypass surgery a few years ago. Both his sons are grown. Emanuel became an attorney and Max followed his father into the linen rental business. He has a close relationship with his sons and talks to them on the phone every day. "Fortunately the younger generation didn't go through what the people of my generation did," says the elder Lateiner. "You are lucky. You live today in a free country. Cherish your family, I tell you. Be together and build a future with them."

For an inspirational father–son story, also centered on the Holocaust and its aftermath, see The Complete Maus, *by Art Spiegelman (New York: Pantheon Books).*

IGNORE THE MEDIA: YOU *CAN* DO IT

One of the obstacles that fathers must overcome today is a persistent media bias against them. Pick up the paper and you will see headlines about "deadbeat dads" (now often changed, so as to be politically correct, to "deadbeat parents"). Movies and television depict fathers as fools or worse. Fred Hayward is the director of Men's Rights, Inc., a national, nonprofit organization whose aim is to raise public awareness of men's issues. A TV talk-show host and lecturer, Hayward has studied how the media depict fathers and how this largely negative image affects the way men view themselves and their role in the family. His observations about *The Cosby Show* are particularly relevant to new fathers who plan to act as childbirth coaches. He is the father of KJ.

Q: *How are fathers generally depicted in the media?*
Hayward: There has been some improvement. Now at least you get to see some competent fathers in the media. Advertising has probably come the longest way. They're more willing to show a competent father, someone you wouldn't be afraid to leave alone with your child.

Q: *What hasn't changed?*
Hayward: Not every parent is shown to be a fool in the media, but when a fool is singled out it is invariably the father. He is seen as the incompetent one, irrelevant at best. This negative public image of fathers erodes our self-confidence, our self-esteem, and affects our treatment in the legal system. It robs men of their confidence that we can care for our children and that we are just as important to our children as the mother. We *are* just as important as the mother, and we can care for our children.

> **"Each person's life is a problem with which he may, to be sure, get help, but which he himself, not someone else, must ultimately work out."**
> **—Father James Harold Flye, advising "foster" son James Agee**

"Almost every avenue, fast lane and alley is either mislabeled or carries no label at all. You therefore proceed at risk, my son. Don't trust any sign that says, 'This Is the Only Way to Go.'"
—Journalist Bob Teague, to his son Adam

Q: Can you give me some examples?

Hayward: Take *The Cosby Show*. That was the number one–rated TV show for many years. I was doing an extensive study of the media at the time, and I watched over one hundred episodes of the show. The star was of course Bill Cosby, a man who in real life has written books about being a father and has a doctorate in education. He played an obstetrician on the show, who delivered babies. He was a medical doctor, and yet even he deferred to his wife on the children's health and even his health. There was a common theme on the show about new fathers, too.

Q: What was that?

Hayward: Since Cosby was an obstetrician on the show, new fathers would frequently appear. One running joke was that new fathers would faint. Another running joke was that they'd forget what they were supposed to do. They'd rush off to the hospital like a scatterbrain and leave the wife at home. If they came into the delivery room, they would either lose control and be asked to leave, or they'd collapse at the sight of the baby being born and have to be carried out. In other words, Dad starts as inept and works his way up to inferior.

Q: Does fainting happen in real life?

Hayward: I have spoken to several obstetricians and none has ever seen a man faint.

Q: What about in advertising? Give me some examples of poor images of fathers.

Hayward: I surveyed a thousand commercials annually for years. Here's one: "Kix. Kid Tested—Mother Approved." Here's another: "Choosy Moms Choose Jif." Both are slogans. They imply that Mom is the parent with the discretionary ability to make nutritional choices for their children. If Mom likes it, it means more than if Dad does. There are many more examples dealing with children's health and other needs.

Q: What should a father do when he sees a portrayal he does not like in the media?

Hayward: Speak out about it. These shows respond to letters, especially advertisers. They really want to sell their products, and they'll change if they see they're alienating potential buyers. Speak out to your wife and friends. Do you know Warren Farrell? He's written two excellent books, *The Myth of Male Power* and *Why Men Are the Way They Are*. He has a great phrase: "Women can't hear what men don't say." Women will speak up, but men have always been reluctant to do that. You have to speak up. Judges and lawmakers are part of this society. As long as we tolerate these pervasive stereotypes, family law will be stacked against fathers. And we need to encourage women to speak up because, ultimately, this hurts them too.

Q: And you can't let these negative images affect your view of yourself as a father.

Hayward: Men approach child raising the way women approach changing the oil in the car. The assumption with kids is: I can't do it. Men say, "No way can I do this." Women also assume that every man is an automotive expert. That's the way a lot of men view women: they're the experts. They're the ones who know. Men are intimidated by women when it comes to kids. They have no confidence in their own ability as a parent, even as they overestimate the woman's ability—and that's wrong.

Q: What do you recommend?

Hayward: You have to do it. Spend time with your child. And seek out other fathers who spend time with their kids. I've found that other dads are very helpful. They'll tell you, "Hey, the kid won't break. It's easy."

Contact: Men's Rights, Inc., P.O. Box 163180, Sacramento, CA 95816; 916-484-7333; www.Mens-Rights.org.

> **"Learn fortitude and toil from me, my son, ache of true toil. Harking back for models in your family, let your father, Aenas, and uncle, Hector, stir your heart."**
> —Virgil, *The Aenead*

BECOMING A FATHER

Here's a story for you, and every word of it is true. It takes place two years after the end of my marriage. A friend of mine said she had someone she wanted me to meet. I said "Great," and she arranged a blind date. This was in late January.

The woman's name was (and is) Jennifer. She was the real deal: smart, great looking, a former actress-turned-communications director. We had an instant attraction.

We survived our blind date and went on other dates. We went to the movies. We went hiking together. I introduced her to my daughter Annie, and they hit it off like gangbusters.

About a month and a half after we met, we slept together for the first time. We spent a lovely romantic weekend in and out of bed. She made risotto and we drank Veuve Clicquot. On Sunday afternoon, we saw a reissue of Taxi Driver on the big screen.

We kept seeing each other, and about a month later, she appeared one day at my house. This was a complete surprise. First, it was the middle of the afternoon. She was supposed to be at work. Nor had she called ahead of time. She drove up in her red Honda Civic just as I was returning from a trip to the video store.

I waited for her on the porch. She looked ashen. Her hands were trembling. "Are you okay?" I asked. She asked if she could come in. She's normally very composed and under control. I had never seen her so upset. When I opened the door, I said to her, half-jokingly, "You're not pregnant, are you?"

She looked at me and said, "Yes, I am."

We had made a baby. It had happened on that lost, romantic weekend. It was March. We had known each other less than three months.

12

We discussed not keeping the baby. But we didn't discuss it for long. I have a daughter and I love kids, and Jennifer had always wanted to have a child of her own. What's more, there was that instant attraction thing I mentioned earlier. We were in love. That helped us make the decision to pitch our tents together and raise our child, you know, like a real family.

I suspect I'm not the only man who's ever fathered a child unintentionally. Sometimes fatherhood calls and you're ready. It's what you've planned for. But sometimes fatherhood calls and you're not ready. Sometimes it is cast upon you. Nonetheless, in my judgment, your responsibility as a man remains the same.

I waited until after Jennifer's amniocentesis to tell Annie the news. I still remember it vividly. Big spender that I am, I bought her dinner at Boston Chicken. We took our trays over to a table by the window and sat down. Then I told her.

She cried. "I've always wanted to have a baby sister," Annie said. She cried some more. These were tears of joy. "I'm going to have a sister. I've always wanted a sister," she said. It was one of the happiest days of my life.

WHAT WE FEAR AS FATHERS

When a man learns he is gong to be a father, he enters a period known as the *couvade* (prounounced coo-*vahd*) or "the brooding season," as one father explained it to me. It is a developmental stage in his life as a father that is often marked by confusion. In some primitive societies, men take to bed to simulate the agonies of labor and childbirth. Contemporary expectant fathers are hardly exempt. Many feel morning sickness or sympathy pains with their partner, and some even gain weight. And yet there's very little social support or understanding for what a man goes through during this time—and the leap he makes from being a non-parent to a parent. Jerrold Lee Shapiro, Ph.D., is a licensed clinical psychologist and a professor of counseling and psychology at Santa Clara University. The author of *When Men Are Pregnant: Needs and Concerns of Expectant Fathers*, *The Measure of a Man*, and other thought-provoking books on fatherhood, Shapiro has seen many expectant fathers (and their mates) in more than thirty years of private practice. Some men think their feelings are unique and that, if they talk about them, it shows weakness or a betrayal of their new family. They even feel shame for having these feelings in the first

"I want to make a life for my kid, get a good job, and support my family. That's the most important thing to do. It's difficult when you have a kid at a young age."

—Eighteen-year-old Anthony Ribeiro, father of Anthony Thomas

> "The first right of every child is to be wanted, to be desired, to be planned with an intensity of love that gives it its title to being."
>
> —Margaret Sanger, birth control pioneer and daughter of Michael Higgins

place. But Shapiro says that all expectant fathers share similar feelings and that these feelings are normal and natural. He is the father of Tasha and Gabriel.

Q: In your book you talk about the fears that expectant fathers have. You say these fears fall into four general categories: performance fears, security fears, relationship fears, and existential fears. What is a man's biggest fear when he learns he's going to be a dad?

Shapiro: A father's first job is also his biggest fear: is he going to be able to provide for his family? Men worry about finances. They don't know if they can support their family in today's world. With most couples these days, there are two incomes for two people. Then suddenly it's one income for three people. A lot of men don't know how they're going to do it. They're concerned.

Q: So these aren't just fears for the sake of fear, are they? They're grounded in reality.

Shapiro: They often reflect very real concerns. Though there's one fear that almost never occurs. Men worry that they won't be able to perform while their wife is in labor. They think they may get queasy and pass out. But that simply doesn't happen. A man is about as likely to pass out as a nurse. Although, of course, there are some men who really can't tolerate blood. And what I would say to them is if you're really concerned, work it out so you won't be in the delivery room. Don't neglect your fears; listen to them and work through them. One of the best fear breakers is to talk to other guys you know, especially new fathers who've been through it. "If Chuck can get through it, I can get through it." That sort of idea.

Q: After performance fears, the next big category is security fears. Redd Foxx has a great line about it: "Mama's baby and Daddy's maybe." Do men really worry that the child isn't their own?

Shapiro: Men don't obsessively worry about it, but it's a passing question in their mind—though men will never talk about it unless you ask them. Even thinking about it seems disloyal to their wife. And they would never accuse her of having an affair, although sometimes, in fact, a woman's husband or partner is not the father of the child. But that's not what this is about. Their uncertainty has more to do with creating life. It's such a giant event, many men don't feel worthy. And that taps into a lot of self-esteem issues.

Q: I would also think it taps into the fourth category, a man's fears about his own mortality.

Shapiro: That's right. You can't be involved in beginning life and not think about its ending. You get pushed back one generation. You are no longer only a son, but a father, too.

Q: Do men have a hard time accepting pregnancy?

Shapiro: I'm seeing a man right now who is. His wife is seven-months pregnant and he's still behaving as if there's no baby in sight. Emotionally, he just doesn't have a sense yet that things have changed. But I feel confident that he's the type who will adjust once the baby arrives.

Q: You've written that childbirth causes a man to fear the possible loss of his partner. Why is that?

Shapiro: It's on a couple of levels. First of all, this is the person he loves most in the whole world. Childbirth is scary, and things can happen. He knows that. It's possible you can lose your baby, and bad things can happen to the mom. There's another, deeper uncertainty. He worries that his wife will become a mother and exclude the father. Most men have had that experience, themselves. They know what it's like to be raised by their mother while their father is out in the garage or some place. They fear that their partner's most intimate relationship will be with the baby and that they will be excluded from it.

Q: That's something I hear a lot of men talk about and it's something I've experienced myself. Mothers pushing fathers away from their children.

Shapiro: I just saw an example of it the other day. It was the Fourth of July and we were out watching the fireworks. We were with a bunch of other families and there was one family with a new baby. They were very excited and happy. Mom was carrying the baby, who was asleep in a belly pack. Dad came over and picked up the covering to look at the baby. Mom slapped his hand away. "You'll wake him up," she told him, and he walked away. Now everyone understands a mother's instinctive need to protect her baby, but that clearly wasn't what was happening here. She told the father to get out of there.

Q: What would you say to a father who finds himself in a similar situation?

Shapiro: If need be, you have to get in your wife's face. She has to know that it's not all right to exclude you from your child's life. Because she wants it that way doesn't mean it has to be that way. You need to develop a space for you and your child. You have to spend time alone

"John's father, Freddie, was a ship's waiter who vanished from his son's life. It would have been a bleak and unhappy childhood for the little boy had it not been for his Aunt Mimi and Uncle George."
—From a biography of John Lennon, about his father Freddie

> "I find myself growing more tolerant of fathers as I become one."
>
> —Poet Vance Crummett, father of Grace Anna

with him. You have to kick Mom out of the house. I tell this to moms, too. If you want your husband to have a good relationship with your child, you've got to get out of the house and leave them alone for a while. Go out with your girlfriends, have a good time. It will be better for you, better for the baby, better for the relationship. Don't stand in the hallway criticizing him. So what if the diaper isn't on perfectly? No baby has ever died from an improperly placed diaper.

Q: In researching this book, I've heard many women complain about how their husbands won't help out with the children or spend time with them. But these same women do not realize or are unwilling to admit how they push men away and help cause the situation they deplore.

Shapiro: Men approach babies differently than women do. These different styles of parenting cause power struggles. Men tend to parent from the outside, as I call it, while women are more from the inside. Women tend to believe they have an intimate emotional bond with the baby, and they operate accordingly. Men do not have the same bond. So their ideas of discipline and the ways in which they interact with the child are based more on rules and an external framework.

Q: One subject I definitely want to touch on is the phenomenon of expectant fathers who have affairs. How common is this?

Shapiro: Far less frequent than the press would have you believe. Read some feminist accounts and you might conclude that only four men in the history of the world have never had an affair while their wife was pregnant. In the course of my thirty-year career, I'd say that I've seen perhaps twenty or so men who actually had affairs during this time. And each time the man felt rejected by his wife. Perhaps he wanted to make love more often and she'd tell him no. In every case, the affair was with a woman they both knew—a sister, perhaps, or a friend. In one case I worked with, the man had an affair with his wife's mother. What happens is that the expectant mother bonds with the baby so deeply and intimately that she shuts the man out, and the man responds in a bad way. But I've yet to hear a man say that he had an affair because his wife was "big" or something of that nature.

Q: What one piece of advice would you give to a man who has just learned he's about to become a father for the first time?

Shapiro: It's very important to talk to other men, particularly to other new fathers. They've been through it and they can emphathize with what you're going through.

BEING A DAD IN A MOM'S WORLD

One of the most intimidating aspects of raising children for men is the simple fact that there are so many women around. Go to a music or exercise class for toddlers or virtually any activity involving young children (except sports), and moms will far outnumber the dads. Curtis Cooper knows all about this. He's an anomaly: a stay-at-home dad. His wife goes to work and earns the paycheck in the family, while he stays home to take care of their two young children, Brett and Brooke. Cooper says there are more than two million stay-at-home dads in the United States. Even so, feeling frustrated and cut off from other men like him, he formed Dad to Dad, a national organization for stay-at-home dads. Being home with his kids full-time, he knows what it's like to be the only dad in a preschool class with twenty moms. For working dads and stay-at-home dads alike, he offers this advice on how to cope:

You're a Dad in a Mom's World, So You Better Get Used to It. Moms still dominate the day-to-day world of child raising. Take your child to the park some morning. Who's watching the children? Women. Some are moms, the rest are caregivers. Most parenting groups and classes are also geared toward moms. *Parenting* is itself a code word for mother. Every man knows this, and that's why so many of them avoid these classes like the plague. Cooper compares it to being "the only guy in an all-girls school."

Don't Be Intimidated. Cooper calls it "the invisible stare"—the look he receives from women who don't know him and yet see him with children in the park. Often they don't acknowledge his presence, and if they do, they regard him with suspicion. Men are seen as shadowy figures of potential harm to children, until they prove otherwise, in contrast to the benign public image of moms. Cooper never pushes a kid he doesn't know on the swing, for fear that someone will misunderstand his intentions. Other dads tell him stories about women rushing up to them in fear saying, "Don't touch my kid" or "Leave my kid alone," and whisking their child away.

When Dealing with Other Moms, Be Yourself. If a mom can't relate to you for some reason, that's her problem. Go about your business with your own kid. Over time, however, most women will come to accept your presence and welcome it. They will praise you for being a dad who cares about his kids. You may even find yourself striking up friendships with moms. If there's one thing every mom likes to do, it's talk about her kids.

"One of the things I wasn't prepared for is that the baby seems to love her mother more than me. One time Maddie put her hand on my chest and pushed me away so she could have her mom to herself. I don't like that. It hurts my feelings."

—Gary Grillo, father of Maddie

"It is sad on the one hand that we have to go to such great lengths to 'prove' the importance of fathers, and sadder still that people will go to such lengths to refute it. We need to put aside our need to validate our own personal lifestyle in favor of what is best for our children."

—Stephen Harris, father and editor/publisher of *Full-Time Dads* newsletter

Seek Out Other Dads. Whereas women will network with other women, men tend to think of their problems as unique. They think they're the only people who've experienced these problems, and thus the only ones able to solve them. Being the father of a newborn is isolating and extremely stressful. You may or may not be able to talk freely about it with your colleagues at work, depending on your job environment. But you can always talk to other fathers. They can relate to what you're going through because they've gone through it themselves.

Think About Joining a Support Group for New Dads. Most men would probably rather have a root canal than join a support group. Still, many new dads find these groups (sponsored by hospitals and other organizations) to be a productive use of their time, especially in the difficult early months after the baby comes home. Children may or may not be present and the topics covered may include last night's game as well as advice and information on fathering. Men tend to be more results-oriented: "My kid craps in his pants six times a day. What do you do about it?" Another great thing about these groups is that you find out that there are lots of other guys in the same boat as you are.

Contact: Dad to Dad provides information and resources for stay-at-home dads. Dad to Dad, 13925 Duluth Drive, Apple Valley, MN 55124. Dad to Dad members may also subscribe to the At Home Dad *newsletter, for $12 published by Peter Baylies, 61 Brightwood Avenue, Andover, MA 01845; 508-685-7931; E-mail: athomedad@aol.com.*

ANOTHER TOOL FOR DADS: THE NET

It may be difficult for some men to go to a new fathers' support group or even call up another man looking for advice. Consider the Internet as a resource. Even dads who have no problem asking for help should get on it. It offers an incredible wealth of information on being a father and virtually everything else under the sun.

One advantage of the Net is that it's anonymous. Nobody needs to know who's asking the questions; you can mask your identity. In a "chat room," where people talk on-line about specific topics, you identify yourself by your "nick"—short for nickname—much the way CB radio users have "handles." It's nearly impossible to find out who Ace or Mack or Lucky is.

There's no such thing as a stupid question. Is your two-month-old crying all night leaving you stumped about what to do? Bring it up in the chat room, and it's almost assured there will be other people on-line who've lived through the same experience and who can make suggestions on how to deal with it. "This is what my pediatrician told me," they'll say, or: "Here, try this. This is what worked for me."

Many web sites that are not specifically parent or family sites may also have useful information. For example, part of the Schwab site (www.schwab.com/college) is devoted to setting up a college savings plan.

Two-thirds of Internet users are male. Some men may be intimidated by colicky babies or potty training a child, but most are not intimidated by technology. Unlike the early days of the Internet, access has become relatively easy and painless. You need a computer, a modem, and an account with an Internet Service Provider (ISP) to get started. A browser—Netscape's Navigator and Microsoft's Explorer are the most popular—allows you to view the World Wide Web.

"Search engines" (such as www.yahoo.com) are like card catalogs at the library; they're basically web sites that are used to find other sites. At one of the search engine web sites, type in your keyword: *parents*. It does a search for you, and a few seconds later two hundred sites (or more) pop up. New sites are being added all the time. One problem is information overload. Utilities like Webcompass and More Like This help you in this battle. They're like little librarians at your fingertips; they pare down the information, visiting the sites and summarizing them for you. If a site catches your fancy, click on and pay it a visit.

Source: Michael Cohen, father of Randi and Becca, is a trained eye doctor who was born and raised in Brooklyn, New York. Michael is now an Internet consultant. His E-mail address is mcohen@crl.com.

"I feel more relaxed than I ever have. Kids prioritize that. You could offer me a hundred Academy Awards, but nothing could compare to a kid."

—Actor Anthony Edwards, father of Bailey

WEB SITES FOR FATHERS AND FAMILIES

Facts for Families. Fact sheets from the American Academy of Child and Adolescent Psychiatry at www. aacap.org/web/aacap/factsFam

Father-L. E-mail conference for fathers to talk about their issues. E-mail address: father-l@tc.umn.edu. Subscription E-mail address: listserv@tc.umn.edu

FatherNet. Electronic bulletin board for dads. *Modern Dad Newsletter* and many other features at www. cyfc.unmn.edu/Fathernet

Father's Resource Center. Includes quarterly on-line newsletter *Father Times* at www.bisi.com/~frc

Family Internet Home Page. Great starting point for families on the net at www.familyinternet.com

Family.Com. Connecting dads with play groups and many other topics at www. familyinternet.com

Get Your Angries Out. Constructive ways to vent your anger—both for your kids and for yourself at members.aol.com/AngriesOut

KidsHealth. Children's health and parenting information at http://kidshealth.org/

National Parenting Center. How-to articles for new and expectant parents, as well as long time parents, at www.tnpc.com

ParenthoodWeb. For new parents and parents of young children at www.parenthoodweb.com

Parents Place. Chat room, support, and information sharing at www.parentsplace.com

Parents Resource Almanac. Activities and information for parents at family.starwave.cm/resource/pra/Table_of_Contents.html

Source: The Internet Kids and Family Yellow Pages, Second Edition *($19.95) by Jean Armour Polly, contains listings and information on thousands of Internet sites. It is available through Osborne/McGraw-Hill, www.osborne.com.*

BIRTH COACH

My best birth story involves my first daughter, Annie. She was eleven pounds, two ounces at birth, but that's not the story. She was born October 20, 1988, two weeks after her due date. The date is crucial because, as it happened, I had both World Series and League Championship tickets that year.

My local team is the Oakland A's. This was in the era of those great A's teams of Canseco, McGuire, and Dave Stewart. They won the American League West that year and faced the Boston Red Sox in the divisional series.

Annie's due date was in early October, around the time that Roger Clemens was using eye black in a vain attempt to intimidate A's hitters who were spraying everything he sent to the plate around the field like Scud missiles. I couldn't use my tickets, though, because we went into the hospital. I sold the tickets to a nurse and watched the games on TV from the labor and delivery room.

We went into the hospital expecting our daughter to be born. But Annie had other ideas. They induced labor with pitocin, but nothing happened. We left the hospital after two days completely frustrated. (The reason Annie wasn't born, we learned later, was that her head was too large—sixteen centimeters—to fit into the birth canal. Lotsa brains, that kid.)

Around this time the World Series began: A's versus Dodgers. I had never been to a series game and I was really looking forward to it when the teams came to Oakland. But there was this little matter of a baby that still needed to be dealt with.

The Dodgers won the first two games played in Los Angeles. In the opener Kirk Gibson limped out of the dugout in the bottom of

> "For the first time I really understand what it's like to look into an infant's eyes and know you would die for this person."
>
> —Actor Sylvester Stallone, on his daughter Sophia Rose (who was born with a heart defect)

the ninth and hit a pinch-hit home run off Dennis Eckersley. The A's never really recovered from that. They lost the second game in Los Angeles and split the next two at home. I had tickets for those games, too, but with my commitments to my family, I couldn't go. Now with the Dodger's Orel Hershiser scheduled to pitch the fifth game in Oakland, it looked like curtains for my guys.

Cut to the morning of October 20. Annie is now two weeks overdue. Something is not right. Things are not moving the way they should. We hold a powwow with the doctors and nurses. They tell us that two weeks after the due date, the placenta begins to deteriorate. They recommend a cesarean section, and we agree. It's time.

They schedule the operation for late in the afternoon. I don't say anything, but Annie's mom mentions that I have tickets for the World Series that night and is there any way they could move up the procedure? Well, you should have seen those doctors jump. Having a baby is one thing, but when you've got tickets to the World Series, that's special. The doctors rearranged their schedule so that I could both see my daughter born and go to the game.

And that's what happened. Annie burst into the world at about 1:20 P.M., bright-eyed and full of life (a nurse nicknamed her "Annie Bright Eyes"). I waited until her mom got out of post-op recovery and saw her hold Annie in her arms. I left the two of them and rushed off to see Hershiser polish off the A's in a masterful display and win the title for the Dodgers.

I arrived before the opening pitch. I sat down in my seat, toting a large beer and a hot dog, and I turned to the guy sitting next to me. "I'm a father," I told him. "I had a kid today."

"Boy or girl?" he asked.

"Girl," I said.

"Cool," he said, and we clicked beer cups and turned our eyes to the game.

WHY YOU SHOULD BE A BIRTH COACH: A NURSE'S VIEW

Nowadays, it's almost routine for a man to participate in the birth of his child. Fathers share their birth stories with other men, genuinely moved and astonished by the intensity of the experience. Health care professionals—not to mention moms everywhere—welcome the presence of fathers in the labor room. But why is this such a good idea? I posed this question to Sarah McMoyler, who has twin credentials as a mother of two and a labor and delivery nurse. She's a perinatal education coordinator and an ASPO certified Lamaze instructor who, over the past fifteen years, has taught prenatal classes to more than two thousand pregnant moms and their sometimes reluctant (at least at first) partners.

Q: Let's say I'm an unwilling birth coach. Explain to me why it's so important for me to participate in my child's birth.

McMoyler: Because Mom needs someone who is able to be there 100 percent of the time. She needs unconditional support. She needs someone who can remind her of what to do. I teach childbirth preparation classes to expectant parents, and they're often surprised to learn that nurses are not able to be with the mother 100 percent of the time. So a partner's presence in the room, to support Mom, is both welcome and needed. It's also an incredible experience which you will miss if you're not there.

Q: What is the attitude of men in your childbirth classes? Are they happy to be there, or not?

McMoyler: Some men are dragged into these classes, especially if it's a six-to-eight-week class. Maybe it takes place on a Monday night and they have to miss Monday Night Football. They sit there with their legs crossed, eyes to the ceiling. But I find that just by the end of that first class, they're involved. They tell me afterward that they never expected to (a) learn anything they could use and (b) enjoy it. And they do both.

Q: What kinds of concerns do fathers have prior to childbirth?

McMoyler: I teach classes of up to twenty couples at a time, and I ask them what their primary concerns are. Some men worry that they'll pass out during childbirth. But in my experience, almost no one ever does. I'm telling you, it is very, very unlikely that you will pass out. Also, couples worry that they'll have the baby while driving there, but this is very unlikely too, if it's your first.

Q: What's the main role of the birth coach?

McMoyler: I compare it to running a marathon. I've run a few marathons and I still remember the people cheering for me whom I didn't even know. These people passed me water and gave me aid and encouraged me on. That's what a coach does. He helps Mom go the distance.

"I have two kids. The second time, I caught the baby. It wasn't supposed to happen that way, but the nurse-practitioner got distracted and the baby kind of dropped out. I was there to catch her."
—Corey MacMullan, handyman and father

"When the doctor handed me my baby, Trey, it was like, figuratively and physically, he handed me this life for me to take care of. When I drove home from the hospital after my baby was born, I obeyed all the traffic laws for maybe the first time in my life. I'd roll down the window of my car and yell at the other cars, 'Hey, slow down!'"
—Actor Will Smith, father of Trey

Q: If you're coaching Mom on this marathon, how do you support her?

McMoyler: You support her physically and emotionally. She is on the ride of her life and she is not getting off. The coach needs to be in the passenger seat with her, providing comfort and support. He gives her back massages, hand massages, cold compresses. He reminds her about drinking fluids and emptying her bladder. He engages her mind. He shows her the breathing she needs to do—not talking about it, but doing it. He reassures her after every single contraction, tells her he loves her, what a great job she's doing. A coach needs to understand the process of labor—how a woman goes through active labor and transition. I call transition "Mr. Toad's Wild Ride." It can be a wild time, and by unconditionally supporting Mom, the partner can help her get through it.

Q: Are men ever resentful that they're in a supporting role and that the focus of childbirth is not on them?

McMoyler: No. Most of them are pretty relieved that they're not the one who has to go through all this pain [laughs]. Historically the focus of childbirth classes has been on the mom. She's the one who gives birth, and that's where we need to put our attention. But if she has a partner who supports her and is tuned into her and who is participating in the process, it helps her so much. In our classes, we speak to both the mom and her partner. He is not a fifth wheel, although sometimes men feel that way. Partners are instrumental in giving comfort to Mom, reminding her of what she needs to do, and supporting her as she does it.

Q: It's hard not to feel like a fifth wheel sometimes. I've participated in two births and still had those feelings.

McMoyler: A lot of men have the impression that when they get to the hospital they'll be greeted by the nurses and the doctor. The paid professionals will take over from there, and then you'll have a baby. That doesn't happen. As I say, the nurses will be in and out of the room. The doctor will appear at the time of birth. That's why it's so important for the partner to be involved and to know what to do.

Q: I'd like to think that perhaps after showing reluctance initially, dads come through in the clutch. Am I right?

McMoyler: Yes they do. I find that men want to feel like they can make a difference. They may not feel invited to participate, or that it's not appropriate somehow. But they absolutely have a place in this process. This isn't the 1950s, when childbirth was considered a woman's thing and men sat out in the waiting room smoking cigarettes. Mom needs to hear from you. You are absolutely essential. She needs to know how proud you are of her, how much you love her. You may tell her that you love her seven thousand times when she's giving birth and, believe me, she'll want to hear it every time.

Contact: Sarah McMoyler, Perinatal Education Coordinator, John Muir Medical Center, 1601 Ygnacio Valley Boulevard, Walnut Creek, CA 94598; 510-947-5219.

HOW TO BE A GREAT LABOR COACH

Pick up a copy of *Who's Who in America* and you will find Harold Hotelling's name. He is an economics professor at Lawrence Technological University in Southfield, Michigan. But he will tell you that his greatest accomplishment is being the father of five children: Harold, George, James, Claire, and Charles. Harold, who assisted in all of their births, offers these handy pointers on how to be a great labor coach.

Go to Class. Attend childbirth classes with your partner. Classes are offered through hospitals and at other places. They will help you overcome your inhibitions and teach you many new things. A labor and delivery room is not your world. It's an unfamiliar environment. Being a labor coach requires a different set of skills than you are used to providing. Men are problem solvers. They like to feel in charge of the situation. Birth is clearly in a different category. Childbirth classes typically give expectant couples a tour of the labor and delivery unit of the hospital. The tour will orient you to this unfamiliar setting and prepare you for the real event.

Pay Attention. It's not enough to go to class and sit there like a lump because you'd rather be home watching Dan Dierdorf and Al Michaels trade scripted one-liners. Be a sport. Participate. Read the printed material they give you. You will learn about the stages of labor. You will learn things about the female anatomy that you never imagined. Show interest in what's going on. Your partner will love you for it, which brings us to the next, vital point.

Be a Caring Partner. Pregnancy is a very sensitive time for a woman (you may have noticed). Many women feel fat and unattractive. They're subject to mood swings and odd food cravings. They feel very vulnerable. Be sensitive to your partner's condition if for no other reason than this: basic self-preservation. Childbirth can be a defining moment in a couple's relationship. She will remember it for a long, long time if you act like a jerk.

25

Drive Safely. Many men feel like a sideshow during childbirth. Well, here's a no-nonsense job for you: get to the hospital safely. It's almost guaranteed that your partner won't give birth in the car if it's her first baby. So don't play Cale Yarborough in the Daytona 500. Also, park in approved parking. It would be a sad thing to walk out of the hospital after helping to deliver a new baby only to find that your car has been towed.

Be Her Advocate. You are your partner's voice, her strongest advocate. There are times when she can barely talk or if she can talk, she does not know what she wants. Be assertive. Help her get what she needs. Nurses go in and out of the room; you're the one who stays by her side. Don't be a pushover. Run interference for her. A doctor may make a suggestion, but it's only that—a suggestion. You and your partner do not have to follow it. Of course, you never want to stand in the way of medical assistance that your partner truly needs.

Communicate Beforehand. A birth plan provides a kind of road map, but you can't lock yourself into it. Flexibility is key. Emergencies arise. Mom wants to give birth without drugs. But what if the pain is too great? Will she accept an epidural? You need to do some contingency planning. Also, think about cesarean sections. Few moms want one, but many end up with them. You need to talk about how a cesarean will be handled if one is needed.

Be Strong. It is hard for a man to see the person he loves in so much pain. But you must remember (a) it's not your fault and (b) this would happen with or without you. Since you are there, lend a hand. Comfort your partner. Make it a little better for her. Also—and this is critical—your partner is enduring all this pain for a reason. She can put up with a lot knowing that it's going to end at some point. Tell her how far she's come, and how close she is to the end. Encourage her. Remind her how long she's waited for this day, and how fed up she is with being pregnant. Most women are *very* tired of being pregnant and more than ready to give birth when the time comes.

Hire a Doula. Hotelling's wife, Barbara, is president of the North American Doula Society, so he has obvious sympathies in this area. But of his five children, three had doulas, and he swears by them. Twelve people, including the doula, were in the room for the birth of Harold's youngest child. A doula is a professional birth attendant who provides comfort measures to the mom, in addition to what you and the nurses give her. She does not displace the father or kick him out. Labor can be very long—from 8 to 12 to 24 to 36 hours long—and you may welcome the break that the doula can give you. A doula gives massages and knows exactly where to put the pressure on Mom's aching back. She is another advocate for Mom in the room, perhaps questioning whether a fetal monitor is really necessary and reminding nurses to take her blood pressure.

Hang in There. Childbirth is an endurance contest unlike any other. But if you're in reasonable shape, you will almost certainly be able to handle it. Pace yourself. Take the attitude: "I'll be here as long as it takes." Pack some food. Step out of the room for a moment and get a bite to eat. Applying back rubs can be pretty taxing after a while. Get in shape by giving Mom back rubs during her pregnancy.

Leave the Video Camera at Home. The trouble with playing Stephen Spielberg in the labor room is that it takes you away from your other responsibilities. The primary question is, What makes Mom most comfortable? There is plenty of time to take pictures after the baby is born.

Be Attentive to Mom After the Birth. Your job's not over when the baby is born. Mom still has some business to do and you need to help her stay on task. She may have needed an episiotomy during the final stages of delivery and must now lie quietly while she is sewn up. She also needs to discharge the afterbirth. Your job isn't over until Mom is given a chance to rest. Then you can stand down, soldier. Job well done.

Hold Your Baby. Hotelling says that neither catching the baby nor cutting the cord constituted a tremendous mystical experience for him. Ah, but holding the baby—that's a different story. Like Mom and you, your baby has had a hard day. She was lying in a nice, warm pool of water when suddenly the walls of the pool began to push in on her, forcing her up through a four-inch hole where she encountered bright lights and all these people yelling at her. Take your baby in your arms. Talk to her and reassure her. Let her get accustomed to the sound of your voice. Let her know everything's going to be all right. Know that childbirth usually lasts only a couple of days. Raising that baby in your arms will take a lifetime.

Contact: Doulas of North America will provide information about doulas and refer you to to doulas in your area. Doulas of North America, 1100 23rd Avenue East, Seattle, WA 98112; 206-324-5440.

> "My ancestors didn't come on the Mayflower, but they met the boat."
>
> —Will Rogers, whose father, Clement Vann Rogers, was part Cherokee

CUTTING THE CORD:
A MAN'S PREROGATIVE

Men feel pressure from women to participate in childbirth. They are also being encouraged these days to cut the baby's umbilical cord after birth.

Should you cut the cord? That's your call, Dad. Cutting the umbilical cord is what film schools and literature classes call "a symbolic act." It separates Baby from Mom. It introduces Baby to Dad and in some ways, to the world. But you don't have to if you don't want to. That's something all men need to know. To cut or not to cut is for you to decide.

Men need to be comfortable during childbirth, too. A lot of dads say cutting the cord is a cool thing. Others say it feels more ceremonial than anything else. Don't sweat it in any case: it is a simple and safe procedure. If you can handle a pair of scissors, you can cut the cord.

But some men may feel funny or awkward about it. It takes place on the business end of childbirth, and they may feel squeamish about it. They may want to stay up with Mom and continue to comfort her. A man can be fully involved in childbirth and snip the cord. He can also be fully involved and support Mom and Baby and *not* snip the cord.

One recommendation if you're unclear on what to do: talk with other dads with children. Did they cut the cord? How did it feel? And if they didn't do it, do they wish they had?

Another way for a man to feel involved is to ask the physician or labor and delivery nurse what's unique about his baby. All babies tend to look alike, at least to a new dad's untrained eye. A physician can point out your baby's unique qualities—what distinguishes him from all other babies born in the history of the world—and this will help you feel more connected to him.

Source: Greg Bishop, Boot Camps for Dads, Irvine, CA; 714-786-3597. Boot Camps for Dads is a program that teaches classes in hospitals for new fathers to acquaint them with the demands of babies and family life. Greg is the father of four.

WHAT TO BRING TO THE HOSPITAL

Be prepared. That's the motto of every Boy Scout and birth coach. Your partner is carrying the baby and her vocal cords; assume that everything else is your responsibility. Wear comfortable shoes; you're going to be on your feet a long time. Drive safely and check Mom into the hospital. After she's settled, go back to the car and get whatever you couldn't bring on the first trip. The following items should be part of every birth coach's bag. You may not use them all, but bring them anyway in case the need arises.

Medical card

Insurance forms, hospital preregistration forms

Written reminder of what you need to do as coach

Copies of your birth plan

List of phone numbers of family, friends, and relatives

Change for the phone and snack machines

Boom box with batteries (for playing music)

Favorite music cassettes (hers, not yours)

Premade lunch and snacks (lollipops, popsicles)

Tennis ball, paint roller, or other massage tools

Pen and writing pad

Massage lotion or unscented oil

Glasses or contact lenses

Playing cards (to help with her breathing exercises)

Her "focal point," such as a photograph or icon

Camera and film (and/or camcorder with tape)

Odorless lip balm

Makeup

Toothbrush, toothpaste

Toiletries (shampoo, conditioner, mouthwash, etc.) and hair dryer

Hairbrush and barrettes or scrunchies

Extra pillows

Slippers, socks, and robe

Extra set of clothing for mom (including comfortable bras)

Baby outfit and blanket

Diapers

Infant car seat for the drive home

CARS

When Annie was born, I owned a 1967 VW bug. I loved it. It was a classic. It had the gas tank under the hood. I'm six-feet, three inches tall, and, unlike with so many cars today, I could drive it without scraping the top of my head against the roof.

People stopped me all the time to tell me their VW memories. Everybody, it seems, of a certain age owned a VW bug or has a story to tell about one. A toll taker at a bridge I frequently crossed always said, "Nice car," every time I drove through. The big problem for me was that the gas gauge didn't work. I kept track of the miles between fill-ups, but it was not a foolproof method, and I ran out of gas with distressing frequency. I kept a gallon container of gas in the trunk for those times when I did.

I always worried about running out of gas with Annie. That never happened. Though something else did that made me reevaluate my thinking on cars. A few years ago, I was working for a magazine and had to drop off some artwork to the art director, who lived in the next town. I was home with Annie. I didn't really want to bring her with me, but her mom wasn't around so I had no choice.

Annie was five—old enough and big enough to ride in the front with me. We had just graduated from car seats. As we were leaving, we saw her mom coming down the street on the way home. That solved the problem. Annie jumped in the car with her and I went off on my errand alone.

A few minutes later a car nailed me from behind after I had stopped at a red light. The jerk was going about 35 mph when he plowed into me. I was furious. I jumped out and was ready to kill. The guy hadn't seen the light and was going straight through the intersection. No insurance, naturally. The rear of the bug was *smashed in but driveable.*

After the initial shock and rage wore off, I felt lucky—lucky that my daughter hadn't been in the car with me. I suffered whiplash in the accident and I have always wondered what would have happened to her if she'd been in the car. At the very least, she would have been scared out of her wits.

That accident prompted a change in my life. Both for my family and for me, I felt like we needed a car with more metal and steel. So I sold the VW to a teenager. It felt like I was saying goodbye to an old friend when she drove off with it.

Every new dad probably goes through much the same thing. Eventually he trades his old, cherished wheels for something that's more suitable for family life (although many men keep their own car and let their partner drive the "family car"). It's like giving up a piece of one's youth. It's definitely a transition, but it's not the end of the world. And if the safety of your children is an issue, it's an easy call.

NOW THAT I HAVE A BIGGER FAMILY, DO I NEED A BIGGER CAR?

Arv Voss knows cars. The first car he ever owned was a 1947 Fleetline fastback Chevrolet. He now drives a 1972 BMW 2002 and collects vintage cars. His collection includes a 1925 Chevy Touring, a 1939 Sedan Delivery, a 1940 Ford street-rod Pickup, and, perhaps his most prized possession, a 1957 Porsche Speedster, one of the greatest ever sports cars in its greatest year ever. Voss is a syndicated automobile writer who test-drives new cars and writes about them for the San Francisco *Chronicle-Examiner, Convertible Magazine,* and other publications. But, no, Arv doesn't think you need to go into debt to buy a new SUV or minivan just because you have a baby. He is the father of Todd, Traci, and Kerry.

Q. Suppose you were a new dad in the market for a new vehicle. What would you be looking for?
Voss: I'd probably say versatility and space. You're going to need more space to haul all the gear. You're going to be hauling things like playpens and diaper bags and a whole ton of other stuff, and it's tough to load it all into a two-door with a small trunk. Also, safety is a big consideration.

Q: How so?

Voss: I think air bags are a great safety feature. Mercedes has a new "baby smart seat," which has a scanner device and, if it's buckled in the front seat, the air bag won't deploy. It also won't deploy if there's less than twenty-six pounds in it. I know there's some controversy about air bags in terms of children, but if you're at all concerned, put the baby in the rear seat. Kids are not supposed to be in the front seat anyway. They should always be in the back and buckled in, in an approved child seat.

Q: If some guy gets a new family car, it will probably represent a change of image for him.

Voss: I'll say. If you were a Ferrari guy or a sports car guy before, that's probably going to change. You're almost sure to feel some pressure from Mom to get out of a two-door into a four-door. She'll be sick of crawling over the seat to put the kid in back, and she'll want to have more access.

Q: What are your choices in family cars?

Voss: People tend to go for the sport utility vehicles now. That's the biggest craze in family vehicles. The old-fashioned station wagons are pretty much a thing of the past, although there are still wagons on the market, of course. Minivans were very popular a few years ago, but there's kind of a stigma attached to them now. You see a minivan on the road and immediately people think "mom."

Q: Why are suvs so popular?

Voss: People want them for the image. They're four-wheel drive. They're secure, although there is a greater rollover factor than say, a wagon, due to the higher center of gravity. You can also use sport utility vehicles for recreation. Guys can use them for hunting and fishing and still use them with the family. Although it's a fact that less than three percent of all sport utility owners actually go off road with them and use four-wheel drive.

Q: What do suvs cost?

Voss: Well, let's see. Roughly speaking, the Kia Sportage starts in the $16,000 range. So does the Geo Tracker. The Suzuki Sidekick is virtually the same as the Tracker, and it's about in that price range. There are probably more Ford Explorers on the road than anything else, but it can jump to over $30,000 in a hurry, almost twice as much as these other models.

Q: What about wagons?

Voss: Well, the Volvo is generally considered to have the premiere wagon on the market. They're built like a tank and reliable. But they're pricey. I think the new models start around $40,000. A couple of more possibilities are the Ford Taurus Wagon and the Mercury Sable Wagon. They're essentially the same wagon and cost less than the Volvo. Toyota's Camry is yet another possibility.

Q: And the minivans?

Voss: Chrysler probably makes the best minivans. As with all these cars, the price depends on the model and features. The Plymouth is the least expensive. Its base sticker is just under $20,000. The Town and Country is higher-end, and it's close to $35,000 depending on features. My wife drives a Plymouth minivan. But you know, minivans are probably for later in the cycle. They're more for when you start carrying your kids around to soccer practice and Little League and you're in car pools where you're carting your kid and his friends around the map. You don't tend to need a minivan as much when you're just starting out with a family. Though many empty-nesters sometimes buy minivans and use them to transport the grandkids.

Q: It's amazing to me. Even the least expensive cars you've mentioned are ridiculously expensive. My parents were able to buy their dream house in the 1960s for less than it costs to buy a new car today.

Voss: I know. But you don't have to get a new car just because you have a new baby. A lot of people make do with what they have. That's a good strategy. Make do with what you have until you feel you can afford to move up.

Arv Voss; 707-644-6802; www.sfgate.com.

SPORTS-UTES: CHOICE OF
THE RUGGED, MACHO FAMILY MAN

Larry Webster is technical editor for *Car and Driver* magazine. Being a single guy, he drives sports cars, but he understands the masculine appeal of SUVs or "sports-utes," as he calls them. "Eighty percent of it is image," he says. "It has a rugged, macho outdoors image. Sports-utes offer more room inside without being a station wagon. A lot of men don't want to drive the car they grew up in or what a soccer mom drives."

The driver sits up real high in an SUV—another reason why men tend to like it. "You can see what's going on around you," says Webster. "It gives you more of a sense of security and safety. Its sheer size and mass make it safer. You hit an Escort with one of these and you're gonna win."

Sitting up so high, however, contributes to a sense that you might roll over. Webster and other automotive experts discount this fear. Rollovers in all automobiles, he says, are almost always due to the driver. The highest rollover rates are in Corvettes, he adds.

Sports-utes generally offer more power than minivans, ranging from a 4-cylinder, 120-horsepower Toyota RAV4 to the 255-horsepower V-8 Chevy Suburban. Most people buy SUVs with four-wheel drive—and almost never use it. Less than 3 percent of the vehicles ever see anything but pavement. "Unless you live in a climate where you need four-wheel drive, don't bother," advises Webster.

SUVs range in price from about $20,000 up to $65,000 for the Range Rovers. Fuel economy is poor; it's in the 15 to 20 mpg range on the highway, though engine performance is becoming more efficient and the styling less blocky and more aerodynamic, which should improve gas mileage. Be sure an SUV is big enough inside. It may look massive from the outside; the reality inside may be a little different. The Suburban seats eight; most sports-utes seat five, some seat seven. Minivans tend to be roomier.

SUVs also handle more like a truck than a car. "They don't drive well. They're like trucks," Webster says. "Sports-utes generally have primitive suspension systems and the sheer mass makes accelerating or turning a chore." Still, even with these drawbacks, Webster might choose a sports-ute over a minivan. "Give me a truck," he says. "At least I'd have a big tough truck."

Tip: Car and Driver *publishes an annual buyer's guide to new cars and trucks that is available in the fall at newsstands and in CD format. Car and Driver, 2002 Hogback Road, Ann Arbor, MI 48105; 313-971-3600.*

MINIVANS:
A MORE PRACTICAL ALTERNATIVE?

You do not have to own a minivan to have a child these days, although sometimes it seems that way. Park any place where families congregate and minivans will dominate the lot. Their popularity, however, has contributed to their staid "soccer mom" image, which turns off a lot of men who prefer the more outdoorsy sport utility vehicles. But minivan manufacturers, says James Hope, associate editor of *Road & Track* magazine's special publications, are sensitive to this and are targeting their advertising more to men. Additionally, minivans now offer features such as traction control and different styling cues that appeal more to the masculine sensibility. Hope says that minivans offer many practical advantages for growing families, and he points out a few of them here:

Easy Access. Minivans are designed to be people movers. They're accessible from the back, and they're easy to get in to and out of. It's a snap to load the baby into the car seat in back.

More Passenger and Cargo Room. Minivans seat seven or eight. Most SUVs seat five (although some models do seat more). Minivans are taller with a lower floor and hold more cargo than SUVs. They do not have as much power, however. There are no V-8s in minivans, only V-6s.

Sliding Doors on Both Sides. Minivans only had a sliding door on the right side when first introduced. Now there's a left sliding door option, allowing people to enter from either side of the vehicle, like a four-door car.

Integrated Child Seat. The child seat is molded into a regular adult seat in back. It is standard in some models.

Better View of Road than a Car. The driver sits lower in a minivan than in a four-wheel-drive SUV, but it's still higher than a passenger car.

Better Gas Mileage. Fuel economy is not as good as most cars but better than an SUV—in the 17 to 20 mpg range in the city, 20 to 25 mpg on the highway.

Rides and Handles Better. It doesn't feel like it's about to tip over, largely because the driver sits lower. A minivan handles and drives more like a car, whereas the SUV rides rougher. Minivans, like all cars today, will make a dent in your pocketbook. They cost from $20,000 to more than $30,000.

Contact: Road & Track's *special publications include an annual* Truck and Van Buyer's Guide, *the* Road Test Annual, *and* Open Road, *an SUV and truck version of* Road & Track. *Available at newstands or by contacting Road & Track, 1499 Monrovia Avenue, Newport Beach, CA 92663; 714-720-5300. James Hope also contributed to the following article on station wagons.*

STATION WAGONS

Once upon a time, wood-paneled Country Squire station wagons were the family vehicle of choice. Those days are long gone.

Station wagons are beginning to make a comeback, but, as James Hope says, they are "more of a sports sedan wrapped in a station wagon body." Station wagons ride and perform like a car yet are often roomier. People like the open boxed area in the rear of an SUV; that's a traditional feature of a station wagon. Car manufacturers see the station wagon as a bridge between the highly popular minivans and SUVs.

Like minivans, station wagons have a sedate family image that does not appeal as strongly to men. But Audi, Volvo, and Subaru all offer popular station wagons with all-wheel drive.

CHILDREN AND CAR SEATS

The safest way to transport an infant in a car is in a child safety seat in the rear seat. It is folly for adults to think that they can hold a child on their lap while riding in a car, even for a short trip. Studies have shown that the impact of a crash pulls an infant from an adult's arms with the force of three hundred pounds or more. Buckle your child into her child safety seat wherever you go, in whatever vehicle you drive, however inconvenient it may seem at the time.

In the event of an accident child safety seats keep children from slamming into the dashboard or windshield, being thrown out of their seat against other passengers, or even ejected out of the vehicle. More children in the United States are killed and crippled in car crashes than any other cause of injury. Auto accidents are the leading killer of children under the age of five.

The National Transportation Board estimates that ten thousand lives would be saved every year if adults buckled their seat belts and children rode in safety seats in the back seat. Nearly one out of three car travelers do not wear seat belts. More than forty thousand people are killed annually in the United States in car accidents. Roughly half of these people are not wearing seat belts.

Never use a car seat that was made before 1981. Also make sure that it has never been in a crash or been recalled. The child safety seats on the market today are all considered safe and effective when used properly. Look for this label: "This child restraint system conforms to all applicable federal motor vehicle standards."

Sometimes, the safety seats that you buy are not compatible with the vehicle you own. It may be too large to put in the back seat, or the base may extend over the seat. Test the seat before you buy it. The best child seat is the one that fits your child and your car and is easy to use.

Child safety seats can sometimes be hard to install. Check over the instructions and your car manual to make sure you're putting it in right. Make sure it is secured properly. Sometimes the safety seat cannot be fastened with the existing seat belt, so you may need to pick up a supplemental belt or locking clip. Don't jury-rig a car seat to work; get a new one if it doesn't work right or fit correctly.

Your child's size and weight determine the type of safety seat to use. For a baby twenty pounds or less, from birth to about nine to twelve months, use an infant seat facing the rear. From twenty to forty pounds, from one to four years, use a convertible or toddler seat. Keep the children in toddler seats as long as they will fit.

Some pregnant women refuse to wear seatbelts while driving because they're afraid the belts will hurt their unborn baby. But there is no evidence that safety belts increase the chance of injury to the baby, uterus, or placenta, regardless of the severity of the collision. On the contrary, a seat belt is the best protection for both mother and child. The main risk to a baby is the injury or death of its mother. Make sure all moms-to-be buckle up, too.

Source: Department of Transportation, National Highway Traffic Safety Administration, 400 Seventh Street, SW, Washington, DC 20590. Contact the Auto Safety Hotline at 800-424-9393 or at www.nhtsa.gov/. The NHTSA provides a shopping guide for child safety seats, recall information, and safety literature on seat belts, air bags, bicycles, car crash test results, antilock braking, and more. The NHTSA also provided the information for the following piece on air bags.

CHILDREN AND AIR BAGS

An Associated Press poll found that nearly nine out of ten adults understood that it was hazardous to put a child in a safety seat in the front seat of a car with passenger-side air bags. Infants under twenty pounds should be in a safety seat in the back seat facing to the rear.

When placed in the front seat, a rear-facing infant car seat sits too close to the dashboard, where the air bag is kept. The bag is designed to inflate with any frontal impact over about 12 mph. It opens with tremendous force. When the air bag inflates, it could hit the back of the safety seat and badly injure the child. It could throw the safety seat up and into the headrest or between the seats. Rear-facing infant seats cannot be used safely in front of an air bag and should always be placed in the back seat.

MORE CAR RESOURCES

A fleet of magazines publish monthly and annual reports on new cars, minivans, and SUVs. In addition to *Car and Driver* and *Road & Track* cited elsewhere in this chapter, they include:

Popular Mechanics: Annual New Car and Truck Buyers Guide. 224 West 57th Street, New York NY 10019; 212-649-2000

Automobile magazine: *Field Guide to Sport Utility Vehicles, Pickups, and Vans*. 120 East Liberty Street, Ann Arbor, MI 48104; 313-994-3500

Consumer Reports Cars: the Essential Guide (CD-ROM). Annual guide to new and used cars, minivans, and SUVs. $19.95 plus shipping and handling. Consumer Reports Cars, 225 SW Broadway, Suite 600, Portland, OR 97205; 800-331-1369

For new car pricing information, contact the Consumers Car Club at 800-CAR-CLUB or www.carclub.com/. Other sources are Edmund's Auto Guides at www.edmunds.com/ and Kelley's Blue Book at www.kbb.com/.

CHILD CARE AND PRESCHOOLS

"Oh, Fester, I'm such a lucky man. I hope some day you'll know the indescribable joy of having children. And of having someone else to raise them."

—Gomez Addams, father of Wednesday, Pugsley, and Pubert

Child care may be the thorniest issue in raising kids today. Life is sweet when you have a good child-care situation. You can go to work without worry or guilt. But when you're unhappy with your child's care or it's unsettled in some way, it's miserable—for your baby, your partner, and you. The best child-care situation is the one that works for you. Families work it out in a variety of ways. The goal of most parents is to minimize the time their son or daughter spends in child care. (I normally refer to child care as "day care," but I'm told that's incorrect, because sometimes day care is at night. So "child care" is the operative term here.)

Mothers tend to take the lead in setting up child-care arrangements, but it's a good idea for fathers to have a hand in what's going on. There were many days when I lost work time and had to stay home because our child care for Annie had fallen through and there was no one else to take care of her.

But I don't think it's fair to leave all the child-care arrangements up to your partner and then blame her if something falls through. I think a lot of men would get a real education if they took over their partner's job and checked out these child-care providers themselves. Some are excellent and supercompetent. Many, however,

39

Ten to twelve million children in the United States below the age of five spend all or part of their day in child care.

are not. And the idea of leaving your child with a member of this latter group—well, it's downright scary.

You may be one of those lucky guys who can afford to have your partner stay home and don't have to worry about child care. For most men, though, child care is a fact of life. Their partner works and they need to share the responsibilities. They share pick-up and drop-off duties, and they may have to stay home some days if the child gets sick and child care won't take him.

We probably tried every conceivable child-care arrangement with Annie, often in desperation. When she was an infant we tried the classic "handoff" technique, where one parent works during the day and the other at night (or a different shift anyway). When you're not at work, you watch the kid. When your partner comes home, she takes over and you go to work. This is a recipe for burnout. Eventually most parents go on to some other arrangment.

When Annie was very young, we moved to a new town where we didn't know anybody. That forced us to rely heavily on my mother. She drove over many times when we couldn't find a sitter and my wife and I had to work. This is another tried-and-true child-care technique: using relatives and grandparents. This has some advantages. It's usually cheaper, and you can trust the people. But again, over time you will probably want to find a situation that's more stable and reliable—something or someone you can always count on.

The first time you leave your infant son or daughter at child care—with someone who is not family—is a big event. It's not just moms and babies who go through separation anxiety. I imagined all sorts of bizarre kidnap fantasies—such as my daughter being abducted and sold into slavery. We interviewed the caregiver and we were confident about her. Still, she was a relative stranger and here we were, leaving the most precious person in the world in her care. It seemed strange somehow.

One of the hardest things about leaving your child is that your child doesn't exactly take it like a man, so to speak. She acts like you've consigned her to the thumbscrews and left her to rot in prison. But it's almost axiomatic that as soon as the parent leaves the baby stops squawking and adjusts to her new world, assuming it's the right one for her.

Word of mouth is probably the best way to find good child care. When Annie reached preschool, one of the parents there told us about a home-care provider in town. We wanted Annie to be in a home setting. Our thinking was, if she couldn't be in our home, she should be in someone else's home. And finally, we found the right situation that worked for us.

The child-care provider we have now is superb. She's a parental figure to Annie: a person of love and trust and stability. Annie has been going to her for several years and has made friends there. Now, it's not as if Annie is being sent to child care; she's going to visit her friends. I don't even think about it anymore, which is as good a sign as any that you've found the right situation for your child.

MEN AND CHILD CARE

Is child care women's work? Most people nowadays would answer with a thunderous no. Why, then, do moms—not dads—mostly take the lead in finding child care for their family? Denise Fogarty is program director for Child Care Aware, a national nonprofit partnership of leading child-care organizations based in Rochester, Minnesota. Its purpose is to help parents find the best child care by connecting them with local referral agencies. An expert on child-care issues, Fogarty talks about how dads fit into an area of family life that is normally associated with women.

Q: My child-care provider tells me that moms almost always take the lead when it comes to child care. Dads may pick up and drop off, but moms handle the primary responsibilities. Do you find that to be true as well?

Fogarty: Yes. We've done focus groups with fathers and mothers and we've found that mothers are the ones who are primarily responsible for child care in the family. They search for the best child care. Once the decision is made, they handle most of the communications with the caregiver. They make sure their child has the right clothes, bottles, that sort of thing. It's rare that a man is involved to the degree that a woman is.

Q: Why is that? Do men not care?

Fogarty: It's not a matter of not caring. Men are genuinely interested in the well-being of their kids. They care. From our focus groups, we found that men generally feel they don't have anything to contribute with child care. They feel that the wife is taking care of it and that it's basically a one-person job.

Four out of five parents of preschool children place their child in some form of child care.

Q: When both parents work, it's certainly more efficient for the woman to handle one set of duties, while the man takes care of his. No one has time to do everything. Assuming that women are going to play a lead role in shaping the child-care decisions, what can the man do?

Fogarty: Finding good child care is one of the most important decisions that parents will make for their children and family. It's an agonizing decision. With both parents working, your child is going to spend a lot of time with your child-care provider. It's a decision about who will be a partner in raising your child. Parents need a lot of information and support at this time. It's an emotional decision. Sometimes parents feel isolated; they don't have all the information they need. That's one way a man can help his partner. The more support he provides, the better.

Q: What kind of support would be valuable?

Fogarty: Perhaps Mom gets the names of child-care programs and caregivers, and she does the first round of interviews. But Dad can be a second set of eyes in checking out the setting and interviewing staff. If you're a manager of a company and interviewing a new job hire, do you make the decision on your own or do you have others review it with you? It's the same idea. Choosing a primary partner in the raising of your child is a major decision, and the support you provide will help ensure a choice that best meets your family's needs.

Q: In talking to a labor and delivery nurse about a dad's role in childbirth, I found that men felt the same about that as they do about child care. They want to feel as if they can contribute and make a difference, and when they don't feel that way, they step back.

Fogarty: There is this idea that child raising comes more naturally to women. Women are often better at tuning in to people and children, and that's why it's assumed they should handle the major child-care responsibilities. But men can bring their strengths to the selection process. They may see themselves as more analytical, logical, and rational. Well, these are very important skills in assessing a child-care situation. Men are able to read people, problem solve, and do comparisons, all potentially very useful skills in making a decision.

Q: How important is child care?

Fogarty: We tend to think in this country that education begins at age five when a child starts school. That's not true. A child starts learning even before she's born. The ages from zero to five are the formative years in a child's development. These early years lay the groundwork for a person's entire life. Recent studies have shown that the first three years of life are critical in a child's brain development. High-quality child-care and early education programs can influence a child's language and thinking abilities and increase his readiness for school. The child-care provider plays a significant role in a child's early development. And when parents understand how important this is, they get more involved.

Q: You've talked about ways in which a father can support a mother. Are there any ways in which men are not helpful?
Fogerty: I don't think it's helpful to view the child-care costs as coming out of the mother's salary alone. The cost of child care is almost always considered to be a proportion of what the wife is making, not the family income as a whole. I guess this goes back to the idea that women are the primary caregivers. And so child-care costs are weighed against their earnings. If Mom can't take care of the baby, then she has to pay for it—that idea.

Q: Women also tend to feel more guilty about leaving a child in child care than a man does.
Fogerty: There are several reasons for that. When a mom takes her child to child care, she feels she loses some level of control in her child's life. Now, some of the values instilled in the child won't all come from her and Dad. She feels she's losing a piece of his childhood—she may miss his first step, his first word, his first "Bye bye." She also feels insecure; she worries that the child might grow more attached to the caregiver than to her. That doesn't happen. Love isn't like that. A child won't have less love for his parents because he loves his caregiver. A strong bond with a caregiver actually helps strengthen the parental bond with the child, assuming the child's needs are met at home. Interestingly, though, single moms who work don't feel guilty about working, because they know they have to. Not so with the moms in two-income families. If there's a choice whether the woman works or not, she tends to feel more guilty about it. So that's another way a man can be supportive—he can understand her feelings and let her share them with him.

Call Child Care Aware for child-care referrals in your area. Child Care Aware also provides at no cost brochures on finding child care, a take-along checklist for interviewing child-care providers, and other information. Child Care Aware, 2116 Campus Drive S.E., Rochester, MN 55904; 800-424-2246; E-mail: HN6125@handsnet.org.

Fewer than 10 percent of U.S. households fit the traditional mold where the woman stays home with the children and the man is the sole breadwinner.

USE THOSE ANALYTICAL SKILLS: QUESTIONS TO ASK WHEN ASSESSING CHILD CARE

What Is the Adult-to-Child Ratio? Staff is critical in any child-care situation. Obviously the fewer the number of children per adult, the more adult supervision each child receives. This is especially important for babies, who need more attention than older kids. The National Association for the Education of Young Children recommends these guidelines: ages zero to twelve months, three to four children per adult caregiver; one to two years, three to five children per adult caregiver; two to three years, four to six children per adult caregiver; three to five years, seven to ten children per adult caregiver; six to eight years, ten to twelve children per adult caregiver; and nine to twelve years, twelve to fourteen children per adult caregiver.

What's the Setting Like? Your child will stay there possibly eight to nine hours a day, five days a week. Is the atmosphere bright and cheery, or cave-like? Is it clean and safe? Are there things lying around that a child might stick in his mouth? Toddlers move all over the place, getting into everything. Is the furniture sharp edged? Can it tip over and fall on them? Is there enough space to move around? Can kids go outside, or do they have to stay in all the time? Is the yard fenced and safe?

What About the Caregivers? Turn a cold, calculating eye on your child's caregivers. Their job is critical, for they may spend more waking time during the week with your child than you do. Do they actually like kids? Do they get down and talk to them on their level? Check out their grooming. Do they smoke? How do they handle temper tantrums? Do they talk on the phone and ignore the kids? Will they be taking your child in the car? Are they licensed with CPR and first-aid training? State licensing is no guarantee of adequate child care. Some licensed providers provide the bare minimum for children and no more. Some moms get into child care because they want to stay home with their own children. They soon grow disenchanted and quit, leaving other parents in the lurch. How long has the caregiver been on the job?

How Do They Care for Infants and Newborns? Newborns pose special challenges for child-care providers. They require more attention than older kids. They need to be held more, picked up, and carried. Is the child held when fed? An infant cannot talk yet, so there's more guesswork in figuring out what she wants. What happens when she cries? Will she have the same provider every day? Are there other babies there? Do they nap each in their own bed? Make sure there's safe, adequate cribbing—not just cots, but cribs. Is there a carpeted area for infants to lie, roll, and crawl on? Unless they're sleeping, infants need to be watched continuously. As a result, child-care providers tend to charge more for newborns.

How About Toddlers? Toddlers have special concerns of their own, some of which revolve around the bathroom. Does the provider have experience in toilet training? Dig around in the toy box. What types of toys are available? Being on the same page with your caregiver on matters of discipline is a must. What happens when a child acts up or doesn't eat? Food is yet another consideration. Are there warm meals? Do you bring food or is it provided? Are the caregiver's cupboards stuffed with Cheezits and Cocoa Puffs? If so, the child may love it but you may not.

Do the Other Kids Like It? You can observe a lot by watching, as Yogi Berra used to say. Usually moms take on the job, but dads have also been known to sit in a child-care situation for an hour or two at a time to see what goes on there. Definitely check out the other kids. Are there kids the same age as yours? You may or may not want to have older children mixing with yours. Do the children seem happy and involved? A place that's too quiet may spell boredom for a child, and yet a place that's too noisy may suggest a lack of control.

What Is the Policy on Being Late or Taking a Child When Sick? These are big issues. Many caregivers charge extra when a parent arrives late to pick up his child. Working parents miss five to twenty-nine days a year due to child-care problems or sick children. Some caregivers are more relaxed about taking a child with the sniffles or a cold, while others sternly refuse. Without exception, you should be able to walk into your child care unannounced, at any time of the day, and feel comfortable. If you drop in and find something that displeases you, or your caregiver objects to this practice, find a new situation for your child. You should also be able to inspect any areas where children go: their beds, bathroom, kitchen, playrooms, or outside area. Again, if the caregiver objects, that's a problem.

What Do Other Parents Say? Talk to other parents; they're the real authorities in child care. Talk to parents with children in the child-care situation that you're considering. Do they like it? Are they happy with how their child is doing? Is the child happy? Your comfort level will increase considerably if other parents recommend the child-care provider. Last but not least, listen to your child and watch him. Does he like it there?

Source: Adapted from material provided by Child Care Aware, Solano Family and Children's Services, and interviews with caregivers. There are more than four hundred Child Care Resource and Referral Agencies in all fifty states. Contact the CCRRA in your area for the names of licensed caregivers and other information. Thanks also to Darlene Dotson, mother of six, for her assistance with this article.

CHILD-CARE CENTERS

There are basically three types of professional child care: child-care centers, family or home child care, and nannies who come into your home. This section and the two that follow contain brief discussions of each type of child care.

A child-care center has a more formal atmosphere than a person's home, which is why many parents like it. The environment loosely resembles a school; it's more structured. There is a designated menu of foods, prepared by a trained cook. Children are segregated according to age. At Kindercare, for example, there are programs for infants, toddlers, preschoolers, kindergarteners, and school-age children. Every age level has its own rooms and activities, and the older children do not play with the infants and toddlers.

Babies must be at least six weeks old to enter. Parents must provide formula, disposable diapers, baby food, and two complete changes of clothes. In the newborn room, each baby has a crib, blankets, and sheets. There are high chairs and a changing table, toys, foam cushions, and balls. Rocking chairs allow the caregiver or teacher to always hold the baby during feeding. Babies can crawl around on the carpet or outside on a blanket in a grassy area fenced off from the other play areas at the center.

The toddler room has scooter bikes, blocks, and educational and fun toys. Toddlers have their own mats with bedsheets for rest periods. There are even porcelain mini-toilets when potty training occurs.

There may be three or four activities going on in a room at the same time. One child may be tending to the fish tank. Others may be playing dress-up, finger painting, or drawing a picture to be posted in the hallway.

Children may be dropped off at 6:30 A.M. and must be picked up by 6:00 P.M. The ratio of newborns to adults is four to one. Parents receive a "daily infant activity record," which tells what a child ate, how many bottles a child had, how many diaper changes there were, how long he or she napped, and other activities and observations.

Source: Adapted from materials provided by Kindercare Learning Centers, P.O. Box 2151, Montgomery, AL 36102; 800-633-1488 or 800-628-2288. La Petite Academy is another nationally known child-care provider with eight hundred centers across the United States. La

Petite Academy, 8717 West 110th Street, Building #14, Overland Park, KS 66210; 913-345-1250.

Families earning below $36,000 annually spend approximately 12 percent of their income on child care.

FAMILY CHILD CARE

Family child care takes place in a person's home. Typically the caregiver is a mom who has chosen to stay home with her own children and takes in other kids in addition to her own.

According to the National Association for Family Child Care, more toddlers and infants are in family child care than any other type of child care in the United States. Many families prefer it because it is in a person's home. Since their child can't be in her own home, this is a close substitute. It becomes a second home for her.

Family child care is usually highly reliable and dependable, with little turnover in staff. The structure of family child care resembles the structure in your home. A caregiver functions as a parent, and many also provide opportunities for learning. They can teach children when they take clothes out of the dryer to sort and match socks, for example.

Naturally, family child care in a person's home will have fewer children than a professional child-care center. This may mean more one-on-one attention for your child. Nor are babies or infants restricted to specific rooms. There is usually a mix of ages in family child care, with younger kids playing with older ones, and vice versa.

Family child care tends to be more willing to take in mildly ill children. Because it is home based, hours can often be stretched to accommodate a parent working late. Some family care homes even take in kids on the weekend and pick them up from school or preschool. Children also tend to have more freedom of movement. They can go outside into the backyard, weather permitting, and come back in again, whenever they please.

You can get a strong sense of who your caregiver is by observing her home. Is the home super-neat and orderly? If so, what are the children doing all day? Are they afraid to touch anything or sit on the furniture? A good caregiver lets the children be themselves in a relaxed, informal atmosphere. One way to measure the quality of child care is if the children form attachments to their caregiver. If they do, you're probably onto something good.

Source: Deborah Eaton is president of the National Association for Family Child Care, which provides referrals to the more than 1,500 accredited family child-care homes in the United States. National Association for Family Child Care, 206 Sixth Avenue, Suite 900, Des Moines, IA 50309; 515-282-8192; www.dms@assoc-mgmt.com/users/nafcc. Lori Triplett of Triplett Day Care also contributed to this article.

Today, 70 percent of women with young children are working outside the home. In 1970, 30 percent of women with young children were in the workforce.

NANNIES

About half a million children in the United States under the age of five receive care from a nanny. Most parents who hire nannies are dual career couples. Mom usually takes the lead in selecting a nanny, though Dad usually has input on the final decision.

A nanny provides in-home care. That's the chief advantage: the child stays in her own home, rather than going somewhere else during the day. She sleeps in her own bed, plays with her own toys, etc. A nanny can be full- or part-time, and may or may not live with the family. People who work at home sometimes hire nannies to take care of the children. The nannies take care of the children in one part of the house while a parent works in his or her home office.

With a nanny, you don't have to worry about picking your child up if you're running late from work. She's already home. (Just remember to give her a call telling her you'll be late.) And the nanny will stay home with the child if she gets sick.

Another big advantage of a nanny: she provides one-on-one care. The child isn't part of a group or center; it is her and the nanny alone. The nanny focuses on the child and doesn't have to take care of other children.

Nannies are overwhelmingly female. A nanny's primary responsibility is child care; she may or may not be willing to do light housekeeping. International Nanny Association nannies must be at least eighteen years old with a high school degree, though many of them have earned bachelor degrees. Nannies fall into three general categories: young, single persons who want to be a nanny for a year or two; older women who have raised a family of their own but still want to be around children; and child-care specialists and professionals who view nannying as a career. Two famous nannies: Fran Drescher's character in *The Nanny* TV series and Mary Poppins.

Salaries for nannies range from $200 to $600 weekly. A nanny typically works five days a week, forty to sixty hours a week. It's a big job; she's with the child an estimated 75 percent of the child's waking hours. Live-in nannies receive job benefits such as paid vacation, health coverage, use of a car, and free room and board. The parents are considered her employer and must pay her Social Security, Medicare taxes, and unemployment taxes.

Source: Wendy Sachs is president of the International Nanny Association, which conducts nanny training programs and publishes an Annual Directory of Placement Agencies *($19.95) to help you find a nanny.*

International Nanny Association, Station House, Suite 438, 900 Haddon Avenue, Collingswood, NJ 08108; 609-858-0808; www.nanny.org.

HOW TO FIND CHILD CARE

The best way to find child care is through word of mouth from other parents. Colleagues at work can also be helpful. Other excellent sources are elementary schools and preschools. Caregivers frequently pick up and drop off children, and they're often well known by preschool and school officials.

Two more sources cited elsewhere in this chapter are: Child Care Aware (800-424-2246) and the Child Care Resource and Referral Agency in your area. Both provide referrals. The National Association of Child Care Resource and Referral Agencies is at 1319 F Street, NW, Suite 810, Washington, DC 20004; 202-393-5501.

The local Better Business Bureau also provides lists of licensed child-care providers, and there's always the phone book.

Yet another source is The National Child Care Information Center, which is a national clearinghouse for information on child-care agencies and associations. Its web site provides links to a number of child-care web sites. NCCIC, P.O. Box 1492, Washington, DC 20013; 202-884-8200; www.nichcy.org.

PRESCHOOLS

The preschool years begin at about age two and a half years and last until five or six when the child enters kindergarten. (Many schools won't take children until after they're toilet trained.) As its name implies, a preschool helps children prepare for school. It used to be known as "nursery school" or "play school." A good preschool is like a good school. It offers an education-based curriculum that promotes learning and childhood development. Children learn as they play and have fun. They listen to stories, paint paintings, sing songs, make crafts projects, and participate in a variety of group and individual activities.

Tom Dalrymple has an unusual perspective on preschools. Not a preschool teacher or director, he is a sales representative for an insurance company that underwrites preschools. His company will not

This generation of American children is the first generation to grow up with the majority of them in some form of child care before the age of five.

insure them if they do not measure up to certain standards. In the past two years, Dalrymple has inspected more than forty preschools in the northern California region. His method of assessing potential clients for insurance reasons can help fathers—and mothers—evaluate preschools for their own children.

Like a parent, Dalrymple talks to the preschool director. It's one of his most important assessment tools. "The way a preschool operates seems to trickle down from the director," he says. Is she organized and on top of things? What are her credentials? It is difficult to have a good preschool without a good director in charge.

Dalrymple walks around the building and the grounds "to get a feel for things," as he says. Preschools are located in churches, rec buildings, schools, offices, former homes, and other sites. He likes to see windows in all the rooms. Preferably there is one large open room where the children play, eat, and store their things in their nooks or cubbyholes. He's not a big fan of homes that have been converted into preschools because they tend to be older, and the facilities are not as good. Although, he adds quickly, there are many excellent preschools located in former residences.

Preschoolers need lots of individual attention. Dalrymple asks questions about the staffing ratios. A ratio of one instructor to four or five children indicates superior quality in Dalrymple's mind. (For NAEYC guidelines on this subject, please see the "Use Those Analytical Skills" section earlier in this chapter.) He takes note of the instructors. Teachers must be eighteen and over. Do they have Early Childhood Education (ECE) credits? Do they seem physically able to handle the kids?

Dalrymple wants to know about school curriculum and programs. Is the preschool just providing child care, or are there educational activities and real teacher–child interaction? He doesn't want to see children sitting in front of a TV screen any more than parents do.

A preschool needs to have age-appropriate activities and age-appropriate equipment, such as books, blocks, toys, and furniture. "I want to know what the school's philosophy is," he says. "What are its objectives?" Dalrymple never walks away from a preschool without one of its parent handbooks or brochures.

Too many "red flags" will make Dalrymple wary of underwriting a preschool. The possibility of child abuse or molestation is also a potential nightmare for insurance companies. Dalrymple asks whether a child ever spends time alone in a room with an adult. The less isolated, the better. No closed doors. He prefers to see two adults in a room with children or everyone all together in a large, open room.

Dalrymple checks out the play equipment. Swings and monkey bars are now considered "high risk" items. They are no longer being erected and are being taken out of many playgrounds. He looks for physical hazards that pose a danger to children, such as a swing situated too close to a fence. When children jump off, will they hit the fence? Soft spongy material under a climbing structure or slide is a must. Kids need to be able to run and fall without landing on concrete.

Pickup and dropoff are yet other considerations. Dalrymple was once sitting at a church preschool waiting for the director to arrive. He saw a parent drive up, sign a registration sheet, let the child out, and then drive off without another adult taking responsibility for the child. Responsibility for the child needs to be transferred from parent to teacher and back again. A preschool should only release a child to a parent or designated person; some preschools have plastic identification cards for security. Parents should feel free to quiz the preschool director about these and other procedures, just as Dalrymple does.

Contact: The National Association for the Education of Young Children accredits child-care centers and preschool programs in the United States. It can provide information on accredited centers in your area. NAEYC, 1509 16th Street, NW, Washington, DC 20036; 202-232-8777; 800-424-2460; www.naeyc.org/naeyc.

CLUBS AND OUTDOOR ACTIVITIES

Kids today have caught a bad break. They play video and computer games. Their tastes in soft drinks, cereal, candy, and fast food bring multimillion dollar corporations to their knees. They watch Nickelodeon and Sesame Street and the Disney channel, often on TVs in their bedroom. They visit dazzling, multilevel toy emporiums that cater to their every whim. They see dinosaur movies at the cineplex and ride dinosaur rides with eighty-foot drops at the amusement park. They own the present, and the future is theirs.

Despite all this, children today have lost something that previous generations of kids took for granted: the freedom to go outside and play. Kids still go out and play, but almost assuredly they do so under the watchful eyes of an adult. Children's activities are almost all supervised now. Everything is structured, organized, and coordinated. For many children, "free play" hardly exists anymore, unless it's in the controlled setting of a school playground.

When I was a kid, we played a game in our neighborhood called "Chase." It was a wilder version of "Kick the Can." We ran all over the place like lunatics and stayed outside after dark until 10 o'clock when our parents called for us to come in. Those days are long gone.

I live in a small town where crime is virtually nonexistent. But I do not feel comfortable letting my daughter play in the front yard unless I'm keeping an eye on her from the living room. The yard of choice for parents nowadays is the backyard; it's safe. The front yard creates unease. Even with a fenced yard, you never know: something could happen. At least, that's the fear.

It's like the crazy fear that your newborn is going to be snatched at the hospital or mistakenly switched with another baby. Parents worry about such things, although they almost never happen.

Here's another thing about kids today: they expect you to entertain them. I have a friend whose two boys will occasionally appear at his side. "What's up?" he asks. "We're bored," they tell him.

"Bored? You're kids! How can you be bored? Furthermore, why is that my responsibility? Now get your paws off my channel changer and clear outta here," my friend will reply, of course always sensitive to their still-developing feelings.

His theory is that children are so plugged in to the boob tube that when they get some free time, they don't know what to do with it. This, combined with their parents' natural protectiveness and the real dangers of the outside world, is why they need so many organized activities.

One of the chief duties of a father is as teacher and coach. This chapter contains information on a number of worthy youth clubs and organizations as well as outdoor pursuits such as bicycling, camping, and fishing. With a newborn on your hands, it will be a few years before you can get involved in some of these activities. But as your child gets older and more self-reliant, the tendency will be to sign him up for everything in sight and fill up every moment of his time.

Let me make an appeal here for unstructured, uncoordinated activities for your child—and for you and him together. He doesn't always have to be involved in an organized activity or playing sports. There may be times when the best thing in the world to do is just hang—no organized activities, no games to play, nowhere special to go—just the two of you, doing whatever, getting to know each other a little bit better.

BICYCLING: PART OF GROWING UP

Bonnie McClun is education director for the League of American Bicyclists, a Baltimore-based national organization of more than thirty-three thousand members. The League promotes and encourages bicycling for families, bicycle commuters, recreational riders, and others. A veteran cyclist and a mom, McClun offers the following advice to new dads who want to get their child's biking career started right.

Start Young. A child can learn to ride as soon as she develops adequate coordination and balance. Start her off with a scooter-style toy. Tricycles have gone the way of the Edsel—too tippy. They've been replaced by Big Wheels. When a child is just learning, find an empty parking lot or playground with lots of room for her to ride. Be prepared to give encouragement. Many parents, of course, take their kids with them when they ride. They use kiddie seats that attach to the bicycle or pull them behind them in trailers. At about age four, the child can move up to a "tag-along" bike. While still attached to your bike, the child can push some of her own weight.

Wear a Helmet. Learning to ride a bike is part of growing up. So is falling off. Get your child in the habit of wearing a helmet even when he's crashing around the house on a Big Wheel or scooter toy. Head injuries are a leading cause of fatalities for youngsters. Blows to the head can also cause brain damage. Adults need to wear helmets, too. If you make your child wear one, but you don't use one, what kind of message does that send?

Buy a Fitted Helmet. Find a helmet that fits your child's head. A helmet should be level front to back with the straps tight. It must be ANIS-, SNELL-, or ASTM-approved. It should cover the forehead with a finger's distance from the eyebrows to the bottom of the helmet. Never let a child ride with her helmet set back on the head. Most biking injuries occur to the top of the forehead.

Get a Helmet Your Child Likes. Your child must like his helmet. If he doesn't like it, he won't wear it. Bright- or light-colored helmets are best. Motorists can see them better.

Buy the Bike That Fits Her Now. Definition of a well-fitting bike: when the child can sit on the seat of the bike with both feet flat on the floor. Many parents trouble over this question: do you buy a bike that your child can grow into (like you do with clothes) or do you get one that fits now? Here's the answer: get one that fits her now. She must know she can control the bike—she must, in fact, be in control. A lack of control due to a too-heavy or too-large bicycle will lead to accidents, frustration, and possibly injury.

Avoid Hand Brakes on a Child's First Bike. Coaster or pedal brakes are the way to go for small children who do not have the strength in their fingers to manipulate hand brakes. Hand brakes are trickier to operate, too, compared to the simple act of using the pedal to stop.

Think About a Used Bike as a Starter Bike. New bikes are expensive. Friends or neighbors may have old bikes in the garage that their children used. All they need is a tune-up. Some old Schwinns are as indestructible as granite. Thrift shops are another good place to look for used bikes, but get it checked by a professional mechanic before letting your child ride it.

Children Like to Ride to a Destination. Don't just go out for a ride with the kids; ride to a specific destination. The best places to go are a park or, better yet, an ice cream shop. The kids have something to look forward to at the end. Even veteran cyclists finish a ride by stopping at a place to eat, which provides an incentive to keep pedaling.

Keep the Bike in Good Working Order. A rusty, clangy, hard-to-pedal bike is a pain. Your job, as father, is to keep your child's bike pain-free (and safe). It's an ongoing project. Kids like to run over everything they see, so periodically check the nuts and bolts for tightness, the chain for cleanliness and lubrication, and the saddle for height.

Teach Your Child the Rules of the Road. A bike is not a toy, it's a vehicle. It gives children freedom, but with that freedom comes responsibility. Teach your children to look both ways before they pull out into the street or cross the street. Ride on the right side of the road with traffic. Obey stop signs, yield signs, and traffic lights. Show them how a driveway is really an intersection, where cars can suddenly appear out of nowhere.

Never Let Children Ride Alone. That is, never let them ride alone until they have demonstrated knowledge of the rules of the road. Studies have shown that children are poor judges of distance. They have not learned to use their peripheral vision the way adults have, and they make spontaneous decisions. Seeing a friend in the distance, they will focus on the friend and ignore the car bearing down on them from the right. Bicycle riding is excellent preparation for driving. Kids who learn the rules of the road on a bike are well prepared when it comes time to take the wheel of a car.

Contact: League of American Bicyclists, 190 West Ostend Street, Suite 120, Baltimore, MD 21230; 410-539-3399; www.bikeleague.org/.

CANOEING: A PASSION FOR TRAVELING ON WATER

Canoeing with a baby or small children may seem a scary proposition to some, but Montana author and veteran paddler Alan Kesselheim says otherwise. He and his wife, Marypat, once took a week-long canoe trip on the Green River in Utah when one of their sons was three months old and the other was one and a half years old. Now with a baby girl in the family, all five Kesselheims have squeezed into a canoe for trips on the Yellowstone River, Smith River, and other rivers of the West.

"We love to paddle, and we're not going to give it up because we have kids," says Kesselheim (who also contributed to the "Traveling with a Baby" section in the chapter "Travel: Business and Family"). "Kids will have a passion for what their parents have a passion about. And we have a passion for being outdoors and traveling on water."

Kesselheim thinks canoeing is a terrific way to spend time with kids, even the very smallest ones. From three months old until about the age of one when they start walking, children are accommodating travel partners. Infants tend to sleep a lot and don't move around like toddlers. They're easy to feed (especially if Mom is nursing) and are fairly self-contained little bundles.

He recommends plastic disposable diapers for short weekend trips. They get "incredibly stinky and toxic" if you carry them any longer. For week-long trips on water, he prefers cloth; about twenty to thirty diapers will cover you. You can rinse and wash them out and then find a laundromat when you take the canoe out of the river. Kesselheim says that sometimes their canoe resembles "a gypsy skow" with all the diapers hanging out to dry.

When you backpack with young children, you need to carry all the gear plus the children. Car camping forces you to use the car as a base camp; you take day hikes only to return in the evening. Canoeing allows you to really get away. Even better, it carries all your gear for you: clothes, diapers, diaper pail, volleyball net, chair, rattle, stuffed animal, etc.

Safety precautions obviously need to be taken. Kesselheim steers away from waves and whitewater and becomes more cautious when the river rises. But he likes the simplicity of being on water—for himself and his family. He looks forward to the day when his children become "great, pure paddlers," who can show the old man how to do it. "It's a huge treasure to share the outdoors with your kids," he says. "They make you see all this stuff that you've forgotten. It's just a tremendous payoff."

Contact: Canoe and Kayak *magazine contains articles about canoeing for families and kids. P.O. Box 3146, Kirkland, WA 98083; 425-827-6363.*

CAMPING: START SIMPLY AND PROGRESS FROM THERE

Jeff Hicks is a former youth minister who now works with at-risk middle school and high school students on wilderness education projects in the San Francisco Bay Area. They study tidepools, conduct butterfly research, plant native plants, and learn how natural resources work. A veteran backpacker and kayaker, Hicks regularly takes his son, Ben, and daughter, Ashley, on camping trips. He wants them to learn what he knows: the values and joys of being out in nature. Some tips from Hicks on family camping follow.

Start Simply and Build from There. You may have climbed Annapurna and rafted the Bio-Bio in your wild and woolly youth. But is that a realistic expectation for children? Take it easy at first, especially with an infant in tow. Undershoot at first, don't overshoot. Progress from simple experiences onto more exciting and adventurous things.

Think Ahead. Camping is no longer a matter of get-up-and-go, a thing you can do on a whim. Make sure your baby and partner have everything they need to feel comfortable and secure. Got all the equipment you need? Sleeping bags, camping stove, tent, etc.? Make a list and check it twice.

Pick a Spot and Stay There. Drive to your campground and park your car. That's home base. Make day trips from there. Staying in one spot allows you to explore an area and really get to know it. Lots of packing and unpacking and driving around will cause misery for you and griping from the peanut gallery.

Do What Works for Your Family. In camping today, you can choose the level of your inconvenience. You can park shoulder to shoulder with other RVs in a campground with as many amenities as a Holiday Inn. Or you can rough it. With a baby in the diaper stage, it's better to stick close to the conveniences. Once he's potty trained, head for wilder destinations.

Keep It Short and Sweet. Go on simple day hikes where you can easily tote your lunch and energy snacks in a rucksack. Take a bike trip or even paddle a gentle river on a canoe. Backpacking trips are out of the question until the children get much older. The gear is too expensive and besides, you will have to carry everything yourself (including your growing child).

Take Your Kids by Yourself if Necessary. Some women like camping; some don't. Your partner doesn't have to come if she doesn't want to. Give her the weekend off, and you take the kids.

Go to Places Where Children Are Welcome. Many state parks sponsor Junior Ranger programs, nature talks, and other activities oriented to children. You may be able to enroll them in a program for the day, giving you a chance to sneak off and have a date with a trout.

Let Your Children Take the Lead. Don't force their experience. Let them suggest what they can handle by the activities they want to do. Remember: they're kids. They may not be used to being dirty. They may get cold at night, and scared. Hicks still remembers the time his kids jumped out of their skins when a raccoon walked across camp. It was the first time they'd ever seen a wild animal.

Be Safe. Be Prepared. Bring mosquito repellant, sunscreen, water purification tablets, and minor first-aid essentials. Weather can change in a heartbeat in the woods. Be aware of the dangers of dehydration, altitude sickness, and sunstroke. You need to know what time it is and where you are when you're hiking, and what to do if someone falls and injures himself. Some basic first aid, such as treating blisters, is useful.

From Time to Time, Venture Out on Your Own. Go get some of what Hicks calls "my personal soul food." Leave the women and children home and bury your head in a free-running mountain stream for a while. Coping with fatherhood and the many other responsibilities in your life will be much easier after that.

Contact: One source for backpacking and camping information is Backpacker *magazine, P.O. Box 7590, Red Oak, IA 51591; 800-666-3434.*

SELLING THE EXPERIENCE OF FISHING

Is there a better outdoors activity for father and son or father and daughter than fishing? A child can learn to fish virtually as soon as she can fold her fingers around the rod (please, never call it a pole). Although don't expect much from her in the beginning. She'll probably pay attention for ten minutes or so. After that she'll be bored and want to go off and skip rocks or something. If she does, let her. Never force an interest in fishing; it will just turn her off.

Pick a day when conditions are ideal—nice and sunny, no wind—just a lovely day to be outside. Keep it simple. Use a bobber and a worm and hook. Try a spin-casting rod and reel. Don't bring out the super-sophisticated fly fishing gear while your kid fishes with the cheapo stuff from K mart. Use the same type of gear she does; stay on her level. If she sees you using something different than what she's using, she's going to want to get her hands on it.

Pick a nice mellow pond. Your five-year-old is probably not ready yet to go sportfishing for tarpon off the coast of Bimini. Find a nice mellow pond stocked with lazy hatchery fish. Bluegills are one suggestion. Trout and catfish are two more.

Fish side by side with your child. During that ten minutes or so when you have her attention, give her your *full* attention. Teach her how to tie a surgeon's knot or splice a fly line. Be supportive, not critical. Don't do it all for her; let her make her own mistakes. That's the only way she'll learn.

Sell the experience of fishing, not just catching fish. Kids love digging around and hunting for worms. That's part of the fishing experience. Being out in nature, getting dirty, spending quality time with the old man—that's a big part of the fishing experience, too. Some kids are happy just to see fish, let alone catch them. And if they catch something, well, that's a bonus.

Catch and release is a good concept to instill early in kids. So is the value of preserving fisheries and wild fish, and conservation basics such as leaving the campsite in better shape than when you arrived.

Source: Ed Goldstein and Andy Martin are staffers of the American Sportfishing Association, which sponsors a loaner program in libraries in twenty-six states where people can check out fishing tackle much as they do books. Its "Hooked on Fishing Not on Drugs" program for children teaches the value of making positive life choices. Educational materials are available for parents from the ASA's Future Fisherman Foundation. American Sportfishing Association, 1033 North Fairfax Street, #200, Alexandria, VA 22314; 703-519-9691. Contact your local bait shop or fishing club for information about fishing in your area.

HIKING: CREATING A LOVE OF NATURE

The Appalachian Mountain Club is one of the nation's oldest and most respected hiking organizations. Headquartered in Boston, it sponsors family hiking trips and outdoor programs to encourage awareness of the natural world. Additionally it operates a network of eight backcountry huts on the Appalachian Trail in the White Mountains of New Hampshire. Backpacking families hike along the trail and stay in the huts at night. Scott Kathan is a spokesman for the club and a longtime hiker. Though not a dad himself, he has three young nephews (one of whom is a newborn). Based on his observations of his nephews, as well

> "It was always important to me to lead my children into real woods, not the woods of Little Red Riding Hood."
>
> —Norman Maclean, author of *A River Runs Through It* and father of Jean and John

"We just blitzed in and
started groping for fish,
while dad cheered from
the bank. My first fish
ever, nabbed with cold
bare hands, was twelve-
inches long. I raised it over
my head and we were all
screaming."
—Writer Dirk Jamison, remembering his first fishing trip with
his father

as his own experiences in the woods, he offers some interesting ideas on how to encourage a love of hiking in children.

Start in a Controlled Environment. An easy, flat walk in the woods is ideal. Remember that the woods can be scary to a young child, especially at night. Animals live there, not to mention dwarves, wicked witches, and other imaginary creatures that populate children's fairy tales. It's probably not a place for a newborn. It's too unpredictable. Wait until he gets a little older, and then bring him along.

Expect to Travel at a Slower Pace. Children, even older children, dawdle. As they walk they become fascinated with tiny, seemingly insignificant objects (just as you are fascinated with things that produce yawns from them). You must by necessity take more of a "stop and smell the roses" approach and become less deadline- and goal-oriented.

Allow for Plenty of Time. It's going to take longer when you hike with children. You can't hike at your normal pace, so don't let that frustrate you. Nevertheless, there will be times when you need to make it somewhere before the sun sets and you have to push them a little. Like so many things with kids, try to strike a balance.

Hiking with Children Changes the Nature of the Experience. This is true for all activities with kids: it's not the same as when you do it on your own or with other adults. In hiking, the pace is slower, the food is different, the company is not the same. You cannot pass a flask of Jim Beam around the fire (at least not for the kids to drink). Realize this before you start, and you'll be better off.

Let Them Carry Something. Obviously, how much they carry depends on their age and fitness. But a dad is not a Sherpa, however much he may resemble one at times. Kids can carry their snacks and water. This will help build a sense of togetherness and teamwork. Everyone pitching in to get the job done.

Listen. Kids like to whine and complain. Oh man, do they. But it is possible amid all that caterwauling that they do have a legitimate gripe, such as a blister. You may also be pushing them too hard.

Get Them Involved. Ask them to help collect firewood. Let them stir the spaghetti. Explain why you need to boil the water before drinking. Involvement builds teamwork.

Keep the Culinary Surprises to a Minimum. A camping trip is probably not the best time to introduce a child to Julia Child's new recipe for frog legs. Stick with the basics—comfort food such as SpaghettiOs or hot dogs. High-energy snacks on the trail are a must.

Create Diversions. The woods are an endless source of "I Spy" type detective games. Kids get into it. They're great at identifying trees and plants, and spotting birds. Point to a flower or tree at the beginning of a hike and count how many times you see it during the hike. They love to find animal tracks and, even cooler, animal scat. In these ways, and in so many other ways, a child's love for nature is born.

Contact: Appalachian Mountain Club, 5 Joy Street, Boston, MA 02108; 617-523-0636. www.outdoors.org.

YOUTH ORGANIZATIONS AND CLUBS

Boy Scouts

Boy Scouts of America was founded in 1910. Since then more than 90 million boys have participated in it. Currently there are 4.4 million members of Boy Scouts of America, with 1.2 million adult volunteers, many of whom are dads with scouting sons. Many of those same dads were Scouts themselves.

Only boys can join the scouting program. However, at the age of fourteen, girls are eligible to join the Explorers, a career-based program sponsored by Boy Scouts. Some famous former Boy Scouts are Gerald Ford, Colin Powell, Stephen Spielberg, astronauts Jim Lovell and Gene Cernan, and Big Daddy Don Garlits, one of the greatest drag racers of all time. A survey commissioned by the Boy Scouts showed that men who had been Scouts for five years or more were more likely to be leaders in their community and have a high school or college diploma than men who had never participated in the program.

The levels of scouting are Tiger Scouts, Cub Scouts, and Boy Scouts. Tiger Scouts is the first level and begins in the first grade. It lasts one year, followed by Cub Scouts and later Boy Scouts, which ends at age eighteen. Boy Scouts earn merit badges by demonstrating knowledge and competency in an array of disciplines such as first aid, swimming, archaeology, computers, crime prevention, rock climbing, spelunking, and communications. The highest honor a Scout can attain is Eagle Scout.

In the past, only women served as Den Mothers for Cub Scouts. But now the position is called "Den Leader" because men do it, too. A dad can become a Scoutmaster, Merit Badge Counselor, Den Leader, or Explorer Post Advisor, or he can simply go along with his son and his fellow Scouts on their camping trips.

Contact: You can locate the local Boy Scout chapter in the white pages of your phone book, or reach Boy Scouts of America, 1325 West Walnut Hill

Lane, Irving, TX 75015; 972-580-2000; www.BSA.scouting.org/. Thanks to Gregg Shields, father of Erin, Kate, and Allie, for his research assistance with this article.

Camp Fire Boys and Girls

About 670,000 boys and girls belong to Camp Fire Boys and Girls nationwide. Girls make up about 55 percent of the membership, boys about 45 percent. Its philosophy stresses the value of coed education—boys and girls learning life skills together.

Formed in 1910, Camp Fire Boys and Girls has grown far beyond its original emphasis on outdoor education. The club program for Camp Fire Boys and Girls begins in kindergarten and runs through high school. Its members earn beads for community projects and other activities much the way Boy Scouts earn merit badges. Volunteer leaders (many of whom are dads) supervise these projects.

There are more than 125 Camp Fire Boys and Girls Councils in the United States. Each council tailors its programs to its community, conducting programs on subjects such as stranger awareness, youth leadership, and resisting peer pressure for teens.

Contact: Contact the national organization to find the Camp Fire Boys and Girls Council in your area or look in your local phone book. Camp Fire Boys and Girls, 4601 Madison Avenue, Kansas City, MO 64112; 800-669-6884 or 816-756-1950; www.campfire. org/.

4-H

The goal of 4-H is to give children the opportunity to become useful citizens and teach them to think, plan, and reason—nice skills for their parents to have as well. It is a service organization for youngsters, encouraging them to work on projects that benefit their community. The four *H*s in 4-H stand for head, heart, hands, and health.

Though originally formed for farm children, 4-H now includes urban and suburban youngsters. Kids raise hamsters, rabbits, and guinea pigs in addition to the more traditional pigs, sheep, and cattle. In addition, 4-Hers can work on a wide variety of non-animal or agricultural projects: rocket science, photography, camping, backpacking, woodworking, cooking, clothing making, and more.

"Mini-members" of 4-H range from five to nine. But most 4-Hers fall in the nine to nineteen age bracket. 4-H clubs operate in affiliation with land grant university cooperative extension offices in every county in the United States. One of the things that distinguishes 4-H from other youth programs is that university academic staff develop the programs and project materials. Adult volunteers (who often work professionally in the project area they're overseeing) serve as mentors. These projects can take months of work and are often judged at state and national competitions.

Contact: National 4-H Council, 7100 Conneticut Avenue, Chevy Chase, MD 20815; 301-961-2820. Contact the university cooperative extension office in your area for information on how to get involved in 4-H.

Girl Scouts

Girl Scouts of the USA is for girls from ages five to seventeen. Its extensive programs and activities seek to help girls make healthy choices in their lives and give them the tools to be successful adults. Some famous former Girl Scouts are Hillary Clinton, Olympic Gold Medal–winners Jackie Joyner-Kersee and Wilma Rudolph, professional golfer Nancy Lopez, and ABC-TV broadcaster Barbara Walters.

There are 3.5 million members of Girl Scouts of the USA, the largest organization for girls in the world. An amazing one out of every four American women has been involved in Girl Scouts since the formation of the first-ever Girl Scout troop in Savannah, Georgia, in 1912.

Like the Boy Scouts, Girl Scouts earn badges to show their competence and knowledge in a variety of disciplines. Girls learn teamwork, go on camping trips, get their first taste of independence, learn to enjoy and appreciate nature, build self-esteem, form friendships, develop skills, enlarge their view of the world, become leaders, and, of course, sell lots and lots of cookies.

Girls can join the Daisy Girl Scouts at age five. Next comes Brownie Girl Scouts in the first, second, and third grades, followed by the levels for older girls. More than 800,000 adults volunteer in Girl Scouts, including many dads. Although men cannot be troop leaders by themselves, they may share that status with women.

Contact: You can locate your local Girl Scouts Council in the phone book, or reach Girl Scouts of the USA, 420 Fifth Avenue, New York, NY 10018; 212-852-8000; www.gsusa.org/.

Indian Guides/Indian Princesses

The YMCA sponsors the Y-Indian Guides program for fathers and sons, and Y-Indian Princesses for fathers and daughters. Children's ages range from five to eight. The Y also sponsors a more loosely structured program for preschoolers called Y-Indian Papooses. Both moms and dads participate in it with children ages three to four.

"A few years ago, my wife and I took our three foster boys huckleberrying along with our five birth children. For most of the day, the boys whined and complained, picking almost no berries. But by evening, they were nearly frantic with a sense of freedom and possibility. They ran up and down the mountain."

—Michael Umphrey, teacher and father of eight

The goal of all three programs is to strengthen parent-child relationships and provide opportunities for a father and child to spend time together. In Indian Guides/Indian Princesses, families form a "tribe." The tribe meets twice a month at a member's house. Activities consist of arts and crafts, games, stories, and songs. Tribes in an area come together as a "nation" for special events and outings.

Of the 2,200 YMCAs in the United States, about six hundred sponsor Indian Guide programs. Two big camp-outs are held each year, often at YMCA-sponsored camps. Kids (and their dads) play games and sports, perform skits, make art projects, fish, boat, hike, and explore nature. In the evening, they gather around the campfire, tell stories, and sing songs under the stars.

Contact: Call your local Y to see if it offers Indian Guides or Indian Princesses.

Tip: For a more comprehensive listing of clubs and organizations, see The Directory of Youth Organizations, *by Judith B. Erickson, Ph.D. It's a guide to five hundred clubs, groups, troops, teams, and more for children and young people. It is available through Free Spirit Publishing, 800-735-7323.*

MORE ACTIVITIES
FOR YOU AND YOUR CHILD

Looking for something more to do with your child, possibly of an unstructured nature? Why not make pancakes, go to a farmer's market, wrestle, see a movie, play Hearts or Crazy Eights, make a fort with blankets, have a water fight, play Junior Scrabble or Junior Monopoly, take the dog for a walk, wash the car, go to the zoo or a museum, draw pictures on the sidewalk, have a picnic at the park, play piggy-back and hide 'n' seek, take a bath, go to a bookstore or library, pick berries, play tag in the backyard, build a tree fort, put up a hummingbird feeder, or go to the beach and feed the seagulls or erect a sand castle.

COOKING AND FOOD

I am not the world's greatest chef, to say the least. But I have cooked for women many times, and not once—never, not in a single solitary instance—has one voiced displeasure or even a hint of criticism. And mostly, they have lavished undue praise on me.

This was—let me emphasize and underline—not because I had created some culinary masterpiece à la Paul Prudhomme. Clearly, it was out of simple gratitude that I had cooked for them.

Lots of fathers cook, and I talked to three of them for this chapter. They are men who cook for their families, and they enjoy it a great deal. They all agree that if you want to be a hero to your partner, cooking is one of the ways to do it. Even if you cook only on a spot basis, she will be truly grateful.

Certainly when both husband and wife work, you can't expect her to cook every night. She may enjoy cooking, but when she has to do it all the time, it becomes a burden. That's just not fair to her.

My experience has been that kids seem to be the neediest in that 5 to 7 P.M. time slot when dinner has to get on the table. You've just picked them up from day care; they're hungry and cranky. They need Mom's attention especially, and yet everybody has to eat.

Things will go a little bit smoother if you step up and fix dinner. Or, if Mom is cooking, you take over with the kid. You're better off working as a team.

That's true on the nutrition issues, too. Many dads would define a balanced meal as a burger, shake, and fries. Roughage is the lettuce in a Big Mac. Pizza supplies valuable protein (cheese) and carbohydrates (crust). Taco Bell introduces the children to international

> "This is not fatherly advice. The only fatherly advice I have ever given you is not to eat your peas off a knife."
>
> —The author John Cheever, writing to his son Federico

cuisine. The people in the Reagan administration who defined catsup as a vegetable were clearly dads.

One of the problems with this attitude is that if you don't care what your kid eats, you force your partner into being the food cop. That's no fun for her and not that great for your relationship, either. Food is like anything else. You lay the groundwork so your child can grow up to be a happy, well-rounded person. You're not doing your job in that area if all she does is eat junk food.

Final point: no matter who cooks the meal or what you're eating, I believe strongly in a family sitting down together every night at the dinner table. To me, the family dinner table is one of the cornerstones of civilization.

Shut off the TV, call everybody to the table, and say a blessing. Over dinner you catch up on the news of the day, trade stories, tell jokes, offer opinions, discuss current events, reminisce, listen, and laugh. As kids get older and their schedules crazier, it becomes harder and harder to preserve this time. But it's worth the effort. It's the one time of the day when you can all come together to acknowledge, and celebrate, the shared blessing of family.

FUNDAMENTALS OF GOOD COOKING

Kent Odell is a man who loves food. Not only that, he loves to prepare and cook it. He is a furniture maker by trade, and whenever he has a spare moment and the wind is blowing, he throws his sailboard on the back of his truck and goes windsurfing. Odell is not a chef or a professional foodie. None of the fathers interviewed in this chapter is, though each is a good cook in his own right. That's the message they all would like to deliver to new dads: you don't have to be a culinary superstar to know your way around a kitchen, enjoy cooking, and prepare healthy, tasty meals. Odell, father of Ashley and Nicole, does most of the cooking for his family while commuting one and a half hours a day and running his furniture-making business. Here, he gives some pointers on organizing a kitchen, stocking the supplies you need, grocery shopping, and other cooking fundamentals.

Get Organized. For things to work well in the kitchen, you need to be organized. "It's like the controls of a car," says Odell. "You want everything where you can get at it." A poorly organized kitchen wastes food and time.

Develop Your Larder. No one with a family who works for a living has time to go to the store every day. So you need to stock up on food and cooking staples. The Odell cupboard always has pasta in it. Red wine can make a pedestrian meal into something tasty. Olive oil is an essential. Basic spices such as garlic powder, onion powder, Italian seasoning, and chili powder are highly useful. Odell sprinkles Italian seasoning on sauteed zucchini rounds.

Take It Easy on Yourself. You don't have to cook elaborately to cook well. One of Odell's staples is chicken stock, which he makes from the bones of a roasted chicken. A whole chicken can feed a family for days. Pull the guts out of the middle, lightly spread melted butter over it, then pop it in the oven at 350 degrees for about an hour. The chicken is done when the thigh juices run clear yellow, not pink, when pierced with a fork. After eating your roast chicken dinner, carve off the rest of the meat and save it for sandwiches. Throw the chicken carcass in a pot of water, boil off the bones and skin, and save the leftover meat and juice. Toss in some celery or carrot tops and you have the makings of a warm, soul-satisfying soup. Odell uses chicken stock for flavoring many of his dishes. He recommends ham for flavoring as well, sprinkling it in scalloped potatoes or bean dishes. Store the ham in the freezer and cut off chunks as you need it. Browned ham chunks in an ordinary canned spaghetti sauce make a tasty spaghetti Bolonaise. Hambone will give a delicious flavor to red beans and rice and navy bean soup. You can make ham sandwiches for lunch or have ham and eggs in the morning.

Keep a List of What You Need on the Refrigerator. When you're a new dad, buy milk every time you go to the store. You'll always need it. Diapers are another crucial item never to be without. Keeping a list means you won't forget anything when you go shopping. Of course, you have to remember to bring the list.

Grab It When the Price Is Good. Buy three boxes of Triscuits when they're on sale, if your family loves Triscuits. The same applies for coffee filters, Diet Pepsi, meat, chicken breasts, granola bars, orange juice, or anything else your family likes to consume. You'll save money and won't have to go back to the store for that item for a while.

Go with What's Fresh and in Season. The key to good cooking? Use fresh ingredients. Take advantage of those luscious green peppers overflowing in the produce bin and make a sweet and sour stir-fry chicken with pineapple and peppers. The best, most plentiful produce is often on sale, making it a doubly good deal.

Always Have Options. You get home late, you're beat, the house is in an uproar. What's a man to do? Make sure you have meals on hand with quick turnaround times. Chicken tacos or burritos are fast, easy, and nutritious. Mexican food usually is a hit with kids. One of Odell's favorites is spaghetti with clam sauce. He mixes two cans of chopped clams, clam juice, olive oil, and fresh garlic and tosses it with pasta with a sprinkling of fresh parsley. It's on the table in ten minutes.

Use Cookbooks. Cookbooks carry recipes and help teach basic techniques. They tell oven temperatures and times, which you can never remember on your own. Odell makes what he calls "a low-rent pot pie" with a biscuit crust. But he can jazz his basic recipe up slightly by using different combinations of spices. If you like a special cuisine, such as Szechwan, East Indian, or barbecue, get a cookbook for it. The women's magazines carry recipes too. (For some basic cookbook suggestions, please see "Cooking Resources" later in this chapter.)

Cook Two Meals at Once. You're in the kitchen whipping up a masterpiece, everything is spread out in front of you, the place is a mess, so why not? It's not as hard as it sounds. Odell was making a chicken dish from a James Beard recipe one night when he had some extra tomatoes from the garden. So he made spaghetti sauce with celery and onions at the same time, and they ate it the next night over pasta. When cooking two meals, he says, always cook the quickest meal first to get it out of the way.

Clean as You Go Along. One of the joys that Odell derives from cooking is to see how efficiently he can do it. Although it's not always possible, he tries to clean as he goes along, not letting dishes and pots pile up in the sink. While sauteeing vegetables, he moves over to the cutting board and chops carrots, then rinses a pot and puts it in the dishwasher. Then he goes back to the vegetables, and so forth. Being organized helps you better manage two or three things at the same time, he says.

Learn to Use a Pressure Cooker. Although intimidating to some cooks, a pressure cooker will help reduce your cooking time considerably. A pot roast that ordinarily takes three hours takes less than an hour in a pressure cooker. A beef stew that might take two hours is ready in twenty minutes. Vegetables are cooked in a twinkling. Odell is not a fan of microwaves, which he says cook things fast but not well.

Get into the Mindset That You're the One Feeding the Family. Some men don't think it's their job to cook. "That's bull," says Odell. When you're the one in charge, you can make sure that everyone sits down as a family and has dinner together. You don't have to eat packaged stuff from the grocery store all the time or fast food. You can trim the fat off the pot roast and eat healthy. Odell thinks it's a good idea to get your kids started early so they're not "cowardly eaters," as he puts it—so they learn to eat spicy foods, not just bland and so they at least have some familiarity with leafy green vegetables. "If you want anything decent to eat yourself," says Odell, "you have to get your kids to go along with it." Otherwise, he says, you'll be stuck with generic brown and white foods permanently. Once he dropped by his brother's house and found them eating corn dogs and Cheetos for dinner. His brother has four kids, and that's virtually the only kind of food they'll eat.

Give Yourself a Night Off. Odell gets tired like anyone else. There are times when he doesn't feel like slaving over a hot stove and wishes his wife would take him out to dinner. When he was a kid, as a special end-of-the-week treat, his family ate burgers and fries and watched TV together on Saturday nights. In a carryover from this tradition, Odell doesn't cook on Friday nights. The family orders take-out Chinese or pizza and they slip in a video and have a good time.

HOW NOT TO BE INTIMIDATED IN THE KITCHEN

For many men, the kitchen can be an intimidating place. Men want to feel competent and respected in what they do. But they are often not the chief cook in the family; their partner is. They cook less and they're not as good at it. Feeling not as competent or as useful, or perhaps deferring to their partner's greater abilities and knowledge, they take a step back, sometimes stepping so far back they remove themselves altogether, creating a void that their partner must fill by herself.

George Calmenson lives in Ashland, Oregon. He is the father of Adam. A former textbook production editor, he now conducts workshops on developmental aging. In the kitchen, at least, he would seem to have plenty of reasons to feel intimidated. His wife Cynthia is a trained pastry chef who studied at a Vienna, Austria, cooking academy. She knows her stuff. And yet Calmenson continues to cook, continues to maintain a place in the kitchen.

"We talked about dividing roles, but I didn't want to be regimented in that way," he says. "I didn't want to say, 'Well, I'll cook Wednesdays and you cook Thursdays'—that sort of thing. We divide the household responsibilities roughly in half. I tend to work more in

> "When you're a parent, you're always giving your child more than they can handle in terms of food. 'Here,' you say, 'it's escargot. You'll love it.'"
> —Writer Mike Finley, father of Daniele and Jonathan

the yard and on the building, while she has a higher standard of niceness and cleanliness, so she's more responsible for the inside. But nobody is solely responsible for the cooking."

When his wife wants to cook, Calmenson asks, "What can I do to help?" Usually this means prep work—chopping, washing vegetables. Sometimes he does the grocery shopping. Other times, when there's nothing for him to do in the kitchen, Cynthia may ask him to pick up around the house. "She wants to feel she's being supported in some way," he explains.

Calmenson doesn't like being told what to do any more than any other man. But he doesn't see supporting his partner in this capacity as being told what to do. She speaks to him (and he to her) using such terms as: "You'll make me happy if . . . you give me this or do this." Other ways to phrase such requests are "It would help me if . . ." or "Could you do me a favor . . ." These are not orders, which imply subservience. They are respectful requests between two equal partners.

Calmenson says, "You want to make your wife happy, right? If she tells you what she wants, it saves you from having to figure it out yourself. It's a gift she's giving you, telling you how she can be made content." He adds, "A lot of men feel resistance to being told anything. They love getting advice, but they don't want to be told what to do. They feel they're being challenged. But by asking the question and your wife giving you the answer, she is acting as a kind of advisor to you. Don't tell me what to do. Rather, tell me what you need so I can choose to do it of my own free will. There is a difference."

What occurs in the kitchen, like in the bedroom, often says a lot about a couple's relationship. It sets the ground rules for how you'll be together. Put a baby into the mix and it makes all of these issues even more potent.

Calmenson says he's learned a lot about cooking from Cynthia—the importance of fresh ingredients, how she uses spices, how to handle knives. But he doesn't try to do the things she does; he cooks what he likes, the way he likes to do it. And when they sit down to a meal of his, he says, "She's very careful to let me know how much she enjoys it."

Sometimes when he's making hummus, a favorite spread of theirs, she comes in behind him and makes suggestions on flavoring. His reaction? "I try to make room for her," he says. "I welcome the input, but I don't give up my position. I don't step aside. You don't have to defer to someone just because they do it better than you," he adds.

If there's hidden resentment in a relationship, sooner or later it will find the light of day, often in the form of big explosions. Being aware of what's going on and dealing with these issues openly will help defuse their power. Then the dinner table can be what it is meant to be, a place of love and nourishment and healing. In observing the Shabbat on Friday, which is the beginning of the holy day for Jews, the Calmensons light candles and say blessings over the food, bread, and wine. Before washing their hands, each takes off his or her wedding ring. At that moment, symbolically, they are unmarried and must decide whether to remarry. Each puts on the ring and says, "Yes," thus renewing their vows.

COOKING RESOURCES

The classic all-purpose cookbook is *Joy of Cooking*, by Irma S. Rombauer and Marion Rombauer Becker. No kitchen is complete without it. The Goethe quote at the beginning of *Joy* mentions fathers: "That which thy fathers have bequeathed to thee, earn it anew if thou wouldst possess it." Two more excellent cookbooks are: *Louisiana Kitchen*, by Paul Prudhomme, and James Beard's *American Cookery*. *Mastering the Art of French Cooking*, by Julia Child, Louisette Bertholle, and Simon Beck is worth investigating. Risotto is a wonderful, soul-satisfying meal that older children can participate in under the watchful eye of an adult. Simple recipes and clear instructions can be found in *Risotto*, by Judith Barrett and Norma Wasserman.

For years *Sunset* magazine had two excellent reader write-in columns, "Chefs of the West" and "Kitchen Cabinet." Both feature straightforward, tasty recipes with a minimum of fussiness. "Chefs of the West," a column by men for men, was recently discontinued, but the older Sunset Recipe Annual Cookbooks carry the recipes. Check your used bookstore for them. "Kitchen Cabinet" is still a revered staple.

Penzeys, Ltd. imports spices from around the world and is a wonderful resource for more than 250 spices, herbs, seasonings, and gift packs. The taco seasoning and Italian salad dressing base couldn't be simpler—and taste much better than their supermarket counterparts. Its catalog is available from Penzeys, Ltd., P.O. Box 933, Muskego, WI 53150; 414–679–7207.

DINING OUT WITH BABY AND OTHER FOOD TOPICS

A recent, well-publicized study by the Department of Agriculture showed that only 1 percent of American children—ages two to nineteen—eat what is defined as "a healthy diet." Kids chow down on too many high-fat, high-sugar foods instead of the proper balance of grains, vegetables, fruit, dairy products, and meat. The study's findings come as no surprise to Mike Finley, a poet, a novelist, and the author of over twenty books. A resident of St. Paul, Minnesota, he writes a syndicated weekly column for Knight-Ridder newspapers. His latest book, *Techno-Crazed* (Peterson's) advises families on how to cope with computers and the brave new world of high tech. As the father of Jonathan and Daniele and chief cook in his family, he has firsthand knowledge of the eating habits of small children. Here, he shares his tongue-in-cheek observations on what kids like to eat (and don't), surviving a night out in a restaurant with a baby, and other useful topics for new parents.

What Children Like to Eat. The rap against kids is that they dislike spicy foods and will eat only bland, predictable foods when not gorging on high amounts of refined sugar. A quick survey of Finley's cupboard—Franco American SpaghettiOs, macaroni and cheese, Ramen noodles, Mrs. Grass dried soup mixes, "homestyle" cheesecake in a box—would tend to confirm this. Finley points out that kids are also suckers for bright packages with gimmicks. In fact, providing bland or highly sugared foods packaged in a brightly colored box with a toy inside is the time-honored sales strategy of most food companies that cater to children.

Finley has observed that children will eat almost anything in the shape of an animal, such as macaroni noodles shaped like sharks. There's a company in Minnesota that makes pasta in the shape of the state. If biogenetics companies could somehow develop cauliflower or broccoli that resembled dinosaurs or sharks or teddy bears, the problem of child nutrition could be solved.

Additionally, Finley's kids enjoy foods that come in bright colors. "My kids will eat anything red," he says. "Also blue. They like blue. But there aren't many blue foods."

What They Don't Like to Eat. In a word, vegetables. Although when they're babies, you can get away with it a lot easier. "When my daughter was a baby, I fed her strained peas all the time," says Finley. "She loved it. I steamed the peas, spread a little butter on them, and she'd roll one around and pop it in her mouth, happy as a clam." But as his daughter grew older, her dietary habits changed. "She hasn't eaten a pea since she was three," he says. "If it's green and it's not lime Kool-Aid, she won't touch it."

Fast Food. Before Finley and his wife had children, they loved going out to new restaurants. They ordered wine and sampled the latest in nouvelle cuisine. Now, budgetary constraints tend to put a damper on expensive nights out. Also, their kids would much rather go to fast food chains that are advertised on television. "Kids like identifiable brand names," explains Finley. "When they're younger, they're more impressionable. They think, 'Oh, we know we're somewhere. We're eating at Big Bob's.'" Finley still fondly remembers taking his son regularly to Fudrucker's or Country Buffet to meet another dad and his son. The boys loved to hog out at "trough buffets," as Finley calls them, running around wild and going back for multiple helpings of jello and slices of salty ham. Neither dad minded because (a) that's what children do, and (b) each of the boys would eat about five pounds of food at a sitting and it would last them for a while.

Dining Out with a Baby. You can take your baby out to dinner with you, says Finley. Don't be afraid. Just remember that babies have good nights and bad nights just like adults. One night they may sit happily content drooling and cooing to themselves. Another night they may resemble Godzilla unleashed on the streets of Tokyo. This is why many parents play it safe and go to a place like McDonald's, where there are other parents with kids screaming and crying and acting up, and so they feel at home. As a regional footnote, Finley adds that the challenge of taking a baby out to dinner is nothing compared to putting mittens on a child in the middle of a Minnesota winter. "Now that's *hard*," he says. Furthermore, no one goes outside during the winter anyway in Minnesota, so the whole eating out with kids question is moot at that time.

Fine Dining with a Baby. Some night you may feel in an adventurous mood and want to go to a tonier, non–fast food restaurant that serves something besides hamburgers or tacos. Bring the baby, says Finley. It's possible you will make it past the soup course before she starts to wail. And if not, you and your partner can still have a nice, relaxing time taking turns walking the baby outside while the other one hurriedly gobbles his meal. Your baby may surprise you and actually get some of that delicious pasta in her mouth. The rest of it will be smeared across her face. The other diners may give you hard looks across the restaurant about your messy-faced baby crying her head off and wrecking your evening out, but that's their problem, not yours.

Fathers and Nutrition. Some fathers, observers note, are lazily content to let their partner stand guard over their child's dietary habits. Since they're not with the kids as much and thus don't have to see the results of their indulgence, they don't have to worry about it. It's said

"We say blessings before every meal. Why? Because it honors our belief in God. It sets a higher tone and keeps us in mind of high and lofty things. It ritualizes and sanctifies our life. And it's something we can share together."

—George Calmenson, father of Adam

that dads tend to be less practical than moms. They want to eat out more and go to more expensive places that bust the family budget. Mothers, on the other hand, are more price-conscious and nutrition-conscious. While Finley concedes that these stereotypes may have a grounding in reality for some families, he points out that both fathers *and* mothers have a hard time getting their kids to eat what's good for them. "I once thought about writing a book with my wife about how to get your kids to eat the right things. But then we realized we couldn't get our kids to eat the right things," he says.

Taking the Long View. Finley remembers how his daughter went through a three-year period where all she would eat were toasted cheese sandwiches. "We counted them," he swears. "She ate 1,500 consecutive toasted cheese sandwiches. Always with the crust cut off, of course. We referred to it as 'The Age of Cheese.'" But Finley notes reassuringly that children do grow and change. After this three-year epoch came to an end, his daughter did agree to sample other types of food. And he finds that as she and her brother have grown older, they have become more adventurous eaters. They're even willing to accompany their father to out of the way, hole in the wall–type eateries in the Twin Cities that they never would have tried when they were younger, which leads Finley to believe that new parents need to maintain some perspective on the whole food issue. "My kids never touch a carrot stick, and yet their minds function," he says. "They're healthy; they can do long division. So I guess they're going to make it."

COOKING WITH CHILDREN: DO YOU DARE?

When your children get older you may want to cook with them. Boys as well as girls can learn their way around the kitchen. What's the right age for them to start? Some experts say as early as three. Expect them to spill things and make messes at this or any other age.

During the week dinners are not the best time to involve a child. Dinners are more complicated; they require more ingredients and preparation and often need to get on the table *now*. Dinners occur at the end of the day when everyone's tired. You won't have the patience to teach, and they'll be too tired to learn. If you're feeling ambitious and want to try a big meal with them, do it on the weekend when you have more time. Take them to the grocery store with you and give them the whole experience soup to nuts.

Generally, kids want to be centered around the stove where the action is. This can cause tension because they're always getting in the way. Give them other things to do, such as chopping and washing lettuce. Although children may resist becoming the designated sous chef, these are important skills to learn. Learning how to safely use knives is an essential culinary skill. Obviously, with burners on and pots of water boiling and pint-sized Power Rangers making like Jim Bowie with the kitchen knives, parental supervision is a must.

When the kids reach school age they can learn to make their own lunches. You don't have to be Julia Child to make a bologna sandwich, and the knife used to spread the mayonnaise won't cause puncture wounds.

Breakfast is the best meal for cooking with children. You can make Dad's French toast or pancakes, and give the kids easy things to do that achieve fast results. Keep it simple. Show them how to crack an egg one-handed. Let them stir the batter and flip the pancakes. They can pour the batter into animal shapes or, better still, the first initial of their name. Let them carry their short stack of pancakes to the table with an A- or G- or S-shaped pancake riding proudly on top.

Pretend Soup and Other Real Recipes, *by Mollie Katzen and Ann Henderson (Berkeley, CA: Tricycle Press), is an excellent source of advice on this subject.*

DIAPERS AND OTHER
MANLY CHORES

I am not the best man to talk about diapers. It's been a few years since I changed one in earnest. But in talking to several bleary-eyed fathers who have recently become diapering experts, I could not help but be reminded of how quickly we parents forget.

Once upon a time all I could think of was diapers, diapers, diapers. Now I can barely remember that time at all. And so I offer this piece of wisdom to all men who are currently knee deep in the Big Huggy (or about to be):

This, too, shall pass.

Another thought: this book, like most books, is divided into chapters. This chapter, like the other chapters in this book, is divided into sections. It's all very neat and orderly.

Family life is nothing like this.

Family life (like changing a dirty diaper) is messy. It is not divided neatly into chapters and sections. Its lessons cannot be contained within the pages of a book. No book, including this one, can tell you everything you need to know about raising children.

Babies learn through experience. So will you.

I am also struck by how one aspect of family life spills into another, like the tributaries of a river flowing into a seldom-tranquil sea. Everything is connected to everything else. How a couple divvies up the household chores says a great deal about their relationship. A simple trip to the grocery store with the baby can bring up discipline issues and call on your emotional reserves as a parent.

Family life is one big simmering pot of stew. Everything blends together—or doesn't. But I'd agree that a house runs just a little bit better when everyone pitches in and does his share.

CHANGING DIAPERS AND OTHER HOUSEHOLD ISSUES

"Housework," says James Thornton, "is the Rorschach inkblot test for a couple's relationship." How you divide the housework gives clues about your relationship. Thornton, who lives in Sewickley, Pennsylvania, is the author of *Chore Wars: How Households Can Share the Work and Keep the Peace* (Berkeley: Conari Press; 800–685–9595). A contributing editor to *Men's Journal* and an award-winning journalist, he is the father of Ben and Jack. Since changing diapers can be one of the messiest issues for new parents to sort out, that seemed a logical place to start the discussion.

Q: I changed diapers. Virtually all of the fathers I know changed diapers. It's pretty much expected of men these days. But there may still be some guys out there who are reluctant to do it. What would you say to them?

Thornton: You want your wife to do all of it and you to do none of it? You're the child's father. You're partly responsible. In my view, it's only fair. You know, before I had kids I thought changing diapers was going to be the hardest job in the world. Just disgusting. But it isn't so bad. Infants have a different kind of body waste than our own. There's a slightly cute aspect to it. You get to see their little bodies. My sons liked it. Having their diapers changed was sort of fun for them. Of course if you have boys, prepare to get geysered every once in a while.

Q: I've had two daughters, so I never experienced that. But I know what you mean about the other stuff. Changing diapers gives you an opportunity to interact with your child . . . again and again and again.

Thornton [laughs]: Right. There are those times when you change a really messy diaper and you think, "Ah, I can finally relax." Then five minutes later, he poops and you've got to do it again.

Q: Any tips for new dads who might be up to their knees in diapers?

Thornton: Both of our kids were born in Minnesota. It was wintertime when they were very little. So we bought one of those warmers for wipes. If you can get them to work right, they're great. Our sons seem to like not having freezing cold wipes on them. Also, when Ben was in preschool, it seemed like I was constantly sick. You know, he'd pick up something there and bring it home and we'd get sick. So I'm big on washing hands. I wouldn't go directly from changing a messy diaper into the kitchen to make a meat loaf.

Q: Changing diapers is such a symbol these days. And the focus is always on the man and whether or not he does it. But I don't see many self-help articles for new mothers on how to change the oil or mow the lawn.

Thornton: Housework is a Rorschach inkblot test for a couple's relationship. The same can be said for diapers. I try to be evenhanded in my approach. That attitude that men are lazy scum, let's-force-them-to-do-more—that's counterproductive. Change is a two-way street. Both men and women today were raised in homes where housework was largely the woman's job. Some guys feel effeminate for even considering it. Most of the guys I know get no satisfaction from it. They're not interested in it. They don't say, "What a beautiful decorative window treatment." Most of us were raised in households where the father played a relatively minor role in these things.

Q: Many couples can work these issues out when it's just the two of them. But when a baby comes, it puts added stress on everything.

Thornton: I tell a story in my book about one couple. They were both lawyers and they had a great relationship. The husband did everything in the kitchen. He cooked, he shopped, he cleaned up after dinner. The wife, meanwhile, did the cleaning and laundry. They had what they felt was a fair division of labor. Then they had a baby.

Q: Uh-oh. What happened?

Thornton: Things went to hell. The male attorney had grown up in a traditional household. When it came to the kids, his father basically said to his wife, "Here, you take 'em. They're yours." And the female attorney grew up in the same type of household. You know, Mom knows what's best for the little tykes. So after the baby came, things started to change between them. Since she was now the mom, she knew what was best for the baby. So she took over the cooking. And since she was doing the cooking, she knew what the baby should eat. So she took over the grocery shopping, too. She took over these jobs and her husband was more than happy to let her. He backed off and let her take over.

Q: Bad move, right?

Thornton: It created an imbalance. The guy was basically living the same life he was before the baby was born, but with less work at home. And the woman, who was still working full time as an attorney, was now overwhelmed. She'd wait till midnight when her husband and son had gone asleep to do work that she'd brought home from the office. Then she'd get up at six to take the child to day care. Finally she filed for divorce and they went into therapy. He could not understand why she had suddenly turned into this chronically unhappy, nagging shrew, and she thought he was being irresponsible and uncaring. She wanted her husband to have a relationship with their son, but she was scared her son wouldn't be safe with him. And part of the reason he wasn't spending time with his son was that he felt pushed aside by her. It was a complicated mess. But they stayed together and worked it out.

Q: That really doesn't sound all that extreme to me. Every couple has issues when a baby's born. What do you recommend?

Thornton: I recommend taking a parenting class together. I think that can be very useful. Both the dad and the mom need to realize that each parent has a different relationship with the child. And each relationship is important. It's also good if you can find another dad with a son or daughter the same age as your child. Then the two of you can go to the park and talk football or whatever, while you're playing with your kids.

Q: Men can't just let this stuff slide, can they? Issues like housework and diapers can spill into other areas of a relationship, like sex.

Thornton: If there's resentment on either side, for whatever reason, it's going to affect sex. Resentment is the saltpeter of romance. It kills romance. If your wife is pissed off at you, she's not going to feel amorous. If she's exhausted, she's not going to feel amorous. What a lot of men don't realize is that the first years of a baby's life require constant vigilance and supervision. From the time they're born up to the age of about four when they reach the borders of reason, they demand so much attention that it almost forces couples to accept a "good enough" standard about housework rather than a perfect standard.

Q: Good enough rather than perfect? That sounds incredibly sane. Your house doesn't have to be spotless, just good enough. That's a statement of family priorities too.

Thornton: Right. I have a great quote from a therapist: "You don't have to have a kitchen floor that's clean enough to eat off of if you have a kitchen table." What's more important in your life? Having an immaculate house or comforting a child who's had a bad day? Obviously we all know the answer to that. My sons once built this huge tent city in the living room. It was a colossal construction but also a colossal mess. But I tried to think ahead to a time when I was older and the kids were all grown up. What would make the better memory? Would it give me more joy to remember a perfectly clean house, or that fantastic tent city?

Thornton has given talks on resolving chore wars at the University of Pittsburgh School of Social Work and Fortune 500 companies, such as Mellon Bank and Bayer Corporation. He can be reached at 412-741-4202; E-mail: jamesthornton1@compuserve.com/.

DIAPERING TIPS

It is one of the great debates of parenting: cloth or disposable? The cloth diaper people claim that disposables are filling up our landfills and that cloth is better for the environment. The disposable diaper people say that disposables are easier to use, more convenient, and work better. They add that disposables are biodegradable and that the chemical processes used in washing soiled cloth diapers are equally harmful to the environment, thus making it an ecological toss-up. *The Daddy Guide* takes no position in this controversy; it merely points out that the baby needs to wear *something*. Here's some advice on diapering for new dads:

- *See diapering as a way to connect with your child*. You can look at your baby's face and she can see yours. You laugh together and teach body parts. Especially for dads with breast-fed babies who don't use a bottle, diapering is one of the few nurturing jobs you can do when the baby's very young.

- *Help out at night too*. The burden of night changings inevitably falls on mothers who breast-feed. Mothers also usually stay home for the first months while men continue to work. Still, you can give Mom a break from time to time by getting up, changing the baby, and then bringing her back to bed for nursing.

- *Put the new diaper under the old one before you make the change*. When you push the baby's legs up and pull the old one out, the new one's already in place. This also covers you if you haven't done the greatest cleaning job.

- *Get a changing table*. It's the right tool for the job. All your diapering gear is stored in one handy spot, the same spot where the diapering takes place. A less expensive option: place a diaper-changing top on a dresser or other flat surface. A diaper-changing top has a wooden or plastic frame with a plastic mattress and works just as well as a changing table. You can put one in the baby's room and one in your bedroom or one upstairs and one downstairs, giving you two places in the house to change diapers.

- *Keep your hand on the baby when she's on the changing table*. Better still, make sure the baby is belted down if she's up high. A baby—even a young baby who is not moving much—can roll off the table if you're not careful. Stand squarely in front of the baby or use the belt. Sometimes you have to reach for things and need to move. There's no worse feeling for a parent than to have a baby roll off onto the floor. The baby gets scared (or worse), and you feel miserable.

- *Use a wipes warmer*. It's like a heating pad that goes around the box of wipes and keeps the box warm. How would *you* like it if someone ran a freezing cold washcloth across your gonads? This is mandatory in frosty northern climates.

- *Check out a Diaper Genie*. A diaper pail apparatus with a roll of plastic inside, it seals dirty disposables like a smelly sausage. When the pail is full, cut the top of the plastic off, tie it up, and open the bottom of the Genie over your garbage can. It's easier than dumping the diaper pail all the time and it helps contain the smell. The eliminations of bottle-fed babies are known to be particularly fragrant.

- *Remember to pack the Ziplocs in your diaper tote bag*. Carrying plastic bags allows you to easily dispose of a dirty diaper when away from home.

- *Make diapering a musical experience*. Turn on a music box (or the music from a mobile) or sing songs with her and let her vocalize.

- *Put a poster or picture of animals above the changing table*. Older babies can stand and point out the various animals in the picture to you.

- *Don't forget to cover the boy's penis when you've got him on the table*. Otherwise you may get squirted as if from a broken fire hydrant. It's also true that girls can pee on you.

- *Expect squirming as the baby gets older.* When a baby is first born, she lies agreeably on the table. As she grows older and more independent, she may not like being changed. She'll squirm and put up a fuss and try to get away, testing your patience.

- *Be in it for the long haul.* It will be a huge event in your life as a father when your child finally grows out of diapers—and further, when she learns to sleep through the night without pull-ups or some other form of protection. But she won't get out of diapers until she's two and a half or three years old or later, and for boys, the sleeping through the night without protection part may take years longer. Until then, hang in there.

Source: Three diaper-changing dads: Steve Cohan, Scott Thomason, and Jon Logan.

HOUSEWORK: DOING A GOOD, CLEAN, FAST JOB

Jeff Campbell has a simple philosophy when it comes to cleaning house: if you mess it up, you clean it. Jeff doesn't have kids ("I have three dogs. Does that count?"), but he knows cleaning the way Harley-Davidson knows motorcycles. He is the author of five books on housecleaning. In addition, he owns his own Clean Team cleaning business that performs eighteen thousand housecleanings per year. You may not incorporate everything he says into your housecleaning efforts, but what he says will help you organize your thinking and do a faster and better job.

Paying Someone Is Only a Partial Answer. The obvious solution to the drudgery of housework is to pay someone to do it for you. Some couples cannot afford this. But even couples who hire out must still grapple with cleaning issues. A professional housecleaner comes in once a week. The house will certainly get messy in the meantime, especially with a baby or small child around. Every household works out its own division of labor. Some couples have an inside-outside arrangement: she takes care of the inside of the house, he handles the outside. However you divide it, a man needs to pitch in. In most households today, both the man and woman work outside the home. Therefore, says Campbell, the housework needs to be divided differently than if only one person paid the bills.

It's Natural to Feel Frustrated When You're Cleaning. Men have a built-in excuse when it comes to a lack of knowledge about housecleaning. Nobody ever showed them how to do it. It's unlikely that a man's mom and dad took their young charge aside and said, "Here, Son, this is how to use the lemon-fresh Pledge." Naturally, when a person does not know how to do something, he feels demoralized and frustrated and finds excuses not to do it. But Campbell believes that once men learn some housecleaning basics, their frustration will fade away.

The Way Your Mother Cleaned the House Was Wrong. Chances are you paid zero attention to your mother when she was cleaning the house when you were young. But if you had, you would have noticed her moving here and there, from room to room as she saw fit. Armed perhaps with a bottle of Windex and an old T-shirt, she might have set about the task of cleaning the glass tables and mirrors in the house. While in the bathroom, she noticed how filthy the sink was. So she set the Windex on the counter, ventured down the hall to a closet where the cleaning supplies were kept, found the 409 behind a jumble of lightbulbs, insect sprays, SOS pads, Spic 'n' Span, and laundry detergents, then returned to do battle with the sink. At the risk of offending sons who will brook no criticism of their beloved mother, Campbell thinks there are better ways to do the job.

1. *Carry what you need with you when you clean.*
    This is the first of Campbell's maxims of cleaning. No one would hire a carpenter who doesn't wear a tool belt, who climbs up and down a ladder every time he needs a nail. It's the same with cleaning house. You need to carry your gear and cleaning supplies into each room with you. You clean that room and *finish* it before moving onto the next. No more going back and forth for supplies, no more wasted steps.

2. *You work from top to bottom, left to right, and back to front.*
    This is another of Campbell's maxims of cleaning. You start from a point in a room, usually the door. Then, as you move to your right, you work from ceiling to floor, finishing up where you started. Apply this method in the baby's room and every other room of the house. (The bathroom and kitchen usually require different starting points, but the cleaning sequence stays the same). Campbell says you can clean a room twice as fast using this approach. It requires less energy and causes far fewer headaches.

3. *The bathroom and kitchen are different.*
    Cleaning these rooms are different than cleaning other rooms in the house. They demand a wetter type of cleaning, with more cloths and sprays, along with a mop. Campbell's teams come prepared for a full-scale assault on these rooms. For the bathroom,

they carry cleanser, cleaning cloths, red juice, blue juice, brushes, toilet brush, tile brush, bleach (for mildew), tile cleaner, feather duster, and other tools. Remove a couple of these supplies and throw in a flat mop for the kitchen.

With a Baby Spill, Do Not Procrastinate. A baby's room requires more wiping and probably more cleaning than just once a week. When a baby spits up, take care of it immediately. A baby's vomit can be very acidic; it will stain a fabric or leave a mark on a countertop if it's left unattended. Allowing it to dry may turn what would have been a small cleaning job into a big one.

Go Easy on the Disinfectants. Some people go crazy with disinfectants in an effort to make everything sparkle for the baby. While disinfectants may be appropriate for the diaper pail and in the wash, Campbell cautions restraint in other areas of the room and house. Disinfectants can be poisonous to humans. What's more, it's nearly impossible to completely disinfect a room, let alone an entire house. If you keep your house clean, wiping surfaces clean and dry, you should be fine.

Vacuum Last. Vacuuming is the last thing you do after you've cleaned the rooms. After vacuuming you are free to return to your normal vegetative state in front of the TV.

Buy Products with Many Uses. Cleaning products should be like utility infielders in baseball; they should be able to handle a variety of jobs. Buy two or three products that do ten jobs, rather than one product that does one job. These are the questions to ask when buying housecleaning products: Does it work? Does it work quickly? Is it personally safe to use?

Let Usefulness, Not Price, Be Your Guide in Buying Supplies. A product may cost less, but if it forces you to spend more time on the job, what's the point? An ostrich-down feather duster costs $25, but Campbell says it actually *attracts* dust, making it far superior to the inexpensive chicken feather duster. Your time is worth more than the pennies you will save on lower-cost supplies. Nevertheless, don't fall into the "it costs more, therefore it's better" trap. Campbell says the best whisk broom on the market today is the cheapest. It's a synthetic whisk broom with bristles that don't break.

Process, Not Products, Are the Path to Happy Housecleaning. Campbell has a mail-order cleaning-products business, but he still says that most household cleaning products will do the job well enough as long as you learn the correct cleaning procedures. Use up the stuff you have on hand; then if you want to graduate to products that Campbell's Clean Team favors, you can.

Work as a Team with Your Partner. Campbell's three-person cleaning teams move through an entire house in an average of forty-two minutes. Working with your partner, you can probably clean your house in an hour. Share a common goal of a clean house and get it done.

Think About Cleaning the House on a Weeknight. Typically people clean house on the weekends when they have more time. Campbell questions that. Why not throw your energy into an hour of housecleaning on a Thursday night, leaving your weekend free? Get the cleaning out of the way so you can go on to do the things you really want.

Tip: Campbell's latest books are Talking Dirt: America's Speed Cleaning Expert Answers the 157 Most-Asked Cleaning Questions *and* Home Care, *a home maintenance guide for CDs, VCRs, and home furnishings (both Bantam Doubleday Dell). The number for his cleaning products catalog, 800-717-2532, also functions as a cleaning hotline for those times when you get stuck and need answers.*

SCHLEPPING THE BABY: PROBLEMS AND SOLUTIONS

Steve Cohan is a licensed marriage, family, and child counselor with the Napa County mental health system. Though he's worked with children and families for years as a therapist, until he had his own child he had never dealt with babies very much. Here are some of the everyday problems he's encountered while doing errands with his daughter Amira, and some of his solutions.

Problem: Baby falls asleep in car, wakes up when you move her.

Solution: Detachable car seat.

You can move the baby without waking her while she's still in the car seat. Remove the car seat and carry it into the store with you. Do your grocery shopping with her riding in the car seat in the shopping cart.

Problem: Baby fights like mad not to get in grocery cart.

Solution: Baby Bjorn front carrier.

Amira hated to ride in a grocery cart. So her father carted her around in a front carrier that she loved. He'd put her in the pack facing away from him and hold the bottoms of her feet. She'd bounce up and down and have a good time, well before she could even roll over.

Problem: Baby loses it in the store.

Solution: Do the best you can.

Try to calm her. Talk to her reassuringly. Give her a bottle. Well-prepared fathers travel with a bottle kit. It's a rectangular padded case with space for a reusable ice pack. It keeps the milk from spoiling. If that doesn't work, head for the exit. Dads need to be aware of their child's schedule. When is it nap time and when does she need to be fed? You and the baby can go places without Mom, but you need plan your trips accordingly. Don't do errands at your baby's eating or nap times.

Problem: Baby is miserable and unhappy at the park.

Solution: Bring her home.

Whether she's at the park or store, sometimes the only thing to do is cut your losses and come home. Pay attention to your child's patterns. It's not a time yet for discipline. The baby is not "acting out"; on some level her needs are not being met. Try to figure out what she needs and comfort her.

Problem: Baby won't get into expensive stroller.

Solution: Get a cheaper stroller.

The Cohans paid $300 for a ritzy Emma Junga stroller. But Amira wouldn't get in it, turning her arms and legs rigid "like a cartoon character," says Steve laughing. When she was about eleven months they bought a $20 fold-up umbrella stroller that fits anywhere and is a snap to carry and fold. Amira loves it.

Problem: Baby cries while riding in the car.

Solution: Howl like a wolf.

Some children love to ride in a car, falling asleep immediately. Amira put up a stink any time the Cohans put her in the car seat to take her for a ride. They found that howling like wolves made Amira curious enough to stop crying and listen to the strange sounds her parents were making. The radio helped too.

Problem: Baby protests when you tell her no.

Solution: Divert her attention.

Children frequently do not like the limits imposed upon them by their elders. But, says Cohan, "It's not good enough to just say no to them. They don't understand 'Don't touch' or 'Don't go there.' So I present an alternative. I give her a toy or a snack or say, 'Let's go find mommy,' trying to find something that interests her and diverts her attention."

Problem: Baby continues to scream and cry despite your best efforts.

Solution: Be patient.

You have to give children the same message over and over again. Try to do it, as Cohan says, "without an emotional charge." If Amira sees that Steve is upset about her eating stones, she only wants to eat more stones. Anger only adds fuel to your child's reaction.

Problem: Nothing you do seems to work.

Solution: Get some answers.

In the short term, do what you need to do to make her comfortable. Take her home. Everybody gets confused from time to time and needs help. Try a different approach if the baby is sick or crying all the time. What works for other people may not work for you. You may need to consult a pediatrician if it seems serious. But as the child's father, you have good instincts. The more time you spend with her, the more confident you will become and the more she will respond to you. Use your common sense, and key into what you think she needs. As Cohan says, "Amira laughs and plays and seeks me out, so I know I must be doing it right."

DISCIPLINE

A few years ago, I went out to my local pitch and putt to hit some balls. I started skulling the ball around as usual when I noticed a man and his son in the stall next to mine.

The guy was hitting the ball better than me (that's not news), but what really intrigued me was his son. He was three or four, about the same age as my daughter at the time. For nearly an hour the boy sat contentedly and watched as his father practiced his driving. He did not complain; he barely said a word. He did not run around; he hardly even squirmed. He did not ask his father if he could hit, nor did his father offer.

I was amazed. I couldn't help but think how my own daughter would have acted if I had brought her. No doubt she would've wanted to hit with me. She would've bounced balls and maybe even tried to wander off. In only a short while, I'm sure she would've whined about how boring this was and bugged me about going home.

So which child, hypothetically speaking, is better behaved? I guess many people would say the boy, although I'm not so sure. My daughter kicks the ball real hard in soccer and chases after it like a dog chasing a cat. She speaks up in class and performs in her school talent shows. I wonder about the boy. Does he speak up in class? Is he too shy to ask for what he wants? Or is he simply a well-disciplined boy, following rules laid down by his parents?

In truth, comparisons of this kind are unfair. They have more to do with the egos of the parents than anything else. Kids are kids. Every child is unique. I bet the boy's brother or sister (assuming he had one) would not act the way he did.

Like all things involving children, discipline is more complicated than it may seem. It's like an onion. Peel it away and there are *layers. Traditional notions of discipline don't really apply with babies, or at least they shouldn't. But the issue does come more sharply into focus when the baby turns into a toddler. You'll have your hands full then; that's for sure.*

Women can be more intuitive on matters of discipline. Men tend to rely more on rules as a means of governing behavior. A united parental front is necessary in any case. For whatever limits or boundaries you set, your child will most certainly push his nose against them again and again. That is his job after all—how he learns about himself and the dimensions of his world. It's said that when a child enters a new room or environment he wants to know three things: (1) what are the rules, (2) who's making them, and (3) what are the consequences when you break them?

Rules must be applied evenly, fairly, and consistently. Never lose sight of the fact that a rule, in and of itself, means nothing. Your goal is to modify your children's behavior and help them learn—though it won't be easy, I'll tell you that. Kids will test your patience as nothing else.

I sometimes see parents who seem afraid of their children. It's as if they can't accept the fact that they're the adults. They want to be "friends" with their children and just get along with them. I want to be friends with my daughter, too, but I know that being a father requires more than just being her friend. You must be willing to risk your children's disapproval in order to do what's right for them.

One last truism (as I see it) about being a parent: everyone can raise everyone else's kids perfectly. But your own kids? Ah well, that's another story.

THE KEY TO DISCIPLINE: REMEMBERING YOUR OWN CHILDHOOD

Discipline is not simply a matter of do's and don'ts. For Eliot Daley, one of the keys to effective discipline—indeed, one of the keys to being a good dad—is remembering your own childhood. A former writer and producer of the public television show *Mister Rogers' Neighborhood*, Daley lives in Boston where he works as a management consultant. In the late 1970s, he wrote a pioneering book about fathering called *Father Feelings* (Morrow & Co.), in which he discovered how events in his children's lives harkened back to his own childhood. At the time

> "You're the father. You're entitled to speak your piece."
>
> —Dr. Laura Schlesinger, radio therapist and mother of Deryk

his three children—Alison, Shannon, and Jad—were ten, eight, and five, respectively. "It occurred to me that I had these three little characters growing up around me and that I should pay attention to them," he says, recalling why he wrote the book. "I wanted to find out who I was to them and what they meant to me. So I reduced my work dramatically to spend time with them and write. It was the single best thing I've ever done in my life." During that year, he says, he not only learned about his children; he learned about himself, too.

Q: Why is it important to remember your own childhood when you become a father?

Daley: It's more than important; it's essential. When you forget what it was like to be a child you begin to have unrealistic expectations about your child. Since disappointment is a function of expectation, you set yourself up as always conveying disappointment to your child.

Q: I know what that's like. I've felt it at times with my own mother—that no matter what I do, it's never good enough.

Daley: Children grow best when surrounded by affirmation, rather than constant correction. A lot of men, a lot of parents, fall into the trap of thinking that your child is a reflection of you. You regard your children as part of your total act, a reflection of who you are. But it may not be in your children to be that. A child's job is not to please you or to make you look good. A child's job is to develop according to his or her God-given gifts, and your job is to nurture him according to those gifts.

Q: When you're a new father with a new baby you don't deal with discipline issues per se. But you definitely have to learn to reign in your emotions.

Daley: It can be frustrating. Your child is crying and crying, and it feels like there's nothing you can do for her. I remember when my oldest was about four months old. I was so frustrated and tired and upset that I was just an inch away from throwing that child against the wall. In that moment, I realized there was a very thin line between me and someone who couldn't restrain himself. But as I say, try not to take it personally. What your child is doing is not a reflection of you, but an expression of him or her. The clearer you can get with this idea, the more you can provide your kids with the nurturing and discipline they need.

Q: Let's talk about discipline. I would think that remembering your own childhood would tend to make most people a little less harsh, less judgmental and punitive.

Daley: Yes. For example it's very natural for a four- or five-year-old child to tell fibs or make-believe stories. Now a parent might say, "That child is lying. I hate lying," and punish him for it. But for some children, fooling around with the truth might be a form of sheer imaginative expressive play. Or it may reflect a sense of inadequacy on the part of children who feel they have to augment themselves in the eyes of their parents, the same way adults do when they embellish their resume when applying for a job.

Q: Yes, but lying isn't right. And there are plenty of times when a child screws up and needs to be straightened out.

Daley: The function of discipline is to teach. The root of the word is from the Latin *disciplina*. It means teaching and instruction. Punishment is not the root of the word. The heart of discipline is the acts of guidance by which you help a child learn what's best for that child. The trick to discipline is to understand why you're doing what you're doing, not just reacting because you're pissed off.

Q: And how do you do that?

Daley: Discipline is related to a parent's expectations and knowledge. Research on young moms has shown that there's a correlation between child abuse and ignorance of normal developmental patterns for children. A child may be doing just what he's supposed to be doing for his age, and yet the parent's response may be to stamp it out. When my daughter was very young, I put a camera on a tripod that was set at her height. I wanted to see what she could see from her level. She was 27 inches tall, and I discovered that she couldn't see the top of the table, only the underside of it. So you can see how it works. A child pulls something off the table or somehow causes an upset, and Mom or Dad comes along and says "Oh, you horrible child," when the child was only exercising one of the most important qualities he can have, which is curiosity and inquiry.

Q: How did you handle discipline in your house?

Daley: My wife, Pat, was much tougher, and more courageous and responsible, than I was. See, my father was born in 1907. He really was the type who, when he got home, would take me over his knee and take a strap to my butt for some alleged childhood offense I'd perpetrated. I knew when I had children of my own I didn't want to perpetuate that model. So I became Mr. Nice Guy with my kids. I basically abandoned that tough love role to my wife, which was pretty unfair.

"You must allow room for disagreement. I always encouraged Tiger to question what I was saying and, if he found me in error, to let me know so I could learn, too. In this way, parents can learn from their children."
—Earl Woods, father of professional golfer Tiger Woods

"The most important thing a father can give his daughter is loving acceptance—a respect-filled approval of who she is. Mothers, no matter how wonderful, cannot be male role models for their daughters."

—Jennifer Kaiser, daughter of Bruno Kaiser

Q: That's a clear case of how a childhood role affected how you acted as a father. I see now what you're saying. Fathers need to become conscious of their childhood patterns, especially the negative ones, so that they don't mindlessly continue the cycle with their own children.

Daley: Right. My wife and I used to occasionally do workshops with parents. The first thing we always asked them to do was write a description of when they were in junior high—where they were, what it was like back then, what they thought about, etcetera. After they did that, it changed the nature of their conversation dramatically. We have this superficial, very romanticized image of childhood. We tend to forget how scary it is sometimes to be a child, how much they worry about everything. Will my parents divorce? Is that dog going to bite me? It's awfully dark out there. What if my friend dies? When you're able to get in touch with your own childhood, you can engage in real empathy with your own children.

Q: Last question: what if a man disagrees with his partner on a discipline issue? What would you recommend he do?

Daley: Husbands and wives have got to support each other. If there's a difference of opinion, try to understand the other person's point of view. It's not your obligation to agree with it. But it is your obligation to understand it. Ask each other. Try to find common ground. You learn a lot about each other in the process, and that can bring you closer.

DO BABIES MANIPULATE?

Dr. Heidi Feldman is a developmental behavioral pediatrician at Children's Hospital in Pittsburgh. A graduate of the University of California at San Diego Medical School, she has a doctorate in psychology from the University of Pennsylvania. She served her fellowship at Children's Hospital in Boston, where she studied under three of the most famous pediatricians in the country: T. Berry Brazelton, Eli Newberger, and Melvin Levine. In her practice at Pittsburgh Children's, Feldman works with children who have developmental delays and disorders. I asked her various questions about babies, and the following paragraphs incorporate her answers and advice.

Do Babies Manipulate? I posed this question to several experts interviewed for this book. All of them answered no. "Babies very rarely self-consciously manipulate," says Feldman. They learn that their cries will gain them attention from their parents. But they cry basically to get their needs met.

When Do Children Learn Right from Wrong? Feldman says that babies do not know right from wrong in the first year of life. "An infant does not deliberately do something wrong," she says. They have short memories and get attracted by something in the moment. They don't have what is known as "means-ends reasoning." Functioning, it seems, in a state of perpetual surprise, babies don't realize that one action—knocking over a cup of milk—leads to another—the milk spilling. Sometime between the first and second birthdays, a child begins to understand these causal relationships and know the difference between right and wrong.

How Then Do You Keep a Baby from Causing Problems? The parents' job is to create a safe environment for their child. Babies do not exhibit good self-control, nor do they know the social rules. Curiosity will compel them to grab for an expensive or fragile object on the coffee table—thus, the need for childproofing. Despite a parent's implorings, a child may still play with the buttons on the CD player. But that's not the fault of the child. It's more the responsibility of the adults in the house who haven't moved the CD player to a place where clutching little hands can't get at it. Now when the child becomes, say, fifteen months old and purposefully stands on a chair to search for an object that is out of reach, the parents have an entirely different situation on their hands.

When Do You Discipline a Child? Discipline, says Feldman, is education, and it is distinct from punishment. "You discipline your child all the time when you teach what's right and wrong," she says. "Punishment is negative consequences for negative or offensive behavior." The time to punish a child is as soon as the offense occurs. If she throws a spoon, she needs to learn the consequences of her action immediately. Waiting until an hour later or the next day doesn't work. The child will have forgotten all about it by then.

Are There "Bad" Babies and "Good" Babies? Feldman resists the characterization of babies as "good" or "bad." All babies are not the same. Some have easy temperaments; some have difficult temperaments. Some are chirpy around people; some are as sociable as trolls. Some eat regularly; some eat in fits and starts. Some are soothable; some are not. Some are passive; some can barely sit still. Some are easily bored and need attention; some can sit happily and entertain themselves. Babies are as individual as the men and women who create them.

Furthermore, there is a difference between "a bad child" and a child who makes a bad decision or does something bad. Don't say, "You're bad" to a child who's done something wrong. Instead say, "That's a bad thing you did" or "I love you, but you shouldn't do that."

> "You take the people you love pretty much the way you find them. Their worst qualities are often linked with their best ones."
>
> —Benjamin Cheever, son of John Cheever

> "My father, whatever you wanted to do, he would just say it was okay. He was a great father, but his way of discipline was to have none."
>
> —Spike Lee, son of jazz musician Bill Lee

Let the child know that he is not a bad person; his behavior needs to be corrected.

How Do You Cope with an Active Baby? Some households respond better to active babies than others. Feldman notes that fathers, because they are more active themselves, frequently have an easier time with active babies than their mothers have. Often it is the father who is gone from the home during the day. Being away, he can appreciate the baby more when he comes home. He's fresher and perhaps more creative than the mom who's been with the child all day and is at wit's end.

What Is the Father's Role in Disciplining a Child? In Feldman's view, the father's role, like the mother's, is as a parent-educator. Ideally the father and mother work together in handling discipline and other aspects of raising a family. "The couples who do the best are the ones who share the responsibility," she says.

Source: Dr. Heidi Feldman, developmental behavioral pediatrician at Children's Hospital of Pittsburgh. She also contributed to the following section entitled "Ten Reasons Not to Spank a Child."

TEN REASONS NOT TO SPANK A CHILD

Lots of parents spank their children. They give them a pop on the butt (or worse) when they act up. It's not the end of the world if you spank your children. They will not grow up to be misfits if you occasionally take a hand to them. Many parents today received spankings when they were children, and they see nothing wrong with continuing the tradition with their own kids.

Spanking roughly divides along socioeconomic lines. Parents with less education and lower incomes tend to spank, while those with more education and higher incomes tend not to. Sometimes spanking seems like the only way to get your child's attention. But there are other, more effective methods to get your child to behave properly. Here are ten reasons why spanking may not be such a good idea:

1. It can hurt your child. You can overdo it and leave bruises and marks. Consequently your child may withdraw from you and learn to fear you.

2. It makes you feel like dirt. When you raise your hand to your child, you don't feel good about it afterward. That should tell you something right there.

3. It is not effective discipline. It doesn't work. A study of children from ages six to nine who were spanked over a two-year period showed that the ones who were spanked two times a week exhibited worse behavior than the kids who were spanked less or not at all.

4. It's hard to control. You're a man. You have a lot more power than a small child. You can raise a welt without intending to.

5. You communicate your emotion when you spank, but not much else. You don't spank when you're calm and under control; you do it when you're upset. It seems ironic, then, that you are trying to teach your child to exhibit appropriate social behavior and self-control.

6. It can escalate. A small tap on the butt may work at first. But as the child grows older and bigger, he may ignore it or rebel against it, forcing a stronger reaction from you.

7. The child doesn't learn anything positive from it. Your child grabs a toy from another child and you give him a spanking. But has it taught him how to share or how to ask for what he wants or how to take turns? He knows his behavior is wrong and must stop. But a child needs to learn what's right, not just what's wrong.

8. It's a general form of punishment, not specific. It tells your child that he's been "bad," without presenting alternatives. The idea is not to punish him for the sake of punishment. You want him to correct his behavior.

9. Time-outs work better. When you give a child a time-out, you take a moment to settle him down. This allows the emotions to die down. All people, including children, learn better when they're in a calm frame of mind. Think of time-outs as a form of grounding, a disciplinary technique well known to the parents of teenagers. When a teenager lips off or flunks algebra or stays out too late on Saturday night, he may get grounded and have his normal privileges revoked for a time. Time-outs are a one- or two-minute "grounding" for young children. Taking away a privilege from a child can also be effective discipline.

10. Spankings don't build good relationships. Men are traditionally less verbal than women and may be less inclined to negotiate with their children when they misbehave. But you don't hit your partner, do you? Then why do you hit your child? Because you have the power, because you're stronger? As Dr. Heidi Feldman says, "All

> "Silent, austere, of high principle; ungentle of manner toward his children, but always a gentleman in his phrasing. He never punished them—a look was enough, and more than enough."
>
> —Samuel Clemens, better known as Mark Twain, on his father John Marshall Clemens

effective discipline rests on maintaining a good relationship with your child."

TIPS ON HANDLING TODDLERS

Toddlers do not run the world, they only think they do. Children enter the toddler phase at about the age of two. Toddlers have not yet learned to govern themselves according to the rules of civilized behavior. They cry and scream and throw tantrums, frequently in public places. Around the age of three, however, a child develops the cognitive abilities to make her own choices. Your job as a father is to teach her to make the right choices—to tell the difference between right and wrong, that it's not okay to hit, bite, or run away. Following are some tips on how to handle misbehaving toddlers from author Donna Corwin.

Know Your Child's Limits. It's virtually impossible to stop a tantrum in full cry. The best approach is to try to prevent one from occurring at all. Your child has limits. She gets hungry, tired, grouchy. The more time you spend with your child, the more you will come to recognize her moods. Know when your child has had enough. Cut your errands short and get her home before she falls apart.

Stay in Control Yourself. Resist the urge to answer her screams with screams of your own. This only makes it worse. Rub your child's back; talk to her in a calm voice. Try to change the subject and distract her from what's causing her unhappiness. It's the same when a child cries. Telling her to "Stop! Stop crying!" as some dads are prone to do, just doesn't work. Demand that your child stop crying and all she does is cry harder.

Make Sure Your Child Is Safe. Suppose your child blows her top in the cereal aisle of the supermarket. Your first concern must be for her safety. Can she hurt herself or others? Pick her up and get her away from the area if it's not safe.

Give the Child a Time-Out. The purpose of a time-out is to stop a situation from escalating further. Children need to know when they've done something wrong. That's the purpose of a time-out. Though it's accepted that a child receive one minute of time-out for every year of life—e.g., a two-year-old gets two minutes—there are no strict time limits. Even one minute can seem like an eternity to a child.

Remove Her from the Situation. If a child acts up in the grocery store or place of worship or when you're eating out, get her out of there. Take her away from people and give her a time-out. But never leave her alone. Just turn your back on her during the time-out.

Watch Your Own Actions. Kids are like sponges; they pick up good and bad habits alike. If you scream and yell or, worse, hit, your child may do the same.

Be Aware of Your Voice. It's very common for young children to think that their father is yelling at them when, in fact, he is speaking normally. Dads are usually bigger than moms. They cut a more imposing figure. They have deeper and louder voices. Your child may feel you are disciplining her when you are just talking. Reassure her that you're not yelling, you're just trying to make a point. Show her the difference between a yell and your regular voice. Tell her, "See, I'm not yelling at you, I'm just talking."

Be Aware of the Image You Project. A father's presence is a source of strength and reassurance to a child. When there's a spider (or Bogeyman) in the room, you will most likely be the one who's asked to get rid of it. But your size and strength can also be intimidating. Don't always loom like a giant. Talk to her on her level; sit on the bed next to her or on the sofa.

Be on the Same Page as Your Mate. One of the toughest disciplinary situations you will ever face is when you and your mate disagree on what to do. Talk things out ahead of time. Try to agree on common approaches.

Never Let Disagreements with Your Mate Affect Your Relationship with Your Child. Here's a painfully familiar scenario for many men: Mom complains that Dad doesn't do enough with the child. So Dad takes the child out for the day, and afterward Mom criticizes him for giving the child too many sweets or whatever. Dad becomes defensive and sullenly resolves not to take his child out anymore, thus avoiding any future reproaches from Mom. Disagreements with your mate are probably inevitable. Never let them affect your time with your kid.

Be Consistent with Your Time-Outs. Use time-outs all the time. Don't use it one time and not another time. If Dad spanks and Mom uses time-outs, it sends a confusing message to the child.

Take Away Privileges. Try taking away privileges if time-outs aren't working. Taking away privileges (or a toy) is another form of discipline and can be one of the most effective things you do.

Let Your Discipline Fit the Offense. A child who is consistently not listening to you may deserve only a time-out. But a greater offense

> "I remember my father busting into my room and grabbing my Buddy Holly record because he'd read in the *Providence Journal* that rock 'n' roll is dangerous. I was about ten years old."
>
> —Jon Katz, former TV producer and father of Emma

∎

> "The rule is, never give a child a choice."
>
> —Robert Frost

"Sidney was arrested for stealing corn and spent a night in jail. . . . He sat for hours waiting for his father to come and bail him out. When his father arrived, he was angry and concerned. On the way home, Reginald told his son wearily, 'You know boy, I can't run after you anymore.'"

—From a biography of actor Sidney Poitier, whose father Reginald had to borrow money to pay for the stolen corn

deserves a stronger response. For example, if a child hits another child with a toy, take the toy away from her and give her a time-out. Take away the source of the problem, especially when dealing with a stronger-willed child.

Source: Donna Corwin is coauthor of the bestselling Time Out for Toddlers *with Dr. James Varni (Berkeley Books). Corwin has also written* The Time-Out Prescription *(Contemporary Books) and five other books on parenting. She lives in Los Angeles with her husband and daughter, Alexandra.*

THE *TOUGHLOVE* APPROACH

When contacted for this book, David York, cofounder of TOUGHLOVE International, said frankly that fathering very young children did not apply to his program, which deals with troubled children ages eight and over. These are at-risk children, children who are acting out against their parents and families. There are more than 250 registered TOUGHLOVE parent groups in the United States and more than one thousand around the world. York, an author, lecturer, and the father of Ilene, Heidi, and Jodi, said that his organization does not work with new parents with babies or preschool-age children. Nevertheless, there are aspects of his approach that do indeed have relevance to new fathers in the realm of discipline. Here are three major points taken from his program.

Get on the Same Page as Your Partner. Many parents who come to York's program are on the verge of divorce. They disagree over everything and blame their partner for the problems their child is having. York is characteristically blunt with these parents. "I tell them I don't care what your disagreements are," he says. "Right now your kid needs help. Once your kid is okay, you can kill each other. But right now let's focus on your kid. That usually cools them off."

It's Better for Your Child When Both Parents Agree. Children and teenagers learn to manipulate their parents when they're divided. When parents actively disagree, kids can play one against the other and split the family further apart. Children may cause internal strife even though they want the family to stay together. York has found that once the parents become united, it helps the child. The power struggles cease and the parents can concentrate on doing what's right for the child.

Use All Your Resources. York believes that the solutions to a child's problems lie within the community and the resources within that community. "Use school as a resource, not an enemy," says York. "If the child breaks the law, use the police as a resource. Use the courts as a resource. Use your priest or minister or rabbi as a resource. Work together with these people and do what needs to be done." It's easy to apply this rule to becoming a new parent. Use whatever resources you can call on—grandparents, friends, neighbors, the medical community, church, or temple—to help you get over the rough spots.

Contact: TOUGHLOVE International, Inc., Box 1069, Doylestown, PA 18901; 800-333-1069. TOUGHLOVE is a registered trademark name.

"If there is anything that we wish to change in the child, we should first examine it and see whether it is not something that could be better changed in ourselves."
—Carl Jung, son of Johann Paul Achilles Jung

GROWING A CHILD: WHAT FATHERS CAN DO

Every stage in the life of a child is special. I know that sounds corny, but it's true. Babies move faster than linear particle accelerators. By the time you catch up with whatever developmental stage they're going through, a stage you couldn't really figure out anyway, they're on to the next one. Don't look past this time. Don't take it for granted. And don't forget to enjoy yourself while you're at it.

As you grow older time seems to speed up. Having children makes it go even faster. You may feel like a spring chicken inside. But when your child turns two, or twelve, or twenty-two, the painful truth becomes clear: you're getting older.

Annie walked when she was ten months. I remember precisely because I was home the day she did it. She had been walking while holding onto furniture for what seemed like months. She was clearly ready to make the thrilling passage into ambulatory freedom.

We were in the kitchen. She was clutching the counter. "You can do it," I said. "Let go." She let go and walked across the kitchen floor— shakily, but unassisted. When she reached me, she fell into my arms as if exhausted. I was ecstatic. I called her mother at work and both sets of grandparents to tell them the news.

Of course, her learning to walk opened a whole new can of developmental worms for her parents. But that's another story.

Jump to the present day. Annie is eight going on thirteen. We're out in the backyard. I keep intending to buy a basketball hoop but never seem to get around to it. Jennifer has just planted a lemon tree *in our yard. The black plastic tub it came in is empty and waiting to be recycled. I get an idea.*

We cut out the bottom of the tub with scissors, à la James Naismith and his old peach basket, and hammer it to a storage shed. Then we play, scoring baskets by shooting the ball through the bottomless lemon tree tub. This crude basket still hangs on the shed. I know I'll replace it one of these days, but right now, we're using it for our pickup games.

In my mind, the time between these two events—Annie taking her first steps and us shooting hoops in the yard—seems like a snap of the fingers. She's growing faster than warp speed. And I'm still playing catch-up—and hoping the whole process slows down.

One more thought: My experience tells me that there really is a corollary between the time you put in with your kids when they're young and the relationship you have with them when they're older. Put in the time; reap the rewards. You will always have to be there for your children, whatever their age. But if you make a good, solid, early connection with them, you have a better shot of hanging together and staying close as time rockets by.

BEING INVOLVED:
GOOD FOR BABY, GOOD FOR YOU

An amazing thing happens to a man who actively participates in his child's life. Not only does his son or daughter grow, the man grows, too. Armin Brott is the author of an excellent series of books on the impact of fathers in early childhood development. His latest are *The New Father: A Dad's Guide to the First Year* and *The New Father: A Dad's Guide to the Toddler Years* (Abbeville Press). A contributing editor to *Baby Talk* magazine and a radio talk-show host, Brott says that studies have shown that men do better in all aspects of their lives—relationships, job, family—when they roll up their sleeves and get busy with their children. He is the father of Tirzah and Talya.

Q: *Why is it important for fathers to be involved with their kids?*

Brott: Fathers have a tremendous amount to contribute to their children, psychologically, socially, emotionally, physically, in every aspect of their growth. Studies link a father's involvement with the development

> "If you have a child, take time each day to really pay attention to him or her. If you have more than one child, try to spend private time with each one individually. You may get to know your children in a whole new way."
>
> —Stephan Rechtschaffen, M.D., father of Eli

■

> "Reading to children at night, responding to their smiles with a smile, returning their vocalizations with one of your own, touching them, holding them—all of these further a child's brain development and future potential, even in the earliest months."
>
> —T. Berry Brazelton, M.D., father of four

of high IQ in children. But many fathers don't know they can have this sort of impact. Men tend to look at parenting as motherhood. But it's not. Fathers can "mother" too.

Q: Let me play devil's advocate. Mothers are good nurturers. They do an excellent job of it. Why do fathers need to do it too?
Brott: The most important thing is that children need two parents. Both are vital. Men and women teach in different ways and kids learn different things from them. Fathers are more physical. Kids laugh more when they play with their fathers. But to deprive a kid of either the mom or the dad is sad.

Q: One of the things you talk about in your book is how being an involved dad not only helps your children, it helps you too.
Brott: Absolutely. There have been very detailed, very high-powered studies that show that guys who are involved with their children have better relationships with their partners. The division of labor in a household after a baby is born is a big stress point in a relationship. It doesn't work for everyone of course, but men who help with the baby will have better and longer-lasting relationships. It also helps in their professional lives. A man learns lessons at home from his child that he brings into the workplace—lessons about patience, perseverance, caring. Men who are involved with their children have better careers, have less stress in their lives, and are professionally more accomplished. It sounds simplistic, but it's true. There is no downside to it.

Q: You read a lot today about the negative impact on children who grow up without ever having a father.
Brott: This is brought up a great deal in the welfare debate in this country. Children who grow up in fatherless homes are more likely to do worse in school, more likely to become teen parents, more likely to abuse drugs, more likely to commit suicide. It's serious business. Now this is not to say that if you dropped an involved dad into these households, all their problems would magically disappear. What I'm saying is that a male role model is necessary for a child. If you have a son, you need to teach him how to be a man. If you have a daughter, you need to teach her how to interact with men when she grows up.

Q: Talk about a baby's first year. In general terms, what things happen?
Brott: It's amazing. Babies go from birth to walking. There's a huge amount of development. They go from learning that they're alive to knowing that they have a place in the world. They go from completely random movements to movements with a purpose. They learn what is called "object permanence." If you show a key to a baby and then put

it in your pocket, she thinks it no longer exists. She thinks it's gone forever. By the end of the first year, she learns that things last, that they have permanence.

Q: That must be why babies put up a stink when you leave them at day care. They think you're leaving them forever.

Brott: That's part of it. When babies are six, seven, eight months old and spending more time with a baby-sitter or at day care, they get freaked out when you leave. They've gotten to know you and accept your presence in their lives. Then you leave and they aren't totally sure you're coming back. Remember, small children have no concept of time. It takes them years before they learn to understand time.

Q: What happens to a new dad in that first year? How does he grow?

Brott: It's almost as amazing. First he's totally clueless. He doesn't know what hit him. He doesn't know how to feed the baby or give him a bath or even hold him. A sense of panic sets in. What kind of father am I going to be? How can I afford this? How do I rearrange my work schedule? How can I support three people? Are we going to make it? He has all these questions. And then, over the course of the year, he gradually becomes more confident. I'm speaking generally, of course. He carves out a spot for himself and his child. He goes from having no confidence to having a lot of confidence. He says to himself, "Hey, I can do this."

Q: Kind of like job training, isn't it?

Brott: Exactly. When you start a new job, you don't know anything your first day. Nor are you expected to. You learn as you go along. It's the same with being a father. We have this idea that parenting requires some sort of innate skills. But as far as I know, there's no diaper-changing gene. There's no genetic predisposition to show that you'll be good at arranging play dates for your child. The best example I can think of is when my now ex-wife was having problems breast-feeding our daughter. So the hospital sent down a lactation consultant who was a man. Here was a man showing her how to do what is supposed to be the most natural thing in the world for a woman—breast-feeding her baby. But it's not natural. It has to be learned, like so many other things with parenting.

Q: Tell me about your relationship with your daughters and the impact you feel you've had on their lives.

Brott: I have a tremendous relationship with my daughters, and it's very gratifying to me. They come to me when they need help. They write me notes. I feel I'm an important person in their life. We'll go

---

"If you have a two-year-old around the house, it keeps you thinking, keeps you young, watching the learning process."

—Actor Clint Eastwood, father of Morgan

■

"From his father, Wells inherited his rich imagination. He saw 'a vein of silent poetry' in his father, who as a youth liked to stay outdoors half the summer night, simply staring at the stars."

—From a biography of writer H. G. Wells, son of Joseph Wells

"It's the greatest joy in my life, spending time with him, hands down. We're so much alike, I look at him and it's like I'm looking in the mirror."

—Baseball slugger Mark McGwire, father of Matthew

over to a friend's house and I'll overhear them talking to their friends, saying things I've told them, lessons I've taught them. And I think, "God, they're listening. I really am making a difference in their lives." You have values as a man and you want to pass them on to the next generation. You can't expect your wife or your partner or your girlfriend to do it for you. They have their own values. I can point to specific things that come from me as their father—their love of music, sports, playing ball. Their interest in those things is because of me and the time I spend with them. I'm very proud of the fact that my seven-year-old is the fastest runner in her grade at school.

Q: A father plays with a child in a certain way, distinct from how a mother plays with a child. And the way a father plays— the simple fact of it—helps the child learn and grow.

Brott: Moms tend to be more forgiving in their play. Men are more rambunctious. They are less likely to treat kids, girls especially, as fragile. They wrestle and roll around on the floor with them. Men are perhaps less concerned with hygiene. It bothers them a little less if a kid has stuff on her face. The classic illustration of the difference between men and women is to imagine a tower falling down. What do you do? Catch it or let it fall? Moms tend to try to catch it, while dads let it fall. Both views are important for children. Neither one is better than the other. It's important for children to know that someone will try to catch the tower and protect them from it. But it's also very important for them to see our point of view. Children can learn to take care of themselves. They can learn independence. They can let the tower fall and then they can build it again.

A CHILD NEEDS DAD IN THE TENDER YEARS, TOO

One of the prevailing myths of raising children is that babies and infants need their mother more than their father—the so-called "tender years" doctrine. Ironically, fathers themselves keep this damaging myth alive by withdrawing from their children and thus becoming less necessary, forcing mothers to fill the emptiness created by their absence. In the following brief remarks, author and therapist Harville Hendrix (who is interviewed more extensively in the chapter "Love and Sex") adds his voice to the growing number of psychologists, social scientists, and others who argue that a father plays a vital, central role in the early life of a child.

"Dads need to be involved in their children's lives every way they can," says Hendrix. "The standard view of fathers is that they come in after the first two years and give the child more structure. But a father needs to be involved in caring, feeding, and holding the child—for the sake of the child and for his own sake. Even if a child is breast-feeding, there may be a supplemental bottle. Get up and hold him and give him his bottle.

"Instead of acting like the child is always bugging you when he is playing, join him in his play. Be a child with the child. When you limit your child, you are speaking from unconscious memory on how you were limited as a child by your own parents."

Hendrix, who has six children, continues. "Children internalize their relationship with their parents. My biggest learning curve as a father has been to discover that how my parents inhibited me as a child was how I inhibited my own children. Children draw out of both men and women a nurturing impulse. They want to experience connection. They climb on your lap and want you to pay attention to them.

"Let them sit on your lap. They don't want to stay long. Giving them two minutes of intense attention allows them to go off and do what they want to do. They just want to connect.

"Nurturing a child is a way for the father to repair some of his own childhood wounds," concludes Hendrix. "You get to provide for your child what perhaps was missing in your own childhood, what you did not receive from your own father. It will contribute to your growth as a person. You will not just be a good dad, you will recover your wholeness as a man."

CONNECTING WITH YOUR CHILD

Nurturing is a buzzword in parenting circles these days. Fathers are being asked to nurture their child, though they may not be sure exactly what that means.

Nurturing, to me, is connecting—imprinting yourself on your child through your voice and touch and sight and sheer animal closeness. It means tending to your child's needs and comforting him. Nurturing builds brain cells. Studies have shown that receiving love and care in the crucial first three years of life can improve a child's language and thinking abilities, and help him succeed later in school.

Today's generation of fathers realize that nurturing is not just women's work. A child needs Dad's nurturing as well as Mom's. Just the way you hold your baby sends a message to him about you and the

"When I was little, my father sang me 'Mairzy Doats.' He patiently held my head when a stomach virus made me vomit all night. He bought me a puppy for my ninth birthday. He sewed button eyes on my teddy bear when its other eyes fell off."
—Writer Cynthia Heimel

■

"I often wonder at the strength and courage my father had in taking me out of the traditional school situation and providing me with these extraordinary learning experiences. I trace who I am and the direction of my development to those years of growing up in our house on the dunes, propelled especially by an internal spark kept alive and glowing by my father."
—Photographer Ansel Adams, son of Charles

world. A mother typically holds her baby so she can face him and look directly at him. A father, on the other hand, turns the baby around and faces him out to the world. The baby rides up on his father's shoulders, astride his kingdom like a little Napoleon on his steed.

Both ways of holding a baby are proper and good. The baby needs the loving security that a mother offers. But he also needs to look out on the world, and that is part of what a father teaches. Nurturing is not the province of experts; you do not need to read a book to learn how. (Many of the experts contradict one another anyhow.) Much of it is common sense. It consists of simple, everyday acts tendered with patient and loving hands. Here are a few ways to connect with your child and nurture him:

Hold Your Baby. The first impulse is to treat him like fine china. But he won't break. Babies are incredibly vulnerable in some ways but remarkably durable in others.

Feed Your Child. Some babies take to a bottle easily; others fight it like it's torture. Don't take it personally; it's not a failure on your part if the baby resists. Rubbing the nipple of the bottle—or your finger—against the roof of the baby's mouth gets his sucking motion in gear.

Give Him Your Finger. Instead of a pacifier, let your baby suck on your finger (wash your hands first). A finger has one advantage over a pacifier in that you always carry it with you. Your finger carries your smell and this increases bonding.

Talk to Your Baby. Let him get used to the sound of your voice, even if he doesn't understand all the words and can't talk himself. It's soothing for him to hear the calm, reassuring voice of his father.

Go Skin to Skin. Lay down on the floor with the baby on top of you. Let him squirm around on your chest and feel his skin against yours.

Let Him Come Into Bed with You. In time, he will learn to sleep by himself. But while he's very young, let him share a bed with you and your partner.

Change Diapers. Many men confess to a secret enjoyment of diapering; it gives them a chance to make eye contact, hold the baby, count toes and fingers, and play Itsy-bitsy Spider. With his clothes off, you can give him a massage, gently rubbing and squeezing his chubby little body. An excellent book on infant massage is Frederick LeBoyer's *These Loving Hands*.

Let Him Play with Your Beard. Small children are fascinated by the roughness of a father's chin and his hairiness in contrast to Mom. Your baby will pull at your beard if you have one and it won't hurt. Gently rubbing your whiskers against your child's face when he's a little older will cause shrieks of laughter.

Bathe Your Child. A baby's so small, you can wash him in the sink. At about age two, you can take baths with him. Baths are a wonderful way to have skin-to-skin contact with your child. It's also a joy, like sharing a bed with a child, that disappears as he gets older. Enjoy it while you can.

Introduce Him to the Park. Even if he's too young to fully appreciate it, take him to the park. Lay him on a blanket on the grass or sit with him on a bench and let him watch the other children. Babies are fascinated to see other small creatures like them. When he's older push him gently on the infant swing or hold him while he slides down the slide.

Take Him to the Coffee Shop with You. Babies are portable and thus easier to include in your round of activities. Take him in a stroller or carrier or simply carry him. When a baby starts to walk, it becomes harder to go places with him because then all he wants to do is move around and get into things.

Feed Him Solid Foods. A baby may begin to eat strained cereal at about four to six months. Gradually he will learn to sit up in his highchair and eat like the rest of the family. Your mission will be to teach him to use a spoon, though he would rather eat with his fingers. It will be years before he actually prefers a knife and fork over his own God-given utensils. Accept that he's going to knock over his milk, spill his food, and make a mess. When you expect a thing to happen, it is not such a big deal when it does happen. Many of the issues in raising children—feeding, potty training, walking, talking, sleeping alone— become crises only if you let them.

Source: Kevin Woodward, father of Lilly, who, for more than a decade, worked as a nurse's aide at a hospital where he fed and held babies in the intensive care nursery. He has returned to college and is now finishing his bachelor's degree.

> "Even as a kid I hated helping him around the house. He loved showing off how handy he was . . . and proving that anything I did was all wrong. He made me completely neurotic about fixing stuff."
>
> —Art Spiegelman, author of *Maus*, on his relationship with his father Vladek

LET YOUR CHILD TAKE THE LEAD: TECHNIQUES FOR PLAY

It's been shown that physical development in children and confidence in movement can lead to academic achievement. Success in school frequently follows early childhood success in walking, running, jumping, climbing, and other activities. Here are some ideas and approaches for helping your child use and enjoy her body through the medium of play:

- Lie on your back with your knees bent and feet on the floor. Let her climb up your knees, much the way a child likes climbing up the wrong end of a slide. Then let her climb or slide down.

- Every father loves to wrestle with his child, but let her take the lead. Her movements and abilities will tell you how much roughhousing you can do. If she comes over and bounces gleefully on your stomach, she may be ready for slightly rougher play.

- Be an obstacle course for your child instead of always wrestling. Let her climb on and over you. A child will learn faster and grow more physically adept when she takes the initiative, rather than having the action done to her.

- Go easy on the bouncing. Many dads bounce, bounce, bounce, forgetting that it can be physically jarring, particularly for an infant. She'll enjoy a gentle rocking motion more.

- Hold your baby securely in your hands and let her slowly "soar." The infant feels the delight and thrill of the ride while being held in her father's strong hands. However, be careful about sudden dropping motions. They can frighten the child and cause you to lose your grip.

- Sit down on the floor and spread your legs. Let your child sit across from you. Then roll a ball back and forth to each other. Your child will have to be a little older, nine to twelve months, and be able to sit up.

- Encourage your child to play on climbers, slides, and other stationary play equipment. The equipment does not move, enabling her to use her muscles and develop coordination. Most children seem to have built-in radar; although they like to challenge themselves, they very rarely go beyond their ability levels when they're climbing.

- Push your baby slowly in an infant swing. It will give her an exhilarating sense of motion and help her establish a sense of balance in space. Make sure the swing has a safety rail that holds her securely in place. After your baby has outgrown an infant swing, you may want to avoid swings until your child can pump independently. Pushing an older child does nothing to help her physical development or her striving for independence. Wait until your child is able to pump by herself before encouraging the use of a swing. Let her try, if she asks, and teach the pumping motion to see if she can master it. Having her learn a skill from you will be a bonding experience for both of you.

- Let your child crawl and move around. Play pens are currently out of favor among parents because they restrict a child's mobility. Crawling is a crucial developmental stage for children. Studies have shown that children with learning disabilities frequently missed the crawling stage.

- Look and listen, rather than always do. One example: a father is intently entertaining his three-month-old with a toy. The toy is a string of shapes linked together. He busily turns the toy this way and that in his hands, not imagining for one minute that the child may be content just to look at it or reach out for it and move it herself.

- Don't push your child too fast. Don't make her do more than she can. Many parents want their children to learn to walk quickly and put them into walkers to encourage them. But what's the hurry? There's no point in doing it too fast. Every child learns to walk when his leg and back muscles have developed the necessary strength.

Source: Ruth B. Roufberg, New Jersey–based author and child-development expert. For Roufberg's views on toys and play, please see the chapter "Toys, Projects, Computers."

OPEN YOUR MOUTH AND SING

Many men feel awkward or embarrassed when they sing around their children. But give those same men a few Stolis late at night and before you know it, they're playing air guitar and howling along with "Stairway to Heaven" at the top of their lungs.

Music is a universal. Everyone loves it and responds to it, especially children. You don't have to be a Sinatra or Pavarotti to sing to and with your child. As Henry Miller wrote, "To sing you must first open your mouth. You must have a pair of lungs, and a little knowledge of music. It's not necessary to have an accordion, or a guitar. The essential thing is to *want* to sing." Don't let Mom have all the fun. Open your mouth and sing. Here are some practical pointers on how to help your child develop an appreciation for music:

- Sing when you're changing the diapers or giving your child a bath. Make up songs. Create chants. Vocalize. Have fun with it.

"My older daughter has been living away from home for well over a decade now. She has a steady boyfriend and we get on just fine. But every so often, when I see them together, a strange urge comes over me to sit him down in the den (I'd need to borrow a den) and ask him if his intentions are honorable."

—Columnist Jon Carroll, father of two

> "Everybody talks about how you need to nurture your children when they're babies. But I have a son who's seventeen, and I still feel the need to nurture him. You need to lay a great foundation, but your job's never over with children."
>
> —School principal Mark Croghan, father of three

- Listen to music. Let your child see you enjoying music, maybe even taking Mom for a spin around the kitchen floor. A child may only sit and observe. But he's watching—and listening.

- Play different kinds of music: classical, jazz, gospel. You wouldn't let your child exist solely on a diet of potato chips, would you? (Well, maybe you would.) Give him a balanced musical diet. And expect to hear the same song over and over. Kids learn through repetition.

- Sing a lap song while you're rocking him. Let him move around and shimmy and shake.

- Sing songs in the car. Road trips are a great time for hoarse-throated dad-led family singalongs.

- Make homemade music in the home. Use spoons, egg shakers, drums, triangles, finger cymbals, even pots and pans. Strike up a delicious cacophony when the whim takes hold.

- Go to church or temple. Houses of worship are houses of song too. Sing hymns together as a family at Christmas or Passover or other spiritual occasions.

- Make music an everyday part of your life. Some children achieve basic music competence—singing in time and keeping an accurate beat—as early as age three. Most children reach it by five or six.

Source: Barbara Lysenko from the Center for Music and Young Children, which offers "Music Together" music and movement classes for infants, toddlers, preschoolers, and their parents/caregivers around the United States. Call or write for the class in your area. Center for Music and Young Children, 66 Witherspoon Street, Princeton, NJ 08542; 800-728-2692.

BECOMING A BETTER LISTENER

Many men would regard the phrase "get in touch with your feelings" as a joke. But the fact is, you can't walk all over your children's—or your spouse's—feelings and expect to maintain a good relationship with them. Adele Faber and Elaine Mazlish are the authors of the bestselling *How to Talk So Kids Will Listen and Listen So Kids Will Talk* (Avon Books) and other books on building better relationships with children. While their advice here applies mainly to fathers with slightly older children, it's still very pertinent to new dads who want to keep the lines of communication open in their family. Listening is one of the most important ways in which you nurture a child. Say the authors (and many other fathers who've had to learn the hard way): listen; don't always tell.

Q. Let me ask you the same question I asked Armin Brott at the beginning of this chapter: how important is it for a father to be involved in his children's lives?

Faber and Mazlish: It is critical. A child's ongoing relationship with his dad can be an enormous source of comfort and strength. Studies have shown that kids who had warm, nurturing relationships with their fathers do much better, emotionally, socially, and academically, than kids who haven't. Girls especially excel, when dad engages them in traditionally "male" activities like fishing or playing ball. Girls conclude that if if they can prove their competency with dad on the basketball court, they can be equally competent in the classroom or later in life in the boardroom.

Q. This is different from the traditional view of the father's role.

Faber and Mazlish: Historically, dads have seen themselves in the limited roles of providers and disciplinarians: "Wait till your dad gets home." One thing that emerges very clearly is that it's not just the child who benefits from a positive interaction with the father. The father benefits, too. It has even been proven that fathers went just as far in their work as comparable men did who were less involved with their kids.

Q. Women are typically seen as the ones with the strong verbal and communication skills. But how many men participate in your workshops?

Faber and Mazlish: When we first started giving lectures and workshops, we would typically have five hundred mothers and about ten or fifteen fathers. But times have changed. I'd say 25 percent of the people who attend our workshops now are fathers. They want to be part of their children's lives, want to be connected to them. And many don't know how because their own fathers were perhaps physically present but emotionally absent.

Q. You talk in your book about the value of accepting and acknowledging your children's feelings. Why is that important?

Faber and Mazlish: Think of it in terms of yourself. The answer is inside you. How would you feel if you said, "It's my first day of school and I'm afraid," and someone said to you, "There's no reason to be afraid." Or you said, "It's hot today," and someone said, "It's not hot." Or you said "I've got a paper cut and it hurts," and someone said, "No it doesn't. Quit crying." Well, a paper cut *can* hurt. And the first day of school can

"I went through Old Spice, Hai Karate—but what I really remember is the smelly stuff my father used to wear. English Leather. The fatherly cologne, yeah, with that wooden top. Sneaking some of his English Leather, spraying it on myself, I'll never forget that."

—Basketball star Michael Jordan, son of James

be scary. There are so many new things to get used to as a child. The point is, children need to have their feelings acknowledged—even the negative ones.

Q. A lot of men—and women—don't do that.

Faber and Mazlish: And when we don't, we're telling our children, in effect, "You don't feel what you're feeling. You don't know what you know. You don't mean what you say." When we deny children's feelings, in a sense we're driving them crazy. But as parents, we want to drive them sane.

Q. I guess in order to listen to your children, you need to respect them as people.

Faber and Mazlish: Ah, respect! That is the foundation stone of our whole approach. But *respect* is an easy word to toss around. How do you remain respectful when a child says "You're mean" or "I hate you." These are the times that try a father's soul. One of the techniques we recommend is to talk about your feelings, instead of attacking the child.

Q. What do you mean?

Faber and Mazlish: You can say, "I didn't like what I just heard. If you're angry about something I did, tell me in another way and then I'll be able to listen." A kid needs a dad who will accept his worst feelings but stop his unacceptable behavior.

Contact: Faber and Mazlish conduct workshops for parents around the country on listening to your children, achieving cooperation without nagging, alternatives to punishment, and resolving family conflicts peacefully. Contact them at P.O. Box 64, Albertson, NY 11507.

HEALTHY AND SAFE BABY

I like doctors. I'm a big fan of doctors. I watch ER on Thursday nights, and when I'm sick, I go to my local HMO. Several outstanding physicians make recommendations on infant care, sleep, circumcision, and other health matters in this chapter. But, as is perhaps fitting with my contrary nature, I am going to use this introduction to say to all to new fathers: trust your instincts. And trust those of your partner.

Listen to what your pediatrician or family physician says. If what the doctor says makes sense, by all means, follow his or her advice. I've dealt with doctors in my life who are honest-to-God heroes. They care about their patients, and they treat them with respect.

Still, trust your instincts above all. You and your partner are your child's chief guardians and protectors. Nobody cares more about him or her than you do. You'd run through a wall for that child, you'd give up your lives. Trust your own counsel over that of physicians, teachers, grandparents, relatives, friends, and whoever else may be offering honest, well-intentioned advice.

When Annie was a baby, she developed a case of salmonella. We never did figure out exactly how she got it. I think it occurred when she was on the changing table. She was always moving and wiggling around, and she may have gotten some of her feces on her fingers. Then she stuck her hand in her mouth without us catching it.

Her stool became runny and grossly discolored, and she got sick. Salmonella is potentially a very grave condition for a baby. But the doctor couldn't figure out what was wrong. Annie's mother suggested the possibility of salmonella, but the doctor dismissed it as highly unlikely. But she insisted that Annie be tested for it, and the doctor grudgingly agreed.

113

Guess who was right. Fortunately Annie's own immune system fought off the disease and cured itself. But we learned an important lesson about sticking to your guns when your child's health is involved.

Nobody knows your child better than you, including your child's doctor. It's comparable to when you go into the hospital to have a baby. You have to stick to your guns there, too. You may want things done in a certain way and you have a right to ask for them. Doctors and nurses will have their own point of view, and this may or may not correspond with yours.

Be informed. That's the first step in becoming an advocate for your child and your partner. Become as knowledgeable as you can. Then follow your instincts. (Please note: The following chapter, "Household and Family Emergencies," contains more health and safety information.)

A THUMBNAIL GUIDE TO INFANT HEALTH

Dr. Chris Graves is a family physician at the Naval Construction Battalion Center in Port Hueneme, California. A lieutenant in the United States Navy Reserve, Graves graduated from medical school at the University of Tennessee in Memphis and completed his residency at the Naval Hospital in Camp Pendleton. His practice, as he says, consists of everything from "birth to grave, outpatient to ICN." He sees all members of the family: babies, pregnant mothers, and fathers. Because of his wide range of expertise, Dr. Graves seemed particularly well qualified to provide a thumbnail guide to infant health. The following section is not intended as a comprehensive look at children's health; its purpose is to generally acquaint new fathers with some of the issues they will be dealing with in their child's early development.

Baby Wellness Checks

Dr. Graves believes strongly in the value of baby wellness checks. They usually occur at two months, four months, six months, twelve months, and fifteen to eighteen months. A common concern among parents is whether the child is developing normally. These exams are an excellent time for fathers to get involved, especially if they have concerns. When will our baby walk? Talk? Sleep through the night? A well-baby check generally includes guidance for parents. A pediatrician or family physician will explain what you can expect in the months until the next visit. It's always better to have both parents at the exams, if possible. Together they can ask questions and gather information, rather than putting the burden on one parent.

Breast-Feeding

Breast-feeding has proven benefits for babies. Mom provides her baby with protection from diseases through her breast milk, and the baby doesn't get sick as often as bottle-fed babies. Not all babies can tolerate certain formulas. This is not true with mother's milk, though. Mom may have to eliminate some foods from her diet because they are transmitted to the infant, causing gas and indigestion. Breast-feeding is also the least expensive way to feed a child. Feed the mother, and her body will convert it into what the baby needs.

Although nursing requires Mom, Dad can easily become an integral partner in this quiet time. By reading a book, caressing the infant, and burping her intermitently, he will not miss out on this very unique experience. Breast-feeding takes time. He can do the chores around the house while Mom is feeding the baby. He can also help bottle feed the baby with milk expressed by the mother for those times when she goes out without the baby. It is especially important for men to be supportive in the early stages of breast-feeding. It takes days to weeks for Mom and baby to adjust to breast-feeding and Dad can help by encouraging Mom if she gets frustrated or insecure.

Bottle Feeding

In general, says Dr. Graves, bottle-fed babies eat what they need. Parents often worry that their child is not getting enough, or is getting too much. They expect him to eat a certain amount which they believe is proper and then worry when he doesn't follow their schedule. Graves says, "When the baby's hungry, feed him. When he's through, leave him alone. A baby will generally eat what he needs." The best indicator of appropriate feeding is the baby's urine output. He is most likely well hydrated if he is producing more than four wet diapers a day. He should be evaluated by his doctor if he has fewer than four diapers a day. His doctor will usually plot his height and weight at every visit to track his growth.

Bowel Movements

The four major activity centers in a baby's life are pooping, peeing, eating, and sleeping. Babies eat and then they poop, especially when they're young. The amount they urinate depends on their fluid intake. Bowel movements are frequently runny and yellow to green. Diarrhea is liquid coming out of the baby's bum, as opposed to stools. Ten to twenty diarrhea diapers in a day, especially if a child isn't drinking or eating, is a cause for concern. A child with diarrhea needs plenty of fluids. Every child is unique in the number of stools she produces. Some babies are "mega-poopers" and stool with each feeding; others stool much less, as little as once every three days. The key, says Dr. Graves, is to learn "what is normal for your baby." If there is an abrupt change or if she stools less than once every three days, you may want to discuss this with your baby's doctor.

Burping/Spitting Up

All babies need to burp, especially bottle-fed babies. They get air in their stomach and need to expel it. All babies spit up, as much as a teaspoon to two to three tablespoons at a time. They may get overfull or some milk may come out with a burp. "Never forget to put a towel over your shoulder when you burp a baby," counsels Dr. Graves with a smile. "You never know how wet or dry it will be." Try feeding your child a smaller volume, more frequently—e.g., two ounces every two hours rather than four ounces every four hours—if you feel he is spitting up a majority of his feeding.

Catching a Cold

It might be wise to keep the baby home for the first month. Take her to the grocery store if you need to, but don't take her to the movies or to any group meetings where she'll be in an enclosed room with other people who may be coughing and sneezing. A grocery store can be crowded, but it's a more open space and people are moving, not sitting in one place. So the risk of infection for baby is less. Be protective of your newborn. A baby is more liable to pick up infection from other people than they are from her. Avoid sick people when you're with a baby. Remember to wash your hands after, as well as before, you handle the baby. That makes you less prone to pick up any bugs yourself.

Circumcision

Dr. Graves believes this is strictly a personal decision for the parents. Medically speaking, in his judgment, a circumcision is a toss-up. The medical arguments to have a circumcision balance out the arguments not to have one. He recommends that parents make the call before entering the hospital to have the baby. A circumcision should take place in the first couple of weeks after birth; it becomes a more complicated surgery after that. Nurses will instruct on circumcision care after one is performed. (See the section on circumsision later in this chapter.)

Colic

Colic is the term applied to "fussy" babies. Characterized by lots and lots of crying, colic occurs in babies up to about three months old. It's hard on babies and parents. For parents, the normal ways in which they provide comfort—changing the diaper, feeding, holding the baby—do not work. The reasons for colic are unclear because infants can't say what's bothering them. It's defined as "abdominal pain presumably of intestinal origin" and sometimes associated with the time after meals. Anti-gas Mylicon drops give relief to some babies. The only proven relief is "time-out" for the parents. New moms and dads may want to go on a date and get some quiet time together, as a colicky baby can be very stressful at times. Just prepare the baby-sitter.

Crying

Sometimes babies will cry just to cry. It's not colic; it's how they communicate. A baby's early life consists of eating, sleeping, pooping, peeing, and crying. Like many child experts, Dr. Graves believes that it is impossible to spoil a child under the age of one. When your child cries, hold him and love him and comfort him. A baby does not know how to manipulate people the way adults understand the term. But over time, he does learn that when he cries, he gets attention from adults. When you put him to bed, he may cry because he doesn't want to go. Later on parents will face the hard task of letting their child cry himself to sleep without intervening.

"Getting her to sleep was a big issue. You hear widely different views on what to do. Do you let them sleep alone? Do they sleep with you? All I know is that someone else's experience may not work for you."
—Steve Cohan, father of Amira

Diaper Rash

This is a very common malady that can often be treated by over-the-counter remedies such as Desenex, Lotrimin, or Balmex. Rashes love moist heat. One solution is to take the diaper off for a while and let the baby run around in her birthday suit. She'll enjoy it, that's for sure.

Discovering the Genitals

Discovering the genitals is normal, natural, and fun. A baby will clutch and grab and wriggle for anything within arm's reach: toes, ears, fingers, and genitals. Not to worry.

Ear Infections

Infections are another normal, if sometimes painful, part of growing up. Never lay a baby down with a bottle, says Dr. Graves. That only increases the risk of ear infections. A baby pulling on his ear does not necessarily indicate an infection; nor are antibiotics always the answer in treating one. Call your pediatrician or family physician with your concerns.

Fever

A baby under three months is considered to have a clinical fever with a temperature of 100.5 degrees Fahrenheit or above. A baby three months or older is running a fever with a temperature of 101 to 101.5 or above. Call your doctor if you have questions about your child's temperature.

Immunization

Beginning at two months, children typically begin receiving immunizations, although some may be started before your baby leaves the hospital. DTP (diptheria, tetanus, pertussis, also called whooping cough), OPV or IPV (oral or intravenous polio vaccine), MMR (measles, mumps, rubella), and Hib (influenza) vaccinations are required in many states for school entry, though you can get a religious or, sometimes, philosophical waiver in some states. People hear horror stories about immunization, but the benefits of immunization "far, far, far, far, far" outweigh the miminal risks associated with it, says Dr. Graves (and virtually all others in the medical community). If your child has a reaction to one of the vaccines, for example the pertussis part of the DTP shot, you can get a medical waiver so your child can avoid any further vaccination with that particular component.

Pacifiers

Some ardent advocates of breast-feeding argue that pacifiers and bottles create "nipple confusion" in a baby, and therefore their use should be discouraged. Dr. Graves does not subscribe to these theories; he sees nothing wrong with pacifiers. Usually a baby is older when he begins using them and breast-feeding is well established by then.

Solid Foods

A baby begins eating cereal at about four months. Eating and nutrition are excellent topics for the two- or four-month well-baby check. Babies tend to tolerate rice cereal well; it's an excellent starter food. New items should be introduced at a rate no greater than one per week to help discern any food allergies she may have.

Skin Care

Your baby has soft, sensitive skin, which you should enjoy by holding and cuddling often. To maintain his skin's delicate state, however, it is important to apply a hypoallergenic, non-perfumed lotion after each bath. Although bathing your baby will be a fun activity, infants do not get very dirty. Make sure his bottom and diaper area remain clean and dry; bathing him more than once every three days is usually not necessary. Remember to apply a hypoallergenic sunscreen if you must take your baby outdoors. Their delicate skin burns easily.

Sleep

Sleep is a big issue for both newborns and their parents. In the first month of life newborns sleep a lot. But it comes in short bursts of two to four hours at a time. Gradually babies begin to sleep for longer periods and even through the night. Dr. Graves recommends that new fathers try to keep the same sleep schedule as their baby. Sleep when the baby's asleep, because you will be up when the baby's up. Understand that a lack of sleep causes irritability—for both you and your baby. It decreases work performance because you can't concentrate as well. It's nearly impossible to maintain normal rhythms and routines during this period. Fathers need to make it a priority to get the rest they need. It can take six to eight weeks or longer for a baby's sleep patterns to stabilize and normalcy to return to the household.

Taking a Baby's Temperature

Dr. Graves hesitates recommending ear thermometers; they are hard to use effectively at home. He says the old-fashioned rectal thermometers are best. The child will make it sound like you're killing him, but, says Graves, "your child really doesn't care and he really won't remember." But never force the issue; sometimes a pacifier will calm a baby who's resisting a rectal thermometer. Lay the baby on her stomach on your lap. Or put her on her back, holding her ankles together and tipping her legs toward her belly. Spread the buttocks apart and gently insert the thermometer. Three minutes is ideal, but one minute gets within one degree of the true reading.

Teething

Teething occurs at about six months, though the timing varies from baby to baby. Teething is when a child's first set of teeth breaks through the gums. Signs of teething are drooling, coughing, biting, pain and inflammation, and irritability. Contrary to popular belief, teething does not cause clinical fever. Graves tells parents not to discount what they think is causing a fever out of a mistaken suggestion by a well-meaning person that the fever is being caused by teething. There are a variety of home remedies for reducing the discomfort of teething. They include giving a baby something to chew on, a cold drink, or something cold to eat. Even a father's finger rubbed on the gums can be soothing. Acetaminophen can also work wonders.

Toilet Training

Potty training typically begins at age two, although some parents start sooner. When a child bids adieu to the diapers it is a transforming event in the life of the child and her parents. Even so, there is no need to rush. The longer you wait to teach your child, the more she will be able to understand the concepts you want her to learn. Try not to give in to peer pressure and "force" the issue of toilet training; your child will let you know when she's ready. Dr. Graves reports that he has seen few children attend their senior prom in Pampers.

Wetting the Bed

A child who occasionally wets the bed at three or four years old is perfectly normal. When a child reaches five and is still doing it, there may be some cause for concern. Consult your family physician or pediatrician on this or any other health issue that causes you concern.

Note: The opinions and assertions expressed herein are those of the author and Dr. Graves and are not to be construed as official or as reflecting the view of the Department of the Navy, the Department of Defense, or the naval service at large.

IMMUNIZATION GUIDELINES

The Center of Disease Control's guidelines for vaccinating young children are as follows:

Birth:	Hepatitis B
2 months:	Hepatitis B, polio, diphtheria, tetanus, pertussis (DTP), Hib
4 months:	Hepatitis B, polio, DTP, Hib
6 months:	Hepatitis B, polio, DTP, Hib
12–15 months:	DTP, Hib, measles, mumps, rubella (MMR)
4–6 years:	Polio, DTP, MMR
11–12 years:	Diphtheria, tetanus

> "To me it's not a big deal if she goes to sleep at eleven. She goes to sleep when she wants to. She has her own body rhythms."
>
> —Gary Grillo, father of Maddie

HOW TO GET A GOOD NIGHT'S SLEEP

Dr. Richard Ferber is one of the foremost experts on children's sleep in the country. A graduate of Harvard Medical School, he runs the Center for Pediatric Sleep Disorders at Boston Children's Hospital. His book, *Solve Your Child's Sleep Problems* (Simon & Schuster), is considered a classic of its kind. The father of two sons, he briefly explains what parents can expect in the first six months of their baby's life:

Birth to Two or Three Months. Babies, as every new parent learns, do not come into this world knowing how to sleep through the night. They sleep at first in irregular intervals. Short periods of waking are followed by varying periods of sleep. As a result, expect your sleep schedule to be disrupted in the first two to three months of your child's life. The baby will need care and comfort at night. She will need her diaper changed. She will need to be fed. "Be sure to participate even if your wife is breast-feeding," Ferber tells new fathers. "You can get up, change the baby, and be part of the process."

Two to Three Months. At about three months or earlier, the baby will show signs of settling down at night. The majority of feedings will be in the daytime now, although Ferber quickly adds that there are lots of variations. A child's ability to settle into a sleep schedule depends on issues such as the timing and frequency of naps and feedings, what the child eats, whether the child falls asleep on her own or in her parents' bed, whether her parents help her fall asleep through rocking or rubbing or other means, and much more.

Five to Six Months. A child will begin to sleep continuously through the night by this time. She will move from three naps a day to two. Her last feeding will occur in the evening before she goes to bed. With the help of her parents, a baby will develop increasingly regular habits. Her life will move in predictable patterns. She will get up at the same time in the morning, go to bed at the same time at night. She will nap at about the same times during the day. Indeed, Ferber believes that having a consistent daily routine will help your child form good sleep habits. "That doesn't mean that you have to do at three months what you did at one day," he says. "It's a gradual evolution. Things change over time. Watch your child and adapt to what she's doing, while moving in the direction of regularity."

CIRCUMCISION: ONE PHYSICIAN'S VIEW

Many physicians take a neutral stance on circumcision, describing it as an individual family decision. Dr. Jeremy Klein is not one of them. He is a family physician in Louisa, Kentucky, in the eastern part of the state. A graduate of the University of Maryland where he also attended medical school, he's been in practice since 1985 and delivered babies every year since then. He, like many fathers today, is circumcised. But his three sons are not. Klein gives these reasons why he opposes circumcision and believes that boys should be left intact:

It Is Unnecessary. Circumcision is the surgical removal of the fold of skin that normally covers the head of the penis. This double layer of skin is commonly referred to as the foreskin. Cutting off the foreskin is elective or cosmetic surgery. "It's not urgent. It's not a diseased piece of skin that's being removed," says Klein, adding, "The foreskin is factory installed equipment. It comes with the model."

The Child Has No Choice in the Matter. One can say with absolute certainty that few adult males would willingly subject themselves to this procedure, if they weren't already circumcised. It is done to babies because babies get no vote.

The Risks Outweigh the Benefits. The most basic oath of physicians is: "First do no harm." In other words, don't do the procedure unless it's the right thing to do. Klein believes that circumcision fails this test. He says that this once-routine procedure carries the risk of possible deformity, disease, bleeding, allergic reaction, and possible damage to the tissue. (As is characteristic of the circumcision debate, not all physicians subscribe to Klein's view. Many of them describe circumcision as routine and safe. It is usually done in the hospital in the first week of the baby's life.)

The Medical Debate Continues to Rage. Few topics generate as much controversy and passion as the debate over circumcision. Both sides cite studies that support their point of view. The proponents say that circumcision prevents cancer of the penis. But Klein says that penile cancer can be avoided by adequate cleaning. Further, he argues, such a disease occurs very late in life among men. Does the benefit toward the end of a man's life outweigh the risk at the start of his life when adequate cleaning will also prevent the disease? Klein doesn't think so.

The American Academy of Pediatrics has stated that circumcision is not "medically necessary." Reports conflict on whether or not uncircumcised males have demonstrated a higher incidence of HIV transmission. One study suggested that uncircumcised boys suffered from a higher incidence of urinary tract infection. Klein cites research that indicates that boys who were circumcised showed more pain at their first immunization than those who were left intact. Another study of adult males showed that circumcised males experimented more with "alternative" sexual practices than intact men. Klein feels the continuing controversy supports his point of view. "If we can't decide that this is a good thing, then we ought not to do it," he says.

Circumcision Is Painful. Klein says that 80 percent of circumcisions in this country are performed without anesthesia. Anesthesia should be used, though injecting a needle in the penis still hurts. Giving anesthesia to a newborn also increases the risk of harm to the baby.

It's an Attack Against Boys. Klein and other circumcision opponents ask why boys are subjected to this procedure. The circumcision of infant girls as practiced in the Sudan—the nicking of external female genitalia and in some cases its outright removal—is rightfully considered barbarous. Why is it different for boys in this country?

Being "Intact" Is Far More Popular than It Used to Be. It's now almost a fifty-fifty split in the United States between boys who are circumcised and those who are intact. This should reassure men who worry that their uncircumcised son will get teased in the locker room

> "As a child, he spent much of his time struggling to get his breath. Often he would have to be propped up with pillows. . . . If this didn't help, his father would bundle him up and take him out in his carriage. Then Mr. Roosevelt would drive his horses pell-mell through the city streets hoping the speed would force air into Teddy's lungs."
>
> —From a biography of Teddy Roosevelt, who had asthma as a child and yet grew to full health with the help of his father, Theodore Roosevelt Sr.

when he reaches high school. It's also probably true that the boy who gets teased will be the one spending his time looking at other boys' penises.

The United States Is in the Minority on This One. Jews and Muslims practice circumcision as part of their religious beliefs. In most parts of the world, however, circumcision is virtually unheard of. In China, Japan, England, France, Sweden, and the rest of Europe, it is hardly done at all.

Why Is It Necessary for Your Sons to Look Like You? Many of the parents in Klein's practice still routinely have their sons circumcised. One reason is that the fathers want their sons to look like them. When Klein's son was about four, he noticed the difference for the first time and asked his father about it. "I told him in terms he could understand," says Klein. "I said that when I was a baby doctors used to think that by cutting off that little piece of skin, boys would have fewer medical problems. But we don't think that anymore." Klein said his son shrugged and said, "Oh," and went back to what he was doing.

It's an Easy Matter to Clean the Foreskin. The foreskin protects the end of the penis. He says that cleaning the outside of the penis is sufficient. But, he warns, don't pull it back. It's not designed to be pulled back on a baby. The foreskin will not get stuck or grow over the penis. It can be retracted naturally without hurting the boy sometime between the ages of two and six. Once you pull it back, wash it, rinse it, and then return it to its natural position. Skin infections are rare. Some men worry about the foreskin being caught in a zipper but, as others point out, that's why they make underwear.

Tip: Klein recommends Say No to Circumcision, *by Thomas Ritter, M.D., and George Denniston, M.D. (Hourglass Publishing, P.O. Box 171, Aptos, CA 94001). The National Organization of Circumcision Information Resource Centers publishes a newsletter and functions as an information clearinghouse for parents and others who oppose circumcision. Contact them at P.O. Box 2512, San Anselmo, CA 94979; 415–488–9883.*

CIRCUMCISION: ANOTHER PHYSICIAN'S VIEW

There are pro-circumcision voices in the medical community. One of them belongs to Dr. Edgar Schoen, medical director of regional perinatal screening at Kaiser Foundation Research Institute in Oakland, California. He says that medical evidence shows that routine circumcision can significantly reduce the risk of urinary tract infection, certain sexually transmitted diseases (STDs) including HIV, and penile cancer.

"Newborn circumcision is a valuable preventative health measure," says Schoen, the former chairman of the American Academy of Pediatrics Task Force on Circumcision who's written on the subject for a British medical journal as well as other publications. He compares the benefits of circumcision to immunization, "which offers protection against a number of diseases throughout a man's lifetime," he says.

Schoen argues that the best time for circumcision is when the boy is a newborn, noting that studies in the past ten years associate circumcision with a lower rate of urinary tract or kidney infections in infants. Uncircumcised infants less than one year old have about ten times the risk of urinary tract infections as circumcised infants, according to these studies.

Schoen points to a greater risk of STDs "involved with abrasions or tears in the foreskin" among intact men. He also says that studies in sub-Saharan Africa indicate a fourfold greater risk for heterosexual HIV infection among uncircumcised males than among circumcised males. In addition, the evidence that circumcision protects against penile cancer is "overwhelming," says Schoen. In the United States, the incidence of penile cancer among circumcised men is essentially zero—about one case every five years. But in intact men, about one thousand cases are reported annually, Schoen says. "When properly done, newborn circumcision is a quick, simple procedure with a low complication rate," concludes Schoen.

Contact: Edgar J. Schoen, M.D., Medical Director of Regional Perinatal Screening, Kaiser Permanente, 280 W. MacArthur Boulevard, Oakland, CA 94611; 510-596-6585.

A SAFE CRIB IS A GOOD CRIB

A crib is a place of rest and comfort. It is the place where your baby will spend most of his or her time. It needs to be safe.

These are the sad facts: more than thirteen thousand children are injured in unsafe cribs every year. Their injuries are serious enough to warrant hospital treatment. In the past decade, more than six hundred children have died from crib injuries. But this may be the saddest fact of all: many of these injuries and deaths were preventable.

The Danny Foundation was founded in 1986 in memory of Danny Lineweaver, who accidentally hanged himself when his shirt became entangled on a corner of his crib. These are a few of the Foundation's crib safety guidelines:

- A crib needs to be solid. Shake the crib after you assemble it. Is it rickety and wobbly? A newborn baby won't move around much. However, a two-year-old will bounce and jump up and down, possibly collapsing an unsturdy crib on top of him.

- Don't scrimp when you buy a crib. Most new cribs comply with safety regulations. But the less expensive ones are not as sturdy and won't last as long. Plan to spend $200 or more for a new crib.

- Don't let Grandma or anyone else foist an older crib on you if you don't want it. Studies show that three out of four newborns are placed in a used crib. There may be as many as 25 million used cribs in the United States either in use or in storage. Your parents may have stored your old crib for the past thirty years waiting for the time when you had children of your own. It may have great sentimental value, but it also may be rickety and unsafe.

- Inspect for corner post extensions. Most of these older cribs have corner post extensions that can catch children's clothing and cause strangulation. Corner posts should be the same height as the end panels and not extend above the end panels. Remove corner post extensions by unscrewing or sawing them off and sanding smooth.

- Check the slats. The space between slats must be less than two and three-eighths inches, and no slats should be missing. Children try to squeeze their feet through the slats, but their heads get caught in them.

- Tighten the hardware down. All screws, bolts, and hardware must be in place and secure. Inspect the crib periodically. Screws can come loose as the baby bounces and becomes more active. The crib should be smooth and free of sharp edges, points, and rough surfaces.

- Follow the instructions when you assemble a new crib. Putting a crib together is not as easy as it looks. An improperly assembled crib can lead to problems. Read the directions and don't throw them away. At some point you will break the crib down and put it into storage. But you may have another baby someday, and you'll need the directions and all the hardware again.

- When in doubt about a crib, get rid of it. It is the only place where a baby will be left alone. It needs to be strong, sturdy, and free of all potential hazards—for your peace of mind and the safety of the child.

Source: The Danny Foundation, 3158 Danville Boulevard, P.O. Box 680, Alamo, CA 94507; 800–83DANNY; www.dannyfoundation.org/; E-mail: dannycrib@earthlink.net/. Its excellent brochure, Is Your Crib Safe? *contains additional crib safety pointers on mattresses, bumper pads, pillows, and many other items. It is available free.*

KIDPROOFING AND BABY PRODUCTS

Some parents get carried away with childproofing the house and do it even before the baby arrives. But you can wait until your child reaches the two- to four-month mark before thinking about it in earnest. It's essential when the baby learns to crawl. It keeps her safe and out of mischief and will save you some headaches. It also protects your stuff. There's no reason to get mad at the baby for being curious and exploring the knobs on your CD player; that's what she's supposed to do. Your job is to put valued (or potentially dangerous) things out of reach or store them away until the baby gets older.

Sample childproof products are corner cushions for sharp-edged furniture, slide locks for cabinets, stove knob covers, security gates, spring latches for drawers and cabinets, outlet plugs and swivel outlet covers, VCR safety locks, cord holders to keep loose cords out of the way, oven locks, double-folding door locks, and more. Pick them up at any hardware store or children's store.

There are thousands of baby products on the market. Some are good, some not so good. Some (like a good crib) are necessary, many are not. *Baby Stuff: A No-Nonsense Shopping Guide for Every Parent's Lifestyle,* by Ari and Joanna Lipper (Dell Publishing), is an excellent buying guide on cribs, changing tables, strollers, rockers, car seats, baby monitors, and more. Another useful resource is *A Guide to Baby Products,* by Consumer Reports Books (800–500–9760). The Juvenile Products Manufacturer's Association (JPMA) publishes a brochure on baby product safety and selection. For a copy, send a stamped, self-addressed business-size envelope to JPMA Public Information, Two Greentree Centre, P.O. Box 955, Marlton, NJ 08053.

HEALTH CARE RESOURCES

Three excellent all-around books on infant health are *The Baby Book: Everything You Need to Know About Your Baby—from Birth to Age Two*, by William Sears, M.D., and Martha Sears, R.N. (Little, Brown & Co.); *Dr. Spock's Baby and Child Care*, 6th ed., by Benjamin Spock, M.D., and Michael B. Rothenberg, M.D. (Pocket Books); and *What to Expect the First Year*, by Arlene Eisenberg, Heidi E. Murkoff, and Sandee Hathaway, B.S.N. (Workman Publishing). All were used as references for this book.

The American Academy of Pediatrics has a referral service that will provide you with the names of pediatricians in your area if you need one. Write the American Academy of Pediatrics, Pediatrician Referral Service, P.O. Box 927, Elk Grove Village, IL 60009. Tell where you live and the specialty you're looking for, and enclose a SASE. The AAP also has videos, brochures, and other information for parents. Contact the same address, Dept. C, Brochures PRG. It will reply with a list of materials available, both for purchase and free. More ways to contact AAP: 800–433–9016; www.aap.org.

The American Academy of Family Physicians is the national association of family doctors, with more than eighty thousand members in the United States. It also has a referral service to help you find a physician and provides health information for new and expecting parents. American Academy of Family Physicians, 8880 Ward Parkway, Kansas City, MO 64114; 800–274–2237; 816–333–9700; www.aafp.org.

Sometimes bad things happen to babies that are beyond the realm of physicians. An estimated seven thousand babies die every year for reasons that are still unknown; these mysterious deaths are characterized as "crib deaths" or sudden infant death sydrome (SIDS). The Sudden Infant Death Syndrome Alliance is a nonprofit research and education organization that provides information and resources for families who've lost a child through SIDS. Sudden Infant Death Syndrome Alliance, 1314 Bedford Avenue, Suite 210, Baltimore, MD 21208; 410–653–8226; 800–221–SIDS.

HOUSEHOLD AND FAMILY EMERGENCIES

I live in California, and it's hard to argue with people who claim that this earthquake-prone, fire-ravaged, flood-possessed state has more disasters than anywhere else. My daughter Annie was born on October 20. The year after she was born, the Loma Prieta Earthquake, one of the biggest earthquakes in California history (and we've seen a few of them), rocked our home a few days before her birthday. Three years later, on the day of Annie's fourth birthday party, a major fire swept through the Oakland hills, killing twenty-five people and burning more than 3,400 houses to the ground in one of the worst disasters of its kind in United States history. Her grandmother drove through the smoke in the hills to be at the party.

Now when Annie's birthday rolls around, we always celebrate it in the underground bomb shelter that we've built under our house. Just kidding. We escaped the brunt of these disasters, and we hope we always will in the future. Still, the Boy Scout motto of "Be Prepared" seems like a good one, especially when you have a family to think about.

Every parent of small children should know infant CPR. I can't recommend that more strongly. Do you know first aid? Do you know what to do if your baby starts choking or suddenly stops breathing? What about if a fire occurred in your house? Do you have a plan on how to get out?

It'd be nice if you could raise kids and never have to cope with a family emergency. It's probably an unrealistic expectation, though. I remember one time when I was a kid and my dad was grilling

Each year one out of every five children has an injury that requires emergency treatment at a hospital.

hamburgers for my brother and me. He wasn't paying too close attention, and the grease in the pan started to smoke. My dad stuck the pan in the sink and turned the water on it. Flames shot up off the pan and caught the window curtains on fire.

"Call the fire department," he told my brother, who did as he was told. I ran down the stairs and out the front door. Then I ran down the street. Don't ask me why. I didn't know what else to do. Running around like an idiot probably seemed like the right thing to do at the time.

My dad put the fire out immediately, but two fire trucks showed up anyway. Their sirens brought half the neighborhood out to watch. Firefighters ran up our stairs carrying a hose, even though my dad assured them that the fire was out. About this time my mother drove up. She nearly had a heart attack when she saw the fire engines and all the neighbors crowded around our house.

The moral of the story is: don't do what I did. Be a person who is cool and in command during a crisis. (Note: more health and safety information is contained in the preceeding chapter "Healthy and Safe Baby.")

INFANT CPR

There is one clear and simple reason why new parents should know infant CPR: they can save their baby's life.

Most parents will never have to use infant CPR on their child. But what if your baby choked on an object or accidentally fell into a pool and stopped breathing? Would you know what to do? Taking an infant CPR class will teach you how to respond—in short, how to save your baby's life. These are the ABCS—airway, breathing, circulation—of CPR for children:

- First, tap or shake the child's shoulders to determine unresponsiveness. Say, "Are you okay?" Shout for help, and ask someone to call 911.

- *Airway.* Open the airway by tilting the head and lifting the chin.

- *Breathing.* Check for breathing. Look, listen, and feel. If there is no breathing, give two mouth-to-mouth breaths. Cover the mouth, pinch the nose, give a breath, and watch for the chest to rise. Allow the child to exhale.

- *Circulation.* Check for the carotid pulse on the neck. If you feel a pulse, do rescue breathing: one breath every three seconds. If there's no pulse, put one hand on the sternum and compress one inch to a half inch, one hundred times per minute. For every five compressions, give one breath. Check the pulse after one minute and call 911 if no one else has. Check for the pulse and breathing every few minutes and continue rescue efforts until help arrives.

These guidelines, however valuable, are no substitute for taking an infant CPR class. Accident prevention is also a major subject in these classes. Among the areas covered are electrical shock, drowning and water safety, swallowing foreign objects, car seats, air bags, and pedestrian safety.

Source: American Heart Association, National Center, 7272 Greenville Avenue, Dallas, TX 75231. Call 1-800-242-8721 for an AHA-certified infant CPR class in your area. Other sources for CPR-training classes are the American Red Cross, local hospitals, colleges, and day-care associations.

BURN PREVENTION MEASURES

Many burns are caused not by fire but by scalding. And children are the ones who are most frequently the victims. A child can be scalded in the most innocent of circumstances. Parents can be drinking coffee reading the paper at the breakfast table and the child can reach over and accidentally knock a cup over, instantly burning himself. Following are some tips for the prevention and treatment of burns:

Never Leave Your Child Alone in the Bath. Accidents can and do happen. Unless he's sleeping safely in his crib, never leave a small child alone anywhere, let alone a bathtub.

Run Your Hand in the Bath Water Before Putting Your Baby in It. Babies are commonly scalded by bath water that's too hot. Tap water scald burns are as serious as hot liquid spills from a stove, and they usually cover a larger area of the body.

Turn Down the Thermostat of Your Water Heater. Water boils at 212 degrees Fahrenheit; steam, which can burn the soft skin of a baby, occurs at 170 degrees. Burn authorities recommend that water heaters should be set between 120 to 130 degrees, not at 155 degrees as is generally the rule. Hot liquid at 155 degrees can cause a third-degree burn in just one second.

Keep Small Children Out of the Way When You're Cooking. Put your baby in a high chair or a playpen. If they're playing or crawling under foot, that's asking for trouble. Make sure that pot handles are turned inward so children can't grab them.

Accidents are the leading cause of death for children under eight.

More than four thousand children are scalded by tap water every year.

In the Event of a Burn, Put Burned Skin Under Cool Water for Twenty Minutes or More. Do not use butter, grease, or ice on a burn. These methods can further damage the tissue.

Be Wary of Microwave Ovens. Microwave ovens are a potential hazard. Never heat baby food in a jar inside a microwave. The contents can be boiling, though the outside of the jar may feel cool to the touch. This is true for other food items heated in a microwave: jelly donut, pop tart, burrito, popcorn. Many microwaves are built over a gas stove. You may have things cooking on the stove, while you reach to get something out of the microwave. Always be aware of where the children are.

Teach Your Children That Fire Is Not a Game. Matches are tools, not toys. As your children get older, they need to know this. Playing with fire is not a phase that children go through or an example of their growing curiosity about life. Children do not realize that when they play with matches, they can burn themselves or be caught in a fire. Educate yourself about the dangers of fire and then educate your children.

Source: The Alisa Ann Ruch Burn Foundation promotes education in fire and burn prevention and provides assistance to burn survivors and their families. Its family burn prevention safety kit contains a thermometer to check the temperature of bath water. Alisa Ann Ruch Burn Foundation, 20944 Sherman Way, Suite 115, Canoga Park, CA 91303; 800-242-2876 (CA only); 818-883-7700; www.aarbf.org.

WHAT TO KEEP IN YOUR FIRST-AID KIT

Keeping a first-aid kit in the house is a smart, sensible idea. In an emergency you may not have the time to hunt around for supplies. The baby may be crying. Your partner may be stressed out or not even present. You want to be able to find what you need quickly and with a minimum of excess motion.

You may want to keep another first-aid kit in your car when you go on trips as a family. You can purchase basic first-aid kits or you can put one together yourself. A good first-aid kit will include these items:

- First-aid information
- Assorted bandages and Band-Aids
- Gauze squares
- Roll of two-inch sterile gauze
- Adhesive tape

- Child's rectal thermometer
- Ice pack
- Hydrogen peroxide (antiseptic solution)
- Dosage spoon, measuring spoons
- Rubbing alcohol
- Syrup of Ipecac (to induce vomiting—only use on the advice of a physician)
- Scissors
- Soap (bar or liquid)
- Tweezers, cotton balls, and swabs
- Hot water bottle
- Calamine lotion
- Disposable gloves
- Petroleum jelly
- Tongue depressors
- Matches (for sterilizing)
- Bee sting kit

Source: Adapted from Childhood Emergencies: What to Do, A Quick Reference Guide. *This easy-to-use, flip-chart manual tells how to handle such childhood emergencies as bleeding, abrasions, cuts, choking, burns, headaches, broken bones, and others. Bull Publishing Company, P.O. Box 208, Palo Alto, CA 94302; 800-676-2855; E-mail: Bullpublishing@msn.com.*

FIRE PREVENTION CHECKLIST

Fire kills thousands of people every year in the United States. Many of these people are sleeping at the time. An intense home fire combines extreme heat with smoke and toxic gases. Temperatures climb to over 1,000 degrees Fahrenheit in minutes. Entire rooms burst spontaneously into flames. Following are methods to prevent a fire from occurring in your home and information about what to do if a fire does start.

- Every member of the family should know what to do if a fire occurs. Know two ways out of every room in case one of the exits is blocked by fire or smoke.

- Establish a meeting place outside the house. Once your family is safe, no one can go back inside for any reason.

There are six hundred thousand residential fires in the United States every year, half of which are set by children.

133

Nearly nine out of ten of the victims of child-set fires are children themselves.

- Smoke and heat rise, creating cooler, easier-to-breathe air closer to the floor. Stay low if you must pass through smoke. Crawl on your hands and knees. If your clothes do catch on fire, stop, drop, and roll while covering your face with your hands.

- If somebody smokes in the house, use large, deep ashtrays. Make sure the ashes are cool before being thrown away. Keep matches and lighters out of reach of curious children.

- Test smoke alarms monthly. Change the batteries at least once a year. Smoke alarms over ten years old should be replaced. More items to check: loose cords and broken wires. Throw away those worn-out extension cords. Replace that old toaster or lamp with the frayed cord. It's a small price to pay to avoid the threat of electrical fire.

- Simple carelessness is the cause of many home fires. Place space heaters at least three feet away from walls and draperies. Check the sofa or cushions if a cigarette smoker drops ashes in them.

- The kitchen is an obvious place where fires start. When you cook, make sure that the pot handles are turned away from your child's little, grabbing hands. (Kitchen accidents cause burns, too.) You can usually stop cooking fires by covering the burning pan with a large lid. A fire extinguisher readily at hand will stop them as well.

Source: National Fire Protection Association. The NFPA provides fire safety pamphlets for individuals and schools. National Fire Protection Association, 1 Batterymarch Park, P.O. Box 9101, Quincy, MA 02269; 617-770-3000; www.nfpa.org. Closer to home, the local fire department is a great source for free fire safety information.

PREPARING FOR A DISASTER

When you were single, you primarily had only yourself to think about. Then you got married and now you have a baby, and now you have to put other people's welfare ahead of your own. You're happy to do it because that's what it means to be a man and a father, but it also entails responsibilities.

If something really huge happened—something on the order of an earthquake or hurricane or fire or big winter storm—would you be ready for it? Disasters of this kind frequently strike without warning. Basic services such as water, gas, phone, and electricity are cut off. Emergency relief will be on its way, but it may take hours—or days— to reach you. You and your family may be forced to evacuate your neighborhood or hunker down in your home until assistance arrives. Here are some suggestions on how to help you and yours ride out a disaster:

Store Water, Food, and Emergency Supplies. Assemble a disaster supplies kit that contains items such as a flashlight, matches, battery-powered radio, and extra batteries. You're going to need to eat and drink if the roads are impassable and stores have closed. Pack a three-day supply of water (one gallon per person per day) and imperishable food items. It is prudent as well to store an extra set of car keys, a credit card, cash, or traveler's checks.

Pack for the Baby, Too. A baby has special needs. Pack a toy or two, diapers, and other supplies she might need. All of you—mom, baby, dad—need to stay warm. Pack blankets or sleeping bags and changes of clothing. Include toilet paper, toiletries, first-aid supplies, and prescription medications.

Pack an Extra Pair of Eyeglasses. One of the most famous "Twilight Zone" episodes told the story of a man who disliked people and only wanted to read books. He got his wish when a nuclear holocaust wiped out all of humanity (except himself), but then he accidentally broke his glasses and couldn't see to do anything, much less read. Do not wander in the darkness if disaster strikes. Pack an extra pair of eyeglasses.

Know How to Turn the Gas and Other Utilities Off. Locate the main electric fuse box for your house, the water service main, and the natural gas main. Know how to turn these off. It is a wise idea for your partner to know how, too. Some people make the mistake of turning off the main gas valve even if they don't smell gas. When you turn the gas off, a professional will have to turn it back on.

Inspect Your House for Hazards. Make a walk-through inspection of your house, looking for possible hazards. Anything that can move, fall, break, or cause a fire is potential trouble. Heavy bookshelves and the hot water heater should be bolted to the wall.

Review Your Insurance Coverage. Are you adequately covered in the event of major loss? This is yet another way in which your thinking ahead can protect your family.

Source: Federal Emergency Management Authority and the American Red Cross. Free family protection publications such as Your Family Disaster Plan *and* Your Family Disaster Supplies Kit *are available through FEMA, P.O. Box 2012, Jessup, MD 20794; 800-480-2520; www.fema.gov. More information can be obtained at your local Red Cross chapter.*

About 75 percent of all fire deaths occur in homes without smoke detectors. More than half of all fire deaths occur at night.

JOB, CAREER, AND FAMILY

*E*verything changes when you have a baby. Early on, I thought it would hurt my career. I thought my responsibilities as a father would take away from the time I had to devote to writing.

To some degree, my fears proved true. I do have more responsibilities. I do have less free time and far less flexibility in my schedule. But you know what? I learned to cope, as I'm sure you will. You'll learn to handle it. You'll find ways to fit it all in and make it work. Or you'll go nuts trying. It's all up to you.

Having a baby actually gave me an unexpected career boost. You can't fiddle around anymore when you have a drooling new mouth to feed. It's like what Johnson said about a man who's about to be hanged: it concentrates the mind wonderfully.

You're the dad. You need to produce income. You clear away all the dross of your life and focus on your mission. You want inspiration for your career? Motivation to get ahead? Go in your baby's room and look at her asleep. That is truly the face of God.

This chapter spells out some workplace options for men who want to spend more time with their family. But I think most men are realistic about their role. We know we have to work. It's our job. And we're happy to do it for the most part. It's how we feel useful and productive as human beings and as fathers.

Fathers support their families and their children by working. It's important to acknowledge and honor that. It's become fashionable these days to put the knock on the previous generation of "absentee dads" who worked all day, came home late, and left the business of raising children to the moms.

Remember who these men were working so hard for: their wives and children, their families. They put in the foundation blocks upon which family life was built. They deserve honor and respect, as do the men and women who work to support their families today.

This generation of fathers is different than the last. We participate in the lives of our children to an unprecedented degree. But what we want, I think, is balance in our lives. That's what we're all striving for and what we'd most like to have: a balance of work and family.

HOW TO BE A RESPONSIBLE FATHER

What does it mean to be a responsible father? Travis Hill, who's a social worker, boils it down to its basics. He coordinates a Proud Fathers program for young, mostly unmarried fathers under the age of twenty-five. In addition, he provides social and resident services for families at a 158-unit, low-income Section-Eight complex in the inner city. In light of contemporary attitudes about "the new father," Hill reminds us that a father's first obligation to his family—the primary way he shows responsibility—is to get and keep a job.

Q. What does it mean to be a responsible father?
Hill: First, let me explain a little bit about what I do and who I work with. A lot of the fathers I deal with are in the nineteen to twenty-five age group. Some live with the mother of their child, in an out of wedlock situation. Others don't live with the mom and see their children on visitation. What we tell them is that not every relationship is going to work out. But what is important is the child in the middle.

Q: What do you mean?
Hill: Most of the time the child stays with the mom. Sometimes he stays with Dad, but mostly with the mother. So that child misses the father in the family structure. That's why it's important to be there, even if you and Mom are not together. The child needs to know that he has a father who's there for him. A lot of kids today don't have that.

Q: Why are so many more mothers committed to their children than fathers?
Hill: That's a big question. The answer probably goes back to the beginning of time. One reason is that women carry the child through pregnancy and give birth. They totally bond with the baby. They feel

the baby in their womb, their body goes through all these changes, all sorts of things. A dad bonds, too, but it's not the same. He doesn't go through the pregnancy and form that strong emotional and physical attachment that the mother does.

Q: Name some practical ways that a young man can show responsibility to his children and his family.

Hill: I really emphasize education for my clients. Finish high school or obtain a general education degree. Then look for further education, say at a community college or a four-year university. Employment is important. Stay employed; keep your job. Even think about doing volunteer work here and there, or becoming an intern. Both of these can expand your contacts and lead to jobs. I know because they have for me.

Q: It's interesting. Some people nowadays would define a "responsible father" as someone who is involved in stereotypically female activities—diapers, child care, cooking, etc.—in addition to providing an income for the family. But your analysis is much more basic. A man first shows responsibility to his family by getting and keeping a job.

Hill: That's right. Much of what we do in the Proud Fathers Program centers on jobs—job placement skills, employment assessment, job search. We help them put together resumes and design cover letters. Even if you're just working at a job that pays $7 or $8 an hour, there's value in that.

Q: Seven bucks an hour? How can someone support a family on that? No wonder these guys get discouraged.

Hill: I tell my guys, you have to look at it as a stepping stone. A lot of people don't like their job and are frustrated, but they don't just quit. They work in their spare time, they start their own business. They go back to school and develop new skills. You don't have to go to college. Some of the most successful people in America never finished college. But you will always be working at the same level if you don't get into a trade or have a specialized skill. You have to focus, find and improve your talents, and explain to people what you can do.

Q: A man shows responsibility by helping to provide for his family, but in so many other ways, too. Talk a little about that.

Hill: There's the whole family structure. Spend time with your family—Mom, baby, and you together, as a unit. Go to the park; walk on the beach. Maybe the two of you work during the week and the baby's in day care. Do all the things you don't get a chance to do during the week. Go to the pool, exercise, play sports together. Take your children with you; do things with them. So they'll know, "Hey,

Dad's here with us. We're here together." Now, maybe they can't verbally say that, but they feel it. And they'll remember. They may not remember the specific things you did together, but they'll know that you were there. They'll always feel the benefits of your love and affection and attention.

Contact: Proud Fathers Program, Family Stress Center, 2086 Commerce Avenue, Concord, CA 94520; 510-827-0212.

WORKING NIGHTS AND WEEKENDS

When a man becomes a father, he has to do things he doesn't like. He works longer hours. He works at a job he hates because he needs to feed his family. He works two or even three jobs at the same time. He puts in for overtime and works double shifts. He does these things because he loves his family and wants to provide a good life for them.

Many men (and women) have to work nights and weekends. They have no choice; it's part of their job. Hours for shift workers vary. But a P.M. shift might last from 4:45 P.M. to 3:00 A.M. The night shift might run from 9:30 P.M. to 7:00 A.M. Working these hours can play havoc with family life.

You're beat physically. You don't eat right. It's not natural to sleep when the sun is shining and be active when the moon is out. It throws your system out of whack. The people who like working nights are usually single. Family men find it much harder. They don't want to sleep all day and miss seeing their kid grow up.

Shift work is not all negative, however; there are advantages. Say you end your work week at 7:00 A.M. Thursday; you don't have to report back until Sunday at 9:30 P.M. That essentially gives you three full days to spend with your family, catch up on the yard work, and maybe take off and play golf.

Another advantage is if you're trying to minimize the amount of time your child is in day care. Your partner works days; you work nights. You drop your child off at day care in the late afternoon before going to work. Your partner then picks your child up after 5:00 when she gets home. Your child has only spent a few hours at the sitter's.

Some shift workers find they can split their sleep up. They sleep a few hours when they get off work, stay up a while, then sleep a few more hours before returning to the job. A better approach might be to hit the sack as soon as you get off work and sleep until mid to early afternoon. When your child gets a little older, she'll enter preschool

"Man ain't got no business on relief as long as he can work."

—Myers Anderson, grandfather of Supreme Court Justice Clarence Thomas, who raised Thomas and his brother after their father disappeared

"We worked. Mom had
our noses in the books.
When they weren't, Dad
had us out there doing
something."
—NFL running back Barry
Sanders, son of William and
Shirley Sanders

and kindergarten. She'll leave in the mornings and come home again in the afternoon when you're waking up. You can all sit down together and have an early dinner as a family.

Working nights is a burnout situation over the long haul. It's hard to do it for more than six months or a year at a time. No matter what, try to get one weekend day off. You need at least one day on the weekend to recharge your batteries and spend time with your child, especially when she's a baby.

Source: Jim Taranto, father of Ariel. Taranto is a police sergeant. He's worked the evening or night patrol for about five of his twenty-four years on the force. He also contributed to the following report on coming home after work.

DON'T BRING IT HOME WITH YOU

Police sergeant Jim Taranto runs a violent crimes unit at a city police department. He sees some pretty ugly things on the job, but he's learned over the years not to bring them home with him. "You can't just come home to your family and dump," he says. "I used to do that. It's not right. I come home pretty stressed sometimes. Not only from the job, but the commute, too. I try to zone out as much as I can—turn the radio up and not let it get to me."

He continues, "The first thing I do when I come home is I get out of my work clothes. When I'm in my work clothes, I'm still in my work mode. But this is home, this isn't work. So I've got to get into my dad mode.

"You know, sometimes you walk in the door and it's like you get hit by a wave. Everybody's coming at you. The baby's crying and your wife is pulling her hair out, or whatever. Or maybe your daughter just wants to show you something great she did at school. Anyway, it's there.

"Sometimes I go straight past Bonnie and Ariel and walk right into my room. I don't say anything to them, not a word. I walk in, close the door, and start shedding my clothes. I change into some shorts and a T-shirt. I put my equipment away and lock it up. I wash my face. It takes a few minutes. When I come out, I'm ready to be with them."

REAL-WORLD STRATEGIES FOR FATHERS WHO WANT TO TAKE TIME OFF WHEN THEIR BABY IS BORN

How to Start. First, talk it over with your partner. How much time does she want to take off before and after the baby is born? How much time do *you* want to take off? And how are the two of you going to swing it financially? You can do it, but you need to do some serious planning and saving.

Read Your Employee Handbook at Work. The handbook will explain your rights and benefits on these issues. Company policies vary widely.

Talk to the Human Resources Office at Your Company. Many companies are too small to have a human resources office (or even an employee handbook). Nevertheless, if these resources exist at your company, take advantage of them.

Vacation Leave. The simple fact is that very few companies will offer paid leave. Your best bet will be to accrue vacation leave. You can start accruing once you know the baby is coming. But make sure you don't exceed your company's accrual cap. Many companies won't let you accrue vacation leave beyond a certain amount—say, four weeks—without you taking some of it. It's always a good idea to have accrued vacation leave when you're in a family because you never know when you may need time off to care for a child or attend a family function.

Pregnancy and Disability Leave. Women can receive paid medical disability benefits for limited periods prior to birth and immediately after. Laws vary from state to state. Though men are not eligible for this benefit, their spouses should definitely apply if they're eligible.

Paternity Leave. Nice concept, but since most companies don't offer paid leave, it remains just that for most men: a concept. Almost no one can afford to take extended unpaid time off from work. And in most households, if one parent is going to take unpaid time to be with the baby, it will be Mom, not Dad.

Family and Medical Leave Act. This federal law applies to companies with fifty or more employees. It allows employees to take up to twelve weeks of unpaid leave in a year for the birth or care of a child (also an adoptive or foster child). Employees must have worked for the company for one year prior to the date of their taking leave. They must take the time within one year of the child's birth or placement, though the weeks need not be consecutive. Employers are legally required to give

> "We were raised to use what you have and not go around looking for more. We were taught not to be greedy or obsessed with what you couldn't have. It was instilled in us as kids."
> —Barry Sanders

employees the job they had prior to departure. They must also continue to pay medical benefits.

Again, the FMLA is a lovely concept, but because it provides unpaid leave, it is not being used extensively. Most parents—mothers and fathers—cannot afford it. Also, for career reasons, it may not look good for employees to take that much time off.

Sick or Personal Leave. Many companies will not allow employees to take sick leave unless they are actually sick. Some, however, allow you to use accrued sick or personal leave if it's counted as part of the Family and Medical Leave Act. Policies vary from company to company. Talk to Human Resources to see how flexible your company's accrued sick leave policies are.

Other Options. Other options exist for men who want to spend more time at home after the baby arrives. These may include telecommuting, job sharing, flexible hours, part-time work, or sabbaticals. Though, realistically, moms tend to use these options more than dads. For many couples, women split time between the baby and work, while the man keeps working full-time. Exempt employees—non-hourly employees who are not eligible for overtime—must be paid in full if they work any part of a day. So if you come into the office for a couple of hours, you still are entitled to a full day's pay. In conclusion, think ahead. The more planning you do before the baby comes, the better off you will be. Your company will also have more time to figure out ways to provide support for you and manage during your absence.

Source: Leyna Bernstein was a human resources executive at Smith & Hawken, The Gap, and The Nature Company. Bernstein is now a human resources consultant with her own practice specializing in nonprofit firms. A noteworthy book on this subject is Working Fathers, New Strategies for Balancing Work and Family, *by James Levine (Addison-Wesley Publishing).*

THE DADDY TRACK AND OTHER HARD REALITIES

The grim reality is that "the daddy track"—a glass ceiling for fathers—exists. Companies demand an employee's time and his undivided loyalty. Many of them look askance at a father who requests time off to be with his newborn baby or child. Such a request by the father may indeed harm his professional advancement. A man with a family is no longer simply an organization man. The company does not come first in his life. He may be offered a challenging, career-building promotion at work, an opportunity he might've jumped at in the past. But if the promotion requires him to travel more and be away from his family, he may see it as a mixed blessing.

Many corporate managers are stuck in the old paradigm: Dad works; Mom stays home with the kids. When your household does not fit this antiquated model, it may affect your standing on the job. You may call in someday and say, "I can't come in today. My kid's sick." And the voice on the other end of the line may answer, "Where's your wife?" You may explain that your wife works, too, and that she's stayed home a bunch of times already and today's your turn. The voice on the other end of the line may respond with a steely silence.

The corporate culture often includes travel. You cannot get ahead unless you are willing to travel (and in some cases, relocate). But saying no to travel may doom you within your company. Sometimes the only thing you can do in a situation like that is grin and bear it.

A navy serviceman returning home to his family after being out to sea for eight months must deal with feelings of obsolesence. While he's been gone, his partner has handled the kids and run the house without him. When he returns, he has to reacquaint himself with his family, including his spouse. After the first fight breaks out, he wonders if it's worth it. His family may think the same cruel thoughts. What do they need him for?

Children need their father. A woman wants to be with the man she loves. But it's hard on a man's family when he works long hours or he's on the road a lot. That old saying about how absence makes the heart fonder does not always pertain to families.

One idea: try to fit into their routine when you come home, rather than making everyone adjust to you. Talk to your partner. Is there anything you need to be aware of with the kids? She'll clue you in. Let things come to you instead of immediately trying to take control. Don't let your (bad) mood dictate the atmosphere in the house. You want your presence to be an ordinary fact of home life, not a disruptive or unique one. Dad travels. He's gone from time to time. But then he comes back and he's home. It's usually the parents who feel guilty about traveling and being away. Children frequently adapt more easily.

Another idea: don't play sixty-four questions with your kids. A lot of well-intentioned men come home from a business trip and naturally want to catch up with their children. So they pummel them with questions. Another natural tendency is to try to compensate for your absence by buying your kids toys or taking them out to eat or to the zoo or always doing "special" things on the weekends with them.

"There's no problem elbow grease can't solve. Old Man Can't is dead. I helped bury him."
—Myers Anderson

Children get tired, too. They may just want to hang out and not do anything on the weekend. Ask your kids what *they* want to do, rather than insisting on an activity that you deem appropriate or desirable.

A third suggestion: listen more than tell. Many fathers who travel can fall into the trap of being "circuit riders." They come home, point out errors or make corrections, and then leave again. Or they try to manage the family on the phone while holed up a thousand miles away in some hotel, making their children—and perhaps their spouse as well—listen only to that harsh, disciplinarian voice that always says no. Just listen on the phone, be less directive. You've got to give up the illusion of control when you're away. And you can't expect your family to be standing on the street corner applauding you when you drive up. Life, especially family life, doesn't work that way.

There are disappointments. You are going to miss landmarks in your child's life simply because you have to work for a living. You may not hear your child's first words or see him take his first step. You are going to go away for a week and when you come home, your child will seem like a completely different human being.

The mother-child bond is the primary unit of nature. Children naturally gravitate to their mother, who usually spends more time with them in the first years of their life. Dad gets left out a lot. And when he travels or works long hours, he gets bypassed for Mom all too frequently. That hurts. Children can seem awfully cruel at times in the way they take a parent's affections for granted. But have no doubt: your children will respond to your steady, reliable, loving presence. They will come to you. Your patience will be rewarded in the end.

Source: Keith Grace, father of Kristen and William, is a corporate bank examiner who relocated to give himself more time with his family. For more tips on how to stay in touch with your family when you travel on business, see the chapter "Travel: Business and Family."

CHANGING JOBS WHEN YOU HAVE A FAMILY

When a man becomes a father, the desire to better himself becomes very strong. He seeks ways to provide more income for his family and wonders if changing jobs will help him do that. But is it a good idea to change jobs when you're a new dad? Scott Thomason, who owns his own San Francisco executive recruitment company, advises his clients to examine their priorities before taking a new job. Scott is the father of Rachel, Jennifer, and Adam.

Q: Let's start with a very basic question: does being a father hurt you or help you in the employment arena?

Thomason: It's a neutral. In fact, if you apply for a job it's against the law for an employer to ask you, "Are you married? Do you have children?" and questions of that nature. And that's good because they're not really relevant to your job performance.

Q: Money pressures get very intense when you have a new baby. Is that a good time to look for a new job?

Thomason: The best time to consider a new job is when you have one. That's my standard advice. You have the greatest degree of strength and flexibility when you are employed. So you always want to keep an eye open for an opportunity that will advance your career. Now when you become a father your life changes in a dramatic way. You have added responsibilities. You have new things to consider. You have to consider your family in any job decision you make.

Q: What factors should you consider in evaluating a new job?

Thomason: Location, for one. Where is the company or the job located? Is it going to increase your commute time, the time you're away from your family? Are there added responsibilities? Are you going to have to work more hours? Is the position truly a promotion or a lateral move? What about compensation? How does it compare to what you're making now? Will you have to relocate? There are so many things to consider. And then finally, you have to ask, What effect is all this going to have on my family? That's what it all boils down to.

Q: So it's not just a matter of taking a new job or not, is that right? It's a matter of setting priorities.

Thomason: Absolutely. Let me give you an example. I specialize in executive recruitment in the nonprofit arena. Typically an executive director for a nonprofit firm makes in the range of $65,000 to $75,000 a year. I was working with an executive in the private sector who wanted to leave his company and possibly take a job with a nonprofit. In talking to him about it, he told me that last year, with salary and bonus, he made about $500,000. I was flabbergasted. I asked him, "Why would somebody want to leave a job where he's making half a million dollars a year for one that pays 20 percent of that?" And he said, "Because four nights a week, I don't tuck my children into bed." That's the reason he gave. He said he had saved enough money, his family's needs weren't that great, and that they wanted to live a different kind of lifestyle. And I admired him for that.

> "I spent most of the first seven years of my life living over my father's saloon. When I wasn't living over it, I was living in it, studying the rough talk of the longshoremen, merchant sailors, roustabouts, and waterfront bums."
>
> —George Herman Ruth Jr., better known as Babe Ruth, son of saloonkeeper George Ruth Sr.

"Sure, we had to move, but a lot of people have to move. Sure, my dad worked hard and was gone part of the year quite a bit, but so were other dads that wanted to reach the pinnacle of their profession."
—Football coach Jim Mora, son of Jim Mora Sr.

Q: Still, sixty-five grand is pretty good money. After a few years of earning a $500,000 annual income, I'd be willing to adopt a life of voluntary simplicity, too.

Thomason [laughs]: Yes, he's a lucky fellow. But we all have to make those choices. It's easy when you're a man and you love what you do to let work dominate your life. I did it myself. In my first marriage, with my first two kids, I worked nights and weekends. I didn't see my kids nearly as much as I could have. Now I have a new family and a four-year-old son. I could make a lot more money than I am now, but I've consciously made a decision not to let work define my life in that way. It's a balance.

Q: What do you mean?

Thomason: Well, when you're working six days a week and traveling 75 to 80 percent of the time as some people do, your life is out of balance—especially if you are a husband and a father. Now sometimes you don't have a choice. You have to do it because you need the money. But in my opinion, your priorities should be family, children, and work. That represents balance to me.

Q: Let's say you're a new dad with young children, and you've just been offered a great new position in a new city. Do you take it?

Thomason: That's a tough call. Obviously it depends on your situation. With a new baby, you need as much support as you can get. Are you moving away from family and friends? Is that where your support network is? A lot of people won't move because their family lives in the area and they can't see living anywhere else. Schools are a real important issue. I just had a man turn down a better-paying job in another city because his children were in good schools and he didn't want to uproot them. Relocating a family is a very stressful thing to do. You're not single, you can't just pick up and go like you used to. You may be moving into an unfamiliar area where you don't know anybody, where you have to find child care and basically start again from scratch. It's tough. But obviously, it can be a great thing, too. People often pursue a new job opportunity because they can move to a better location and find a better quality of life. They like the schools better, it's a better neighborhood, whatever. Certainly if you do make a move like that, you have to give yourself time to make it work.

Q: Money is not the chief reason that people change jobs, is it?

Thomason: Not in my experience. Compensation is not the driving motivation. The primary reason that people change jobs is job satisfaction, or lack of it. Maybe they hate their new boss or a new management team has come in and they feel threatened. Or maybe the company is struggling and you need to protect yourself.

Q: Children represent a big change in a man's life. So does changing a job. You really need to consider everything before you act.

Thomason: Absolutely. I always have people say to me, "I need to sit down and talk to my wife." And I understand, because you *should* consult with your family. It's really a collective decision. It has to be right for all of you. You ultimately have to trust your gut. If it doesn't feel right, don't do it. But what makes it hard sometimes is that what's best for your career may not be best for your child and your family. That's where your priorities come in.

Contact: Scott Thomason, The James Scott Group, 555 Montgomery Street, Suite 1155, San Francisco, CA 94111; 415-837-3782.

DOWNSIZING YOUR LIFESTYLE: PLUSES AND MINUSES

Men are still mainly the chief breadwinners in the family. They don't have the option of not working when a baby comes; that's usually not even considered. Still, many fathers want more flexibility at work and if they can't get it, they're willing to consider a change that gives it to them. But leaving one job for another that allows more time for the family is not an easy call; like so many choices in life, it's a trade-off. More flexibility usually equates to less money. Every man needs to weigh the pluses and minuses as he ponders the work–family balance that's right for him and whether he should "downsize" his career in favor of more involvement in his family life.

Pluses

- *Better relationships with your children.* You spend more time with them. They know you'll be around and involved in their lives. You not only watch them grow up, you participate in it.

- *More flexible schedule.* You have the time to coach Little League or volunteer at school. Women teachers and mom volunteers dominate the elementary grades. When you volunteer at school, not only does your child benefit from having you around, but other children get to have a man present, too.

- *Fewer work demands*. If you workd for a corporation, you probably only see your children at night or on weekends. Travel may be part of the job. You are often required to work late or on Saturdays. If you make a career change to a more flexible (though lower paying) job, you're more in control of your schedule and less subject to the politics and games of corporate life.

- *More day-to-day involvement with your kids*. Instead of Mom always being the one to walk your child to the park or take him to preschool, some days you do it. This in turn gives your partner more freedom and flexibility to pursue her own interests, including a career.

- *You learn how to make do with less*. Even when you make a lot of money, spending usually rises to match income. Now that you earn less, you learn to manage. You cut back on your wardrobe, take more sack lunches to work. Commuting costs may also go down because you've chosen a job closer to home.

- *You realize that you can make moves and not be hurt by them*. Before leaving a company, you wonder if you'll be able to survive. Your success teaches you that you can make different choices and they can work out for you.

- *Simple happiness*. A less demanding job gives you more of the life you want to lead: more time with your family, more time for yourself.

Minuses

- *Economic uncertainty*. There's less money, at least in the beginning. You may make good money in your current position. You may be able to support your family on one income without your partner having to work. This may change with a change of jobs.

- *Less security*. The days when a person worked at a company for life (and the company showed similar loyalty) are gone forever. Still, a corporate position does provide a level of security. When you leave, you are, in effect, rolling the dice.

- *Reduced benefits*. Your company may offer a full benefits package: medical, dental, life insurance, etc. It may be hard to match that coverage in a new position at a reduced salary. Retirement may also be affected. It may take a while before you can feel comfortable enough to begin saving for retirement again.

- *You lose potential future earnings at the company*. Walk away from a company and you walk away from the chance for bonuses and promotions with raises in pay. But promotions can be a double-edged sword for a family man. While a new title may increase your paycheck, it also increases the demands at work.

- *Saving for college may be jeopardized.* You'll have less to put away for your child's college education if you're earning less. Your dreams of sending him to Stanford or Harvard (if such dreams exist) may be postponed or abandoned.

- *Less spending money.* A new "downsized" job inevitably pays less, sometimes a lot less. You won't be able to go out to dinner or the movies as much as you did in the past. Popping for a baby-sitter for an evening out will seem an extravagant act.

- *This may not be your last stop.* Once you leave the security of a corporation, it may take a while—and one or two more jobs—before you settle into something that's right for you.

- *Possible stresses in your relationship.* Maybe you were a career go-getter when you met your partner. She may feel betrayed by your change of jobs. She may have to make up some of the lost income by taking a job herself. That's why it's always a good idea—vital, in fact—for you to talk it over with your partner before you act. Let every decision you make be a family decision.

Source: Mike Maggart, father of Dave, Dan, and Matt. For himself personally and in order to spend more time with his sons, Maggart gave up a management position in the insurance industry to take a job that paid $15,000 less per year. He coaches his sons' soccer and Little League teams and volunteers at their schools.

RUNNING A SMALL BUSINESS AND BEING A NEW DAD

It is the dream of many men to own their own business and be their own boss. There is no reason why having a child should stop you from achieving this dream. But it is probably not wise to start a new business—or any large project—in the first year of your child's life. You're only going to create problems for yourself if you do.

A new business is like a baby. Both need time and nurturing. Both make tremendous demands on you. It's not fair to lay all your family responsibilities on your partner; she carries plenty as it is. Nor is it fair to your child to spend so much time at work. Finally, your business will suffer if you don't get enough sleep or your home life creates conflict or unease.

"What is this rich man, this busy father, doing? Paying another man to discharge his duties which are peculiarly his. Can you believe money will buy your son another father?"

—Jean Jacques Rousseau, eighteenth-century philosopher

> "Joe's first pass receiver was his father. Joe would often sit on the front steps at home waiting for Joe Sr. to return home from his job. Joe Sr. would be tired sometimes, but he'd always make time to play with his son."
>
> —From a biography of football great Joe Montana, son of Joe Montana Sr.

Some small business owners make the mistake of thinking they can bring their baby into work with them. Immediately they see the folly in this; the baby creates too much distraction. She needs to be changed, she needs to be held. Her place is at home or in child care. When she grows older, of course, you have the luxury of bringing her into the family business and putting her to work.

A nanny might be a wise child-care choice when you run your own business. Sometimes things come up and you cannot get away at exactly 6:00 P.M. The nanny will still be home when you get there. Whatever child-care arrangements you have, you will still always have to coordinate with your partner.

Ideally, you would be able to take a break in the middle of the day and go home to see your family. But for most small business owners, this happens only rarely. There is too much to do at work.

Small business owners do not only have responsibility to their own family. They employ the fathers, mothers, sons, and daughters of other families. They all feel the squeeze if the business doesn't make money. That can be one of the drawbacks of running a business: income goes up—and down. You can't count on a steady paycheck anymore. Then again, you may make far more in your business than at a regular job.

Your priorities will change when you have a family. When you first started out you were undoubtedly focussed completely on your business, spending more time there than at home. A baby has a way of changing that. Herein lies one of the chief benefits of owning your own business: you're the boss. You make the rules. Your baby may not fall asleep for the night until 11:00 P.M. But that may not bother you because you know you can sleep in the next morning. You can adjust your schedule or reduce your hours to give yourself the flexibility that every parent is looking for these days.

Source: Gary Grillo, father of Madeleine, is the owner of Blue Moon Textiles, a textile sales firm in Los Angeles.

WORKING AT HOME

John Godfrey is news editor at *Home Office Computing* magazine in Manhattan. A resident of Brooklyn, he worked as a freelance writer before joining the staff of the magazine. While he worked at home, his wife went to the office, leaving their two infant sons, Jack and Owen, in his care. This experience taught him some valuable lessons about working at home with children that may be useful to other new dads who find themselves in a similar situation.

Lesson #1: It's Virtually Impossible to Be a Good Dad and Do Good Work at the Same Time. In order to save money and be with his sons, John kept them home with him at first. But it didn't work out. "I was trying to do two things at once and I wasn't doing either of them well," he confesses. His children interrupted him frequently. It was hard to concentrate when they were around. When he was at the computer, they'd want to crawl on his lap and play. He'd ask them to come back in five minutes. Thirty minutes later they'd come back and ask again. Godfrey knew that what they were asking for—their daddy's attention—was reasonable. But he was trying to concentrate and get his work done. Something would happen almost every day to make him lose patience and snap at them. "I had no sense of accomplishment either as a parent or a writer," he says.

Lesson #2: Children Have an Innate Sense of When You Are Trying to Concentrate, and That's When They'll Interrupt. Owen and Jack often played together in another room while John worked. But when the phone rang, the boys seemed to always choose that moment to get into a fight or spill a cup of milk or tug on their dad's sleeve to get his attention. Jack would sometimes interrupt his father's conversation to speak to whomever he was talking to. The person on the other end of the line was frequently understanding, but this nagged at Godfrey's sense of professionalism. "I didn't want to give people the impression that I was wearing shorts and a T-shirt with two small kids in the background, which of course I was," he says. There's sometimes a stigma attached to people who work at home, and Godfrey did not want to interrupt an interview with an IBM product manager so his son could talk baby talk to him. He'd fall into this pattern of getting mad at his sons and raising his voice at them and then feel horrible about it afterward.

Lesson #3: You Must Be Prepared to Be Flexible When You Work at Home with Children. Eventually the Godfreys enrolled Owen and Jack in a co-op child-care center in their neighborhood on a part-time basis. They'd go in the mornings for three or four days a week. While an improvement over the previous arrangement, Godfrey still had to juggle his schedule to make it work. He'd conduct his interviews or do his writing while they were gone. When they came home, maybe they'd take a nap or he'd put in a video and get more time to work. But by two or three in the afternoon, they'd be ready to play and there'd be very little chance to do anything more. So when his wife Nicola came home in the evening, Godfrey would often take his laptop to a coffee shop and finish up what he didn't get done earlier.

"It's a full-time job being a parent these days. You're always on."

—James Atlas, writer and father

Lesson #4. Be Prepared to Help Out More with the Children When You Work at Home. Like all 9-to-5ers, Nicola needed to be at work by a certain time. His schedule being more flexible than hers, John almost always took the children to day care in the morning. Then he'd pick them up in the early afternoon. He also made their lunches every day. Godfrey is the type who eats when he feels like it. But that didn't work for his sons at all. They liked the routine of eating and napping at the same times every day. Getting his kids into a routine made it easier for him as a parent, too. Now he and his wife plan everything they do. There's no more "winging it"; they always plan ahead, even a day ahead.

Lesson #5: There Are Some Big Pluses to Being a Work-at-Home Dad. Work permitting, Godfrey set aside Tuesdays as his field trip day with his sons. They'd go all over New York City: Central Park, Metropolitan Museum of Art, the Aquarium, Bronx Zoo, and their favorite haunt, the American Museum of Natural History. "We must've gone at least a thousand times to the dinosaur exhibit," he says. The time he spent with his children made a palpable difference in his relationship with them. His younger son came to him for comfort, not just Mom. "I got to spend time with my kids that lots of parents, particularly fathers, don't," he says. "I'll never regret spending that time. I got a chance not just to watch them grow up but to be an everyday part of it."

Tip: Godfrey's magazine, Home Office Computing, *contains useful information and articles for home office people, often targeted to parents who work at home. Home Office Computing, 411 Lafayette Street, 4th Floor, New York, NY 10003; 212-505-4220.*

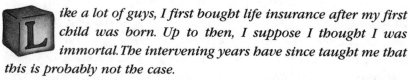

LIFE INSURANCE

ike a lot of guys, I first bought life insurance after my first child was born. Up to then, I suppose I thought I was immortal. The intervening years have since taught me that this is probably not the case.

I'm lucky in that my mother is a financial counselor who sells life insurance. I follow her advice, which allows me to not think about subjects like death and my mortality any more than I have to.

My mom recommends term insurance and that's what I have. But I know there's considerable disagreement about what's the better deal for people: term or whole life insurance. Whichever type of insurance you choose, it's just important to get it. Don't overpay, but get it. I don't like giving money to insurance companies any more than anyone else. But life insurance will protect your family in the event that something happens to you.

My dad died when I was thirteen. He served two tours of duty in the jungle hell of the South Pacific during World War II. When he got out of the Navy, he enrolled in the University of Oklahoma in Norman, where he met my mom. On his check-in physical for the university, the doctor informed him that he had developed diabetes. The horrid conditions of the war brought it on.

In time the disease steadily did its dirty work. He lost his eyesight and his kidneys shut down. He lapsed into a coma and died in a hospital bed at the age of forty-seven. As a boy I didn't understand how young he was, but I sure do now.

My dad carried life insurance of course, but after he died, my mom didn't want to put any of the money she received in the bank. It just didn't seem right to her. So the following summer, she took my brother and I (and a close friend of my brother's) on a six-week trip to the British Isles.

It was pretty gutsy of her. Age forty, a widow traveling in foreign lands with three teenage boys, she rented a car and drove the four of us around England, Scotland, Wales, and Ireland. My mom was a big fan of Mary, Queen of Scots, and we trooped around to some of the castles where Mary liked to hang out. I got so jaded that I wouldn't even get out of the car to see a castle if it was built after the thirteenth century. Too modern, I felt.

At the end of the six weeks, we flew out of Shannon, Ireland. The night before we left, I cried about my dad's death. I'm not sure why I cried at that moment. Maybe I was sad about the trip being over or maybe I was just overdue. I hadn't cried since the funeral eight months before. My mom held me in her arms.

I still remember that trip with great feeling. I know my mom and brother do, too. Maybe it wasn't your typical use of a life insurance policy, but it was inspired. It was important for us as a family to have that time together and it was important for me as a young boy trying to deal with such an unfathomable loss. In a way, the trip was one more gift for us from my father.

NOW THAT I HAVE A CHILD, DO I NEED LIFE INSURANCE?

Having a baby is a life-affirming act. But ironically, it also makes you aware of your own mortality. Dan Crouch is director of communications for California Association of Life Underwriters. He's worked in the insurance industry for more than twenty years. But even if he didn't work in insurance, he'd still have life insurance for his family. He thinks it's crazy not to, and in this interview, he tells why. He is the father of Emily and Sarah.

Q: The first time that a lot of men think about getting life insurance is when they have a baby. Why does a father need life insurance?

Crouch: The main reason you have insurance is to cover debts that are left behind when you die. You don't want to leave your wife saddled with debt and you want your family to be able to maintain the same lifestyle they're living now. Your salary is supporting them in their lifestyle and with you out of the picture, it could really affect them.

Q: Isn't it kind of ghoulish to think about life insurance?
Crouch: Some people are uncomfortable talking about their own mortality. In some cultures, it's almost a taboo to talk about death. But it happens to all of us. There's a hilarious Richard Pryor routine called "Eulogy" where he talks about surviving death as "the ultimate test. So far nobody we know has passed the ultimate test."

Q: What is life insurance exactly?
Crouch: Essentially everyone contributes to a large pool. If one person dies, his beneficiaries receive benefits from the pool that he's been contributing to. Virtually every financial expert across the board recommends life insurance, whether it's whole or term. You rarely run into someone who says it's not a good thing. Some so-called experts will refer to life insurance as a gamble, but not purchasing it is a bigger gamble, in my opinion. People who are uncomfortable thinking about death might prefer to think of life insurance as an investment. And it can be a pretty good one. You can pay, say, $200 for one year of term life insurance, and in the event of your death it will pay your beneficiaries $100,000. That's a pretty good return on your dollar.

Q: What types of things does life insurance cover?
Crouch: Funeral expenses, mortgage, rent. You have to remember that if the mother of your child is using your salary to pay rent, she may have to move if she doesn't have that salary anymore. Life insurance can help pay for a college education for your kids or even for private school. It can pay for unanticipated medical expenses and general lifestyle expenses.

Q: I know a guy who owns his own business. For many years, he was the only breadwinner in the family. His wife stayed home and took care of their two daughters. He said he simply could not afford life insurance. What do you say to someone like that?
Crouch: I think he's taking a pretty big risk. Some people take an attitude of: "What does it matter what happens after I die? I'll be dead anyway." It's true you won't know the difference, but your surviving wife and kids sure will. It's going to have an impact on the way they remember you. Some agents say that life insurance is a kind of bequest, even an expression of love. You're leaving behind support for your family, even though you're gone. Also, term insurance can be pretty cheap, if you break it up into monthly payments.

Q: What types of insurance are there?
Crouch: The two basic kinds are term insurance and permanent, or whole life, insurance. Term insurance only lasts for a period of time—

ten, fifteen, twenty years. And there's no cash accumulation. Whole life or permanent insurance is in place permanently for your life. It has a cash value. The cash is invested in everything from straight interest-bearing accounts to securities—the whole gamut.

Q. What is better for families with young children—term or whole life insurance?

Crouch: That depends. It's really impossible to say. Everybody's situation is different. Term insurance has some advantages for younger families because it's less expensive, but it's also temporary. It's only less expensive in the short term, and if you really look at it over a longer period like a person's lifetime, the permanent types of insurance—whole life, universal life, variable life—look better. Some people have both term and whole life insurance. But this is really where you need to talk to an agent or maybe even more than one to find out what's right for you and your family.

Q: Can you use life insurance for your own retirement?

Crouch: Yes. It does work well for a person saving for retirement. That's another thing. When you retire, you want to be able to support yourself, because you don't want your kids to be stuck supporting you. A cash accumulating life insurance account is a good way to save for retirement.

Q: What about pension plans from your job? Won't that work as well as life insurance?

Crouch: There are different types of pension plans. If you've been working twenty-five to thirty years at the same company, your pension may be substantial. But if you're just starting out in your job, your pension is not going to be very big and it takes years to accumulate. Whereas with life insurance, if you died your beneficiaries would get $100,000 or $200,000—or whatever you're insured for—immediately. The best advice is to check into exactly what you have at work. All pension plans are different. You want to make sure your family is protected.

TERM OR WHOLE LIFE?

The two major types of insurance are term and whole life, or permanent, insurance. Term insurance provides protection for a specific period of time and pays a benefit only if you die during the term. Permanent or whole life insurance provides lifelong protection, as long as you pay the necessary premiums.

Advantages of Term

- Less expensive. This allows you to buy more coverage when you are younger, may have less income, and the need for protection is greater.

- It covers specific needs that disappear over time, such as mortgages or car loans.

- The amount you save in insurance can be put into retirement accounts or other investments.

Disadvantages

- Premiums increase as you grow older and as they increase, they may get too expensive to afford.

- No cash value.

Advantages of Permanent Insurance

- Guaranteed protection for life, assuming you pay the premiums. Premiums can be fixed or flexible according to a family's finances.

- Sense of security because the premiums do not go up.

- Policy accumulates cash value, which you can borrow against.

- Option to buy more insurance without taking a medical exam.

Disadvantages

- More expensive than term.

- Higher commission for agents who sell whole life.

- Cash value does not increase the face value of the insurance. Cash value lessens the amount the insurance company is liable for upon death. If you've borrowed against the cash value and not paid off the loan, the amount owed to the insurance company is deducted from the face value of the policy.

Source: Adapted from materials provided by the American Council of Life Insurance, 1001 Pennsylvania Avenue NW, Washington, DC 20004; www.nich.org. Its National Insurance Consumer Helpline, 800-942-4242, answers insurance questions and provides informational brochures.

"Fatherhood starts the minute the pregnancy is confirmed. You now have a family you have to protect. If anything happens to you, you've left your wife and baby hanging. You have to provide them with a financial cushion."
—Harold Hotelling, father of five

FINDING THE RIGHT AGENT

Once you decide to get life insurance, the next step is finding an agent. You may already have an agent. If not, ask your friends and family. They can recommend someone whom they trust and feel comfortable with.

The professional organizations are another resource. The Life Underwriters Association (1922 "F" Street NW, Washington, DC 20006; 202-331-9606; www.agentsonline.com) can refer you to agents in your area who belong to the association. The American Society of CLU and CHFC (270 South Bryn Mawr Avenue, Bryn Mawr, PA 19010; 610-526-2500) is a group of chartered life underwriters and chartered financial consultants. Agents with these credentials have passed a series of exams on insurance, taxation, financial planning, and other subjects. Call for chartered agents in your area.

Trust is important in choosing an agent. Do you feel comfortable with him or her? Insurance agents can represent one company or a number of companies. An agent working for one company chooses insurance products within his company, while an independent agent can evaluate several different insurance carriers.

There are several important questions to ask yourself when buying life insurance: Would your beneficiary need help in paying the mortgage if you died? Would you want to help your children with their college education? Would your spouse need continued income to help raise the kids and maintain their lifestyle? Your answers to these and other questions will help determine the amount and type of insurance you need, based on your budget.

Source: Joseph Curtis, CLU and CHFC, independent insurance agent; 510-938-3399; E-mail: josephp@hooked.net.

LOVE AND SEX

*M*ake it a daily practice. That's about all I know about relationships, and the line isn't original with me. Jennifer uses it to talk about our relationship and how to keep it vibrant and strong.

What does it mean? Somehow, every day, you've got to connect with your partner. You don't have to spend an hour together in deep and intimate conversation. But you do have to touch base with each other every day, even if it's only for a moment.

Practice is a central part of the idea. Most everyone would agree that you have to work at having a good relationship. You work at it every day, and you never quite get it perfect. Or if you get it perfect today, tomorrow is another day and you have to put in more time and work.

It isn't easy to make a daily connection. It especially isn't easy with a newborn baby squawking and screaming and wailing and moaning and tugging at Mama's breasts every ten minutes. Both of you are tired and distracted, and the baby sucks up every particle of energy you have like a vacuum.

One of the emotions I remember having to deal with is jealousy. I didn't like it that the baby commanded so much of her mother's time and attention. I wanted some of that attention too. And the baby seemed equally jealous of me, at times trying to break in between us when she saw me hugging her mother.

Then there's sex—which definitely becomes problematic when you have kids. When I told a friend of mine I was writing this book, his first words were, "And what about the sex thing? Put in something about that." He's been married fifteen years, has two kids, and is still trying to figure it out.

> "And so I advise you, both of you, to think and to live as lovingly as possible. Your aim in life should not be the joy of marriage, but that of bringing more love and truth into the world through your life."
>
> —Leo Tolstoy, to his son Ilya on his impending marriage

All I know is that amidst everything, you have to find a way to make that connection. Do that, and the "sex thing" will work itself out. (See "Sex and the New Father" later in this chapter.) Having gone through a divorce, I know that it's absolutely vital to work it out one way or the other. Your baby needs both of you, living under the same roof, making a life together.

The heart of every family is not mother and child or father and child, it is father and mother, man and woman. Your love and ongoing commitment to each other is what makes a family strong—indeed, it's what makes a family a family. Lacking this bond, every family is potentially at risk. Every man owes it to himself and his family to maintain a vital, growing relationship with his partner. Put in the time; do the work. It's essential.

The best thing you can do for your child is have a loving, caring relationship with your child's mother. Make it a daily practice.

MAINTAINING CONNECTIONS WITH YOUR PARTNER AND CHILD

"The best gift we can give our children is a good marriage. If you're a single parent, the best gift is a good relationship with the person you're intimate with." These are the words of Harville Hendrix, Ph.D., author of the bestselling *Getting the Love You Want: A Guide for Couples* and *Giving the Love That Heals: A Guide for Parents*. The founder of the Institute for Imago Relationship Therapy in Winter Park, Florida, Hendrix is a nationally respected therapist and educator with more than twenty-five years of experience in working with couples and families. No less a personage than Oprah Winfrey has credited him for helping her in her relationships. In this wide-ranging interview, Hendrix talks about how crucial it is for fathers to make and maintain connections with their partner and child. He is the father of Hunter, Leah, Kimberley, Katherine, Mara, and Josh.

Q: A man with six children obviously loves and enjoys children. Let's start there. How has being a father affected your work as a therapist?

Hendrix: Two things come to mind. Being a father helps me go through my own childhood and see the world in a fresh way. Children are always asking universal questions. They see things in a universal way. The other day my son and I were driving somewhere and he asked me what pain is. I began to give him a scientific explanation and he stopped me and said, "I know how it works. What I'm asking is, what is it? What is the experience of pain?" I realized he was asking me something very profound. So instead of giving him answers, I asked him to speak about what was on his mind. As adults we tend to come to conclusions about things and form our reality around those conclusions. Children are more open to the freshness of experience. The second thing is, my children have made me aware of how imprisoned I can be in my own experience.

Q: What do you mean?

Hendrix: As parents we tend to want to impose our perceptions on our children's experience. But we need to back off from that. We need to relate to our children in a way that supports their perception of experience rather than replacing it with our own. It's true for you and your child as well as for you and your wife. You both may be living through the same event, but you're not going through the same experience.

Q: One of the biggest jobs in being a father is transmitting values to your children. Aren't your values, in effect, your perception of experience? Shouldn't your children know that?

Hendrix: That's one of the flaws in parent-centered parenting—that children need to be shaped as if they were were clay. Children are natural organisms who need to be allowed to grow and find who they are, within appropriate boundaries. Parents have failed to grow moral children if they simply impose their own morality on them. Every parent knows the truth of the axiom: children pay attention to what you do, not what you say. Children absorb the experience of the parent, not the words of the parent. Children demand consistency and integrity. They're very sharp in this area. "Dad, you told me to obey the laws and yet you're driving past the speed limit." They're constantly evaluating and internalizing. How did you react when you had to wait in line a long time at the grocery store? Did you get mad about it? That's what children pick up: how you actually live. The phone rings and as your child is about to pick it up you say, "Tell him I'm not here." That's very different than saying "I'm not available." Kids are like sponges. They soak that stuff up. They identify with parents and they reenact the issues in their parents' lives.

Q: So if you're not good to your partner, the child is going to pick that up, is that right? There's really no separation between the two. Being a good dad means being a good husband or partner, too.

Hendrix: Like it or not, the child is going to mimic us. The way you relate to your child will be internalized by the child. The child will also internalize how the parents relate to each other. The best gift we can give children is a good marriage. If you're a single parent, it's a good relationship with whomever you are intimate with. The goal is to make and maintain connections with your wife and your child. A child who feels connected lives in a very different world than a child who is isolated and alone.

Q: *After a baby is born, the focus is all on the baby. You're exhausted, you're not sleeping, there's no time to do anything. How do you make and maintain connections with your partner in that atmosphere?*

Hendrix: You do it by creating a conscious relationship with your spouse. As I said before, your spouse is going through the same event but she's not having the same experience—whatever it is you're going through: the later stages of pregnancy or staying up nights with a crying baby. You need to stay in dialog and maintain a connection with her. Sometimes one of you has to go the extra mile and be the container in the relationship.

Q: *The container? What's that?*

Hendrix: Say, the mom has been staying up three nights in a row with the baby. She's stressed and frustrated. There are two types of people. One type dumps it all out, and the other type doesn't dump it all out but acts it out. It comes out in their behavior. So the mom breaks down and tells the dad, "You're not helping enough. I'm doing it all. I need help." Now what a lot of people do is react defensively. "What do you mean I'm not helping?" they'll say. "Look at everything I've done. I change diapers, I made dinner on Tuesday"—and so forth. When you respond defensively, you amplify the negative energy by contributing your own negative energy. It escalates. The tension and friction increase. The single biggest growth point in a person's life, in whatever he's doing, is: what do you do when negative information is directed at you? Most people say they're innocent and counter it in a defensive way.

Q: *I have that problem myself. When I feel like I'm being criticized, I respond by criticizing the person who's attacking me.*

Hendrix: Consider this approach. When you're the "container," you stay with your spouse's experience instead of going into a defensive reaction. You contain the negative. You engage her in dialog. You say, "Let me see if I understand what you're saying. You're feeling strung out. You're tired of this baby. You're so tired you don't even know if you like having a baby anymore." You move toward validation. You continue, "That makes sense to me. You've been up three nights. I can see why you're so strung out." What I find is that the person's frustration lessens. She's been heard by you, received, seen. Never deflect, always reflect. That's a good rule. There was this idea in the seventies of let it all hang out. Just be yourself and everything will be fine. That was wrong, that was bad advice. You need to be conscious of what you're doing in your relationships.

Q: I can see the value of being an empathetic listener. But there's still a problem between the couple that needs to be solved, isn't there?

Hendrix: One of the exercises I recommend is what we call "the behavior change request." After you've mirrored the other person, after you've really understood and listened to her, then you can ask: "What do you want me to do differently?" Invite your partner to suggest concrete, specific changes in your behavior. "Well," she might say, "I'd like you to respond to the child in the middle of the night for the next three nights so I can sleep." Behind every frustration is an unmet need. You must address the unmet need. Also, don't forget the absolute necessity of intense positive input. We have what we call our "flooding" exercise. The wife, let's say, sits in a chair while her husband walks around her flooding her with positives. "You're a fantastic mother," he tells her. "You're so faithful to our child. Look at all the things you do for him." This lasts one to three minutes. The research I've read says that for every negative comment or interaction, you need five positives to counterbalance it. But I've found that it takes twenty positives to overcome one negative. I compare it to a wound. It takes a second to cut yourself. But it takes a long time for it to heal. And then it has to heal in a certain way and you have to take care of it. It's the same thing in a relationship. One thing you can do is increase the amount of positive feedback you give your wife. "Wow, you are a terrific mom." Do it spontaneously. Make it a part of your daily interaction.

Q: I have to confess, all of this seems like a lot of hard work to me.

Hendrix: Everyone wants to maintain connection, and it's the hardest thing to do. But you need to maintain connection at all costs. It's not just a good thing to do, it's essential. You need to act in ways that promote connection with your child and with your spouse.

Contact: The Institute for Imago Relationship Therapy, 335 North Knowles Avenue, Winter Park, FL 32789; 800-729-1121 or 407-644-3537. For Harville Hendrix's thoughts on the central role of a father in the early life of a child, please see "A Child Needs Dad in the Tender Years, Too," in the chapter "Growing a Child: What Fathers Can Do."

"There are several kinds of love. One is a selfish, mean, grasping, egotistic thing which uses love for self-importance. The other is an outpouring of everything good in you. The first can make you sick and small and weak but the second can release in you strength and courage and goodness and even wisdom you didn't know you had."

—John Steinbeck, to his son Thom

"Because of you I can accept everything that's ever happened to me and not regret any of it, and look at life and my own future life without any reservations."

—Poet Randall Jarrell, writing to his wife Mary

BEING ON THE "SAME TEAM" WITH YOUR SPOUSE

Daniel Ellenberg is a nationally renowned expert on the male psyche. A therapist with a doctorate in counseling psychology, he is the author of *Lovers for Life: Creating Lasting Passion, Trust, and True Partnership* (Aslan). He leads "Strength with Heart" men's groups and over the years has worked with thousands of men, including many new fathers, in his practice. Here, Ellenberg gives five pointers on how a new dad can improve his relationship with his partner and family. He is the father of Kiva.

Recognize Your Feelings of Loss. Every man has what Ellenberg calls "a core emotional reaction" to the birth of a baby or the news that his partner is pregnant. For many men, this gut response may be markedly different than hers. She sees the baby as a gain; at least initially, he often fears the loss—the potential loss of his partner. Women are fabled for their ability to join support groups or reach out to friends who help them in their daily life as well as in the tough times. For many men, their partner represents their chief (and sometimes only) pillar of support. They fear they'll lose this support when the baby comes. And, to some degree, this is what happens. The woman plunges into her new role as mother. Her time and energy are almost completely absorbed in caring for the perpetually needy baby, often leaving the man feeling adrift.

Don't Act Out These Feelings on Your Partner or Child. When new fathers feel jealous or competitive with a new child, they are not proud of their reaction; they feel shame and generally don't want to talk about it. They know they should be more understanding, more tolerant. But, says Ellenberg, it's important to realize that these feelings are very common. Men like to feel loved and competent, and suddenly they feel less loved and frequently useless. Initially the baby seems completely dependent on the mother. What's the man's job in all of this? A new father must grapple with a whole new set of issues, issues he's never dealt with before: the emotional loss of his partner, a nagging sense of incompetence, the lack of a support system, and feelings of loneliness. Every new father, to some degree, needs to come to grips with his new situation and not take out his frustration, anger, or hurt on the baby or his partner.

Talk to Other Men. It takes guts for a man to admit that he's feeling a little overwhelmed and needs to talk to someone about it. Sometimes that's all you need—just a little venting with a buddy. You can't assume that others will reach out to you. You may have to be the one to pick up the phone and make the call. One reassuring note that you will hear from other fathers is that this intense phase doesn't last forever. Some men think, "My life as I knew it is over. It will always be like this." But as the baby gets older, your load will lighten (to be replaced by other challenges and demands).

Be on the Same Team with Your Mate. In his couples workshops, Ellenberg has found that this concept seems to resonate with both men and women: be on the same team. Find out what your partner wants and try to supply it for her. Know that she'll be stretched to the limits by the baby. Understand that there may be weighty emotional issues lurking beneath the surface for both of you, and that these emotions can erupt over seemingly trivial matters such as making the bed or doing the dishes. When conflicts arise, get beyond the "fight or flight" syndrome. Try not to respond defensively to being criticized, as if your very survival is being attacked. See yourself as on the same team as your partner, rather than flexing "the muscles of separation" (Ellenberg's phrase) as you may have instinctively done in the past. Of course, communication is a two-way street. If a man opens up and says, "I know it's crazy, but I feel jealous of the baby," and the woman replies, "You're so immature," that's not very helpful to him.

Open Up to the Larger Organism of Family. You are now a member of a unit that is larger than yourself. Your ego and your needs are no longer the primary focus. But fatherhood is not a contraction of your life, as you once feared, it's an expansion. By supporting your partner, you support your child. The reverse is true as well: by supporting your child, you support your partner. Include them both in your life. Make them both part of your team.

Contact: Daniel Ellenberg, Conscious Relationships Institute, P.O. Box 840, Fairfax, CA 94938; 415-457-7705.

SEX AND THE NEW FATHER

The best birth control device ever invented is a newborn child. Based on my experience and the experiences of other dads I've talked to, a baby can play havoc with a couple's regular sex life. Dr. Jama Clark is a licensed psychotherapist and a therapist in marriage, family, and child counseling. She is the author of *What the Hell Do Women Really Want?* Based in Seattle, Washington, she gives lectures around the country on men's and women's relationships. In this interview, she talks frankly

"She is only a little body, but she hasn't her peer in Christendom. I gave her only a plain gold engagement ring, and told her it was typical of her future life—namely, that she would have to flourish on the substance, rather than luxuries."

—Mark Twain, on his wife Olivia Langdon (they had two children, Clara and Jean)

about some of the sexual issues that men face after a baby joins the household.

Q: Sex is always a big issue with couples, but it is a particularly sensitive time right after the birth of a child. Why is that?
Clark: There are lots of reasons. First of all, the woman is usually not interested in sex right after she's given birth. If she is, she's a rare bird. There are things going on with her body. There are emotional issues she's dealing with. And her focus is on the baby.

Q: Where does this leave the man?
Clark: Well, this is a time when a man might wonder, What have I gotten myself into? He might even want to roam at this time. The baby is crying in the middle of the night, he's getting up, Mom's getting up. You're both exhausted. Maybe the mother-in-law is staying in the house. Mom is distracted, and there's pressure on the man because he's not getting his needs met.

Q: What should he do?
Clark: First he has to realize that he has a sex drive going on and that's normal. Some men think, "There must be something wrong with me. My wife is dealing with the baby, and I shouldn't be thinking about these things." Men like to beat themselves up in that way. But that's not a healthy approach.

Q: What's a healthy approach?
Clark: You need to engage in healthy, sublimating activities. I recommend masturbation all the time. It's okay to look at *Playboy*. It's been shown that men are more visually oriented than women. You're normal. There's nothing wrong with masturbating. Now don't go off into the other room and masturbate while your wife is taking care of the baby in the next room. That's what some men do to punish their wives and show their frustration.

Q: What if your partner doesn't approve of it?
Clark: Then you do it on the sly and you don't talk about it. Certainly having a fight with the woman in the early stages of raising a child is not going to help the woman or the child. Or your relationship, for that matter. Later on, if it remains an issue, you can talk about it with her.

Q: Some men may try to "sublimate" their desires through exercise. But that only seems to work for so long.
Clark: You can't exercise your sex drive away. I know when I exercise, I feel sexier. That's one reason why people do it. Most men want to have sex an average of three times a week. There are some men who want it every night, but on the whole most men are happy with sex three times a week.

Q: Women are great networkers. They tend to talk with their girlfriends about these sorts of issues. But men don't do that.

Clark: Most men don't feel comfortable calling their buddy and saying "Hey, my wife's not having sex with me." But they can get involved in a new dads' support group. That's great. There is also counseling. One of the things that makes a relationship is a healthy sex drive. If the sex drive goes away over a period of time, you need to get into counseling. I compare counseling to changing the oil in your car. It's not for crazy people. It's a necessity. And don't wait until it's too late before you get into counseling.

Q: Everybody leads busy lives, and having a baby adds one more huge demand on your time. That isn't very good for your sex life, either.

Clark: I think that's an excuse. If you like sex and it's a goal in your life, make time for it. Cut out the TV. People don't realize how much time they spend watching TV.

Q: That's true. When the baby is sleeping and you finally do get some time alone with your partner, you don't want to spend it always sitting in front of the TV.

Clark: The courtship is really important in any relationship. It's important to extend the courtship through the early period of having a baby. Buy your wife lingerie. Hire a sitter and go out together. It's okay to leave the child for one evening, although I know it will be difficult for some moms to do. It will help the child and it will help her be a better mom. Your wife doesn't feel confident about her body at this time. Get down on the floor with her and do light exercises with her. That will make your bond stronger as a couple. Anything you do together with her will strengthen that bond, and your child will grow because of it.

Q: I guess a man needs to keep some perspective on these issues.

Clark: Every father needs to understand that the psychological issues that a child faces in this critical period of early development have greater long-term ramifications than the ones he faces. A baby bonds with her mother first. The mom usually picks up the child more and the child in turn picks up her strengths and weaknesses. And if a mom is having problems emotionally in her relationship because of pressures she's getting from dad, it can affect the child. A father needs to consider this.

Contact: Dr. Jama Clark at 206-557-8796 or 800-BOOKS41.

"It's burning hell without you . . . I'm lost without you. I love your body & your soul & your eyes & your hair & your voice & the way you walk & talk."
—Dylan Thomas, to his wife Caitlin

> "She was only sixteen and I was twenty. I strung rackets and worked at the tennis shop and she was a young gal who came over there. We got married a year later. She deserves a Congressional Medal of Honor for living with me."
> —Famed prosecutor Vincent Bugliosi, on his wife Gail

TIPS ON HAVING A HEALTHY SEX LIFE

Make Small Connections. Sexually speaking, men tend to focus on the Big Connection. But making the Big Connection becomes far less frequent after the baby comes; thus the need for small connections, such as holding hands or cuddling in bed. Just making eye contact with your mate can be meaningful and sexy. Because sex occurs less often, some couples make the mistake of abandoning physical contact altogether. Then they're awkward and out of touch with each other when they finally get a few moments in bed. Small connections lead to more frequent, and possibly even better, Big Connections.

Grab Small Moments Whenever You Can. Even ten seconds of stolen intimacy can be wonderful, such as a warm embrace in the kitchen or gentle stroking of the face or neck. And with a new baby bawling in the next room, sometimes that's all the time you get together.

Be Attentive. Listen to your partner, really *listen* to her. Women get turned on by men who listen to them. To borrow a line from Diane Sawyer, who was quoting someone else, "The greatest act of romantic love is to pay deep and undivided attention."

Give, Don't Just Take. Cuddle her. Give her back rubs and foot massages. Be together as lovers rather than just having sex. Look at sex as a chance for connection, rather than just getting your rocks off. And don't always expect something in return.

Take Your Time. How do you slow down when there's so little time for sex as it is? That's a good question. Men are like microwave ovens; they heat up very quickly. But women build up heat more gradually, like crockpots. This is especially true after a woman has a baby. Your body hasn't changed at all but hers certainly has, and it's harder to arouse her. Still, you need to slow down and let her come along for the ride.

Touch Her All Over. Because men tend to fixate on what John Hiatt calls "the little head," they make the mistake of thinking that women are similarly fixated on their sexual organs. But a woman does not always want her breasts and vagina groped, at least not right away. Let your hands (and tongue!) explore other parts of her body.

Make Time for Yourselves as a Couple. This is easier said than done when you're first-time parents with an itty-bitty baby on your hands. Neither of you, but especially the mother, is going to want to leave the child in the first months or year or perhaps even longer. But it's a necessity. Ask your partner out for a date. Put it on the calendar. Find a baby-sitter that you both can trust. Then go to a movie or have dinner out, like real adults.

Go on a Romantic Getaway. A romantic weekend or even just a night in a no-tell motel is equally vital for your relationship. Your child will be better off in the long run by having two parents who love each other and feel romantically connected. Though, realistically, you will probably have to wait until Mom feels up to it or the baby is a little older and can be left overnight with the grandparents or a friend. But once you finally do get away, you will rediscover why you fell in love with your partner in the first place.

Source: Daniel Ellenberg is an author and therapist, who also contributed to the section "Being on the Same Team with Your Partner," in this chapter. More tips on how to maintain intimacy with your partner after a baby can also be found in the chapter "Supporting Mom."

A funny thing happened as I was writing this book: we conceived a child. The other day Jennifer noticed—uh-oh—that she had missed her period and was over a week late. We stopped in at Raley's over the weekend and picked up one of those home pregnancy tests. With this particular test, two pink lines are supposed to appear if you're pregnant. Well, one line was solid as a felt pen marker, but the other—the most critical line—was so faint as to be almost invisible. Nevertheless, it was a line and it was there. So were we or weren't we? We couldn't tell.

On Monday, Jennifer went to the hospital for a urine test to put an end to the mystery. On Tuesday, the answer came back loud as a thunderclap: yes, we are going to have a baby!

This will be my third child and it's all pretty exciting. I'm delighted, as is Jennifer, though we're scared and worried at the same time. Once more, we are setting out on a big risky adventure. We have many months to go. Lots of things can happen, and some of them aren't good. We know all of that, but still, we're happy and grateful for the chance.

My mother told me something once that I've always remembered: every baby brings his own luck. I believe that. Every child has his own destiny. As parents we try to point our children in the right direction, fill their knapsack with love, and give them the tools they need for their life's journey. But their path is their own. Only they can walk it.

It's a great honor to be a father, and it's extremely humbling. Sometimes I think, "Man, I can barely manage my own life," and yet here I am, entrusted with this new life to care for and provide for.

Certainly I'm as excited about this child—no name yet—as I was about my first two. I plan to go with Jennifer to her ultrasound exams and the amniocentesis, and I want to participate and be as helpful as I can during the birth. Even so, this baby is different. I'm far more relaxed and calm this time around. I've got some experience in this business; I've done it before. We both have.

I've learned a few things since my first child was born, but do I know it all? Heck no. As every dad will tell you, you never stop learning as a father and your kids never stop pointing out your mistakes. Anyhow, this chapter contains some miscellaneous advice that every new and expectant father would do well to heed.

NAMING YOUR CHILD

Names are a clue to identity. They often evoke a person's heritage and family history. What to name your child is a monumental decision. Power struggles can erupt between couples, with the mother insisting on her favorite name while the father doggedly hangs onto his. George Foreman simplified the process by naming all of his sons George: George Jr., George II, George III, George IV, etc. Deion Sanders took this one step further, naming his son *and* daughter after him: Deion Jr. and Deiondra. With names as in everything else, what works for one set of parents—and their child—may not work for another. Taste, pure whim, personal experience, the aspirations and expectations you have for your children all play a part. In choosing names for his two sons, my father Delmar Nelson, a lifelong newspaperman, insisted on short, succinct names that would look good in a byline.

Michael Connell Lester is an editor and journalist and a "Family Matters" columnist for *Diablo* magazine. He knows names; in fact, he has three of them, one of which was his wife's. After he was married and his wife, Margaret, adopted his last name, he thought it was only fair to take hers, too. So he substituted for his birth middle name—Caleb—her maiden name of Connell, forming his current pen name.

Names are of no small import in the Lester family. Before Margaret would agree to conceive their first child, she wanted to first settle the business of his or her name. So Lester obligingly submitted a list of first names he liked, including Mayor, Mister, Project, Lord, and Lester. His personal favorite: Downtown Lester. Needless to say, his wife rejected them all.

Because he has such a common first name, Lester wanted something uncommon for his prospective son or daughter. When he was in elementary school, there were three other Michaels in his class, two of whom also had last names beginning with *L*. Says Lester glumly, "I couldn't even be the only Michael L. in my class." The problem persists even to this day. A psychiatrist with the same name as his lived in his area code and for years, his patients left messages on Lester's machine, thinking they were talking to their shrink. "I kept getting calls from people complaining about their dreams," Lester the journalist says.

In the hopes of finding something a little different—and yet suitable—Margaret and Michael went shopping for names. They looked at all the books, of course. They discussed it with friends and family. One boy's name they liked was rejected after a visit to their local school, where they found far too many Joshuas on class rosters to suit them. They spoke to a pediatrician, who advised them on what was trendy among his preschool patients.

The girl's name they liked was Molly. With Josh stricken from the list, the front-running boy's name now became Miles. In the manner of fathers everywhere, Michael wracked his brain for possible nicknames that could subject a boy named Miles to teasing and thus haunt him all his life. He could think of none. He thought of name associations: Miles Standish and Miles Davis, in addition to miles or kilometers. Lester asked the pediatrician if he had any patients named Miles. "No," he said. "I've never had a Miles patient. I do know a Miles, but he's much older." That settled it. The Lesters flew off to Greece for a wild and wonderful vacation where they conceived a child who later was named Miles.

The Lesters conducted a similar name hunt for their second child, also a boy. The only rule was that like Michael, Margaret, and Miles, his name had to start with an *M*. Rejecting Matthew as too popular and Madison as perhaps too obscure, they settled on Mason. "I think it has unique appeal," says his proud father, whose mailbox at home reads "The 4-M Corporation." Lester adds that new parents do not have to decide on a name until after the child is born. If they're troubling over two or three names, the child's personality may dictate the one for him. Anyway, Lester is glad they took the time and trouble to get it right. "It's real important to raise a child with a sense of identity, and part of his identity is his name," he says.

Tip: Leaf through the pages of The Daddy Guide *if you're stumped on what to name your child. Most of the fathers interviewed for this book have listed the names of their children, and these may give you some ideas. For an unserious look at baby names, check out* What Not to Name Your Baby, *by Andy Meisler and Michael Rey (Ten Speed Press). Some names to avoid for your children: Sherlock, Shorty, Pee Wee, Jack Daniel, Orenthal, Zsa Zsa, Polly Esther, Clytemnstra, Spanky, Sparky, Pickles, or Kathie Lee.*

EIGHT REASONS TO CELEBRATE YOUR CHILD'S BIRTH WITH A CIGAR

1. *It's tradition.* When cigars fell out of favor a few years ago, new fathers distributed bubble gum cigars—a paltry candy substitute. Now cigars are popular again and you can pass out the real thing.

2. *Having a baby is a special moment in your life and it deserves to be celebrated in a special way.* Inexpensive cigars even have preprinted blue or pink cellophane wrappers that say, "It's a boy!" or "It's a girl!"

3. *Cigars promote bonding.* After your baby comes home, invite your brother or father or father-in-law to step out onto the porch with you and have a cigar. Maybe even uncork a bottle of Glen Fiddych as well. Sip your drink, smoke, and talk in the cool evening air.

4. *Passing out cigars helps others share in the event.* Most cigars are sold in boxes of twenty-five. Inexpensive brands cost less than $2 per cigar, mid-range premiums $2 to $6 per. Fine cigars, such as those made with Cuban tobacco prior to the 1962 United States embargo of Cuba (or contemporary Cuban-made cigars), cost $25 apiece and up.

5. *Cigars make a statement.* They're like a business card, advertising who you are. The finer the cigar, the better the impression. Two excellent popular brands: Macanudo and Partagas. The Arturo Fuente Opus X is a limited production Dominican cigar. Though illegal, the practice of bringing Cuban cigars into the United States is not unheard of. Cuban cigars make a definite impression.

6. *Cigars are manly.* Though women do smoke cigars, most cigar smokers are still men. Some new fathers create a keepsake out of the cedar cigar box. In it, they store a lock of the baby's hair, a copy of the birth certificate, hospital bracelet, photographs, and other memorabilia.

7. *Cigars are associated with the good life.* Cigar smokers like to match the cigars they're smoking with their food and drink, much like wine drinkers. Drinking a single malt Scotch demands a

stronger cigar, for example, while a cognac or light wine would call for a mild-flavored smoke.

8. *Cigars are a grand gesture.* Some men may come into possession of a Cuban-made Cohiba or some other great cigar and put it in safekeeping until they have reason to celebrate. There's no better reason to celebrate than the birth of a child.

Source: Mike Travis, a cigar smoker for more than nineteen years, runs the five hundred-square foot walk-in humidor at Art's Premium Cigars and Accessories on North Orange Avenue in Orlando, Florida. Call 888-770-ARTS or 407-895-9772. You can also drop by your local cigar store or consult Cigar Aficionado *magazine. Its* Buying Guide *($12.95) contains ratings and prices on more than one thousand cigars, cigar-friendly restaurants, and other information. You can contact them at 800- 992-2442 or www.cigaraficionado.com.*

COPING WITH IN-LAWS

Before he was married, Gene Brissie thought that in-laws didn't matter. After he was married, he realized how wrong he was. "In-laws are almost as important as your spouse," he says. "You spend lots of time with them and deal with them a lot. They become your alternate family." This becomes even more true after the baby arrives. The in-laws become an often-present fact of life, and every new father must learn how to deal with them as surely as he learns how to change diapers or give his child a bath.

Brissie is vice-president and editorial director of Prentice Hall Press in Paramus, New Jersey. He and his wife, Lisa, are the parents of Anna and Elizabeth. He says Lisa's parents were a godsend in that hectic first week after the baby was born. "There comes a time when you bring your baby home from the hospital, especially if it's your first child, and it's just the three of you. You look at your spouse and you think, 'What do we do now?'" With the in-laws (or your parents) present, you are less prone to push the panic button. Brissie continues, "They provide a sense of continuity. They've done it before. The baby's crying, what do you do? You pick her up. Why's she crying? Well, she's hungry or wet or just needs comforting. You need all the help you can get that first week, even with a second baby, and it's nice to hear some of that reassuring common sense maternal wisdom."

For each of the Brissie children, his in-laws came and stayed a week in a guest room in their apartment. They helped with the 3:00 A.M. feedings, changed diapers, cooked meals, and gave Lisa a chance to catch a catnap now and then. These days this kind of assistance is invaluable since many insurance providers require the woman to leave as early as a day after giving birth.

But you can't count on the older generation to know everything, says Brissie. It's been a while since they had babies of their own, and they forget. The Brissies didn't have a dishwasher in their apartment, so they had to boil the baby bottles to make them sterile. Brissie checked all the reference books to see how long to boil them. As the books so often do, they disagreed on what was appropriate: one said five minutes, another ten minutes. Brissie asked his mother-in-law, and she couldn't remember what she did. They ended up (as is so often the case for new parents) relying on their own best judgment.

Because the in-laws are family and because they're parents (and therefore experts) themselves, they feel little restraint in offering advice. Sometimes this advice is helpful, sometimes not. What they think is good for the child may not be what you think. Brissie's solution? "We do what we want, and we yes 'em to death." It doesn't make any sense to get into fights over these matters. Because they're not his parents, Brissie can maintain more of an emotional distance than his wife. He sees his job as supporting Lisa if any disputes arise between her and her parents, but not getting in the middle of it.

Brissie thinks it's worth keeping in mind that your in-laws have a different perspective than you do. "It's helpful to remember that they don't see the baby as your child, they see her as their grandchild. Unless, of course, she misbehaves, in which case she's your child." The in-laws focus on the child, making you more of a minor player in their eyes. Still, says Brissie, it's always a good idea to keep on solid footing with your in-laws, for they provide many useful services, such as:

- *They baby-sit.* "At some point you're going to have that first baby-sitter," says Brissie. "Whether it's two weeks or two months or two years, there will come a time when you leave the child with someone else. It's much easier that first time if the baby-sitter is your wife's mom." Everyone has heard stories about new moms being so freaked about leaving their child with a baby-sitter that they run out in the middle of a movie. Enlisting your wife's mom and dad as baby-sitters will ensure that the two of you last all the way to the final credits.

- *They take the child overnight, allowing you to arrange a romantic getaway with your partner.* Brissie thinks the ideal location for in-laws is thirty to sixty minutes away. "You want them near but not too near," he says. Four hours away is too far, but five minutes away—allowing them to drop in all the time—may be a little too close.

- *They take the child in a pinch*. There are certain things that are simply impossible to do with children, such as house hunting. While looking for a place to live in Chicago, the Brissies had no choice but to bring the rug rats. "By the seventh apartment they were running around, picking things up and banging on the pianos," he says. "It was wild."

- *The in-laws give you things, and they give your children things*. They may still have a crib or stroller left over from when their kids were young. These can be useful items (though make sure you check out the crib or any baby item thoroughly for safety). The grandparents can buy savings bonds for the children and contribute toward their college education.

- *Your wife sometimes takes the child and visits her parents, giving you some much-needed R&R time*. You can eat what you want when you want, rent the videos you want to see, and maybe even call up a few old buddies you no longer see much of anymore. This last can actually be a very instructive experience for a new father. Beset by a blizzard of diapers and responsibilities, unable to go out on the town anymore, he may think fondly back on the good old days and wonder what he's missing. When his partner and child leave for a few days, he gets a chance to sample that old life again and realizes that he's not missing a thing.

RAISING TWINS

Phil Maggart has a unique perspective on twins. Not only is he the father of twins, he is himself a twin. (His twin brother, Mike, contributed to the "Downsizing Your Lifestyle" section in the chapter "Job, Career, and Family.") Phil, a manager for a reinsurance company, offers these tips to new and expectant fathers of twins:

- *Don't sweat it*. It's going to work out. Even though he's a twin himself, Maggart said he was "shocked" when he learned he was going to be the father of twins because he had always thought they skipped generations. Once he adjusted to the fact that he was having two, not one, he was fine.

- *It's not that much harder to raise two than it is one*. Maggart can say this with some assurance because after having twins (Andrew and Teressa), he had another daughter (Elizabeth) three years later. Nevertheless, it *is* different. And that first year will be a challenge, make no mistake. Breast-feeding two hungry babies will test the patience—not to mention the nipples—of every new mom. "And you can pretty much forget about sleeping through the night," says Maggart. Twins tend to do things together when they're babies, including waking up at night. When one starts crying, the other wakes up, and now there are two babies who need to be changed or comforted. When you have one child, parents can take turns getting up in the night—Mom gets up one time, Dad the next, and so on. But with twins, it's nearly impossible to alternate because both sets of parental hands are demanded. Expect a bumpy time of it until they get into regular sleep patterns.

- *There will be additional costs initially, but it won't break you.* Some extra expenses are unavoidable with twins, the largest being the child-care bill. Paying for one child in day care, let alone two, is tough enough for many working parents. "But you can find a way to make it work," says Maggart. "It's manageable. You can make ends meet." The twins share their bedroom. They also share clothes when they're young, and it's not that much more expensive to feed two mouths than one. This changes though, as the twins get older. Which brings up his next point:

- *You've got to do more financial planning with twins.* Maggart wants to underline this; he wishes he had done more financial planning—for example, with college. "When you think about helping your kid go to college, you can probably get by okay if you have one," he says. "But it's not so easy with two." And don't forget: those two will reach college age at the same time. But it's not just college; they'll need braces at roughly the same time, they'll go to parties and the senior prom, they'll get their driver's licenses and want a car, etc. These sorts of double hits to the bank account can be tough to absorb unless you've planned ahead.

- *Twins always have a playmate and companion: their other twin.* This can be extremely reassuring to new parents of twins, especially if they have to leave them in child care during the day. "You don't worry as much about them," says Maggart. "They're always with someone they know. They're never a single kid in a new environment. My kids always had each other when they were in a new environment." This unique kinship carries through even into adulthood. "I'd say we have intuition about each other," says Phil, in speaking about Mike. "If we're discussing something, I kinda know what he's going to say before he says it." Both share similar likes and dislikes. Both are soccer coaches, and both love hanging out at the beach. Phil says that if the two of them went shopping at the same store at different times, they'd probably emerge with similar duds: shorts, sandals, and T-shirts.

- *Treat your twins as individuals.* Despite their similarities, each twin has his or her own personality. Just because they look alike doesn't mean they act or think alike. As their father, you need to give each child individual time and attention. People tend to treat twins as a package. They're always sharing things—birthday parties, clothes, toys and what have you. But spending time with them individually will strengthen your ties with them and you'll get to know them better. Twins are often highly competitive with each other. Phil and Mike ran track against each other in high school and "our whole life we were competitive," says Phil.

- *Just because you have twins once doesn't mean you'll have twins again.* Phil was scared to death about having another child after having twins. "I'm thinking, Will it happen again? Will I have two . . . or three . . . or four?" As with so many of his fears about twins, it never materialized. "What I'd tell new dads with twins is relax, don't worry," says Maggart. "All in all, it's a really enjoyable experience."

Tip: The National Organization of Mothers of Twins Clubs provides support and information for families of twins. Call 800-243-2276 for referral for support groups in your area. Two national organizations assist families with "supertwins"—triplets or more. Each publishes a newsletter and distributes prebirth planning packages for a fee. The Triplet Connection, P.O. Box 99571, Stockton, CA 95209; 209-474-0885 and MOST (Mothers of Supertwins), P.O. Box 951, Brentwood, NY 11717; 516-434-MOST.

WHEN TO HAVE ANOTHER CHILD AND WHAT TO EXPECT IF YOU DO

Inevitably, when you have a baby, someone will ask, "So when are you gonna have another?" The answer varies from family to family. For many parents, one is plenty. Others think that two provides balance and symmetry and gives each child a potential friend and playmate.

For Michael Corbo, father of Grace, Emily, and Daniel, the right number (so far) is three.

Corbo is the deputy general manager of the elevator and escalator division of Mitsubishi Electronics America Inc. He claims only to be an expert on elevators, not child development. But based on his experience, he recommends waiting at least a year before trying to have another child. "For us it wasn't even an option," he says. "It was so hectic that first year after Grace was born, different than anything we expected. You can't understand what it's like until you've gone through it. It's like going to Mars or something. You can't describe it to someone unless you've been there."

Another common sense reason for waiting is to give your firstborn plenty of what she needs before a brother or sister enters the picture. "You don't want your first child to feel shortchanged," says Corbo. "You want to give her enough time and focused attention to minimize the potential jealousy between the two. In our case, we wanted Grace to be old enough to know and welcome a newborn."

When you only have one, all the focus is on that child. Corbo laughingly remembers "hovering" around Grace so she wouldn't bump into walls when she was a toddler. There's far less time for such individual attention when a second comes along. "Adjusting to a newborn is a big step. Every step seems difficult," he says. "But when Emily was born I'd look back and think how easy it was with only one. Someone always has a free hand when you have one."

Corbo went to every one of his wife's doctor visits when she was pregnant with their firstborn. He says he canceled any business meeting that would have conflicted with a doctor visit or some other fatherly responsibility. Naturally his attitude for their second child was more relaxed. He did not accompany his wife to her ultrasound exam. He never went to the doctor's office for any of her appointments; nor, in fact, did he even meet the doctor because, as fate would have it, Emily was unexpectedly (and safely) born at home before they could get to the hospital.

For the second child, says Corbo, "you're not as suprised by things," although Emily's unplanned home birth certainly threw them for a loop. You've seen how the process works and been through it once. You know what you need to do (or at least you think you do). Your partner is also more confident and as in Corbo's case, may not need the level of support she did the first time around. Or she may need different things from you. Corbo often took his older daughter to the park, giving his wife some uninterrupted time with the baby.

Corbo came from a family of five, his wife, Diana, from a family of three. Both wanted to stretch the envelope and go for number three. At the time of this writing Grace was almost six, Emily, three, and Daniel, five months. With two kids, as the saying goes, you're playing man-to-man defense: one parent for each child. With three children, you switch to zone.

Corbo admits with a smile that, with each child, he's gotten "progressively worse as a husband." He has yet to change a single diaper of his five-month-old son. Daniel was born at home (this one was planned), and Corbo's chief job during labor and delivery was to cook breakfast for everyone afterward.

Three is different than two, just as two is different than one. Family roles and relationships shift with each new child. The Corbos are especially sensitive to Emily, the child in the middle, not wanting her to feel shortchanged. Again, Corbo takes both Emily and Grace to the park to give their mom some time with the baby. Grace is old enough to want to hold Daniel and help take care of him. But Emily's younger and more headstrong. Her parents must keep an eye on her to make sure she doesn't pat the baby too hard. Daniel, meanwhile, seems to mildly take it all in, basking in all the attention. The Corbos believe in what is known as "attachment parenting," holding and hugging their children as much as possible. "We believe that if you give your child more attention in the younger years, they'll grow up to be more independent in the later years," says Corbo. Time will tell.

Tip: Diana Corbo recommends Siblings Without Rivalry, *by Adele Faber and Elaine Mazlish (Bantam Books), for advice on how to help your children get along with each other. Adele Faber is interviewed in this book. For her thoughts on how to communicate with kids, please turn to the chapter "Growing a Child: What Fathers Can Do."*

MONEY

*recently started giving my daughter an allowance. I'm try-
ing to teach her responsibility and how to handle money.
I'd say the results are mixed so far. Based on my conversation with Elissa Buie (one of the experts interviewed in this chapter),
I give Annie eight dollars a week. Out of that money she pays for her
treats, Giga-pets, and anything else she wants. Saving money is a
very tough concept for an eight-year-old—hell, it's tough for a thirty-
or forty-year-old—but I'd like her to see the value of it.*

*The other day I asked Annie what she thought about receiving
an allowance. She said she didn't like it. Why not, I asked.*

*"I want you to buy me everything I want," she said. Well, at least
she's honest.*

*The tendency is to spend, spend, spend when a new baby
arrives. You want to buy her everything she wants. Maybe you didn't
get everything you wanted when you were growing up, and damned
if it isn't going to be different for your kid.*

*Trouble is, as everyone knows, money is a finite resource. A
baby puts an unbelievable number of demands on your wallet, and
they come at a time when one of the breadwinners in the house—
usually Mom—has taken time off work, reduced her hours, or quit
her job altogether to spend more time at home.*

*There are two basic approaches to money: earn more or spend
less. I try to do both, though I'm not always successful at either. In
one of our periodic family financial crises a few years ago, I sat
down to look at all of our spending to see what we could cut. After
itemizing every household expense, I came up with one single solitary thing: the subscription to our local paper. Cost per month: a
lousy four bucks.*

> "He was one of those quiet heroes who worked until the day he died. He was also a man who could do a financial transaction on a handshake; he bought our first house that way. What spare time he had was spent in public service; what spare cash he had was given away. This remarkable man filled a church when he died, and the planet was diminished."
>
> —Author Carol O'Connell, paying tribute to her father in the dedication to one of her novels

It's easy to tell new fathers to plan, plan, plan. But it's hard when your children ask for something and you have to tell them no. You'd much rather be a man who says yes, a man who gives them what they want.

If it's any comfort, I've found that the financial pressures in raising children tend to ease up a little bit as they grow older, though the pressures never go away. You've always got to juggle their wants and needs with your finite resources. The main point is to be wary of those credit cards. When your child reaches three or four, you do not want to still be paying for something that you bought her when she was six months old.

HOW TO GET OUT OF DEBT AND STAY THERE

Money is a tough issue for new fathers. It's almost a manhood thing. They want to be seen as the provider, and yet sometimes that yearning clashes with the reality of what they can afford. The National Foundation for Consumer Credit is a nonprofit organization with 1,300 offices around the country. It works with new families and other people to help them manage their money and stay out of debt. Tina Powis-Dow is a director of marketing and education for the organization. Not only does she know the problems that you can run into as a new head of a household, but she can help you get out of them, too.

Q: *How do new families run into problems with debt?*
Powis-Dow: What we find with new families is they often underestimate how much it costs to have a child. They don't tend to plan for the time when the woman is on materinity leave. When she's off work, you're going to lose almost half of your household income. Then there are the extra expenses: doctor visits, diapers, shots, food. Clothing and the crib can be expensive. It adds up.

Q: *What do you recommend?*
Powis-Dow: First, find out how much you're spending. Get a handle on your money now, before the baby comes. Go into it with your eyes open. Having a child is seldom thought of as a monetary commitment, which is unfortunate, because it's a lifelong monetary commitment.

Q: *What do families forget to consider?*
Powis-Dow: Well, one thing that new families often forget to consider is space. They sometimes need a bigger space—a bigger house.

Another thing to consider is day care, or is one parent going to stay at home with the child?

Q: What happens when new families go into debt?
Powis-Dow: Many times they turn to credit cards instead of spending less. We still have a philosophy in this country that if you make more money, everything will be okay. But it isn't true. Studies have shown time and again that when people get a raise, they will spend that much more. Sometimes new parents also don't do a good job of differentiating between what they and their new child need and what they and their new child want.

Q: What do you mean?
Powis-Dow: Some new parents will buy top-of-the-line stuff for the kid, more than they can afford—top-of-the-line cribs or $100 Nike sneakers, for example. Parents will buy things for their child that they didn't have when they were kids. But remember, kids outgrow things in a matter of months. Spending time with your child creating memories costs much less and lasts much longer.

Q: The kids have grown out of the shoes, but the parents are left with the bill.
Powis-Dow: Right. Parents want the best for their children, and that's understandable. That's why many couples turn to their parents or grandparents to buy the big items. Throw a big party and cook a bunch of food. Invite your friends, and let them give you the stuff at a shower.

Q: What else do you recommend?
Powis-Dow: After you've figured out how much you're spending now, estimate how much it's going to cost to have this child. Don't let it be guesswork. Really look at how much it will cost. For diapers, day care, everything. Day care is expensive. Add up these expenses while considering other factors. How much time are you going to take off work? Are you going to reduce your hours to spend time with the baby? What if Mom stays home? When you take time off, it costs money. So what do you do? Well, there are different alternatives, but you need to look at them.

Q: So figure out what you're spending now. Then estimate what your expenses will be when the baby comes. That sounds simple, but do people actually do it?
Powis-Dow: Most people underestimate the cost of having a child. Generally the costs wind up being about twice what the new parents anticipated. Some new parents don't plan at all. New parents can get frustrated and angry with the added costs, especially when the finances were tight prior to having a child. One person may feel that

the other one isn't contributing enough monetarily. Don't let this happen. Figure your expenses now, estimate the additional child expense by doing a little research. With a little planning, you'll avoid a lot of problems.

Q: What should you do if you get into debt you can't handle?
Powis-Dow: Call 1-800-388-2227 for the local consumer credit office in your area. Tell CCCS what's going on. You're behind on your payments, having trouble making ends meet, whatever it is. We can even counsel people over the phone. It only takes about an hour. We send out a worksheet ahead of time for the client to complete. The worksheet contains questions about income, basic living expenses, and consumer debt (e.g., credit cards and personal line of credit). A certified credit counselor will look at all these things and explain what your options are. The average person who comes to CCCS is thirty-eight years old, has ten credit cards, and has $23,000 in consumer credit. But we don't just help people with debt, we also help people learn how to develop and stick to a savings plan, how to manage the emotional aspects of money management, and how to manage money as a couple.

Q: What else do you do?
Powis-Dow: We have a Debt Management Plan (DMP) where we negotiate with their creditors to reduce or eliminate their interest rates, so the client can pay the money back within a reasonable range. Our DMP fees range from zero to $20 per month and the average client is debt free in thirty-six months. We also do housing counseling for people who are behind with their mortgage. And we refer clients to outside sources when appropriate, such as Debtors Anonymous. We try to help the whole person as much as we can.

Q: I know people with psychological blocks about money. They can't deal with a budget because for them money represents more than just money.
Powis-Dow: Oh yes. Money represents many different things for different people: love, approval, power, etc. Money beliefs come from society, family, religion—a person's sphere of influence. From those beliefs, people form behaviors. For example, I have clients who are afraid to open their bills. We try to work with them on the emotional aspects of money as well as the technical aspects.

Q: I suppose the main thing for people to realize is that if they have problems with debt, they're not alone. There's no shame in it.

Powis-Dow: That's right. It's something that can happen to anyone and help is available.

Contact: The National Foundation for Consumer Credit at 800-382-2227.

TAKING CARE OF THE NICKELS

There's an old saying: "Take care of the nickels and the dollars will take care of themselves." Here are forty-one ways to take care of the nickels:

1. Bring a sack lunch to work.

2. Rideshare or join a commuter van pool.

3. Pump self-serve gas and do oil changes yourself.

4. Sell any vehicles that you don't need.

5. Remove or cancel any unnecessary phone features.

6. Reduce the use of calling cards.

7. If you pay for trash pickup, limit your trash service to one can per week (recycle as much as possible).

8. Raise your deductibles to lower the cost of car insurance.

9. Drop comprehensive coverage if you have an older car.

10. Buy term life insurance instead of whole life or permanent insurance.

11. Quit smoking. It's good for your health and pocketbook.

12. Barter talents and resources. Trade your services in exchange for someone else's.

13. Pay off your credit cards in full every month.

14. Pay your car insurance premiums in full in order to avoid interest charges.

15. Wash and wax your car yourself.

16. Purchase airline tickets in advance.

17. Avoid duplicate insurance coverage when you rent a car.

18. Buy a used car, not a new one.

19. Comparison shop on car and homeowner's insurance. Check with three different companies to see who gives the best deal.

"Now I heard you say the other evening when we were discussing your career that you were after the big money. Now that I don't approve of. . . . Service to the pleasure of people will make you great. And I mean service to the higher instincts of people."

—President Harry S. Truman, to his daughter Margaret

> "It isn't your success I want. There is a possibility of your having a decent attitude toward people and work. That alone may make a man of you."
> —Writer Sherwood Anderson, to his son John

20. Put your money in a bank, savings and loan, or credit union that does not charge minimum fees. Maintain an adequate balance to avoid fees.

21. Use direct deposit. Many banks reduce fees with direct deposit of a paycheck.

22. Avoid the ATM. If you don't have cash to spend, you won't spend it.

23. Switch to lower interest credit cards and reduce the interest owed.

24. Refinance your mortgage.

25. Drive less. Combine many errands into one trip.

26. Buy generic products over brand name.

27. Get at least two bids in writing for major home improvement projects.

28. Cancel subscriptions of unread magazines or newspapers.

29. Don't subscribe to cable TV, or subscribe only to basic cable, not expensive add-on channels.

30. Turn off the lights in rooms not being used (somebody has to do it).

31. Turn down the heat in the house. Wear sweaters.

32. Delay the purchase. Let a little time pass, and you may find that you don't need the thing you were planning to buy after all.

33. Empty the coins from your pocket at the end of the day into a jar. You'd be amazed at how that money grows.

34. Recycle aluminum cans for a cash trade-in.

35. Open a money market account which pays more interest than a regular bank savings account.

36. Trade baby-sitting with friends. They watch your child one time, you watch theirs another time.

37. Go to bargain matinees or reduced-price twilight matinees.

38. Find cheaper forms of amusement, such as a family picnic where you make a lunch and spend the afternoon at the park.

39. Avoid buying new baby stuff. Other parents will give you things, and you in turn can give your old baby clothes to others who may need them.

40. Shop baby consignment shops for strollers, clothes, and other baby gear—much cheaper than department stores.

41. Stop thinking about money so much. It only causes stress, which hurts your health, hampers your productivity, and reduces your earning potential.

Source: Adapted from materials provided by the National Foundation for Consumer Credit and the Consumer Federation of America. For a copy of 66 Ways to Save Money, *contact the Consumer Federation of America, 1424 16th Street NW, Suite 604, Washington, DC 20036; 202-387-6121.*

CREATING A STRESS-FREE FAMILY BUDGET

Steve Bragonier is director of finance for Silicon Graphics International, one of the leading computer workstation manufacturers in the world. Helping to manage the finances of a $4 billion global corporation is one thing, but handling the budget for a family of four represents an entirely different set of challenges. Bragonier, who is the father of Aimee and Danny, offers these thoughts on taking the stress out of creating a family budget:

"I have my job and Shirley sells real estate, so we both have incomes," says Bragonier, speaking of himself and his wife. "I'm pretty good at handling money, it's something I like to do. So I usually take care of the budget, although we switch off from time to time. Shirley has done it, too. I know money can become a control issue with some couples. I know, too, that some couples keep their money separate. We throw everything into the same pot, so to speak. That's worked well for us. No matter what, though, you have to be on the same page with your wife. You have to talk to her. You have to agree on things."

Bragonier, who has a master's degree in business from Stanford University, says, "I use Quicken. It's a money management program. Once you get into the habit of inputting the checks you write, it's great. It totals everything up and shows you what you're spending and where it's all going.

"When we plan our budget we have short-term goals and long-term goals. We sit down at the start of every year and figure out where we want to go as a family. We talk about where we want to be at the end of the year. Those are our short-term goals. Then we look at the long-term, maybe two or three or even five years down the road. What do we want for the kids? What do we want for us? Maybe we want to renovate a room in the house or landscape the yard or even move.

Those are costlier projects, and so we know we have to adjust the budget for them.

"Okay, so you start with the major categories: house payment, property taxes, vacation, recreation, insurance, child care, groceries, auto payment, utilities, cash, miscellaneous, etcetera. Some people pay for private school. It blows my mind, thinking about how much it's going to cost to send my kids to college. But that's part of the budget, too. It's the same with retirement. Actually, no, that's an off-budget item. That money has to be taken out of your check before you even see it. Put it in a 401(k) or a stock purchase plan or something like that. Retirement has to be the first thing that happens; the money won't be there if you deal with it last. And if you do have some money left over, you'll find reasons to spend it on a new CD player or sofa or whatever.

"A good thing to put in the budget is date nights with your wife. You know, take her out to dinner and see a movie without the baby always tugging at her. You need to give her a break and keep your relationship going strong."

Bragonier, who has been married fifteen years, continues, "One of the hot points of every budget is clothing. Women tend to spend more than men on clothes; can I say that? The way we deal with it is by establishing a set amount of money for clothing at the start of the year. That's the figure we both agreed on and so we stick to it. What every spouse wants is to have money that's not accountable to anybody. To spend however you like. So you have to build that into the budget, too.

"Sometimes you overspend in one category. Well then you know you have to spend less in another category. What you're trying to avoid is a situation where you get to the end of the month or the pay period and you're broke. Then the fights start and nobody needs that.

Bragonier adds, "It's more difficult when one person is a spender and the other's a saver. What might help is talking about the future together, kind of painting a picture for her. How do you see yourself in the coming years? Living in a house on the ocean? Riding horses on a ranch in the country? Well, then, it's going to be very hard to get there if all anyone does is spend.

"You take a hit with a firstborn baby. There's no doubt about that. There are all these expenses: crib, portacrib, stroller. But people give you things and you get hand-me-downs, and that helps reduce the cost. You have eight months warning before the baby comes. It's like a hurricane warning. Get ready for it as much as you can.

"What you spend is fairly predictable. Sometimes there are surprises, things break down that you didn't anticipate. The car's a good one for that. But unless something huge happens, your spending last year will roughly resemble your spending this year. Print it out on

Quicken and see what the patterns are. The groceries are higher at Christmas and Thanksgiving. Vacations come in the summer and costs go up. You pay your insurance bills at certain times of the year. Your taxes are due in the spring and fall, and so forth.

"A budget is not foolproof," concludes Bragonier. "And it's hard to stay on it all the time. But what you want to try to do is get the emotion out of it."

MARDE'S MONEY ADVICE

Marde Nelson is a grandmother, mother of two sons, and the daughter of Dr. O. I. Green, the first ear, nose, and throat doctor to practice in Bartlesville, Oklahoma. She has bought and sold properties and, as a registered representative for a brokerage firm, provided investment counseling to her clients for over twenty years. She recommends these basic steps for any new family trying to put itself on a solid financial footing:

Pay Off Your Credit Cards. Interest is wasted money. Nobody benefits from paying high credit card interest fees except the credit card companies.

Pay Cash. Don't buy it if you can't afford to pay cash.

Save. Try to have six months worth of salary in the bank. You need cash protection in case of an emergency.

Make Your Money Work for You. Put your money in safe places, but make sure it's working as hard for you as it can. Invest in mutual funds as a solid long-term method to grow your money.

Open a Money Market Account. Money market accounts are not insured and checks must be written for at least $100, but they do pay more interest than bank savings accounts, charge no fees for minimum deposit, and can be opened for as little as $100. They are a good place to keep emergency funds.

Get Health Coverage. Medical and disability insurance are a must (many receive coverage through their job). Suffering an injury or accident without adequate health and disability coverage can be disastrous for your family.

Buy Term Life Insurance. Term is less expensive than permanent insurance. You can buy more coverage for less.

Make Out a Will. Some states accept "holographic" or handwritten wills. Take a clean sheet of paper with no marks. Write down your assets and how you want them distributed in the event of your death, sign and date it. Store the document in a safe deposit box or another

> "Neither a borrower, nor a lender be;
> For loan oft loses both itself and friend,
> And borrowing dulleth the edge of husbandry."
>
> —Polonius, father of Laertes (or William Shakespeare, father of Susanna, Hamnet, and Judith)

> "With my school lessons father made me learn hymns and Bible verses. For learning 'Rock of Ages' he gave me a penny and I thus became suddenly rich. Scotch boys are seldom spoiled with money."
>
> —John Muir, recounting a childhood memory of his father Daniel Muir

safe place. If you want to have an attorney draw up your will, bring one or two other couples into the office with you; some attorneys give group rates.

Get Professional Advice. Talking to a financial planner or brokerage representative is one more step that you can take to protect yourself. Talk to friends and family. Whom do they use and trust? Buy service as well as investment products. One question to ask your representative: where does he put *his* money?

Save for Retirement Ahead of Saving for College. You can pull money from retirement to pay for college if you need to. But your children can be drained financially by you in your later years if you haven't taken care of yourself.

Save for College in Your Own Name Rather Than Your Child's. When a child has her own college savings, she needs to spend more of it if she applies for financial aid than if the same money were in her parent's name. You also have more flexibility when you're in control.

Risk More When You're Younger. The further you are away from your savings goal (e.g., college, retirement), the more you can risk because you have a longer period to make it up if you lose it. The closer you move to your goal, however, the safer you need to be because you have less time to recover from losses (and yes, you *can* lose money in investing).

Protect Yourself and Your Family First. Take care of the necessities first. Pay the bills, put the food on the table, then worry about saving for college and paying for frills for the children. Your kids will be fine as long as you are.

Tip: Consult Nolo's Will Book, *by Denis Clifford, to learn more about the legal requirements for drawing up a will. Nolo Press (800-992-6656) publishes self-help legal books and software on retirement planning, family law, travel, insurance, and other consumer-oriented topics.*

FINDING OUT WHERE YOU STAND

Having a baby forces you to assess so many things in your life. One of them is your finances—present and future. Stu Stein is an associate financial planner for MetLife in New York and a member of its elite group of "Hall of Fame" advisors. The father of Matt and Allan, he frequently advises families on how to to put their financial house in order and grow their investments.

Each of his clients fills out a financial questionnaire that asks for information on personal and business assets, debt, insurance, and other areas. Every family's situation is different, so Stein—like all financial planners—needs to know a client's entire financial picture before he can know what to recommend. These are the types of questions he asks his clients:

- What are your most important personal and financial goals?

- Do you want to save for your children's education?

- How do you feel about renting versus buying a home?

- How would you assess your career?

- Are you saving for retirement?

- At what age do you wish to retire?

- How long could you live on your reserves if you were disabled tomorrow or had major medical expenses?

- In your opinion, what percentage of your income would you like to save?

- When investing money, would you take substantial risk, not any risk, or are you somewhere in between?

- What is the most important thing to you in the world?

Most new fathers will answer the last question, "My family,"—which is, after all, the reason for all this hard thinking about finances. Whether or not you seek professional investment advice is up to you, but you need to sit down with your wife and figure out what needs to be done. "Most people are real bright about all of this," says Stein. "They know the value of these things. It's just a matter of finding the money."

Contact: Stu Stein, MetLife, 145 Pinelawn Road, Melville, NY 11747; 516-249-3110. MetLife's Consumer Education Center publishes several free Life Advice booklets. Titles include Creating a Budget, Choosing a Financial Advisor, Planning for College, *and others. To order call 800-METLIFE or go to their web site: www.lifeadvice.com.*

A FEW WORDS ABOUT RETIREMENT

The financial demands of being a parent do not magically disappear as the children grow older. Years from now, your kids may want to go to college. This could occur at the same time as they are handing you the gold watch at work and you are pulling up stakes to Boca Raton for that condo on the seventeenth fairway. So the financial juggling act of being a parent—balancing their needs against yours—will continue indefinitely.

There is one indisputable maxim of retirement planning: the sooner you start saving, the more time your money has to grow. You may be in your twenties or early thirties and feel that time is on your side. Just don't put it off too long, or you may find yourself playing catch-up. Time, as Mick Jagger said, waits for no one.

It's better to start early than late, but late is better than not at all. Saving is important, whatever your age. The problem, of course—well, it's not a problem, it's a "challenge"—is that you are now the head of a growing household with a baby and a partner who has probably reduced her hours at work (or wants to). You may want to have another child down the line.

As Steve Bragonier recommends in the earlier section, "Creating a Stress-Free Family Budget," you have to take retirement off the table. It can't be the last thing considered in the family budget. There are too many other demands on your money; it will be gobbled up before you get to it. You can't even *see* that money; invest in a 401(k) plan at work through an automatic payroll deduction plan.

It's a no-brainer: max out your 401(k) if you can. Many employers have programs where they match a portion of your investment. There are also considerable tax advantages. The National Association of 401(k) Investors (P.O. Box 410755, Melbourne, FL 32941; 407–636–5737) can provide more information.

An Individual Retirement Account (IRA) is another method of saving for retirement. Put $2,000 a year into an IRA and delay paying taxes on investment earnings until retirement age.

Social Security currently pays the average retiree about 40 percent of his preretirement earnings. You can find out how much money Social Security will pay you based on what you've earned to date. Call Social Security (800–772–1213) for a free personal earnings and benefit estimate.

A central tenet of every good investment program is diversity; don't put all your retirement eggs in one basket, spread them around. Consider all of your resources—pensions, 401(k) plans, IRAS, Social Security—in your planning. Family crises inevitably arise and sometimes you need to call on every available financial resource. But once you build up a nest egg, resist the urge to raid it. That can hurt you taxwise and affect your principal and interest as well.

The average American spends eighteen years in retirement. Watch your investments with an eagle eye. Be informed. Talk to your employer, bank, union, or financial advisor if you have questions. Be sure the answers they give you make sense to you.

Source: Adapted from materials supplied by the U.S. Department of Labor and other materials. Two recommended books on retirement planning are: Get a Life: You Don't Need a Million to Retire Well, *by Ralph Warner (Nolo Press) and* Your Next Fifty Years: A Completely New Way to Look at How, When and If You Should Retire, *by Ginita Wall and Victoria Collins (Owl Books).*

TEACHING KIDS ABOUT MONEY

Children need to learn how to handle money just as their parents do. Elissa Buie, Certified Financial Planner, owns her own financial planning company in Falls Church, Virginia. She is widely regarded as an expert on teaching kids about money. She offers these suggestions on when to give children an allowance, how much to give, and whether or not it should be based on chores.

First, Set a Good Example. A child gets the wrong message if you constantly replace broken toys or lost clothes. Money is not a limitless resource. Show that money does not control you; you control your money.

Involve Your Child. Let your two-year-old hand the money over to the clerk when you buy something at the auto parts store. The child won't know exactly why he's doing it, but over time he will understand that you do not receive these items for free—that you pay money for them. An ATM is another potential learning opportunity. Let the child punch in your pin number. Explain afterward that this isn't the bank's money; it's your money. You and Mommy earned it at work, the bank is keeping it for you, and now you're withdrawing some of it.

Give Your Child an Allowance of $1 per Week for Each Year of His Life. Buie thinks that an allowance can begin as early as age five or six. A five-year-old receives $5, a six-year-old $6, a seven-year-old $7, etc. It's important to think of this money not as a new budget expense but as transferring funds. You spend money on the child anyway, right? Now instead of you making all the decisions on how the money is spent, the child becomes involved.

Allowance Should Be Paid Separate from Household Responsibilities. A child shouldn't be paid for making her bed, feeding the cat, or other household responsibilities. Each member of the family is expected and required to help out and do their jobs. Sometimes a child does something extra and deserves to be paid for it.

"His mother worked as a nurse and his father worked nights at a grocery store to keep the family going. But they couldn't afford any extras. When Ray's class went on a field trip, there wasn't the money for Ray to go. So on field trip days, Ray stayed home."

—From a biography of champion boxer Sugar Ray Leonard, whose parents Gertha and Cicero raised seven children including Ray

193

Generally though, an allowance is what a child receives for being a contributing member of the household, and it's not tied to specific jobs.

An Allowance Should Be Broken Up Into Three Uses: Immediate, Short-Term, and Long-Term. A child wants candy at the store. That's an immediate use. Instead of her asking you for the money, you ask her: does she have the money in her savings? If she does, she can buy it. If she doesn't, well, tough. Short-term uses for her allowance might be birthday gifts for friends—a budget item that you formerly paid for. Now it's her responsibility. Long-term uses might be high-priced items such as clothes and sports equipment, or a week at camp. Say your son wants an $80 pair of sneakers. Instead of you popping for the whole thing (or not), he puts in $30 of his money and your share is reduced to $50.

Let Your Children Really Make the Buying Decisions and Live with the Consequences. You have to give your children the tools for success. Sit down with them and discuss their clothing budget for the school year. Show them how much it costs to buy pants, blouses, shirts, a jacket, shoes, etc. Discuss how much money is in the budget and what clothes she can buy for that. Now this is the hard part: when your daughter wants to buy a $125 denim jacket that has caught her eye, blowing the budget to shreds, let her do it. She won't learn if you rescue her. All the lessons you're trying to teach will be for naught. Kids learn fast. They won't make the same mistake twice.

Open a Bank Account. An elementary, but important teaching tool. Kids can watch their long-term savings grow. You might even institute savings incentives with a matching program. For every dollar your son puts in the bank, you contribute one dollar into his account.

Involve Your Child in Family Budget Planning. Children do not need to know how much you make, the amount of your mortgage, things of this nature. But you can involve them in a limited way in the planning for big family events, such as birthday parties and vacations. Say you've decided to spend $1,200 on your vacation this year. You can discuss with your children the pros and cons of how this money can be spent. The family can, let's say, stay in an expensive hotel on the beach. However, that means you won't be able to dine out very much or go on day trips. Another option is to stay in a cheaper motel, which is not as nice and farther from the beach, but it does allow you to dine out every night, rent a car, and have more flexibility. Now, as parents, you've set the budget limits on the vacation. But your child feels more involved and better understands the choices that you have to face.

Teaching Children About Money Is Not Just About Money, but a Way to Teach Values. Children need to learn about money. It's a complicated, demanding world. Knowing how to use money will help them succeed and prosper. It will foster self-reliance and resourcefulness, making them less dependent on their parents. They will learn restraint. They will learn about trade-offs—that you can't have everything in life, that sometimes you have to take more of one thing and less of another. They will learn the truth of the axiom about money and trees, and that they need to manage their resources wisely to get what they want.

Contact: Elissa Buie at 703-538-2116; E-mail: ebcfp@aol.com.

OWNING A HOME

ike many men, I occasionally suffer from "house envy." I feel lucky to own a house, but it's a small, ancient cottage that is extremely modest compared to what some of my friends live in.

The other day, Annie and I drove to a friend's house to pick up his daughter for soccer practice. When we pulled into the driveway, Annie, gazing upon the size of their house, said, "Wow. Are they rich or something?"

It was a new, upper middle class home in a pleasant residential neighborhood. Upstairs and downstairs, new carpets, landscaped backyard, and lots of space for the kids to run around in. Though the house really isn't my style, I can't help but think how nice it'd be to live in a place with more room.

But then I think about what it would cost to trade up to a bigger house—and I get suddenly depressed. It feels like an impossible dream—that my family and I are going to be stuck in this tiny place forever.

There's an old saying: "You pays your money, you takes your choice." I've made my choice, and for the most part, I'm happy with it. My friend with the nice house travels constantly on the job. When his company tells him to go, he goes. Many weeks he says goodbye to his family on Monday morning and doesn't see them again until Friday. I don't envy him a bit in this regard.

Yes, my friend has a bigger house, but this Friday, he'll be working while I'm sitting in the stands watching my daughter run the seventy-five-yard dash in her school track meet.

My friend also has a new car, but this summer he was planning to coach his daughter's soccer team until they pulled the rug out from under him at work. They're sending him out on the road and forcing a change in plans.

So who is the richer man? My friend has nicer digs by far, but I spend more time—lots more time—with my daughter and family. I don't want to seem smug or self-superior; that's not my point at all. My friend would spend more time with his family if his job let him. All of us are forced to do things we don't want to do because of the need to make a living. But over time, I think, you can make choices in your life, and these choices will ultimately reflect what you value and hold important. And these are the values your children will learn from you.

Most families who live in an apartment will probably want to move into a house as soon as they can afford it. That is, after all, the American dream. But with a new baby on your hands or on the way, I'd be cautious about tying yourself down to a big mortgage payment. Enjoy your new baby now and put off going into debt until later, when life has calmed down a bit. Although others may disagree (such as Charles Gaines, whose interview follows), that's my advice.

THE DIFFERENCE BETWEEN A HOUSE AND A HOME

Having a baby can sometimes make men feel inadequate. Their job no longer pays enough because they now need more income to support their family. Their car is suddenly too small (or too old). And their house or apartment, which was fine for two people, is no longer big enough for three. They need a second bathroom, more bedrooms, a yard. To make up for these perceived inadequacies (and for personal reasons too), men set about doing what men do best: they go to work. But ironically, their work often draws them away from their families and creates a gulf between them and the people they love.

Charles Gaines knows all about this. The author of *Stay Hungry* and other novels (his latest is *Survival Games*) and a screenwriter, Gaines wrote the book *Pumping Iron*, which was later made into a movie starring the then-unknown Arnold Schwarzenegger. (Gaines also wrote the screenplay and acted as associate producer for the film.)

While researching the world of bodybuilding, Gaines, a former weight lifter himself, came to know Schwarzenegger, and the two have since collaborated on a series of children's fitness books. In the summer of 1990, feeling that his life was out of balance, Gaines and his artist wife, Patricia, bought some land in a remote part of Nova Scotia and, with the help of their children, built a cabin in which to live. His book, *A Family Place: A Man Returns to the Center of His Life* (Grove-Atlantic Press), tells the story of this adventure. "He makes you understand that 'a family place' won't be found on any map or purchased through any Realtor," writes Joyce Maynard. "It is a place within ourselves." The father of Latham, Greta, and Shelby, Gaines now splits time between Nova Scotia and a home in Alabama. But the lessons he learned while building the cabin in Nova Scotia have great relevance to new fathers trying to balance family responsibilities with the pressures to work and succeed, make money, and accumulate.

Q: Many couples think seriously about buying a house when they have a new baby or are about to have one. Do you think that's a good idea?

Gaines: Yeah, I think it is. I don't see any reason not to get a house unless, say, you're in the Army or working for IBM and you're being shifted around the country every year or two. Then buying a house makes no sense at all until you get more stability. But having a home is important. It gives your family a venue, a cave of its own. Those are the walls that distinguish your family from everyone else. It's where you develop as individuals and as a family. I think a lot of the unhappiness in families today comes from the breakdown of those walls of privacy and intimacy. When you're living in a one- or two-bedroom apartment in a gigantic building in downtown Detroit you have very little intimacy or privacy.

Q: But I know you'll agree there's a difference between a house and a home. You can live in a house that's not a home to you. And yet you can make a home for your family in a tiny apartment.

Gaines: Absolutely. You don't have to have a house to have a home. A house provides a structure, a very helpful structure for a family. But you can create a home in a tent if you want to. It's more important to develop an interior sense of family, a place with an atmosphere of intimacy, affection, mutual attention, and self-respect. Make those the four walls of your home.

Q: When you start a family and buy a home, it's very easy to get caught up in the "Keep up with the Joneses" syndrome. How do you avoid that?

Gaines: Well, when we were living in rural New Hampshire, we were the Joneses. We had forty acres. We lived in a very nice home that was 4,700 square feet. We had a tennis court, a trout pond, a 3,000-square-foot horse barn. We had by far the most elaborate home in the area. What got to us wasn't so much the pressure of keeping up, but just the pressure of ownership, of tending to all our possessions. The house was this gigantic old Colonial that we had renovated. We raised sheep. My wife, who's a painter, had a studio and I had my writer's cabin. We had a guy who cut the lawn for us, another guy who helped tend the sheep. My wife figured out that while we spent less than three months of the year in the house, it was costing us $40,000 annually in upkeep. Finally we had to ask ourselves, "What the hell? Why are we doing this?" We felt like a slave to all these things.

Q: I can imagine some guy reading this and thinking, "Man, I wish I had his problems," but every new father faces a similar dilemma, even if he doesn't have your resources. He's got to find a balance in his life, because the job of supporting a mortgage and all his possessions is going to take him away from his family.

Gaines: That's right. There are lots of hassles attached to ownership and mortgages. You have to carry liability insurance, there are all these riders to your coverage. It's an endless cycle. Your possessions dictate to you what you have to do to protect them. And finally you reach a point of diminishing returns. You realize that you're giving up too much. By being away from your wife and family, you're giving up essential things that hurt you later on. Some guys may think, "Well, in another twelve or fifteen years, I'll have made my nut and I'll have plenty of disposable income and then I can spend time fishing or whatever with my kid." It doesn't work that way. You make the best connections with your children when they're very young.

Q: You talked about reaching a point of "diminishing returns." Is that when you left New Hampshire for Nova Scotia?

Gaines: That's correct. We lived in New Hampshire twenty years, but our lives had gotten out of hand. I had made mistakes and put our marriage in jeopardy. I'd almost blown it. Patricia and I wanted to put our marriage back together. So there was that element. We decided to start over, to try to get back to the kind of close-knit family we had when the kids were younger. So we bought three hundred acres of land in northeastern Nova Scotia, near St. George's Bay—windswept and desolate and really wild. No one had ever lived out there before. We cut a road into it, and over one summer we lived in tents while we built a cabin—a twenty-four by twenty cabin where we lived. We wanted to

> "One bedroom in Queens is fine. If we had kids—*if we had kids*—it'd be another story."
>
> —Nicolas Cage in *It Could Happen to You*

reclaim a kind of personal simplicity that had gone away. We wanted to see if we could maintain as high a quality of life as we had before, but without all the possessions.

Q: It sounds like an amazing adventure. What are some of the things you found you could live without?

Gaines: TV, for one. I've never had a TV in the cabin and never will. Television, computers, telephones—it's amazing how much better your life gets when you get rid of all that electronic stuff. You go back to entertaining each other. You go back to attending to each other, to tending to each other's needs. I know it sounds corny, but we even told ghost stories again. We ate breakfast together. We helped cook the meals. I went out and flew kites with my son. I hadn't done that with him since he was seven.

Q: I'm struck that when you went to Nova Scotia, what you wanted to re-create was the time when your kids were young. A lot of new dads may be looking past this time, thinking they'll work hard now and reap the benefits later. But based on your experience, when you have a new family may be one of the best times you'll ever have.

Gaines: It is the best time. It's very hard to appreciate your life in the time you're living it. But those early years with your family, if you miss them, will come back and haunt you later on. In so many families, the man disappears from the house. He's off working. There's a lack of intimacy between fathers and children. It's a failure of our culture really. So definitely, appreciate this time. Cherish it. Take full advantage of the time you have with your kid. Those early years for a father are so crucially important. Once they're gone, you never get them back.

FAMILY AND HOME

Gordy Kulis is an equipment operator specializing in graders. He drives a 14 H Caterpillar Grader leveling roads so they drain and slope in the right direction without bumps. He's now building the roads for a planned development community under construction in Reno, Nevada. In twenty-three years of marriage, he and his wife, Patty, have moved seventeen times. When their son, Chris, was born they were renting a solar-heated home. They've moved several times since then and they're now looking to buy a house.

One reason for all the moves is the nature of Kulis's work. In the past, he drove heavy equipment for a ski resort where the work was seasonal. Many days he reported to the job site at 5:00 A.M. and didn't get home until 9:00 P.M. Some years ago, he and his family had to leave the mountains he loves in search of work and greater opportunity in the city. There, they lived in a condominium complex with a pool and a view of a traffic-clogged valley with parched brown hills. Eventually they left the city and moved back to the mountains. Now they live in a duplex in Gardnerville, Nevada, and when they go to the grocery store, there are slot machines.

"In all the places we've lived, this is the first time I've ever had a garage," says Kulis with a laugh. Now he's got a place to work on his boat and keep his cars. Before he and his wife were married, they lived together in a tent on a wilderness ridge overlooking Lake Tahoe. Nowadays they prefer to live in new, clean places—no fixer-uppers (or tents) for them.

They once bought a house and rented it out while living elsewhere. They thought they could make money on the deal, but it didn't pan out. They had to pay out more money than was coming in, and finally the bank foreclosed. "I'm not too much of a real estate tycoon," says Kulis. "I'll build the streets to the houses, but I'm not too good at the financial part of it."

Kulis likes where they live now because the schools are good and Chris doesn't have to ride the bus as far as he used to. Now they're looking to get into the market again. "That's the tough thing, because we'd like something nice," he says. "Our dream home is probably over our budget, so we're wondering what to do. We may keep renting and wait until we can afford what we really want."

Like all families, the Kulises have had their ups and downs. They've rented houses, bought a house, owned a condo, and rented condos, duplexes, and townhomes. They've lived in big, spacious mountain homes and places that were so small, as the joke goes, you had to go outside to change your mind. They've heard their neighbors arguing on the other side of their apartment wall. They've lived in different cities, states, and geographical regions. It's a simple point, but an important one: throughout all the moves, the one constant is family. They've stuck together. "You've just got to go with the flow," says Kulis. "I'd move to Alaska if I thought it'd be comfortable for us and if it was something we all wanted to do. I wouldn't be afraid to live anywhere if I was with my family."

QUESTIONS TO ASK YOURSELF
BEFORE YOU BUY

Can I Afford It? Look at the numbers. Do the math. Does buying a home make sense for you and your family economically? Look at the tax advantages you'll receive from owning a home versus what you're paying in rent. Your mortgage payments may be higher than your rent, but the write-offs will bring the net mortgage cost down. Still, you have to be able to afford your mortgage payments in order to receive the tax benefits.

Is My Partner Willing to Make the Commitment, Too? You may be able to qualify for a home on your income alone. Lucky you. Other couples will require two incomes. But taking on a new mortgage may force your partner back to work sooner than she likes. She may have to go back full-time, thus taking her away from the baby. Will she be happy with that? Will you? Buying a new home may be the single biggest economic transaction of your life. Talk it out thoroughly with your partner so you both understand all the ramifications.

Where Do I Want to Live? Location, location, location—these are the three tried-and-true rules of buying real estate. Schools and neighborhood are the biggest selling points for families. Another tried-and-true rule: the better the neighborhood and school district, the more expensive the home.

Do I Plan to Be in the Area for a While? Don't buy unless you plan to stay in the area for at least a couple of years. There are lots of costs associated with buying and selling a home—closing costs, broker costs, loan fees—and if you buy and sell too quickly, you may lose money.

What Am I Looking for in a Home? Many couples with a child on the way like a clean and tidy atmosphere—new carpets, new fixtures, fresh paint. You may want to look into a more affordable townhome or condo if that's the case with you. Later on, when the child gets older and the need for space greater, you can move up to a house. Outside, yards that are flat are most desirable. Some older homes have unfenced backyard pools. Many parents shy away from homes like these for fear of possible swimming accidents with small children. Buying a less expensive fixer-upper is a proven way to enter the housing market. But do you really want to deal with the dirt and dust of a major home renovation with a new baby in the house? If there are home improvement projects to be done, finish them before the baby arrives.

Do I Have a Good Realtor? If you don't, talk to friends, family, people in the area. Get a referral from someone you know. A good Realtor is a person who knows the area and is easy to work with.

Have I Spoken to a Lender? Some home buyers speak directly to a lender. Others go first to a Realtor, who refers them to a lender. A lender tells you what you can—and cannot—afford, based on your household income, down payment, and other factors. A visit with a lender is a cold dose of reality for many couples, who often have three-bedroom, two-bath fantasies but only two-bedroom, one-bath wallets.

Do I Have the Down Payment? Many first-time buyers must rely on their parents for the down payment. Other sources are friends and relatives. You cannot borrow a down payment; it must be yours free and clear. Other people draw on their 401(k) savings and cash out stocks, or use other financing methods.

Am I a First-Time Buyer? First-time buyer programs offer options with 0 percent down or as little as 3 or 5 percent down. One strategy for a new family is to make a lower down payment and finance more of the mortgage. The advantage is that it leaves you with more cash on hand. Situations can arise with a new child, and you may need to have available cash.

Do I Know What to Watch Out for When Buying a House? Be wary of buying on a busy road or of a home that backs up to a busy road. Nobody likes cars whizzing by an area where children may be at play. Never buy near railroad tracks or an airport. Is the home in a moun-

HOME BUYING RESOURCES

Basic handbooks for buying and financing a home, such as *Home Buyer's Vocabulary*, *How to Buy a Home with a Low Down Payment*, and *The HUD Homebuying Guide*, are available free or for a minimal charge at the Consumer Information Center, 7-C, P.O. Box 100, Pueblo, CO 81002; 719-948-4000; www.pueblo.gsa.gov.

The Federal National Mortgage Association (Fannie Mae) is the largest supplier of home mortgage funding in the United States. Two informational booklets, *Opening the Door to a Home of Your Own* and *Choosing the Mortgage That's Right for You*, are available at 800-688-HOME or Fannie Mae Foundation, 4000 Wisconsin Avenue NW, Washington, DC 20016.

tainous area with soil or drainage issues? Some parents even worry about their children living too close to power lines. Neighborhood zoning is crucial. Residential zoning is best; a mix of residential and commercial is not as preferable. Buying a place to live in a strictly commercial area, while adventurous, may be foolhardy.

Source: Glenn Mendell, father of Evette. A longtime real estate broker, Mendell owns Fox Real Estate in San Ramon, California.

OWNING A HOME: A MATTER OF VALUES

Bill Mowry is the owner of Prime Equities, a commercial real estate firm in Charlotte, North Carolina, and the father of Eva, Diana, and Gracie. Though his specialty is industrial property, not residential, he owns his own home and knows firsthand what it's like to buy a house while starting a new family. A graduate of the University of North Carolina with a master's degree in business, Mowry believes that home ownership is more than just an economic proposition; it's a lesson in values, too. These are some of the values he has learned:

- *The value of waiting.* It makes no sense to rush into buying a home, especially with a new baby. Why not spend time getting to know your child before taking on the burden of a mortgage?

- *The value of family.* The Mowrys lived four years rent-free in a house owned by his father. During this time, Bill developed his business, and he and his wife, Donna, saved money. After their second child was born, they bought the home where they now live.

- *The value of thrift.* The Mowrys came up with their down payment the old-fashioned way: they saved it. Since he was self-employed, Mowry felt it was necessary to save the entire down payment and have a half-dozen mortgage payments in the bank before taking the big step of buying a new home. Steady wage earners may not need to set their savings goals as high as Mowry. The loan qualifications are generally tougher for self-employed people, often requiring more cash up front.

- *The value of prudence.* Typically couples buy on the high end of what they can afford, but Mowry counsels caution: you don't want to get in over your head.

- *The value of being smart.* Mowry heard about a house for sale that had suddenly become available in a subdivision they liked. The intended buyer had dropped out at the last minute. The Mowrys got the house they wanted for a good price. You can be smart by investigating the various loan programs that are available to first-time home buyers. Some programs offer 100 percent financing with nothing down.

- *The value of neighborhood.* When you buy a home you will fill out many forms and be asked many questions. Even more important are the questions you ask yourself. Who are you as a person? How do you want to live? What kind of life do you see for your children? All this will be reflected in the home you choose, within the limits of what you can afford.

- *The value of your home as a home.* Never view your house solely as an economic investment. It does have an economic value, which can appreciate over time (unfortunately, it may also go down), but that's not the primary way to look at it. Your home is a sacred place. It is where you live. It is where your kids play and grow up and, in the case of the Mowrys, go to home school.

- *The value of talking things over with your partner.* Having a baby requires financial readjustments. Buying a house demands still more changes. Your entire family may be affected dramatically. It's important to hash out all of this with your partner before making any big decisions.

- *The value of faith (suggested by Donna Mowry).* You may want to buy a house but can't afford it right now. It's frustrating and disappointing. Have faith that things will work out and in time they may.

- *The value of roots.* Home ownership gives you a stake in the world. You no longer are accountable to a landlord. You build equity. Studies have shown that a man's view of the world expands when he becomes a father. He becomes more aware of his community and society at large because now his child is going to be part of it too. Owning a home helps a man throw down roots. Mowry, who teaches classes in North Carolina history, thinks this is especially vital in his region of the country, the South. A home helps instill in your children a father's love of place and the land.

PETS

At some point in your life as a father, your child will run up to you and say, "Daddy, can we have a dog (cat)?"

But what he is really saying is this:

"Daddy, can we have a puppy or a kitten? I love puppies. They're so cute and cuddly. I have posters of puppies on my wall. I love holding them and I'm going to love sharing them with my friends. But"— and here's the unspoken part of his request—"when it comes to feeding or taking care of the animal, that's pretty much going to be your job. Matter of fact, I'll probably be bored with this cute little cuddly creature in about five minutes and want to go on to other things. So when he poops on the carpet, I expect you to clean it up. And when he gets older and needs to take walks every day, that's your job too. And if he chews up your shoes and books and anything else he can stick in his mouth, I only ask that you make sure he doesn't wreck any of my toys. And when he tears up thousands of dollars worth of new landscaping in the backyard, I don't really care about that because I'm too young to understand a concept such as 'property values.' Anyway Dad, can we huh? Can we?"

If you are like most fathers on this planet, when he looks at you with those big, expectant, impossible-to-disappoint brown eyes, you are going to say yes. But don't say I didn't warn you.

We have a dog and a cat. They're both completely neurotic. The dog is named Patch and the cat is Blackjack. Patch is a black Lab of mixed parentage. Some people think he has Chow blood in him because he has a spotted tongue. But when we picked him out of the pound, they told us he was a Lab-Shepherd mix. (By the way, although the experts in the next two sections represent purebreds, *never forget your local SPCA or Humane Society if you're looking for a pet. They have animals that make wonderful companions for children.)*

Dogs and cats teach kids to care for something outside themselves. That's what I've always heard. I find them especially useful in creating safe topics of conversation at functions and gatherings. Everybody, it seems, likes to trade stories about their pets.

Idiosyncracies and all, pets become part of the family. We have a new pet rat named Little Guy. Little Guy is actually a little girl, though she doesn't seem confused by this. My advice on rats is: keep an eye on 'em. Some nights after Annie goes to bed, Jennifer brings Little Guy into the living room with us to watch TV. Little Guy likes to crawl onto the back of her neck and hide under her hair. One night I went into the kitchen for a few minutes, forgetting that Jennifer still had Little Guy. When I returned, I sat down on the couch next to Jennifer and, in an amorous mood, started to kiss her neck when Little Guy jumped out at me from under her hair. Jennifer had to peel me off the ceiling.

CATS AND BABIES

Cats are not human beings. They are, well, cats. They do not share your boundless feelings of love for your baby. In fact, they may feel jealous of this strange new arrival in the house.

Consider it from the cat's point of view. Your cat may be used to snuggling up on your or your partner's lap. But his lap time gets severely curtailed after baby appears on the scene. Your cat may have had the run of the house. He may think he's the king of the household. Baby's arrival—the new King or Queen—usurps him from his throne and restricts his liberties. This can cause your cat to become jealous of the baby and perhaps even hostile toward him. It helps to give your cat some lap time and attention now and then.

Always be aware of where your cat and baby are. Never leave them alone together. The baby may grab the cat's foot in play and the cat may respond with a left cross to the nose. The baby cries enough as it is. You do not need him to cry more. It is unwise to lay a baby on a blanket on the floor with a cat nearby. The cat may want to lie there too, causing a potential rift.

There's an old wives' tale about how cats suck the life out of babies. Babies drool. Their drool tastes and smells of the milk they drink. Cats have been known to lick the drool from a baby's mouth—thus, the origin of the tale. Babies do smell good. Cats like their smell. They also like to eat baby food, so at times your cat will get close to your baby—until your baby starts to crawl and then walk, at which point, your cat will run in the opposite direction.

Cats are like children. They need to be taught boundaries. They need to be taught that a crib is off limits. Like children, you may need to tell them more than once. Some families place netting over the crib to protect the baby. Another solution is to keep the door of the baby's room closed. At night, if you want to leave the door open, make the cat sleep in a big cat carrier.

Babies will put almost anything in their mouth. Be careful that your child does not sample the contents of a kitty litter box. Your child probably gets enough roughage in his diet as it is; he does not need more. He may also eat any cat food left on the floor, but at least this won't cause any harm.

Petting a cat is a learned skill. Young children tend to pound on cats and wonder why the cats get upset. Show your child how to gently stroke a cat. Every cat loves to be stroked.

Cats provide companionship. They also teach limits to children, such as never putting their face directly in front of a cat. Having a cat at home helps children better understand how to deal with animals outside the home. As children get older, they can take over the job of feeding the cat and changing the litter box. That can be one of their household chores and help teach them responsibility.

Source: Linda Etchison is executive director of the American Cat Fanciers Association, a national organization for owners of purebred cats. It publishes a quarterly bulletin and yearbook about cat shows, clubs, and other feline pleasures. American Cat Fanciers Association, P.O. Box 203, Point Lookout, MO 65726; 417-334-5430; www.acfacat.com.

DOGS AND BABIES

Dogs are wonderful companions for children. But like cats, they need to learn how to behave around them—just as children need to learn how to behave around dogs.

Advice to those who are thinking about getting a dog: spend time finding the right one. If you get a purebred, make sure its breed and temperament are suitable for children. Disney's *101 Dalmatians* spawned requests from little people all over the country for cute black and white dalmatian puppies. But dalmatians are active dogs that need involvement from their owners and frequent exercise. They are not recommended for children under five.

If you already have a dog, introduce him gradually to this new and very important member of his pack. Allow him to sniff items the baby will be using so the dog's scent will be on them. Dogs have incredible noses. They can pick up scents even after clothing has been washed. More important, bring something back from the hospital that the baby has already worn while Mom and Baby are still in the hospital. When they do come home, the baby's scent will be familiar to your dog.

When the baby first comes home, enter first without the baby. Then introduce the baby's items to the dog and, finally (ta-da!), the baby. Allow him to investigate this wide-eyed gurgling presence but only with all four feet on the floor. As with cats, never leave your baby alone with a dog. Make him sit or lie down whenever he is near the baby.

Try to keep a regular schedule with your dog. It is hard to keep a regular *anything* with a baby around, but feed your dog at the usual time, walk him, and play with him. Walking the dog is a good way to clear your head if you need to take a break from family life for a while.

Dogs were bred from wolves. A genetic study published in *Science* reports that man may have first domesticated dogs 135,000 years ago, around the time of the Neanderthals. These domesticated wolves need obedience training, but especially with a baby in the house. A dog needs to be taught what's right and wrong. He needs to know how to sit and heel.

Toddlers pose their own special challenges for dogs. It's best to introduce a toddler to a dog away from his territory, then on his property, then in the house. Toddlers like to pull and squeeze ears and other body parts, and dogs do not as a rule appreciate this. Help your child recognize when he's got a Hulk Hogan chokehold on the dog or he's being too rough. Also, a child should never disturb a dog at mealtime.

Before you get a dog, include the whole family in the decision. Never get a dog for a baby so they can "grow up together"; the baby's too young and you have too many things on your mind to fully tend to them both. Children clamor for a dog but inevitably leave the feeding, walking, and training duties to their parents. One dad came up with a novel answer for this. He gave his children a leash and asked them to take a walk in the neighborhood every day for a week. No dog, just a leash. If they followed through and did it every day, that would indicate they were ready to have a dog.

Source: Jeanine O'Kane works for the American Kennel Club, which, in addition to its purebred registry services, offers a free Dog Buyer's Education Kit *and other dog pamphlets and brochures.* The Complete Dog Book for Kids *($22.95) is loaded with color photographs of dogs and fascinating canine tidbits. It is available in bookstores or through the AKC. American Kennel Club, 5580 Centerview Drive, Raleigh, NC 27606; 919-233-9767; www.akc.org.*

WE HAVE SEEN THE FUTURE, AND IT IS FURRY

Most new parents might anticipate that they'll be asked to get a dog or cat if they don't have one already. But they may not expect their child to approach them at some later date with a request for a pet rabbit, rat, guinea pig, or hamster. The acquisition of a pet means a lifetime commitment to that animal. A hamster may only live two to four years, a dog up to fifteen, and several decades for some birds and tortoises. Be sure your family is ready for the joys and responsibilities before taking the big step.

Use common sense and safety-first rules: make sure the animals have fresh food and water daily and clean, safe shelter. Protect them from extreme heat and cold, and never tease or kiss your pet's mouth. Read on for more of a look at what your future may hold.

Rats

For some big city dwellers, it may be impossible to conceive of ever having a rat for a pet. They'd just as soon put a leash on a cockroach. But rats actually make very fine pets. They're smart, curious, and friendly—also very quick. A rat will scamper up a woman's arm onto her neck. Being a nocturnal creature, it seems to find comfort and security under her hair. In contrast to their public image, rats are not dirty creatures—at least not when kept in a cage in the home. They're constantly cleaning themselves, although they do litter the bottom of their cage and it needs to be cleaned frequently. They love to eat nuts and pieces of apple. Consult *Rats, A Complete Pet Owner's Manual*, by Carol A. Himsel, D.V.M. (Barron's).

Rabbits

Rabbits—or "wabbits" as Elmer Fudd might say—come in a variety of sizes. But don't put one in the same hutch with another; they'll fight like Tyson and Holyfield. Tame rabbits would rather associate with people than their own kind. A child who has grown up with visions of the Easter Bunny or Peter Rabbit may think that having a live rabbit is like having a stuffed one. But a live rabbit will not lie passively on a bed or sit on the shelf gathering dust. It likes to play and really should spend more time out of its cage than in it. When you open your home to a rabbit or a rat (or any other rodent), keep an eye on your cat. He may think that you've provided him with a nice new plaything. The rabbit version of the American Kennel Club is the American Rabbit Breeders Association (ARBA), 1925 S. Main, Box 426, Bloomington, IL 81701.

Guinea Pigs

Guinea pigs, hamsters, and rats are all rodents. Guinea pigs hail from South America and are as sociable as Charo. Consider buying more than one. Guinea pigs sleep much like parents with newborn babies: five hours a day, about ten minutes at a time. They need daily grooming and lots of activity. If your guinea pig seems starved for companionship, introduce him to your rabbit. The two get along pretty well, although they shouldn't be housed together because then it apparently turns into a nasty Oscar and Felix type of thing. Guinea pigs possess plump bodies and short legs; they have good hearing and sense of smell. Put the cage in a place where the guinea pig can see you; he likes to nibble all day and gnaw on tree branches. The ASPCA Pet Care Guides for Kids are excellent, easy-to-use beginners' guides. Titles include *Guinea Pig, Rabbit, Hamster, Kitten, Puppy,* and *Birds*.

Hamsters

Hamsters possess sharp front teeth perfect for gnawing. They will gnaw everything, so nothing loose in the cage should be made of plastic. Hamsters in the wild run as far as five miles in search of food. At home they eat the usual pellets, fruits, and vegetables. Syrian hamsters, tamed since 1940, must live alone; house them separately if you own more than one. Hamsters have been known to suffer heart attacks. Like dogs and horses, they compete in running races, putting their fragile little tickers to the ultimate test. Hamsters are nocturnal fitness buffs; they like to do their treadmill workout after hours. So put its cage in a safe place, but not in your child's bedroom. The last thing you want is for your child to wake up in the middle of the night because of an overzealous hamster.

Source: Jennifer Kaiser is communications director at the Lindsay Wildlife Museum, which is one of the largest and oldest wildlife rehabilitation centers in the United States. It treats injured native birds and wildlife in order to return them to the wild. It has an exhibit hall where visitors can see live bobcats, coyotes, eagles, and other animals. Its nature and animal education programs include a pet library where children can check out a live rabbit, guinea pig, hamster, or rat. Lindsay Wildlife Museum, 1931 First Avenue, Walnut Creek, CA 94596; 510-935-1978; www.wildlife-museum.org.

READING ALOUD

Like many families, we make reading part of our bedtime ritual. Annie, Jennifer, and I pass the book around and take turns reading. We read for twenty minutes or so before we turn out the lights and Annie goes to sleep.

For me, being a dad gets better as your child grows older (even though it's still cool when they're babies). Reading is one example of that. When Annie was younger, her attention span was about as long as a gnat's. Her motto, like Alice's, was: "What good is a book without pictures in it?" As she's grown older, we can read real books where the words matter, where the authors care about their choice of words and how they arrange those words on the page. Though there are some nights when I'm tired and my mind drifts elsewhere, these authors draw me into the worlds they've created, almost against my will.

Kids today watch so much TV and so many videos and movies. It's nice to be able to introduce them to the original works upon which these spinoffs are based. I remember when I was a kid reading The Wizard of Oz for the first time. I stopped after only a chapter or two, complaining wimpily that it was different than the movie. Later I came back to the book, read it all the way through, and enjoyed it even more than the truly wonderful film.

We recently read Charlotte's Web, by E. B. White. Mark Twain defined a "classic" as a book that everyone admires but no one reads. In the case of Templeton, Fern, Wilbur, and Charlotte, the maxim does not apply. My mom gave Annie both the book and the video of Charlotte's Web. I thought that was a pretty good idea. That way Annie gets exposed to both worlds—print and film. Next on our E. B. White reading list: Stuart Little.

One well-worn book in our house is The World Treasury of Children's Literature, Volume Two, *edited by Clifton Fadiman. I loved reading a story called "The Stupids Step Out," by Harry Allard, with illustrations by James Marshall. It's about Stanley Q. Stupid and his family including their wonderful dog, Kitty. Very funny stuff. William Steig's "Amos and Boris" and Arnold Lobel's "The Bad Kangaroo" are wonderful, too. So are poems by Edward Lear ("The Owl and the Pussycat") and David McCord ("Bananas and Cream") and Dr. Seuss's autobiographical "And to Think That I Saw It on Mulberry Street."*

Somehow I lost Volume One of the series. It contains Judith Viorst's "Alexander and the Terrible, Horrible, No Good, Very Bad Day," and I had a terrible, horrible, no good day when I realized it was gone.

The True Story of the Three Little Pigs, *by Jon Scieszka and Lane Smith, is hilarious. It's told from the point of view of the wolf. Some nights, all we do is read Shel Silverstein.* Where the Sidewalk Ends *and* A Light in the Attic *never seem to run out of surprises.*

When Annie was a toddler we endlessly read Goodnight Moon *and* Runaway Bunny, *both by Margaret Wise Brown, and of course Beatrix Potter's* Peter Rabbit *series. Another favorite was* Mike Mulligan and His Steam Shovel, *a tale about a hardworking equipment operator. Annie still enjoys some of the books we read when she was younger. We just reread* Where the Wild Things Are *the other night.*

That's the great thing about reading. You can come back to these stories and poems again and again and again. I'm a sports junkie, so I love it that Annie enjoys "Casey at the Bat" as much as I do. Another wonderful poem, on a wholly different subject, is Milne's "The King's Breakfast." It's about a king who asks for some butter on his bread, but the Queen, the Dairymaid, and the Alderney suggest marmalade instead. The King replies, "Nobody, my darling, could call me a fussy man. But I do like a bit of butter on my bread."

Many of the fathers I've talked to say that one of the best things about being a dad is being able to relive aspects of their childhood. It's true with reading to your children, too. One of the joys of reading aloud is being able to rediscover books that you enjoyed as a kid, even as you uncover new treasures with your own child.

DO THE RIGHT THING:
READ ALOUD TO YOUR KIDS

There's a great moment in the movie *Three Men and a Baby* when Ted Danson's character reads an article from *Sports Illustrated* to the baby. While his choice of reading material may not have been ideal—hey, at least it wasn't *Playboy*—Ted's heart was in the right place. Dads need to read to their kids. Jim Trelease will tell you that. He is the author of *The Read-Aloud Handbook* and two other books. First self-published by Trelease, *The Read-Aloud Handbook* has sold more than one million copies since 1982. A father of two, with boundless enthusiasm and passion for his subject, Trelease talks to dozens of schools and civic groups every year on the virtues of reading aloud to children. He is the father of Elizabeth and Jamie, and, fittingly perhaps, he lives in Springfield, Massachusetts, the birthplace and former residence of Doctor Seuss.

Q: Why should fathers read aloud to their kids?

Trelease: There are two purposes. When you read to your children, you accomplish all of the things that you do when you talk to them. When you talk to them, your words inspire them, caution them, spiritualize them, instruct them. When you read to them, you do the same thing but in the form of a story. You may read them a Bible story. That story inspires, cautions, spiritualizes, and instructs them. Below the surface, you increase the child's listening comprehension. A child must hear a word before he can understand it. Say a child has never heard the word *patio* before. When he comes across it in a book, he won't know what it means or how to pronounce it. If a child has heard a word and said it, it's easier for him to write and read it. That's the first purpose of reading aloud.

Q: And the second?

Trelease: You want to show your kids how good books taste. You have to make reading a pleasure-connected experience. If you go to church and like it, you'll go back again. If you have a donut that tastes great, you'll have another. It's the same with reading. When you read one of Dr. Seuss's books, say, *Yertle the Turtle* or *The Lorax*, the child hears the rhythm and rhyme of words. When you're finished he says, "Read it again." It's safe to say that most of the reading that a child does in school is not pleasure-connected. It's boring or painful reading. If the child's only connection to print is pain, he will withdraw from it. If no

"That boy! Always stuck in the library. What he needs is fresh air and exercise. . . . What sort of child is he anyhow?"

—Giuseppi Marconi, father of Guglielmo Marconi, whose early interest in reading enabled him to become a pioneer in the development of radio

■

"I had the lonely child's habit of making up stories and holding conversations with imaginary persons."

—Eric Blair, better known as George Orwell, whose father Richard Blair served in India and almost never saw his son until he was eight

> "Keep reading to your kids even after they can read on their own. What's important is not the reading but the relationship."
> —Ron Lee Davis, father of Rachel and Nathan

learning is fun, he won't learn. He'll become only a school-time reader. He'll reach a plateau and won't get any better. Because the only way to get better at reading is to read. Studies have shown that the kids with the highest scores are the ones who have been read to the most.

Q: Isn't reading to your children Mom's job?

Trelease: If speaking to the children is Mom's job, then I suppose it is—because reading and speaking accomplish the same objectives. There's a crisis among men in this country in terms of intellectual endeavors. Blue collar men, working men, don't read as much as they used to. And there's a lack of role models for boys. They seldom see a man who reads. They seldom have a man take them to a bookstore or the library. Seventy to 75 percent of the students in remedial reading classes in this country are boys. This is true in both Canada and the United States, and it's true nowhere else in the world among industrialized nations. Their teachers in the elementary grades are almost all women. The principal might be a man, but they never see him reading. Reading is for girls, that's the message boys receive. Dad works; he plays ball; he works around the yard; he fixes the car. But the son doesn't see Dad open a book, unless it's a how-to book on fixing a car.

Q: Isn't it true that historically boys are drawn to math and the sciences, while girls have greater verbal skills?

Trelease: That's changing. Girls still score high in verbal, but they're catching up to boys in math and science. Fifty-two percent of the students taking college-entrance SATs are girls, 48 percent are boys. There are now more female college students than male. Boys tend to identify with their fathers, girls with their moms. There was a research project conducted in a Modesto, California, school district. One group consisted of boys who were not read to. The other group consisted of boys who were read to by their fathers. The boys with fathers who read to them showed significant reading gains over the other group.

Q: Most men work. When they come home at the end of the day, they're tired. They may not have the energy to read to their kids.

Trelease: The average children's picture book takes five to six minutes to read. Read two or three of those and talk about them a little bit, and it only takes about twenty minutes. That's all that's required. You can always find energy and time for the things that you like. But you're going to have trouble reading to your children if you're exhausted. If you're too tired by eight or nine o'clock when the child goes to bed, switch your reading time to after dinner. Many adults find that they get drowsy when they read. They raise their feet up and get comfortable before they start a book. As soon as you elevate your feet, it sends a

GREAT READ-ALOUD BOOKS

Wordless Picture Books

Puss in Boots, by John S. Goodall (Simon & Schuster)

Good Dog Carl, by Alexandra Day (Green Tiger)

Deep in the Forest, by Brinton Turkle (Dutton)

The Silver Pony, by Lynd Ward (Houghton Mifflin)

Infant Books

Chicken Soup with Rice, by Maurice Sendak (HarperCollins)

Goodnight Moon, by Margaret Wise Brown (HarperCollins)

Millions of Cats, by Wanda Gag (Putnam)

If You Give a Mouse a Cookie, by Laura Numeroff (HarperCollins)

Picture Books

Alexander and the Terrible, Horrible, No Good, Very Bad Day,
     by Judith Viorst (Atheneum)

The Complete Adventures of Peter Rabbit, by Beatrix Potter (Warner Books)

Curious George, by H. A. Rey (Houghton Mifflin)

Frog and Toad Are Friends, by Arnold Lobel (HarperCollins)

Mike Mulligan and His Steam Shovel, by Virginia Lee Burton
     (Houghton Mifflin)

Miss Nelson Is Missing, by Harry Allard (Houghton Mifflin)

The True Story of the Three Little Pigs, by John Scieszka (Viking)

Chapter Books and Novels

Baseball in April, by Gary Soto (Harcourt Brace)

Charlotte's Web, by E. B. White (HarperCollins)

The Indian in the Cupboard, by Lynne Reid Banks (Doubleday)

James and the Giant Peach, by Roald Dahl (Knopf)

The Thanksgiving Visitor, by Truman Capote (Random House)

Where the Red Fern Grows, by Wilson Rawls (Doubleday)

Poetry

Casey at the Bat, by Ernest L. Thayer (Godine)

Where the Sidewalk Ends, by Shel Silverstein (HarperCollins)

Kids Pick the Funniest Poems, compiled by Bruce Lansky (Meadowbrook)

Source: These books were suggested by the author and by Jim Trelease, who has compiled two excellent story anthologies, Hey! Listen to This: Stories to Read Aloud *(K-4) and* Read All About It! *(preteens and teens).*

neurological message to your heart to pump less oxygen. And the reduced oxygen tells your brain it's time for sleep. If you get drowsy when you read to your children, sit up straight. Put your feet on the floor. Your body position has a lot to do with your fatigue level.

Q. Lots of men and boys are interested in sports. Can you recommend any sports-oriented books for them to read together?

Trelease: Sure. Here are three novelists who write sports-oriented titles for boys and girls. Matt Christopher has written fifty or sixty books. He's excellent. He writes for kindergarten through third grade. A wonderful one of his is *Centerfield Ballhawk*. Alfred Slote writes for the middle grades, fourth through sixth. *Finding Buck McHenry* is terrific. Thomas Dygard writes sports novels for seventh graders and up. *Winning Kicker* is one of his good ones. But you can find a good book on almost anything. If you're a father with a son who's interested in fishing, go to a library or a bookstore and look around. You'll find something.

Q: At what age do you stop reading to your kids?

Trelease: I read to my kids into high school. That's one of the worst mistakes parents can make: to stop reading to their children. Children can hear more complicated stories than they can read. And when they hear really interesting stories, it gives them incentive to read better stuff than what they're getting in school. You don't always have to read storybooks. You could read an op-ed piece in the newspaper. Seventh and eighth graders can understand that. Afterward you can ask, "What do we think?" and discuss it with them. Reading builds a bond between parent and child. You sit side by side with him, and share these stories together. I've cried with my children over things we've read. Nothing replaces reading.

Contact: Jim Trelease, Reading Tree Productions, 51 Arvesta Street, Springfield, MA 01118; 413-782-5839; E-mail: 437-0936@mcimail.com.

READING TO YOUR KIDS: AN ACTOR'S PERSPECTIVE

Rodney Hudson is assistant professor of musical theater and drama at Syracuse University in Rochester, New York. A professional actor for more than twenty-five years, Hudson has appeared in the New York Shakespeare Festival's *Travesties* and *Alice* (with Meryl Streep), *Waiting for Godot* for the American Repertory Theatre in Cambridge, and other prestigious productions. He says that fathers can become better at reading aloud—and enjoy it more—by borrowing a few simple techniques from the stage.

"Whenever I do a reading, I act like I'm on the radio. As if no one can see me and I'm acting all through my voice. Dads should do the same thing. Act like you're reading for radio. If you're reading a scary passage, make your voice scary. If you're reading something that's happy, make your voice happy. I say that to my students all the time. How can you be portraying a sad character with a happy voice? Or a happy character with a sad voice?

"Kids love characters," Hudson continues. "Have one voice for your narration and different voices for the different characters. It doesn't have to be perfect; you don't have to be a genius. Just make each character sound distinct from the others. Maybe one character has a growly voice, another has a happy voice, and a third has a high-pitched voice. As we get older, we don't pretend as much. But children love to pretend. The best pretenders are the ones who have the most fun. Pretending is the basis of acting. It's a sophisticated form of pretending. If kids see you pretending and having a good time, they'll have a good time."

A man's voice, says Hudson, is a powerful instrument. But it can seem as loud as a bass drum to a small child. Hudson says his father used to yell a lot when he was a kid and to this day he cannot abide anyone yelling at him. Men should be aware of the power of their voice when reading—and talking—to their children.

"Kids respond to the melody of the voice," says Hudson. "Use the whole range of your voice, not just part of it. Go from really low and growling to really high and almost sopranoish. Tension makes your voice go up. I'm naturally a tenor, but when I concentrate I can drop my voice and make it lower. You can't read a kid's story like it's a textbook. The actor's job is to make the story on the page come alive. The story comes alive for a child when he sees his parent enjoying it."

He adds, "What's wrong with putting on a hat for different characters? Wear a cowboy hat when you're Pecos Bill or a conductor's hat for John Henry. The visual element never fails with children."

Hudson realizes that many men are tired when they come home from work. But fathers, like actors, can draw inspiration from their audience. "We'd do four shows a day when I was doing children's theater," he recalls. "I was exhausted. But the kids would look at you like you were ten feet tall. You'd think, 'Oh well, another half hour and then I can rest.' It's the same when you read to a child. A little more effort and you'll be done.

"Many years ago, when I was a boy brought up in my village in the Transkei, I listened to the elders telling stories."
—South African President Nelson Mandela, whose father Henry Gadla Mandela was a member of the Thembu tribe

"Frida's father often shared books and his interest in nature with her. Sometimes she watched while he enjoyed his hobby of painting with watercolors."

—From a biography of the painter Frida Kahlo, on the early influence of her father Guillermo Kahlo

"But it needs to be a pattern," he adds quickly. "You can't read to your kid once in a while. It has to be every night, or every night you can be there. Maybe Wednesday nights are Dad's Night—just you and your child reading together. Maybe you and your son or daughter can get together and create a play that you present to Mom."

Hudson concludes, "Don't read to your child just to make him tired or to get him to go to sleep. Reading is one of those intimate times between a father and child. It's true quality time. It's one of the things he'll remember about you years from now. And it has nothing to do with discipline. It has nothing to do with go to your room without your dinner, and all of that. Find the fun in it. That's my main advice. If you can find the fun in it, it will translate."

POETRY: FOR MEN AND BOYS, TOO

Poetry is for sissies. Poetry is for girls. We've all heard such things, and there may even be some people who believe it. If you're one of those people, you've no doubt never met Andrew Carroll. He is the executive director of the American Poetry and Literacy Project. Its goal is to encourage people to read poetry. Project volunteers give away free books of poetry in schools, nursing homes, subways, airports, and other public gathering places. Carroll loves poetry with a passion and offers these reasons why every man should make poetry a staple of his family's reading diet:

Poetry Makes Kids Smile. Children love the rhythm and sound of words. They love puns and jokes and word games. Remember that famous book, *Off to the Bathroom*, by I. P. Freely? Generations of kids have laughed at that joke. Children love to sing words and scream words and shout words, and poetry is at its best when it is read or spoken aloud.

Poetry Is for Everybody. Poetry is not just for girls and women, it's for boys and men, too. Some of the greatest poems ever written are love poems penned by men trying to woo (and bed) women. Truck drivers love poetry. So do farmers, cowboys, carpenters, plumbers, fishermen, and many more.

The Subjects Are Limitless. Some people have the mistaken impression that poetry is just about butterflies or sensitive, touchy-feely subjects. Other people may still feel pain from those syrupy or dainty poems that teachers made them memorize. Forget all that. There are wonderful poems about baseball (e.g., the legendary "Casey at the Bat," by Ernest Thayer), sports, the outdoors, nature, fishing, automobiles, airplanes, trains, and other traditionally masculine interests. One of the greatest of all lyric poems, *The Illiad* by Homer, is the epic story of the Trojan War. Homer's *The Odyssey* is one of the greatest adventure stories ever written. Edgar Allan Poe's poetry is passionate and morbid, just like the man himself.

A Good Poem Works on Many Levels. Kids and adults respond to poetry on many levels. They may simply enjoy the sounds and arrangement of the words. On a first reading, a poem may have one meaning. Read the same poem a year or two later (or twenty years later) and it takes on a whole new meaning. One example is Robert Frost's classic "Stopping by Woods on a Snowy Evening." It seems a nice quiet poem, very simple. Further readings reveal a dark and foreboding quality. Both father and child can read a poem like that and get something different from it.

Poetry Expands the Vocabulary. You hear words in poems that you don't hear in everyday speech. Take the nonsense poems of Edward Lear or Lewis Carroll's marvelous "Jabberwocky" ("O frabjous day! Callooh! Callay!"). For a more contemporary poet, try Shel Silverstein. *Where the Sidewalk Ends* and *The Light in the Attic* are filled with treasures. His poems expand and excite a child's imagination. He writes about things that a child is not supposed to talk about, and he does it in unusual and comical ways.

Poetry Helps Children Look at the World in New Ways. Poetry makes the familiar new and the new, familiar. It helps children express themselves. Children experience despair and loss just as adults do, and they look for ways to cope. Poetry shows them that other people—other children—have gone through similar experiences. After the 1995 bombing of the Oklahoma City federal building in which 168 people were killed, including fifteen children, schoolchildren in the area wrote poems to express their shock and grief.

Poetry Teaches Children How to Think. Poems must be crafted. They cannot be tossed off willy-nilly. Even seemingly simple poems, such as Williams Carlos Williams's "This Is Just to Say," are extremely well thought out. Poems tell stories in unique and surprising ways. Vachel Lindsay's "Euclid" is about a boy who sees outlines of the moon in geometric shapes.

Experts Need Not Apply. You don't have to be an expert or an academic to read and enjoy poetry. Go to a bookstore and pick up an anthology of poetry. There is great stuff out there; it's just a matter of having the will to find it.

> "My father is still my 'muse,' the one whom I turn to for the right words."
>
> —Writer Len Roberts, son of Raymond

"Though we have raised you for this moment of departure and we're very proud of you, a part of us longs to hold you once more as we did when you could barely walk—to read you just one more time *Goodnight Moon*."

—President Bill Clinton, speaking to his daughter Chelsea's class at high school graduation ceremonies

Source: Andrew Carroll, American Poetry and Literacy Project, 1058 Thomas Jefferson Street NW, Washington, DC 20007; 202-338-1109.

READ, READ, READ

As your child grows older, you'll find that it's easy and natural to make reading part of your daily life together—not just at bedtime, but at other times too. Opportunities to read with your son or daughter are everywhere. Here are a few suggestions:

- Read the back of a cereal box or the cover of a newstand magazine when you stand in line at the grocery store.

- Play an alphabet game on the walk to the park. Ask your child to identify something that starts with *A*. Then you find something that begins with *B*. She follows with *C*, you do *D*, etc.

- Bring books on a family picnic. Set aside some quiet time for reading aloud under a shady tree. The best advertisement for reading is for your child to see you with a book in your hands.

- Get your child a library card. Go to a library and let her check out some books to read or look at.

- Browse in a bookstore. Let her pick out a book, while you pick out one for yourself.

- On a driving trip, highlight your route with a yellow marker. When she asks, "How much farther?" let her find it on the map. Show her your town on the map and then let her discover the other cities that you will be visiting.

- Put up a bulletin board. Make it a family communications center. Post notes, cards, clippings, homework. Leave messages there for her.

- Require a thank you note from her when Grandma, Grandpa, or anyone sends a gift. They will be eternally grateful, and her writing will improve.

- Tape record your child reading a story or poem. Then send the tape to the grandparents as a gift.

- Kids love to receive mail. Send your children postcards when you're away on a business trip.

- Read the newspaper together. Children love the weather page and of course the comics.

- Some morning when you're feeling frisky, leave your child a cheery message on the bathroom mirror using shaving cream. Make it clear, however, that this is a one-time only use of shaving cream and that she is not permitted to repeat the act elsewhere in the house.

Source: Adapted from materials provided by Reading Is Fundamental, a national nonprofit organization that gives free books to children to encourage reading. Its Parents Guide brochure advises parents on how to inspire their children to read. Reading Is Fundamental, 600 Marly Avenue SW, Suite 600, Washington, DC 20024; 202-287-3257.

KID 'ZINES

Babybug. Ages six months to two years; $32.97 per year; 800-827-0227

Ladybug. Ages two to six; $32.97 per year; 800-827-0227

Sesame Street. Ages two to six; $19.91 per year; Children's Television Workshop; 212-595-3456

Your Big Backyard. Ages three to six; $14 per year; National Wildlife Federation; 800-588-1650

Highlights for Children. Ages five to nine; $29.64 per year; 888-876-3809

Ranger Rick. Boys and girls seven to twelve; $15 per year; National Wildlife Federation; 800-588-1650

Sports Illustrated for Kids. Boys and girls eight and up; $17.95 per year; 800-826-0083

Stone Soup. Stories and poems by children, eight to thirteen; $26 per year; 800-447-4569

"His father, Donald, deserted the family when Stephen was young. To make up for not having a father, Stephen invented a daredevil named Cannonball Cannon who 'did good deeds.'"

—From a biography of author Stephen King. When his father deserted the family he left behind paperbacks by H. P. Lovecraft and other writers, forming the basis for his son's early interest in horror writing.

SAVING FOR COLLEGE

ike most parents, I'm trying to pinch pennies and figure out ways to send my daughter to college. College is a great thing, and I want her to have every advantage that I can give her. I know you're supposed to start saving early, and it already feels like I'm slipping way behind.

College gives your children an opportunity to broaden their horizons. Then they come home on break and tell you how corrupt your values are, all the while asking you for more money for next quarter.

That's the way I acted certainly. I don't expect my daughter to be any different. In any case, I want her to go to college and I want to help her do it. It's part of my job, my commitment to her as her father.

One of the most encouraging things I learned while researching this chapter is that you don't have to shoulder all these costs yourself. When your children reach high school, they can get part-time or full-time jobs. When they start college they can work in the summers and save money to help defray expenses. Financial aid and loans are also available. Some kids get scholarships. Others go to community college for two years before moving on (or not) to a four-year institution. All these are viable possibilities.

One financial analyst compared the idea of saving your child's entire college education with buying a house in cash. Nobody can do that. Many young couples need financial assistance from their parents to buy their first home. This may hold true for your child's college education, too. Grandparents can start an investment program for your child or contribute to one that you've set up.

Saving for college is like climbing Mt. Everest. It is intimidating and complicated. The sheer mountain of money that's required, as well as the decisions and sacrifices that need to be made, overwhelm some parents. But the worst thing you can do is nothing.

Saving for college is a long-term investment goal, and like any long-term goal, it won't happen overnight. It takes time to grow money. You have to plan for it and prepare. You have to make a commitment. And the sooner you get started, the better off you and your family will be.

SAVING FOR COLLEGE: AN OVERVIEW

Many men could look a firing squad in the eye and not blink. But the thought of paying for their child's college education makes their knees buckle. Bob FitzSimmons is a registered investment advisor in Lincoln, Nebraska. A certified financial planner and registered broker/dealer, he regularly conducts educational classes and workshops on college investment strategies for parents. He has three sons, Curtis, Blake, and Clark, each of whom he put through college in part with investments started when they were young children. In this lengthy and at times highly detailed interview, FitzSimmons provides solid information about the importance of getting started early, the pros and cons of custodial accounts, financial aid, mutual funds, and other issues in saving for a child's college education.

Q: Private and even public college tuition is astronomically expensive. Is it still possible to save enough to send a kid to college these days?

FitzSimmons: Yes, but a new parent needs to get started when a child is very young. I urge my clients with a new baby to visit me as soon as they have received the child's Social Security number. It's very difficult to properly pre-fund a significant portion of college education expenses if a parent waits until the child approaches the high school years. A few of my clients have been fortunate to come into extra money through job promotion, sudden growth in cash flow from business ownership, or a family member inheriting a significant sum. But such events shouldn't be counted on to properly fund college expenses.

Q: So get started early in a child's life. That's your first advice.

FitzSimmons: Absolutely. I want to see new parents within the first few months after a child is born. In some cases the grandparents may also establish an initial college investment program for their grandchild.

Q: *Once you decide to start saving for a child's education, what's the first step?*

FitzSimmons: One of the critical first steps is deciding whether to open a custodial investment account versus simply earmarking an investment account for your child and opening it with the parent's name and Social Security number. Now parents can also open a new educational IRA for up to $500 per child per year until the child is eighteen. The annual contributions for this new educational IRA are nondeductible. But the growth in the account is tax free, assuming the monies are solely used for postsecondary education expenses before the child turns thirty. The educational IRA is phased out, however, if the parents' income exceeds certain levels.

Q: *This stuff can get pretty complicated at times. Explain the difference between the three investment programs: the earmarked account, custodial account, and the new educational IRA.*

FitzSimmons: Essentially, an earmarked account is established using a parent's Social Security number. This is contrasted with a custodial account that is established under the child's Social Security number. There are several critical tax planning and account control issues surrounding all of these approaches. For example, the major advantage of a noneducational IRA custodial account and the new educational IRA is that, in most cases, you will potentially save on federal income taxes. You are essentially gifting the money to your child in a custodial account, and the IRS requires the monies to be used for the child's benefit. Some parents prefer the earmarked account because they could lose control of the custodial account when the child reaches nineteen or twenty-one in some states depending on the nature of the account.

Q: *What about an earmarked account? What are some of its advantages?*

FitzSimmons: Historically, the major advantage of an earmarked account is the parent has more control over the monies and can potentially use it for non-college activities, such as a household emergency or a special one-time purchase. In addition, a child is more likely to qualify for financial aid if the monies are invested in the parent's name and Social Security number. However, many of my clients are not likely to qualify for any significant financial aid, except for loans, even when they have earmarked an investment in their name and Social Security number. The Taxpayer Relief Act of 1997 complicated the rules on how much income tax savings may accrue to the custodial account versus the earmarked account. Now with a custodial account (typically referred to as Uniform Transfer to Minors or Uniform Gift to Minors), the investment account is titled "for the benefit of the child" and generally not liquidated until the child's college years. In other words, there's a much greater chance that parents will keep the monies invested long term for college expenses in a custodial account. From my experience, parents rarely liquidate a child's custodial account for their personal use.

Q: How much should parents invest at first?

FitzSimmons: It depends on the family budget, but if the account is opened with a mutual fund it can be as low as $25 per month. The most important thing is to get started, preferably between $50 and $100 per month. I usually recommend about $50 a month for a baby less than a year old, as most of the popular mutual fund families generally require a miminum of $50 per month.

Q: And you put that in every month?

FitzSimmons: That's correct. Hypothetically speaking, an investment of $50 per month for eighteen years into a growth-oriented investment will cover a significant portion of the estimated expenses at a state-supported public university in the child's state of residence. Over time it may be possible for the parents to increase their monthly contribution. In addition the Taxpayer Relief Act provides for a nonrefundable tax credit for up to $1,500 of postsecondary education expenses during the first two years of college.

Q: The idea is that over time your monthly investments will grow into a sizable chunk.

FitzSimmons: Right. You have to do it systematically. Allow your mutual fund to systematically withdraw the $50 per month from your bank account. Now there's another conceivable approach. A few clients are able to invest up to $10,000 to $12,000 in a lump sum investment when the child is less than one. In the past this approach has generated most of the funds necessary for a typical state college for an in-state resident. Realistically, though, very few parents have that kind of money to invest at one time.

Q: A lot of parents ask their kids to help finance their own education themselves.

FitzSimmons: That's right, and that definitely should enter into your discussions. I rarely meet with clients who expect their child to pay a majority of the college bill. When a child is first born, it's very difficult to predict how much a child may earn during his high school years and

"Things not to worry about: Don't worry about popular opinion. Don't worry about the past. Don't worry about the future. Don't worry about growing up."

—Scott Fitzgerald, advising his daughter Frances when she was away at school

227

save and invest. A child might eventually qualify for a scholarship. In addition, many college students have a part-time job during school and work full-time during the summer. It seems reasonable to expect a child to pay for up to 25 to 33 percent of the total college bill, again assuming the child attends a state university.

Q: Financial aid is another possibility, isn't it?

FitzSimmons: Yes, as it's very difficult for most parents to pay for all of their child's college education. Most parents expect their child to borrow some of their college education expenses. But I've found that financial aid is generally stacked against the upper middle and higher income families in terms of getting grants. I certainly wouldn't want my clients to rely heavily on financial aid by itself to fund college expenses, especially if the aid is primarily in the form of low-cost college loans while the child is in school.

Q: You've referred to mutual funds as an investment vehicle for funding a college education. Explain how they work, would you?

FitzSimmons: Basically, growth-oriented stock mutual funds are neither insured nor guaranteed by the U.S. Government. They present a greater risk than, say, U.S. savings bonds or a bank savings account. Lower-risk investment vehicles generally have less volatility and provide lower long-term returns. For a parent to achieve higher rates of return, they must accept a greater degree of risk. Growth-oriented mutual funds have historically, over long holding periods, offered investors a higher potential return and provided superior returns to fixed income investment. Of course, past performance is no guarantee of future returns.

Q: One last question. Should a person save for his retirement and save for his child's college education at the same time?

FitzSimmons: Yes. As a child gets ready to enter college, the costs can adversely impact a parent's preretirement accounts, especially if you borrow against a 401(k) at work. The Taxpayer Relief Act also permits penalty-free withdrawals from traditional IRA accounts for qualifying postsecondary education expenses. It's not going to be easy for a family to do both college and preretirement investment programs and still maintain the lifestyle they established when their child was younger. The key is for each family to establish realistic goals and objectives based on their specific financial situation. Then they can lay out a workable plan that accumulates and preserves wealth while at the same time giving them the flexibility to address potentially unexpected contingencies.

Contact: Bob FitzSimmons, Greentree Court, 210 Gateway Mall, Suite 426, Lincoln, NE 68505; 402-465-5678; E-mail: fitzcfp@aol.com/.

HOW TO DEVELOP A BUNDLE FOR COLLEGE

The College Entrance Examination Board of New York estimates that in fifteen years the cost of a four-year public university education, including room and board, will surpass $120,000. The projected four-year cost of a private college education for the same period will be more than $280,000. In a sentence, it's going to take a bundle to send your child to college in the future. Here's more sage advice on how to get a bundle for your bundle of joy:

Just Saving Your Pennies Will Not Do the Job. College costs historically rise faster than the rate of inflation. Many people, perhaps wary or even fearful about investing, keep their money in bank savings accounts or CDs. These are considered "fixed income" investments that guarantee your principal yet give you a low rate of interest. That won't cut it. The interest on bank passbook accounts does not keep up with inflation. You can't expect to build a college fund without growing your money.

Mutual Funds Are an Excellent Means of Growing Money. When you invest in mutual funds, you invest in a family of stocks. This family includes many companies, rather than just one. It is diversified and professionally managed. Many mutual funds are global in nature, investing in an array of companies around the world. Some mutual funds have seen a 30 to 50 percent rate of return per year in recent years. And yet it is possible to invest in mutual funds—and start the big job of saving for college—with as little as $50 per contribution.

You Won't Save What You Need Without Some Risk. The diversity of mutual funds helps spread the risk, and you can buy in small lots. There is risk in buying mutual funds, however, and it is possible to lose money. Mutual funds can go down, not up. But one of the basic principles of investing is that the more time you have, the more aggressive your investment strategy can be. You can be more conservative as your child enters high school and gets closer to his college years.

Reinvesting Your Dividends Is an Easy, Yet Sometimes Overlooked, Way of Growing Money. You're saving with a long-term goal in mind. Rather than cashing checks that are usually very small amounts anyway, reinvest the dividends. Dividend reinvestment can really add up over a long period of time.

"In order to become a respected and useful member of [society], young blacks must strive for and scheme for even the skinniest chance to reach college, because everybody knows that's where it's at."

—African American Journalist Bob Teague, writing to his son Adam

"Anyone calls you nigger, you not only got my permsission to fight him—you got my orders to fight him."

—William Marshall, to his son Thurgood Marshall in segregated Baltimore in the early 1900s. Thurgood Marshall grew up to become the the first black Supreme Court justice of the United States.

Grandparents May Have to Pitch In. It is estimated that 60 percent of the nation's wealth resides in the hands of people fifty-five or older. Younger parents are working and have less discretionary income. Grandparents can help fill in the gap by starting investment programs for their grandchildren and buying the occasional savings bond as a gift.

You May Need to Pay a "Load." For many men, "doing it yourself" is a badge of honor. They'd rather do a so-so job themselves than ask someone else for help. But unless you're willing to commit the time and do the background research, you're probably better off working with an investment pro and paying a commission (or "load") for his or her advice. No-load funds are essentially commission-free; load funds carry a commission.

Savings Bonds Make Nice Gifts, But You'll Need More to Subsidize a College Education. When aunts, uncles, godparents, or grandparents ask you for birthday gift ideas for your child, suggest Series EE savings bonds. They're sold at banks; the price of a savings bond is always half its face value. A $100 bond, for example, costs $50. Interest rates on bonds vary, and Series EE bonds reach their face value in seventeen years. Backed by the U.S. government, they are a safe, low-yield investment. But to keep up with college education costs, you need to grow your principal through a systematic program of investment, and that brings you back to mutual funds.

Building Up Your Retirement, and Then Borrowing Against It Later Can Be a Viable College Investment Strategy. Many parents use the money they've sheltered in 401(k) and 403(b) accounts to help pay college expenses for their children. Beginning in 1998, you are exempt from the usual 10 percent penalty for early withdrawl of 401(k) funds when you use the money to pay higher education expenses for your children (or for yourself, your spouse, or your grandchildren). You will have to pay regular income taxes on the amount withdrawn, but you still may come out ahead because you've been collecting that money on a tax-deferred basis over the years. It functions as a low-cost loan. Additionally you have the advantage of keeping the money in your own name, allowing you to use it for your retirement if you don't need it to pay for college. Maintaining control is one reason why many financial experts do not like custodial investment accounts. They give fewer options to parents. For example, if a child comes of age and decides not to go to college, he's legally entitled to the money in the custodial account and can use it for whatever purposes he desires.

More options are available. Up to $1,000 of interest on a student loan for yourself, your spouse, or a dependent is now tax deductible. Credits for higher education expenses for the first two years are also allowed. You may also be able to contribute up to $500 each year to an Education IRA for a person under 18. The contributions are not deductible, but the earnings grow on a tax-deferred basis.

Don't Let the Projected Cost of a College Education Scare You. Don't worry about numbers so much. Fix on your goal. Start putting money away. Get into a growth-oriented investment program that beats inflation. There are other options available, such as junior college, scholarships, financial aid, and the child helping to foot some of the bill. Find out where you stand financially, figure out what you can afford to do, and then do it.

Source: Joe Fuccy, father of Kirsten, Becky, and Lesley, and a former teacher and high school basketball coach, has worked as an investment advisor for more than twenty years. Advisory Financial Consultants, 39210 State Street, Suite 117, Fremont, CA 94538; 510-795-1122.

COLLEGE INVESTMENT PLANS

Some investment companies offer specific college investment plans. Others do not label their plans as such but can enroll you in long-term growth plans whose investment goal is saving for college. The minimum initial investment at Charles Schwab is $500. Others may ask as much as $2,500 to get started, although this may be waived with participation in an automatic investment program.

The following companies offer savings plans for college. They will provide brochures and other information on their specific plans. You may want to contact several different ones to compare their respective programs.

American Century Investments, P.O. Box 419200, Kansas City, MO 64141; 800-345-2021; www.americancentury.com/

Dreyfus, 144 Glenn Curtiss Boulevard, P.O. Box 9316, Uniondale, NY 11553; 800-645-6561; www.dreyfus.com/

Fidelity Investments, 82 Devonshire Street, Boston, MA 02109; 800-544-3902; www.fidelity.com/

Janus, P.O. Box 173375, Denver, CO 80217; 800-525-3713; www.JanusFunds.com/

"I don't care what you do in life, but whatever you do, be the best person in the world when you do it. Even if you're going to be a ditch digger, be the best ditch digger in the world."
—Joseph P. Kennedy, whose sons, Jack, Bobby, and Edward, did not grow up to be ditch diggers

Pioneer Funds, 60 State Street, Boston, MA 02109; 800-225-6292

Charles Schwab, 101 Montgomery Street, San Francisco, CA 94104; 800-435-4000; www.schwab.com/

Vanguard Group, P.O. Box 2600, Valley Forge, PA 2600; 800-962-5235; www.vanguard.com/

MORE OPTIONS AND RESOURCES

At least a dozen states have prepaid tuition plans. One such plan is the Texas Tomorrow Fund. Begun in 1996, it allows parents to prepay their child's tuition and fees with monthly installment payments or a lump sum payment. For Texas residents only, for attendance at a state-supported college or university in Texas, residents pay a fixed amount that is designed to cover the projected cost of tuition and fees when the child enters college. You can find out more about this by contacting Texas Tomorrow Fund, P.O. Box 13407, Austin, TX 78711; 800-445-4723. Residents of other states should contact their state department of education to find out about the availability of prepaid tuition plans where they live.

The Department of Education publishes a helpful booklet entitled *Preparing Your Child for College: A Resource Book for Parents*. It contains information on financing, long-range planning, state-by state financial aid agencies, educational resources on the Internet, and other topics. Write the Consumer Information Center–7C, P.O. Box 100, Pueblo, CO 81009; or see their web site at www.pueblo.gsa/gov/.

Sallie Mae, formally known as the Student Loan Marketing Association, is the nation's leading educational lender. It provides funding for four in ten of all insured educational loans today. Its pamphlets, *Paying for College* and *Borrowing for College,* explain financial aid and other college education issues. For these pamphlets, write to Sallie Mae, 1050 Thomas Jefferson Street NW, Washington, DC 20007; or call 800-222- 7182; or see their web site at www.salliemae.com/.

SPIRITUALITY

When I was a kid we went to the Methodist Church on A Street in Hayward, but my dad often worked at the paper on Saturdays, and on Sunday he wanted to sleep in. So there were a lot of Sunday mornings when we didn't quite make it to church, which was okay with me. The minister seemed awfully boring, and the seats were uncomfortable.

When my dad died, a Lutheran pastor befriended the family and helped my mom get through the funeral and some of the hard times that followed. After that she started taking us to the Lutheran Church in Castro Valley, in part, I think, out of gratitude and loyalty to the pastor.

But there was more to it than that. My brother and I were both teenagers, and, having lost our father, my mom wanted to give us as much direction as she could. The church could help in that department. It could give us direction, supply a rudder, if we ever needed it.

A funny thing happens when you have kids. You start thinking like a parent. Your thoughts turn to such concepts as guidance and direction and God and faith. At least mine did.

The Gulf War occurred in 1991. It was over in a flash, but it shook me up pretty good. I grew up during the Vietnam War, but that was different for me somehow. Now I was a father. I had a daughter. Young American men and women were putting their lives on the line because their country asked them to. Someday my daughter could be one of them. Now I could truly see what was at risk—not just for the troops themselves, but for their families as well.

That was when we started taking Annie to church. My then-wife was a lapsed Catholic. There is a lovely, thriving Catholic Church in *town and so that's where we went. It was great to hear the singing and the voices. You know you're getting old when the only place you hear live music is at a church or temple.*

As time went on, we decided to have Annie baptized. A bunch of friends and family came to the church and afterward we invited them over to the house for food and drink. One of Annie's godfathers was Max, who's Jewish. It was his first time in a Catholic church. Before he went in he raised his head to the sky and said, "God, forgive me." Annie was three. I asked her what part of the ceremony she liked best and she said, "When they threw the water on me."

As part of the ceremony, the parents were asked to explain why they wanted to baptize their child. It was mainly the dads who did the talking, who stood up in front of the congregation and spoke for their family. For me, it had to do with giving Annie another choice.

When times get tough, she can turn to her friends. She can turn to her family. She can turn (I hope) to her father. Here, I said to the congregation, is another place for her to turn. It reminded me of what my mother did for my brother and me after my dad died.

That's all a parent can do, it seems to me. You cannot guarantee that your children will always make the right choices in life, but you can try to provide them with guidance and direction.

FATHERHOOD AS A SPIRITUAL JOURNEY

When a child is born, a mother and father are born too. It's not just the baby who begins a new life. His parents, if they keep their hearts and minds open, each embark on a journey of self-discovery as well.

Gerald Hair is a former Roman Catholic priest. He graduated from Xavier College in Cincinnati and later formed its counseling department. After receiving his master's degree in theology, Hair cofounded the Jesuit Renewal Center in Milford, Ohio, which organized spiritual retreats. He served as a priest for twelve years and a Jesuit for twenty-five years before leaving the priesthood in 1987. "I knew in some sense I had to go," he says in explaining why he left. He went on to marry and become the father of a daughter, Grace.

Though he has spent a lifetime in religious study and teaching, Hair says that becoming a father has made him grow as a human being. "Being Grace's father calls me to a kind of loving I've never known," he says. "I've never had to open myself this way before."

Hair says that children open a person up to what Thomas Aquinas cited as the four "transcendental" qualities of life: the oneness of God, goodness, truth, and beauty. He explains, "When I think about Gracie, there's so much that's beautiful about her. There was beauty in the sexual act of creating her. There's the beauty of Maureen when she was pregnant. We could talk all day about each of these qualities. Certainly, a baby is goodness in its essence, in its purity. Everyone melts around babies and there's a reason for that. There's truth in babies. This is life at its most precious. Gracie is the lens through which I look and see that all of life is precious. A child embodies the profoundest mysteries of God, the oneness of Creation. I'm one with this child in some way that I've never known before. Men know this feeling. They may be called away to work or have to leave the home for a time, but their heart remains with their family."

Hair adds a fifth transcendental quality that children bring to your life. This quality, first remarked upon by the author Peter Berger, is "risibility" or humorousness. "I equate this with play, laughter and play," says Hair. "I'm probably like a lot of fathers in this way. I've always been very serious. But my daughter has shown me a playful side to my personality that I'd never explored."

Hair believes that the foundation of fatherhood, indeed for all of life, is love. He says, "If your child is being pissy, I should say *when* he is being pissy, when you have love underneath it, even if you lose your temper you can come back to that love afterward and ask forgiveness from your child." A lot of fathers, he admits, may have trouble doing that—acknowledging being wrong in front of their child or spouse. That is something Hair himself has had to learn. As he puts it, "I've never had to die to myself so much as since I've become a father."

By "dying" to himself, Hair means that time after time, he's had to swallow his ego. The other night he was cooking dinner and his daughter wanted to play with some friends. Hair said no because it didn't fit with what he wanted to have happen at that moment. After a while he reconsidered, allowing his daughter to play with her friends. "I think our egos can get in the way of us loving our kids," he says. "I think it's true too with our spouse, our coworkers, other people we know, in other situations. Our egos tell us we need to be in control."

Not just your ego, but your pride sometimes takes a beating, too. Gracie has a scooter, but all her friends have bicycles. The other day Hair watched as her friends pedaled off and left Gracie taking up the rear on her scooter. "I feel that," he says. "It hurts." But he simply can't afford to buy her a bike right now. He talked it over with her, and she seemed to understand.

> "I hope you let not a day pass you without prayers to the glorious God. And that all the vices of dishonesty, debauchery, and false-speaking are abominable to you."
> —Cotton Mather, to his oldest of fifteen children, Increase Mather, circa 1715

"After all, Cathy my love, He's right there in your very own heart so whenever you are in doubt about the right or wrong thing to do, think of Him by closing your eyes and being real still until presently, if you stay very quiet, a warm feeling will creep over you and presto! the right way will pop into your mind."

—Beat poet Neal Cassady, writing to his daughter, Cathy, from jail

These seeming insults to pride and ego are a form of spiritual teaching, says Hair, if a man is willing to let these lessons in. A truly strong father can show weakness to his child. A truly strong father can let go of the need to always control and can serve his partner. "Someone asked me what is the best thing a father can do for his children, and I said, 'Love their mother.' Love her in a way that's filled with the reverence she deserves," says Hair.

Hair, who now works as a "spiritual director" helping men and women maintain an active relationship with God, believes that children are open to spiritual life. They love myth and ritual especially when it's connected to the changing seasons. But he's reluctant to emphasize specific religious practices for children, arguing that ritual, although often useful and necessary, becomes "empty and undone" if practiced for its own sake only and not connected to the source of things.

Says Hair, "When you become a father, a spiritual bond with your child takes place. You participate in this stunning mystery, this wonderful miracle of creation. If you're ever in doubt about it, go to where the love is. The love you feel for your child is divine love. For there's only one love in the universe—and that's God's love. When you practice love you are doing what God is."

Tip: Raising Spiritual Children in a Material World, *by Phil Catalfo (Berklee Books), gives practical pointers on how to bring spirituality into everyday family life.*

IS FAITH IMPORTANT IN A FAMILY?

Most men would probably agree that faith is an essential ingredient in a healthy family life, although they're unsure about what to do about it. Isn't that another one of those jobs that Mom is supposed to take care of? Dr. Ron Lee Davis is a pastor at Bear Creek Community Church and a leader in the national Promise Keepers movement. He has worked with families and youth organizations for more than twenty-five years. He believes not only that faith is very important in families, but that fathers must take a leadership role in the spiritual life of their family. He is the father of Rachel and Nathan.

Q: Why is spiritual faith important in a family?
Davis: I think it's essential to a family in a number of ways. Every family goes through struggles, whether they're marital struggles or a child is having problems with drugs or a member of the family is critically ill

or whatever. I've found that families with a deep faith in God tend to cope better in crises than families who do not have such faith.

Q: What spiritual role does a father play in a family?

Davis: He helps set the tone, he acts as leader. When difficulties come, he takes the attitude that with God's help, we're gonna get through this. As a Christian the way I say it is this: with God's help, and because of our strong faith in Jesus Christ, we're gonna get through this.

Q: What are the elements of a strong family?

Davis: I believe there are five traits that characterize a strong family. The first is that they intentionally spend significant time together. They challenge the myth that quality time alone is enough. Every dad knows that if there isn't a lot of quantity, you're not going to have the quality. In our family Monday nights were sacred. We took turns choosing what we'd do on Mondays—bowling or pee-wee golf or whatever. But we always spent them together as a family. One thing I was able to do, because of the flexibility of my schedule, was take my kids out to breakfast every week. I took Rachel out to breakfast on Tuesday mornings and Nathan on Thursdays. They called it the Tuesday and Thursday Morning Breakfast Club. We'd just get a bagel or an Egg McMuffin before school, it wasn't any big deal. But they will always remember that their dad cared enough to block that time into his schedule.

Q: All right. You must consciously spend time with your family. What else?

Davis: I believe a strong family expresses specific appreciations for each other. The dad specifically expresses appreciation for his wife in front of the kids, and affirms his kids as well. Not just saying to them you're a good person or a good guy, but telling them, "You really worked hard on that math test" or something else specific. You know, psychological studies have shown that 81 percent of what a child learns is through modeling—what dad actually does, his behavior, his actions. Eleven percent of what a child learns is through shared events—working together fixing a car or playing a game, say. Only 8 percent of what a child learns is through words—you know, telling them what to do and what not to do. But of course all the focus is on the words.

Q: What are other traits of a strong family?

Davis: Strong families have a deep spiritual commitment and, in my belief, a shared love for Jesus Christ. God is a natural part of their life as a family. Nathan and I pray together every day before he goes to

"Music is serious. Music is like a prayer, and you just don't put anything in a prayer, you say important things. You pray for people who are suffering."
—Singer Bob Marley, father of Stephen

"What kind of example are you giving your children if you're not taking care of your own soul?"
—Mark Gerzon, father and activist

school. One thing a dad can do if a kid comes home from school with a problem is pray with him. Let's just ask God to work this out and let's pray. Faith in God is not just a matter of observing rituals. There are religious families who go to church who are not very spiritual. God is not a central part of their daily life. I try to help my children look at events from a Christian perspective. What that means to me is suppose a kid they knew got arrested. Instead of just criticizing or judging him, we would want to have compassion for his family, and for the boy.

Q: What you seem to be saying is that spirituality is not just about believing in God. It's about how you treat your kids, too.
Davis: One dimension of spirituality is that you would never demean your kids, never emotionally abuse them. Because as a spiritual person, you know that they are created in the image of God. For that reason alone, I am going to value my children and esteem them. I will never abuse them and never call them names. That is true for your wife, too.

Q: I want to make sure that I cover all five elements of a strong family. A strong family intentionally spends time together, expresses specific affirmations and has a spiritual bond. What are the other two traits?
Davis: They solve problems in a crisis, and they have excellent communication skills. Many families can go along okay on the daily stuff, but when a person gets cancer or a kid develops a drug problem or something major occurs, that's when a lot of families break down. Whatever comes in life, Mom and Dad have to have tenacity. They have to say, "We're gonna get through this." That's where having faith in God comes in, as well as communication. This is really hard for a lot of dads. They need to talk to their pastor or a counselor or read books about it because they really need to be good at communicating.

Q: Give us some examples.
Davis: If you want your child to make her bed, deal with that specific issue instead of criticizing her in a general way. If an argument arises with your wife, try to be a resolver instead of trying to be the winner or trying to force your convictions on her. Dads have a tendency to want to fix things right away. A lot of times what Mom and the kids need is for you to listen. Put down the paper and listen to them. Though I know that's hard for men because we're so oriented toward solving problems.

Q: What is the Promise Keepers?
Davis: Promise Keepers is a national men's movement. It seeks to call men to take responsibility for their families by loving God. It asks them to keep their vows as fathers and husbands and nourish their families.

Invest time. Be there. Spend time with your families, not at work. Put God, family, and work in that order.

Q: Final words of advice for a new dad?

Davis: Love your children not because of their performance, but because they're your kids. Working with kids for over fifteen years, I've noticed that a lot of dads seem to say, "I'll love you if. . . ." It's conditional. Not enough dads are telling their kids, "I have high expectations for you, but that doesn't affect my love for you in any way." Give your children your love and give it to them unconditionally.

Contact: Promise Keepers, P.O. Box 103001, Denver, CO 30250; 303-964-7600. An eight-tape audio series, "Habits of Healthy Fathers," by Dr. Ron Lee Davis, is available through Bear Creek Community Church, P.O. Box 690989, Stockton, CA 95269; 209-951-9229.

WORSHIPPING WITH YOUR FAMILY

Why take your family to church or temple? Why worship at all? Lots of men wrestle with these questions. Wade Malloy is the minister of South Lake Presbyterian Church in Lake Norman, North Carolina. He says that some men are threatened by the idea of church because it indicates they may need help in running their lives. "Men like to feel they're doing a good job of controlling their lives," says Malloy, who operated a lucrative north Florida car dealership before giving it up to join the ministry. "But life is chaotic. By their presence in church they are saying, in effect, 'I need guidance.' Men won't stop to ask directions when they're driving. So they sometimes have trouble admitting they need guidance in other ways, too." Once you overcome this hurdle (and other possible misgivings), there are lots of reasons to bring your family to church. Malloy, the father of Steve, Sarah, and Anna, suggests a few of them here:

Going to Church May Be Different than What You Remember. "When I was a kid," says Malloy, "going to church was roughly akin to going to the dentist." But not all churches or synagogues are the same. Churches have different personalities. Congregations vary. Ministers, rabbis, and priests are not all alike. Their messages differ in style and theme. One church may not be right for you, but another one might be.

You May Meet People at Church Who Share Your Values. For many fathers (and mothers), so much of modern life seems inconsistent with the values they want their children to learn and live by. In church, you'll find people who want to live according to those same values.

> "When I was young, and my father could see that something was bothering me, he used to suggest that I might try saying a prayer. A prayer for strength, or a prayer for courage."
> —Writer Susan Cheever, daughter of John

> "Prayer is a sense of belonging. Belonging is the basic truth of our existence. We belong here. Life belongs here. When we say 'Thank you' we really are saying 'We belong together.'"
>
> —Elias Amidon and Elizabeth Roberts, parents of Jesse, Hanah, Aura, and Aquila

Nobody Will Ask You for Anything. All churches and temples, whatever their denomination, welcome new members, especially families. But you won't be rushed or pushed into joining anything. Just come for a Sunday (or Saturday), and check it out. You may like what you see and want to explore further. Malloy estimates that 75 percent of his congregation consists of families with children.

It's a Good Environment for Kids. Many churches and temples offer child care while their parents attend services. There are also religious studies classes for older children and many other youth programs. Malloy encourages parents to worship with their toddlers and babies. "I believe children need to learn to worship the same as they learn to eat at the table," he says. "And you know what that's like. It's pretty messy at first. But you don't shut children out. You bring them in."

Even Adults Can Learn a Few Things in Church. Not only do children learn when they go to church; their parents do, too. They read the Bible and think about God. Malloy believes that some people steer away from church because they know in their heart there's a difference between how they're leading their lives and how God wants them to lead their lives.

They Make a Joyful Noise on Sundays. Now that you are a parent, your chances to hear live music will be fewer and far between. On Sunday mornings at church they sing hymns and play toe-tapping music. Whitney Houston, Wynnona Judd, Aretha Franklin, and other famous names got their start singing with their families in church.

You Can Pray with Your Family. At South Lake Presbyterian, worshippers stand up and ask others in the congregation to pray with them. They pray for a loved one suffering from cancer, a father who's out of work and needs help finding a job, and many, many things having to do with children.

When You're in a Crisis, the Church Can Help. Much of Malloy's congregation has lived in the Charlotte area for less than five years. Their blood ties often reside elsewhere in the country. A good church can act as a kind of "an extended family," he says. It will act as a support network in a time of crisis. Church members will sit and pray with you if your kid is sick in the hospital. They will cook for you and bring you meals.

Worshipping Together Is One of the Ways to Show Your Child What It Means to Live a Moral Life. Every parent wants their child to grow up to be a decent, moral human being. But how do you do that? You do it, says Malloy, by leading an "intentional" life. Fathers need to take a leadership role in this area. Children will not learn what's important in life by chance; they must be taught. And the best way to teach them is by example.

Contact: South Lake Presbyterian Church is a member of the Presbyterian Church in America (PCA), 1852 Century Place, Suite 190, Atlanta, GA 30345. Call 404-320-3366 for a PCA church in your area.

FISHING AND THE SPIRITUAL LIFE

The happiest times for many fathers and children are when they are fishing together. A survey by the Lutheran Brotherhood showed that nearly four out of ten adult men said that fishing or some other outdoor activity was what they enjoyed doing most with their father.

Jim Grassi is the father of twin sons, Dan and Tom. He is also an outdoorsman, pastor, author of two books on Christian spiritual life, and founder of Let's Go Fishing Ministries, an interdenominational ministry that sees fishing as a means to encourage spiritual growth and family togetherness. He points out that eight of Christ's disciples were fishermen. In other sports, fathers can handily beat their young children. But in fishing, the child can sometimes pull off surprises.

"It's an even playing field," says Grassi. "When that hook goes in the water, the fish isn't concerned with whose rod it's attached to." Going to church can be awkward and intimidating for some men. Fishing is a way to share experiences with your children in a relaxed, outdoor environment. It gives you time to talk about things, the things that really count in life. "No time is ever wasted when you're spending time with your kid," says Grassi.

Contact: Let's Go Fishing Ministries, P.O. Box 434, Moraga, CA 94556; 510-376-8277. Its A Kid's Guide to Fishing *pamphlet gives practical pointers on catching, cleaning, and eating fish, as well as spiritual lessons about Christ. Another contact is the Christian Sportsmen's Fellowship International, a national organization of evangelical Christian fishermen and hunters; CSFI, P.O. Box 566547, Atlanta, GA 31156; 800-705-7892.*

TRANSMITTING VALUES TO
YOUR CHILDREN

One of a father's biggest jobs is in transmitting values to his children. But how do you do it? And what are the right values? Aryeh Hirschfield is a rabbi for P'nai Or of Portland, a Jewish congregation in

Portland, Oregon (503-248-4500). A leader in the international Jewish Renewal movement, he has done religious and spiritual work for more than twenty years. In this interview, Hirschfield talks about how to transmit values, specifically values of God and faith, to your children. He is the father of Aviel, Jonathan, and Isaiah.

Q: When we raise children, we want them to grow up with certain values. Let's talk about that. How do you transmit values to your children?

Hirschfield: That's a big question, that's a very big question. For our family, prayer is an important part of our lives. We celebrate shabbat every Friday evening, which is the start of the Jewish holy day. We do it every week. We come together as a family, and it centers us in the home and in our spiritual selves. We light candles, say a special blessing, and be together as a family. I have a five-year-old, Aviel, and sometimes he wants to be a part of this and sometimes he doesn't.

Q: What do you do when he doesn't want to be part of it?

Hirschfield [laughs]: Aviel can be contrary at times. Sometimes Beth, my wife, creates his own little table for him with his own candles. He appreciates that. She incorporates him into the ceremony and lets him participate. You've got to be a storyteller sometimes. Aviel really gets into the music. You have to address a child in simple terms that are still meaningful to adults. It's often a struggle.

Q: What's the point of these rituals? What do they have to do with transmitting values to children?

Hirschfield: Raising children is such a tricky thing. Kids have all this stuff coming at them. In order for them not to be lost, we try to give them a sense of place that's holy. Kids especially get swept away, you know, by the mall and TV and peer pressure. When they get to be teenagers, they're lost. In Judaism, we emphasize two central elements: home and community. Whenever I do a bar mitzvah or bat mitzvah, I always tell the young person that we have come here to acknowledge you, that you are an important person, that we care about you. You're part of a community, you're not just lost out there. There are all these things vying for kids' attention. When the family has some kind of faith at the center, there is something to bring them back home.

Q: A lot of people of my generation—now parents themselves—attacked religion when they were younger because of its empty rituals. But you're saying that ritual can be very meaningful.

Hirschfield: I have two grown sons, Jonathan and Isaiah. On Friday nights and into Saturday, they participated in making shabbat with me. And those were the times when we were really close. During shabbat, after the lighting of the candles and the blessing of the wine, there's a part of the ceremony in which you bless the children. You put your hands on their head and say a blessing. We did that when they were kids and it was very sweet. Well, once Jonathan said to me, "You gave us a blessing, now we want to give you one." So I knelt down to be at the same height as they were and he put his hand on my head and Isaiah put his hands on my shoulders, and Jonathan said, "I bless you that you should become a rabbi." This was at a time in my life when I was still debating whether or not to become a rabbi, and it just went through me like a lightning bolt. It was very powerful. It is the same in any religion. These rituals give us a place where we can share our feelings in an open and loving and holy way. They're a kind of channel for these feelings.

Q: You talk about openness. That's a constant question in my mind. How open should we be with our children?
Hirschfield: There are levels of truth that a kid can handle. When my grandfather died, I wasn't allowed to go to the cemetary to see him buried. I was ten years old. I felt terrible about not being able to go. Aviel's grandfather died last year. Aviel was not quite four. But he was very close to my father-in-law and so we took him to the cemetary. In Jewish custom, people drop handfuls of earth on the coffin, as a final goodbye. Aviel dropped a handful of dirt on his grandfather's coffin. On some level, he could be part of it and understand it. That's what I'd say: whenever it seems that it might be better to let kids know and be part of it, I'd let them. Whatever they can handle. Ever since his grandfather's death, Aviel talks about how Gramps is in the spirit world and how he misses him. I think we handled all this in a good way with him.

Q: What about doubt? Should you share your doubts with your children? Some men want to be a rock for their children, and they equate having doubts with weakness.
Hirschfield: I remember I had a talk with my son Jonathan before his bar mitzvah. It was very open, we shared a lot of things. He was thirteen. We talked about how his mother and I had split up, and how that must've caused him great pain. He talked to me about how hard it was to be the rabbi's son, and how everyone expected him to be such a good student and a role model. And I talked to him about how hard it was to be the rabbi. I shared how I had screwed up in my life, how I felt I lacked courage. And you know what, the more I shared how I screwed up, how I fell short, the closer we became. Be truthful. Don't hide stuff. When your kids get older they'll know that their parents had doubts. But they'll know, too, that you were truthful and real with them.

"It was Reverend Robeson who had the strongest influence on Paul's life. The reverend's unbending belief in the importance of personal integrity and achievement shaped Paul's character."
—From a biography of actor Paul Robeson, son of William Robeson, a Presbyterian minister

Q: Transmitting values to your children, then, is not a matter of just filling an empty vessel. You have to look at yourself and your own actions.

Hirschfield: Children will pick up on what you do. If you drop them off at religious school and then you go off and do something else during that time, they'll pick up on that. It's not so much what you tell your children. The question is, How real are you in your own spiritual life? Look to yourself. If you walk the life, you stand the chance that your children will get it, too. There's a Jewish phrase, "*heshbon hanefesh.*" It means an accounting of the soul. When you become a dad, you have to do your own soul accounting. If you really care what values you transmit to your children, you have to ask yourself: What are my values? What path am I on? Kids push your buttons all over the place. They make you angry sometimes. But instead of blaming them, I try to look at myself in the process. I try to see my shortcomings and learn. Even as you instruct a child on his or her path, you must always be in the process of finding your own path.

Contact: Jewish Renewal is a growing international movement within Judaism that incorporates music, artistic expression, personal prayer, and other expressive elements into traditional practices. It emphasizes spirituality and social action. Aleph, Alliance for Jewish Renewal, 7318 Germantown Avenue, Philadelphia, PA 19119; 215-247-9700.

SPORTS

Sports is one of the traditional ways that fathers participate in the lives of their children. They may not want to change diapers. They may think pushing a stroller makes them look silly. But they want their kids to play sports.

Men—that is, fathers—dominate the coaching ranks of virtually every sport. You see more and more women coaches, and God bless 'em. But if your child signs up to play youth soccer or Little League or CYO Basketball, his coach will likely be a man.

If you've been away from youth sports for a while, you'll notice that something has changed since the days when you were young. Now, girls play baseball, basketball, and soccer, in addition to gymnastics and swimming and other sports. The entry of girls into team sports is a boon not only for the girls themselves, but for guys like myself. It is no longer just the fathers of boys who get to have fun in youth sports, the fathers of daughters do, too.

I once did an interview with a man who coached high school boys' basketball and girls' volleyball. I asked him what was the difference between coaching girls and boys.

He said, "Well, you can yell at the boys, and, while they don't like it, they pretty much accept it. But," he added, "if you yell at a girl, she has an identity crisis for a week."

I have a daughter, so I'm real aware how sensitive girls can be. I just try to be as supportive as possible and not act like a big jerk, which many men are prone to do. Maybe these men had fathers and coaches who yelled at them all the time, so they think it's the way it's done. I don't think so. Sometimes you have to yell. Your players are off chasing butterflies or whatever, and you've got to get their atten-

"For three or four years, every day after school, my dad would teach us how to hit, throw, and run the bases. I grew up into a good baseball player because of him."

—Yankee centerfielder Bernie Williams Jr., son of Bernie Sr.

tion. But you can coach without becoming a drill sergeant. There are other ways to get through to your players and motivate them.

One thing I'll never understand is dads who coach and are tougher on their own kids than they are on other players. Their child does something great, and they're mute as stone. But when he screws up, they're all over him. Meanwhile they're very tolerant when another child messes up. I don't get it. I've also noticed that dads tend to be tougher on their sons than their daughters.

I coached my daughter's soccer team with Mike Maggart, the father of three boys whose youngest son Matt was on the team, too. They started playing when they were five. I still remember our first practice. We made them run to a hill a hundred yards away and back. After five years of my daughter wearing me out, I finally got a chance to wear her out. It was great.

One of the questions I puzzle over from time to time is, do you let your child win when you play against him? You're an adult. You're bigger and stronger, and when they're younger you can win every time if you want. But that has to be discouraging for the child. So I win some and lose some. Every athlete needs to know how to win and lose.

When you're a new dad with a new baby, you may start out thinking you're going to raise the next Tiger Woods or Lisa Leslie. When my daughter was a baby, I got down on the floor and rolled a ball to her. The first few times I did it, she basically blew me off. It discouraged me. I wanted her to play sports just as I did.

But over time, she got more and more interested in playing with the ball. Thinking about it now, I realize she probably wasn't interested so much in the ball, although it was fun to play with. Rather what she must have thought on some level was, "This ball is important to Daddy. Therefore there must be something to it."

And that is what's important. Your child may or may not grow up to be an athletic superstar, but she will benefit all her life from the time she spends playing sports with you. Assuming, of course, you cut her a break now and then.

BASKETBALL: THERE ARE ONLY BARRIERS OF THE MIND

Alan Taback is the basketball coach for Princeton Day School in Princeton, New Jersey. A hoops coach off and on since 1970, he is a member of the coaching staff at the renowned 5-Star Basketball Camp in Honesdale, Pennsylvania, where college recruiters watch high school stars play against one another. Michael Jordan and Patrick Ewing played at the camp when they were preps. Additionally Taback has coached professional basketball in Greece and for the minor league Trenton Flames, as well as running a summer basketball camp for local kids in the Princeton area. A lifetime of teaching basketball to youngsters has taught Taback that joy is an essential part of the game. He is the father of Jennifer.

Asked what he would say to a father who wants his son or daughter to play basketball, Taback replies, "Pay attention to your child's interest. Give him balls at a young age and let him play with them. Let the child get a feel for things. You don't immediately have to become a coach.

"If your child's interest continues, put up a hoop at the house," says Taback. "Get a hoop with an adjustable rim and lower the basket so your child has success. You want the rim low enough so your child can reach it and not become frustrated because he's shooting at something that's too high. Play a little with him, one-on-one games. Horse around. Don't worry about the score. Keep it light, so joy is a big part of it."

Taback has seen fathers who let their expectations for their children get the best of them. They become critical of their children and their children's coaches. They "muddy the waters," in Taback's words, interfering too much and creating problems. "You don't want it ever to be less than fun for your kid," says Taback. "You don't want him to do it just because he wants to please you. You want him to love it. You want him to gain an appreciation for the game."

Whatever the father's intentions, ultimately it is the child who will decide whether he's having fun, whether he wants to keep playing.

Basketball leagues begin in the elementary grades. There are recreational leagues, AAU leagues, private leagues, CYO leagues, and others. When children are young, Taback thinks their coach should be "an encouraging guy. You don't want your child to get disappointed and frustrated and turned off by someone's zealousness," he says.

"I just hate it when I see kids playing video football. I want to tell them, 'That's not the point.' If I had a son, I'd really want him playing Pop Warner football—with good coaching, of course—because I think football teaches some valuable lessons."

—49ers quarterback Steve Young, great-great-great-grandson of Brigham Young

"The best age to start a child in golf is the time he or she becomes interested in the game. I don't believe in parents forcing the game on kids. But if a little child is eager to go out and play with Dad or Mom, then it's time to start."

—Golf teacher Harvey Penick, father of Tinsley

That would be a shame because basketball and sports teach wonderful lessons for kids. "At its best basketball teaches sharing," Taback says. "Making a nice pass, setting a pick. You learn to be unselfish, you learn that it's fun to do something for someone else." He goes on, "and there are so many other things you learn when you play sports, not just basketball. Being part of a team. Learning to set goals and reach goals. You learn there are no barriers, only barriers of the mind. You learn mental discipline and how powerful a person's will is. You learn not to be thrown off course because you've suffered a disappointment. You learn that it's not a put-down to lose, that you are a winner every time you play and compete and enjoy it."

GOLF: TEACHING THE GAME FOR A LIFETIME

Marty Parkes is director of communications for the United States Golf Association. His dad taught him how to play golf. "I learned to play because my dad was a golfer and I caddied for him," he says. Now the father of Nicole and Trevor, he offers these ideas on how to raise a golfer of your own.

Get a Club That Fits Him. A child doesn't need to play with new clubs. He can play with those old clubs gathering cobwebs in the garage. Take one of the clubs to a pro shop. Get it regripped and cut down to your child's size. He doesn't need an entire bag; one or two clubs, fitted to his size, will do.

Play with Him. Play with him in the backyard with a net and plastic balls. Take him to a park or an athletic field and practice chipping. Play target practice games by chipping to different areas. Take him to a driving range and let him hit some balls with you. Even miniature golf can promote a feel for the game, especially putting.

Teach More than Just Stroke. There is more to golf than hitting a golf ball. It is a game of great tradition and history, centuries old. It is played outdoors in nature. Birds and wildlife frequently abound. An obsession on stroke and score (often fed by the dad's own obsession) can rob a child of the simple joy of playing.

Teach Sportsmanship and the Rules of the Game. Golf teaches self-control, respect for the rules, and honesty. There is a code of conduct for golfers. Count all your strokes. Replace your divots. Rake the bunker after using it. No talking during someone's backswing. There are rules that every golfer must abide by, including the young.

Bring Him onto the Course with You. A child ought to know at least some basics of golf before he ventures onto the course. As long as you're not holding anyone up behind you, drop a ball and let him hit from time to time. Don't force an interest. He'll tell you how much—or how little—he wants to be involved. Expose your child to golf and give him the opportunity to play. He will take it from there.

Play for the Long Haul. A child can start playing golf whenever he seems ready. Legend has it that Tiger Woods shot a forty-five on a nine-hole course at the age of three. But not every kid is a Tiger Woods. Golf is a lifetime activity, one of the few games that the entire family can play together. If your child is still playing the game when he's your age and older, then you've done your job right.

Contact: Call the USGA or your local golf course for more information. Golf pros offer free clinics for juniors from time to time. City park and recreation departments also hold golf clinics, or just do it yourself. USGA, P.O. Box 708, Far Hills, NJ 07931; 908-234-2300; www.usga.org.

GYMNASTICS: DEVELOPING COORDINATION, FLEXIBILITY, AND SELF-CONFIDENCE

All children are at heart gymnasts, whether or not they formally participate in the sport. They love to run and jump and climb and roll around and do cartwheels and headstands and test their balance by walking across a narrow ledge. These activities form the basis for gymnastics.

Toddlers at a very early age can participate in body movement classes with their moms and dads. They do forward and backward rolls, climb ropes, crawl through tunnels, throw balls into baskets, and other activities. They learn concepts such as up and down and in and out, while moving their body around. Gymboree and other groups hold these types of classes.

When your children get a little older, you may want to enroll them in a gymnastics school. Gymnastics classes begin as early as age three or four. Taught by a gymnastics teacher, they are more structured yet still similar to the earlier body movement classes.

USA Gymnastics is the governing body for gymnastics in the United States, overseeing men's gymnastics, women's gymnastics, and rhythmic gymnastics. Girls far outnumber boys in this country in terms of number of competitors. There are 51,000 female gymnasts, 9,800

"One day I waded out neck-deep on the slimy, smooth-stone bottom and slipped into a hole that was over my head. When I broke the surface and coughed in a breath of air, I was startled to find that my father wasn't running toward me. He just stood on the shore and laughed. And then I realized that I was swimming by myself."

—Charles Lindbergh, on how his father, C. A. Lindbergh, taught him how to swim as a boy

> "Love is given and respect earned. Convey to the child that you care, that you are there like an oak in support. Counsel only when needed. Laugh and cry with your child. Above all, be consistent."
>
> —Earl Woods, father of Tiger Woods

males, and 1,100 rhythmic gymnasts. Girls cannot compete in USA Gymnastics–sanctioned meets until the age of six, although many girls do not compete until age eight or older.

Gymnastics develops coordination, flexibility, strength, and self-confidence. It provides a sound physical basis for children to play other sports. A four-year-old, for example, cannot dribble or throw a ball very well, but she can develop fitness and agility. For girls, it is an excellent starting point for aerobics and cheerleading.

One fatherly concern about girls in gymnastics is: will they be judged on their looks and body image, instead of their ability? Gymnastics officials reply that all competitors are judged on their skills and how they perform on the floor, not their looks. Judging is subjective and a gymnast's presentation does matter, but it remains an athletic competition.

As to the concern that young girls will be asked to diet and lose weight in gymnastics, possibly weakening an already fragile sense of themselves and their bodies, a 1996 study showed that gymnastics proved superior in building bone density in females, ranking above swimming, bicycling, and other sports. Additionally, gymnasts act as positive role models for young girls. Look at the 1996 Olympic Gold Medal–winning U.S. Women's Team or Mary Lou Retton from the 1984 Games—all healthy, vibrant, and physically powerful young women whose confidence and self-esteem shine forth like the rays of the sun.

Source: Luan Peszek, Director of Public Relations, USA Gymnastics, Pan American Plaza, 201 South Capitol Avenue, Suite 300, Indianapolis, IN 46225; 317-237-5050; www.usa-gymnastics.org. To find the gymnastics school in your area, contact USA Gymnastics or look under "Gymnastics" in the yellow pages of the phone book.

HOCKEY: LET YOUR KID PLAY OTHER SPORTS TOO

Ken Johnson lives in Deerfield, Illinois. He's played and coached hockey virtually all of his thirty-seven years. A former Miami of Ohio star, he now runs "Summer on Ice" hockey camps in Highland Park and Winnetka. He also conducts hockey clinics and acts as director of hockey for the local Falcons Hockey Association with over eight hundred participants. But like other coaches interviewed for this book, he deplores the trend among parents of starting children in sports when they're five or even younger. He is the father of Annie and Kimberley.

"Kids who focus on a sport at five are often done playing it by the time they're eight," says Johnson. "There's no such thing as just playing in the backyard for kids anymore. Everything's structured and organized. But look at the kids who are forced into playing. Are they the best players? I don't think so.

"There's no correlation between the kids who are good at a sport at eight and the kids who are good when they're eighteen. Too many things happen in between. They get injured. They burn out. They don't grow as much as the other kids. Their grades are poor and they can't play."

When Wayne Gretzky was a youngster his father built an ice rink for him in their backyard. When asked about this, Johnson says, "First of all, Gretzky enjoyed playing. And somebody's backyard is different than a five- or seven-day-a-week structured program at a rink. Anyway, how many Wayne Gretzkys have there been in the last ten years? That's like saying your kid is going to grow up to be the CEO of General Motors. Now he may do it and if he does, good for him. But that's a lot of pressure to put on a kid."

Johnson continues, "A lot of parents around here sign their kid up for skating lessons at the rink. Then if the kid enjoys it, everything mushrooms from there. A lot of it depends on geography. Roller blading is getting big. My kids strap roller skates onto their tennies. I read somewhere that the two fastest growing sports are roller blading and hockey. Six or seven is about the time when most kids start playing league hockey. That's our Mighty Mites. Then comes Super Mites for eight- and nine-year-olds, and so on up the ladder."

Youth hockey has a reputation for being expensive. Ice time *is* costly, Johnson admits. But except for skates, which need to be replaced from year to year as a child's feet grows, his pads and other equipment can last two to three years. Johnson adds that hockey is safer than many other youth sports. The only part of a child's body not protected by pads or a helmet is the back of his legs.

Johnson thinks it's sad that hockey is steadily becoming a year-round sport. "There are so many complementary activities, especially for younger kids," he says. "Riding bikes builds the leg muscles. When I was a kid we had three ways to get somewhere: walk, run, or ride a bike. Now everybody hops in a car. I think swimming's great. A kid who swims uses muscles that will help him in hockey. Even baseball builds hand-eye coordination. These days we're developing terrific hockey players and soccer players and tennis players, but not terrific athletes. I think kids should play different sports when they're young. That's what's so fun about being a kid."

Contact: Summer on Ice at 847-940-7756.

> **"If he had a dollar for every hour he spent with me, my stepfather would be a millionaire. He loved me so much."**
>
> —Martina Navratilova, on her stepfather, Mirek Navratti (Martina seldom saw her birth dad, who committed suicide when she was nine)

LITTLE LEAGUE: STAY POSITIVE AND KEEP THE FOCUS ON FUN

When should your child start playing organized baseball? It depends on the child. Many children start with tee ball, which begins at age five. Tee ball is noncompetitive with a very low injury rate. Players hit off a batting tee. The score is not kept, and nobody makes an out. One team hits around while the other team plays the field. When all the players on one team have hit, they take the field and the other side bats.

The secret of success in baseball, as in life, lies in preparation. Fathers cannot push their children out onto the field and expect them to be an instant success. Help your children overcome their natural jitters by playing and practicing with them. Help them get the feel of throwing a baseball and swinging a bat before they are called upon to do it in a game.

When the child is very young, get down on the carpet and roll a soft ball back and forth with her. It's true for baseball and so many other sports. Everything starts with a ball.

There are many ways to promote an interest in baseball in your child. Take her to a game—a tee ball game at a field in town or a major league game. A good glove and the right equipment are a must. Both girls and boys can play Little League.

Little League organizers urge parents to get involved with their children. Don't just drop your kid off at the practice field and disappear for a couple of hours. Become a Little League coach or a volunteer. No experience or even knowledge of baseball is necessary. Parents can learn the game along with their children.

About 75 percent of all current major leaguers played Little League. But they represent only a miniscule fraction of the 40 to 50 million boys and girls who've played Little League in this country since its inception in 1939. Dads need to be realistic: is your child *really* the next Barry Bonds or Ken Griffey Jr.? Stay positive, and keep the focus on having fun.

Source: Lance Van Auken is media relations director for Little League Baseball and father of Lance Jr. and Sarah. To sign up to play Little League, contact the league in your area or Little League Baseball, P.O. Box 3485, Williamsport, PA 17701; 717-326-1921; www.littleleague.org. The national office will refer you to your local Little League. It also offers the Parents Guide to Little League, *a baseball rulebook, and other publications.*

FOOTBALL: LEARNING TO PLAY
—AND CHEERLEAD

Pop Warner Little Scholars, Inc., as it is officially known, is a football and cheerleading program for boys and girls ages five and up. Pop Warner is named after the legendary college football coach of the late 1800s and early 1900s. The league was founded in 1929 by Philadelphia businessman Joe Tomlin, who wanted to provide a healthy sporting outlet for Depression-era youngsters. Now, more than 275,000 kids in forty-one states play and cheerlead in Pop Warner. There are 5,000 tackle teams, 4,300 cheerleading squads, and about 800 flag teams.

Flag football begins at age five. Tackle begins at seven. The Mitey Mites is the first level of tackle football, played by seven-, eight-, and nine-year-olds between forty-five and eighty pounds. The next level is Junior Pee Wee, for eight-, nine-, and ten-year-olds from fifty-five to ninety pounds. The ages for the cheerleaders correspond to the players, so that cheerleading squads root for teams on the field. Girls dominate the cheerleading ranks, although some girls do play football and some boys cheerlead.

Some parents initially have qualms about their children playing a contact sport such as football. But Pop Warner officials say their sport is safer than many other sports played by youngsters. Kids in Pop Warner only play against other kids of a similar age and weight. Weigh-ins take place before every game. Every player always plays with a helmet and full tackle gear.

Pop Warner coaches are encouraged to play their players in different positions, not just putting the big kids on the line and the fast ones in the skill positions. Every player must play a minimum number of plays per game. No one just rides the bench.

A child must show proof of progress in school—i.e., a report card—in order to play Pop Warner. Participation in other school activities, such as student council, is encouraged. Pop Warner picks Academic All-Americans at the end of the season. One way to encourage an interest in football in your child is to watch games together on TV. Another way is to go outside and play with him. Manufacturers make smaller junior and youth footballs that allow a seven- or eight-year-old to grip and throw a ball to his father on a down-and-out pattern.

Source: Ron Dilatush is spokesman for Pop Warner and father of Ron, Clark, and Chelsea. Pop Warner Little Scholars, Inc., 586 Middletown Road, Suite C-100, Langhorne, PA 19047; 215-752-2691. Call national headquarters for the Pop Warner League in your area.

"Set goals for yourself, not just in football, but in the rest of your life as well. Even if you fall a little short on some of them, the time and effort put into reaching these goals will have made you a better person."

—Former football star Joe Theisman, father of Joe, Amy, and Patrick

"My dad never tells me I
did great. He may tell me
what I did good, but he'd
never say, 'My son did
great.' He thinks my head
would swell."

—Boxing champion Oscar De La
Hoya, son of Joel

SOCCER: DOES YOUR CHILD ENJOY PLAYING WITHOUT YOU?

Soccer may be the fastest growing youth sport in America. More than 2.3 million boys and girls play for the United States Youth Soccer Association. The sport got a big boost in 1994 when the United States hosted the World Cup in cities around the country. The U.S. Women's Team dominates international soccer. It won the first-ever World Cup in 1991 and the 1996 Olympic Games in Atlanta.

A child can learn soccer as soon as she can stand on her own and kick an object. Buy a nerf ball—a ball with a soft cover—and let the child play with it. Make it available to her. As dad, you can model how to play soccer. Instead of picking the ball up with your hands and throwing it, use your feet. Move the ball around with your feet, both left and right.

Let your children play, rather than forcing them to compete. Children can play soccer as early as age five. This may or may not be a good thing, depending on the child. The tendency among parents is to put their children into game settings and expect them to perform. They encourage these young players by yelling at them. And they yell these instructions during a game, when the child is least able to absorb them. The adult perspective (shared by many coaches) is focused on getting the children ready to play the next game. Coaches and parents mistakenly believe that children can learn the basics of the game while competing and being watched by critical—that is, adult—eyes.

Your goal as a father is to create an atmosphere where your child will enjoy playing the game without you. That is when true learning will take place. The first years that a child is exposed to soccer are crucial. Does she like it, or not? Is it fun to play, or is it more pressure and yelling? A child will answer these questions in her mind very early on.

Think of teaching soccer in terms of levels, much like a video game. Level one: keep things simple. Make sure the child succeeds. Level two: gradually introduce more activity, yet continue to ensure that the child succeeds. Level three and beyond: as the child grows and keeps succeeding, introduce more pressure, more activity, more competition. Always, feed your child a steady diet of success.

The best way for a child to learn soccer is with you—or Mom—playing one-on-one games in the backyard. Make sure there is a goal to attack and defend. But offer little resistance, so the child isn't discouraged. Give her as many ball touches as possible. Let the child score. If it's too simple for her, as she improves, allow her to score less. But, as an adult, never hog the ball. Never make fun of your child. Never make her look or feel silly. Sometimes dads will block the ball easily or keep it away from their child, as a joke. When your child quits and gives up playing in discouragement, you will find that it was no joke after all.

The United States Soccer Association can put you in contact with your state soccer association and local clubs and leagues. United States Youth Soccer Association, 899 Presidential Drive, Suite 117, Richardson, TX 75081; 800-476-2237.

Source: Karl Dewazien, father of Darcy, is the author of FUNdamental Soccer Guide *and five other instructional books on soccer. He is the coaching committee co-chairman of the U.S. Soccer Association. His books and a videotape series on teaching soccer to kids are available at Fun Soccer Enterprises, 2904 Fine Avenue, Clovis, CA 93612; 209-291-5798.*

SWIMMING: A GIFT FOR LIFE

Give your child the gift of swimming and you have given him something he can use all his life. A child needs to be water-safe by the age of five. He must know how to make it to the edge of the pool if he falls in.

Your child must be comfortable in the water and not afraid of it. When he gets older, other children will invite him to pool parties. As his father, you want him to go and not be excluded, but he needs to know how to swim.

Besides, swimming is great glorious fun. Share in the joys of water when you give your child a bath. Bathtime can be playtime (assuming you don't get too much water on the floor). Take baths with your child. Let his mind associate water with pleasure, but never leave your child alone in the bath.

Another way to introduce a child to the fun of water is to set up a little backyard pool that he can splash around in without fear or worry. The idea is to let a child first have fun in the water without putting pressure on him to learn to swim.

Parent–child swim classes, such as Water Babies, begin when the child is at least six months old. Parents (including many dads) get in the water with the child. Swimming lessons, where the child gets in by himself, begin at age three. Don't force an interest in swimming; some children are scared out of their wits by a too-abrupt introduction to water. One approach is to take your child to the pool and sit with him on the deck for a while. Let him watch the other children splashing around and going nuts. Let *him* want to get into the water.

Competitive swimming begins at age eight or younger, with competitors grouped by ages. The younger you start your child in swim-

> "The thing I've tried to do is keep focused on each game or play, not get caught up in looking too far ahead. That's what my dad told me. I talk to him about everything, which is kind of nice to be able to do."
>
> —Major league third-baseman Bill Mueller, son of Bill Sr.

> "A true baseball fan, Mutt named his first son after catcher Mickey Cochrane. And almost as soon as little Mickey could walk, Mutt had him swinging a bat at tennis balls."
>
> —From a biography of Mickey Mantle, son of Elvin "Mutt" Mantle

ming or any other sport, however, the greater the risk of burnout. Olympic-caliber swimmers may indeed have started when they were barely out of diapers, but of all the children who swim, how many actually make the Olympics? Many kids who are stars when they're under ten drop out by the time they're teenagers. Or if they're still competing, they've been surpassed by other athletes their age. Sometimes letting your child sit out a year is the best thing you can do for him.

Another tip: if your child doesn't want to join the swim team, don't say to him, "Okay, if you won't swim, then you can play Little League." That's a surefire way to make your child hate baseball, too, because he sees your actions as punitive and rebels.

Competitive swimming is an intense year-round sport. Competitive swimmers work out every day with meets on the weekend. When they get older, they swim twice a day. Because they're in the pool so much together, swimmers develop great camaraderie with one another. Many parents like swimming precisely because it *is* daily; it provides their children with a routine and teaches discipline.

One possibility to consider is a recreational swim league or pool team. Enter your child as a nine- or ten-year-old and let him swim for a season during the late spring and summer. Nothing will improve his stroke faster than competing against other swimmers his age. He does not have to be a star, and he still can play other sports the rest of the year. That one season of swimming will give him a solid base as he grows older. Who knows, maybe later he'll join the high school team.

To evaluate a good swimming coach—or any other type of coach, for that matter—watch how he or she handles the average ability kids. Anyone can coach the gifted ones; they almost don't need coaching. But the best coaches will pay attention to the swimmers in the middle of the pack or below. They're the core of a program. They tend to work harder and improve more dramatically, often beating the kids who supposedly have more "talent" but who haven't put in as much time in the pool.

Source: Mark Croghan, father of Trevor, Troy, and Tristen and a former high school All-American swimmer, has coached competitive swimming at all levels, including college. He is now an elementary school principal. U.S. Swimming is the governing body for competitive swimming in this country. Contact them at One Olympic Plaza, Colorado Springs, CO 80909, or call 719-578-4578 for referral to the local swim club in your area.

TENNIS: PLAYING WITHOUT ADULT RESPONSIBLITIES AND PRESSURES

Tennis is the sport of phenoms. Girls especially can achieve quick success at a relatively young age. Chris Evert, Martina Navratilova, Steffi Graf, and now Martina Hingis all rose to fame while only teenagers.

Kids can start playing tennis at four years or even younger. Jimmy Connors started when he was three. Instructional classes are held for youngsters between the ages of four and eight. Most junior tennis programs begin at age eight.

The emphasis in tennis for youngsters should be on having fun. Go at the pace of the child, not the adult. If the child succeeds and can handle new challenges, your job as a parent is to help her. Don't push your own agenda or compete vicariously through your child; that's when trouble starts.

Some young tennis phenoms never got a chance to be children. They showed early prowess, and adults loaded pressures and responsibilities onto their still developing psyches. Girls under the age of sixteen can now enter only a certain number of tournaments based on their age. Many youth tennis programs, such as USTA/National Junior Tennis League and USTA Junior Team Tennis, sponsor team play, much like the Davis Cup and Fed Cup. In ordinary match tennis, the spotlight is on the individual. But in team tennis, pressures are diffused. A player still plays her match individually but participates as a member of the team. If she loses her match, it's not the end of the world; she doesn't walk off a loser. She can still root for her teammates and participate in the fun and excitement of the game.

Some fathers want their children to be tennis stars, but all they do is sign them up for lessons and then shout at them while they're playing in a match. A better tactic is to make tennis a family activity. Play with your child. Roll a ball back and forth to her, then play bounce and catch. Equipment is available for young kids—junior racquets, bigger than usual balls, foam tennis balls, mini courts, and modified nets that allow toddlers to hit winners over onto your side.

The United States Tennis Associaton, the governing body for tennis in this country, has many programs to teach youngsters to play tennis. Play Tennis America for Kids is a program designed to teach tennis quickly and inexpensively. Children have short attention spans and when they can't succeed in something right away, they often move on to the next activity. The USTA also offers the National Junior Tennis

"We just tried to let him grow up. We didn't shove track in his face. We didn't put pressure on him to be great."

—Bill Lewis, father of multiple Olympic gold-medal winner Carl Lewis

League for advanced beginners. Founded by tennis legend Arthur Ashe, it teaches children tennis in a low-key team format.

Usta Junior Team Tennis is comparable to Little League baseball. Boys and girls compete in a coed format. Local winners play in the AAU Junior Olympics.

Source: Bill Leong is recreation coordinator for the United States Tennis Association and father of David. USTA, 70 Red Oak Lane, White Plains, NY 10604; 914-696-7000; www.usta.com. Contact the USTA for information on programs in your regional section. Tennis clubs and city park and recreation programs also offer youth tennis classes.

SUPPORTING MOM

Jennifer went into labor at 1:00 A.M. on a Sunday. I was asleep. When I got up to go to the bathroom, I saw a light on in the living room and found Jennifer on the couch. She looked ill. "Is this it?" I asked. She nodded.

After a few hours things seemed to speed up. This was Jennifer's first child but she appeared ready to give birth any second. I tried to stay cool. My first daughter was a cesarean baby and I had never really gone through any of this before. I called the hospital and described Jennifer's condition. They said they'd pull her chart and told us to come down.

One minor complication: Annie was sound asleep in the next room. It was about five in the morning, still dark outside. I called our day-care person and woke her up. Fortunately we had discussed this possibility ahead of time. "Sure," Lori said, "bring her up."

I woke Annie up and bundled her into the car. She was a real trooper, groggily wishing us both luck. I drove up to Lori's and back in five minutes. By the time I got home, Jennifer's contractions had slowed to a near stop.

When you go to the birth classes, they always tell you, "Wait before you go to the hospital if it's your first time." Well, they're right. Just the thought of going to the hospital seemed to make Jennifer tense and put the brakes on everything. I called the hospital and told them we weren't coming in after all. They said, "Fine. We'll be here when you're ready."

Jennifer remained pretty miserable throughout the morning. She kept having contractions but not making much progress. At 1:00 P.M. the 49ers game came on. I felt kind of guilty because I got caught up in it and neglected my coaching duties. Luckily Jennifer is an understanding person and didn't throw anything at me.

"Right from the start, I understood that I was, in some fundamental way, a bystander. Marypat had an interaction with the baby growing inside her that was physically, chemically, and intuitively profound."
—Writer Alan Kesselheim, husband of Marypat and father of Eli, Sawyer, and Ruby

At about 6:00 P.M., things got moving again. The contractions became more intense and closer together. No false alarm this time. I walked Jennifer to the car, loaded up our stuff, and off we went.

When we got to the hospital, Jennifer was fully effaced and dilated to about five centimeters. A woman must be dilated to ten in order to give birth. We were halfway there. One of the nurses said, "You'll have your baby before I get off my shift."

It didn't happen. When the nurses changed shifts at 11:00 P.M. we still didn't have a baby, though Jennifer was working hard and in plenty of pain. It was frustrating.

At midnight, they gave Jennifer something to help her sleep, and I nodded off on a bed in the room. At about 2:30 A.M. Monday—more than twenty-four hours after she started having contractions—her bag of waters broke. Jennifer screamed in pain, and I jolted awake.

At 7:00 A.M. the morning shift came on. These nurses had lots of energy. They were determined to help us make it through and deliver our baby. I ate breakfast and psyched up for the final stretch drive. Jennifer couldn't think about food. We were both exhausted. Little did we know we had hours of work ahead of us.

In the movies, pushing lasts about thirty seconds. In real life, it can last an hour or more. Jennifer pushed and pushed and pushed, and finally, a little head appeared. I glanced up at the clock. It was a little after 1:00 P.M. when our daughter was born, a seven-pound, thirteen-ounce heartbreakingly beautiful girl whom we named Leah. Total number of hours Jennifer was in labor: thirty-six.

In looking back on this incredibly intense experience, I am not entirely proud of myself. I hung in there all the way, that's not what I mean. I stayed on my feet and helped every way I could. But I'd still describe my actions as selfish.

Jennifer's sister Cynthia had wanted to participate in the birth. She showed up at the hospital that night, hoping to get involved in some way. But I wanted it to be just Jennifer and me. I didn't want to share the experience with her sister or anyone else.

I was wrong. Cynthia might have made a difference. She could have given massages or just spelled me for a while. She might have made her sister feel better, and what's wrong with that anyhow?

What I am struggling to say is that sometimes the best thing you can do as a father is step back—put your ego on hold, not be in control all the time. Put yourself and your desires second (or third). To love is to serve. Show your partner love and support, and serve her.

TAKING CARE OF MOM
DURING PREGNANCY

Everyone tells you how your life changes when you have a baby. Well, here's one change: your schedule is no longer your own. You may run the show and set the rules at work, but not at home—not anymore. A subtle but fundamental shift has occurred. Now your world runs according to baby's clock, and the shift begins even before the birth. Your focus changes, shifting from yourself to your pregnant partner, who is carrying your most precious cargo.

In this section, author Beth Wilson Saavedra talks about how to cope with the changes in your partner and in your life during pregnancy, and how a man can support his partner (and growing baby) during this most sensitive of times.

Zero to Three Months

It's as simple—or as complicated—as this: when you support your partner at this time, you support your child. Pull back from your partner and you pull back from your child. But why pull back? Listen to her. Try to see things from her perspective and understand what she's going through. Morning sickness strikes in the first three months. What's morning sickness like? Wilson Saavedra uses a description her father gave her about being seasick: "First you feel like you're going to die, and then you wish you would."

In the throes of morning sickness, your partner feels rotten and tired much of the time. Her body has begun to change. These changes create excitement as well as anxiety. She's more emotional—in fact, expect a rollercoaster ride of emotions. She may even break into tears because she can't fit into her jeans.

Whether she can tell you or not, your partner needs you now more than ever. Wilson Saavedra says not to argue with her about her feelings. She feels what she feels. Draw on as much patience as you can muster. She may need to turn to you after other women tell her their childbirth horror stories. She may have strange dreams about giving birth to animals or deformed creatures (very common, actually). Realize that it's a time when she's less willing to engage in small talk; all her energies and attention are being drawn inward.

Husbands sometimes feel "sympathy pains" similar to what their partner is experiencing. These may include backaches, exhaustion, and even nausea. These pains are a signal saying, Hey, pregnancy is happening to you, too. Wilson Saavedra believes that having a child for a

> "Women want full partners, not just someone to pick up a sock now and then. Raising a child is an overwhelming task. Women can feel pretty hostile at the end of the day if you want something from them but you won't help them."
>
> —Authors Adele Faber and Elaine Mazlish, interviewed for this book

"Our whole family was musical. Poppa could play the violin. Momma sang. We had a family orchestra going there on the front porch at night after dinner."

—Babe Didrickson Zaharias, the daughter of Hannah and Ole Didrickson, who contributed to the family orchestra by playing the harmonica and who grew up to become an Olympic gold-medal winner and one of the greatest athletes of all time

man represents a shift away from what she calls "uni-focus": focusing solely on work and career. Now a man must grapple with the less familiar realm of emotions and the needs of mothers and children. Accept that these are big events, and work through them.

One of the early hurdles a man faces when his partner becomes pregnant is making it all seem "real." After all, the child is growing in *her* body, not his. But once he comes to grips with the emotional truth of fatherhood—that it's his child inside the womb, and that he is responsible for it—he can more readily accept the changes that are coming in his life.

Go to the ultrasound exam and Ob-Gyn appointments. At the ultrasound exam, you hear the heartbeat for the first time and see an image of your baby. The baby's heartbeat is faster than an adult's and clearly not the mother's. (Please see the following two articles for more on the ultrasound.) You may also want to go with your partner to her Ob-Gyn appointments if you're concerned about what's going on or need more information. If that's not possible, write down questions for the doctor beforehand so your partner doesn't forget to ask them when she's at the appointment.

Another way to make it more real is to look at a book together. Expectant dads do not tend to read volumes upon volumes about pregnancy, as expectant moms do. But photography books such as *A Child Is Born,* by Lennart Nilsson (New York: Dell Publishing) chart the development of the child in the womb as well as provide a very readable text.

Three to Six Months

Your partner's attitude usually lightens and improves in the second trimester. Morning sickness lifts, and she feels better physically. She's showing more, and so people realize that she is indeed pregnant and not just putting on weight.

Usually you can feel the baby kick between four and six months. This is truly a wonderful thing; it's as if your child is sending you a message from another world. See this as an opportunity for intimacy with your partner. But don't feel bad if you don't share the same enthusiasm as she does to feel the baby kick over and over again.

Though you can't see your child, she's there. Talk to her. Studies have shown that an unborn child responds to sounds and voices in the later stages of pregnancy; many parents play soothing music and read aloud together.

Often with a baby's first kicks comes a desire to start making the nest. Your partner may want to prepare the baby's room and buy baby clothes. Do your part by stripping wallpaper, painting, and, later, assembling the crib and helping babyproof the house.

It may feel like you're being asked to take on more than you ever have before. In fact, you are. Both of you are. Your partner is carrying the baby while probably still maintaining a full-time job. You're cooking more, cleaning, doing the laundry—all this, in addition to your regular chores and possibly working longer hours to save money. This doesn't let up when the baby comes; it intensifies. All things considered, though, the burden of having a baby becomes a little easier when both parents pitch in and act as a team.

Six to Nine Months

Coming down the homestretch. By months eight and nine, the baby is taking on heft and so is your partner. Her body will seem large and unwieldy to her. She may grow out of her shoes. None of her clothes fit, and she's sick of wearing the same old maternity things. By the end of her term she'll be more than ready to give birth.

Everything revolves around a mother's needs during pregnancy. But this is a dicey time for you, too. You are in the midst of a major life passage. Your body isn't changing but your world is. You may feel anxious about a loss of control. You may look uneasily into the future and think, Can we afford another mouth to feed? Your sexual relationship with your partner may have changed—and possibly not for the better.

Why not talk to your partner about it? You won't feel as connected to her if you can't talk to her. Ask for some time to talk about *your* stuff. Say to her, "We talk about your experience a lot. I want to talk about mine for a minute." You may need to ask for this time because she will probably be caught up in her world and less tuned to yours.

Sex during pregnancy can be wonderful. It's often freer and more spontaneous because you no longer have to worry about birth control. You can be in the same positions as before, at least in the beginning. Be on top, or let your partner be on top, until the baby's growing presence becomes impossible to ignore. By the final trimester your partner will clearly and definitely look like a . . . *mother.* Her belly will be rounded and full, and her nipples will have changed. She may even be able to express milk from her breasts. Some men take these changes in stride; others may associate motherhood in their mind with baking meat loaf and attending PTA meetings. But many couples report satisfying sex into the final weeks of pregnancy, although their choice of positions may be limited to "spooning" with the woman on her side in bed and the man snuggling behind her.

"When I look back on it, I really have to tip my hat to my mom. She took me to all of my games, congratulated me if I did well, consoled me if I didn't."

—Future Hall of Fame ballplayer Cal Ripken Jr., son of Vi Ripken, and Cal Sr.

Think of the final months of pregnancy as your last chance to be alone with your partner, *sans infant*. Take advantage of it. Touch and explore her body. Get naked together. Turn off the phone and take your time. Tickle her arm, rub her stomach. Take her voluptuous body in through your hands and eyes. Let her press her belly up against your back so you can feel the baby kick. By staying in tune with the amazing changes that occur in a woman's body during pregnancy, you will feel less detached and more like the father you are. "Wow! What a trip! There really is a baby growing in here!"

Source: Beth Wilson Saavedra is the author of Restoring Balance to a Mother's Busy Life *(Contemporary Books) and other books on parenting. She conducts couples workshops and creativity workshops for women and new mothers based on* Restoring Balance to a Mother's Busy Life. *Contact her at P.O. Box 1131, Belmont, CA 94002; 415-654-1202.*

THE ULTRASOUND EXAM: IS IT A BOY . . . OR A GIRL?

For many men (and women), the ultrasound examination is when it (the pregnancy, the baby, even parenthood) becomes *real* for the first time. Yes, we are having a baby! Yes, I am going to be a father!

An ultrasound or sonogram is routinely performed in the first trimester, allowing physicians to closely predict the mom's due date. Another ultrasound usually takes place at about twenty weeks. In the case of twins or high-risk situations, more ultrasound exams may be required as the pregnancy develops.

First-time parents view their first ultrasound with giddy expectation. They can see, with their very own eyes, an image of their child. It is a profound moment. They often cry, laugh, and touch and caress each other. Their dreams are coming true.

In addition to seeing their baby and hearing the heartbeat, many couples want to know the sex of their child. Some couples choose not to be told, but most can't wait to hear the news: Is it a boy or a girl?

For some fathers, though, it's a moment of mixed emotions. They turn away in disappointment or walk away from the fuzzy image on the screen and sit down. Their enthusiasm drops; their attention strays elsewhere. They pick up a magazine and leaf through the pages.

What happened? What caused the man to sulk like a child? Only the news that he was having a daughter, not a son—a girl, not a boy.

If you feel let down, it may be a good idea to remember how boys and girls are made: a man's sperm fertilizes the woman's ovum. Each parent provides twenty-three chromosomes that determine the genetic makeup of the child. Twenty-two pairs of chromosomes are exactly alike. The twenty-third pair determines sex. A female's twenty-third chromosome is XX, a male's is XY. When an X sperm fertilizes the X egg, it forms an XX, or female. When a Y sperm fertilizes the X egg, it forms an XY, or male.

It is a random act, an act of fate—a matter of Xs and Ys. No one controls or decides the sex of a child. It's nobody's "fault." Some men blame women. They think it's a sign of virility to have a boy. They think having boys or girls is a trait that runs in families. It's not true.

You may understand this intellectually, but your emotions have a truth of their own. You may, in fact, be disappointed that you're having a girl. Or if you have boys and want a girl, you may be disappointed about having a boy. Whatever is going through your mind at that moment, the woman you love is lying there on the table, part of her body and all of her soul exposed to you. She's searching your face for a reaction. It's your baby, too. How are you going to respond?

Source: Robin Cunningham, an ultrasound technologist at a medical group, has conducted ultrasounds for thousands of couples in nearly twenty years in her profession. She also contributed to the following section.

MORE ABOUT THE ULTRASOUND AND HOW YOU CAN HELP

There is no more vulnerable time for a woman than pregnancy. She has fears about her baby, about herself, about her relationship with you. She feels ugly and fat and, at times, despite everything you may do to show her otherwise, unloved. Even she makes jokes comparing herself to the side of a barn or calling herself "an old cow." (Word of advice: never, ever share in those jokes. Let her make them if she wants to, but you tell her how beautiful she looks.) Pregnancy is like walking along the edge of a cliff for a woman. It's very powerful and exciting but scary, too.

How can a man show support for his partner at this time? Compliment her on her appearance, for one. Show affection to her. Anticipate her needs. Ask what you can do for her, and give her time to rest. Take over more of the cooking and the household chores. Help out with the older children if there are any.

What you do matters. Be there. Participate fully and willingly. Show your partner that the two of you are in this together. Many

"When I was just a little boy, I always wanted my momma to smile on me."

—Former heavyweight champion Joe Louis, son of Lillie Reese Barrow

"The one thing that's changed is my view of women. Going through my wife's pregnancy had a really powerful effect on me."

—The Artist Formerly Known as Prince

women have vivid dreams the night before an ultrasound; it's an emotional experience. An amniocentesis can feel much riskier. In an amniocentesis, the doctor inserts a needle into the woman's uterus to sample a small amount of amniotic fluid; it's a test for possible birth defects. The procedure carries a small risk to the baby but a large amount of anxiety for the mother. Some cry as it is being done. Not tears of pain, but rather out of worry and fear.

Give your partner a hand to hold. Yes she can drive to the appointment, but she really doesn't want to go alone. The old days when nurses and doctors treated men like unwanted strangers are long gone; your presence is welcome. In fact, if your partner's willing, invite the grandparents and friends to the ultrasound. Include the extended family and let them share the excitement. Some medical offices make videos of the fetus; you will certainly get a black and white picture, your first baby picture. And if you do have a boy, you can make jokes about the size of his penis, commenting how "huge" it is or asking the technician to measure it for you. Just realize that jokes of this nature are about as stale as week-old bread and that gazillions of other dads have made similarly dopey comments before you.

AFTER THE BABY COMES HOME

A newborn baby places huge demands on both Mom and Dad. It's no longer an abstraction; now it's very real. This is a time of high anxiety, intense joy, and not nearly enough sleep.

One thing to remember: your partner is a novice, too. On a first-born, you're both learning on the job, probably with less support than your parents received when they were new at the game. Past generations of parents could often call on their parents, grandparents, uncles, and aunts who lived nearby. That's not as true anymore. Nowadays, both men and women work. Fewer people are home during the day, so it's harder to get immediate assistance from friends. Here are some tips on making the transition easier:

- *Hang in there*. Coping with a newborn—indeed, raising a child at any age—is a challenge. There's a steep learning curve. You will feel frustrated and inadequate at times. You may feel like giving up. But both your partner and your baby need you.

- *Don't let your partner always rescue you*. When she's on the phone with a girlfriend and that familiar wail sounds from the next room, first try to comfort the baby yourself. When you've never had kids, holding a baby is like holding an antique vase. You feel like it'll break if you touch it. Once you have your own child, you realize a baby is not as fragile as all that.

- *Change diapers and help out around the house*. Many men take great pride in the speed and skill in which they change diapers. Anything you can do to help out—laundry, cooking, grocery shopping, running errands—will be appreciated.

- *Put yourself in your wife's place*. Your job as a father is to nurture the baby and to support your partner as she nurtures the baby. A woman needs plenty of liquids when she breast-feeds. Would she like something cold to drink? Ask your partner for a list of things that she needs done. When you've checked off everything on the list, take a break.

- *Support your partner in her breast-feeding*. Breast-feeding is healthier for the baby, but many women experience problems in getting started, and extreme soreness once they do. Their nipples can be rubbed so raw that the simple act of putting on a blouse will send them up a wall.

- *Go easy on sex*. What with baby always tugging at her breasts, your partner may not be in an amorous mood. Ask ahead of time. Vaginal dryness is also common among women after giving birth. It may be painful for her to have intercourse for months afterwards.

- *Don't be a jerk about her weight*. Sure, you want her to take the weight off. She wants to take it off herself. But give her a chance. Think about it: you're not going to get the result you want by telling her she's fat and that she needs to lose weight. That will only hurt her feelings and alienate her.

- *Give each other breaks*. Take the baby for a couple of hours on the weekend so your partner can get out of the house. Then she can take the baby so you can exercise or enjoy a game on TV.

- *Get involved in finding a baby-sitter or child care*. Your partner will be most anxious about leaving the baby in the first year. That's also when the baby will be the clingiest. Understand this when you look for a baby-sitter. Don't blow off your partner's concerns by telling her to quit worrying. She may never want to go out if she feels like she's the only one who cares about who you're leaving the baby with, and she may resent you for not taking her concerns seriously.

- *Keep talking*. Your partner may be depressed about her weight or anxious about going back to work and leaving the baby. Many

> "As far back as he could remember, the Sandburgs had gathered around the kitchen table to listen to his mother's storytelling. . . . After the storytelling August Sandburg would take up his accordion and play a Swedish folk song."
>
> —From a biography of the poet Carl Sandburg, son of Clara and August Sandburg

women experience "the baby blues" or postpartum depression. She may simply need to vent her feelings. Listen, if you can, without thinking that you have to provide solutions or fix what's wrong. Your partner will probably feel better just being able to talk and that will be solution enough. Don't forget to give her reassuring touches of affection, either. Let her know she's beautiful; it's possible, to be overweight *and* beautiful. Cherub dumplings are great to hug, too.

Source: Beth Wilson Saavedra, author of Meditations for New Mothers, Meditations for Mothers of Toddlers, *and other books on parenting.*

TELEVISION

et's face it: television is a drug. Need proof? Put a can't-sit-still, always wiggling, always-getting-into-something, can't-leave-her-alone-for-one-minute toddler in front of the TV and watch what happens.

What happens is nothing. She goes practically comatose. Her eyeballs glaze over. She sits as if in a drug-induced trance. She is hypnotized, and she will sit like that for hours.

Every parent soon discovers the value of TV—"the one-eyed baby-sitter," as it's called. Plunk your child in front of that cathode tube cyclops, slip in a video or flip on a Bugs Bunny cartoon, and finally you can have a few minutes to yourself.

And what's the harm in that? You need a break from your child—and vice versa—from time to time. You may want to have an uninterrupted adult conversation with your spouse or perhaps even sneak off into the bedroom for other adult activities. TV will occupy your child's attention for a while and let you have that time.

Still, based on my experience, television resembles a Trojan horse. It seems like a gift at first, but over time you realize the enemy is lurking within. Even so-called quality television, such as Sesame Street, offers only passive learning; the child is still sitting, often for hours at a time, in front of an electronic box—entertained but largely unengaged. Furthermore, much of what is on TV is not even close to the quality of Sesame Street. It's mindless drivel (or worse) that frequently conveys messages, images, and values that are antithetical to what you are trying to teach as parents.

I used to have a more relaxed attitude about TV, but my views have changed over the years as Annie has gotten older. We have rules in our house about TV. It's never on during dinner, nor can Annie watch it after dinner, unless it's a special occasion or we're watching a movie together on the weekend. We've just recently instituted a new rule restricting her to thirty minutes a day on weekdays. As long as I draw breath, she will never have a TV in her bedroom.

Nevertheless, it feels like a losing battle. Annie's a great kid, but sometimes she comes home and immediately plops down in front of the TV. Whenever she's bored or looking for a way to kill time, she asks to flip on the tube. It's nearly impossible to monitor everything she watches. There have been power struggles over what she can watch and for how long, and we've been thinking lately about maybe junking the TV altogether (but keeping the monitor to watch movies).

Now you may be a new or expectant father and these kinds of issues may seem as far away as Pluto. You may be just trying to get through the night, and I sympathize. Consider all this food for thought. You've got time to figure it all out. But take it from me: the habits that get started early with children are sometimes hard to break later on.

HOW TO TAKE CONTROL OF YOUR TV

Carleton Kendrick is a family therapist with a master's degree in education from Harvard. Some years ago, he served as program director for Action for Children's Television, which lobbied Washington for improvements in children's television programming. Now, in addition to his therapy practice, he acts as consultant for the Family Education Company in Boston where he answers questions from parents on television, computers, and many other family issues. Kendrick, father of Jason and Alisa, doesn't regard TV as "the enemy," although he does think it should be treated it as a controlled substance. Here, he gives some pointers on how to take control of your television.

Be Aware of How Much the TV Is On. In some homes (and child-care situations), the TV is on all the time, functioning as background noise. As children get older, turning on the TV becomes almost an involuntary response. "They walk into a room and turn the TV on just like they're turning on the lights," says Kendrick. Watching TV is not per se a problem; but watching it too much can be. Studies have shown that children are basically putting in a work week—forty hours or more—in front of the television.

Once You Become Conscious of How Much the TV Is On, Take Responsibility for It. One of the problems with TV is all the things children are *not* doing when they're watching it. They're not reading (or being read to). They're not playing. They're not exercising their limbs or brain cells. Most parents are aware of this, consciously using the TV as a free baby-sitter to give themselves a break. But young children especially do not have the cognitive ability to interpret the images they're seeing, says Kendrick. They cannot separate the reality of man–woman relationships from the fantasy of TV soap operas. The unrelenting cascade of violent imagery is another worry. Kendrick cites a landmark University of Michigan study that followed groups of young people over a period of years, observing their TV-watching habits when they were eight years old and then later as teenagers and young adults. The children who watched the most TV were more likely to get into trouble as teenagers. Ten years later these same people were more likely to be convicted of serious crimes and more inclined to inflict violent punishment on their own children. "There are long-term, lasting effects on character and development from watching television," says Kendrick.

Cast a Critical Eye at So-Called Quality Programming. Some parents tell Kendrick that they don't worry about violence on television because they only let their child watch nonviolent, politically correct children's videos. "That's not the operative issue," he says. "The operative issue is their child is still sitting in front of the TV for three hours doing nothing." Parents also sing the praises of *Sesame Street* and other so-called quality programming on the Discovery Channel and Disney Channel. Kendrick attended Harvard when *Sesame Street* was being developed, and, while he still enjoys parts of the show, he's not sold on it. "Children are cued into short attention spans," he says. "There are all these fast-paced images under the guise of teaching numbers or letters. It's far too frenetic a pace for children."

Watch What Your Children Watch. When children are very young, this is easier to do. You may sit and watch *Sesame Street* with them (or at least a portion of it). But as children get older and watch more TV, this becomes harder. It may be a sign that they're watching too much TV if you can't keep up with their viewing habits.

Discuss the Programs with Your Child. Kendrick says that TV can be turned into a beneficial learning experience if it serves as a grounds for discussion with your child. Have a running discussion about the show you're watching or talk about it during commercial breaks.

"At night in our house, it's reading time. We don't allow the TV."

—Comedian Jeff Foxworthy, father and star of his own TV show

"I grew up listening to arias the way kids now listen to television commercials. It was a matter of repetition. When I hummed my favorite tune, it was an aria."

—Opera legend Beverly Sills, daughter of Morris Silverman

Talk Back to Your TV. Commercials are good for this. After watching some blatant huckster appeal, you might say to your child, "A candy bar so big it will feed six people? You know they're not that big. Are they trying to con us or what?" thus encouraging discussion with the idea that what's on the tube can be challenged.

Encourage Them to Watch Specific Programs. One of the problems with TV is that once it's on, it stays on. Children flip it on (or their parents set them in front of it) and they watch show after show after show for hours at a time. Encourage selectivity. If your children have a specific program they want to watch, fine. But turn it off after it's over. "If kids say, 'I want to watch more.' I don't go for that," says Kendrick. "Then it's just more."

Don't See Computers as a Cure-All Substitute. Parents sometimes see computers as a "healthy" substitute for TV. While severely restricting TV or even banishing it from the house, they let their child stare into a computer screen for two or three hours. Kendrick himself receives letters and E-mail from parents asking him how they can start their three-year-old in computer training. "It's too much," says Kendrick. "Where are they learning social skills? Where are they learning anything but being a passive recipient?" Because of TV, videos, and computers, Kendrick thinks youngsters today have far less interest in the natural world than past generations.

Don't See TV Time as Family Time. Most every family comes together to watch a movie or a special TV show. Just don't make it an everyday routine. Kendrick says, "Parents are fooling themselves if they consider this quality family time. Everybody sits passively and watches and nobody says anything for two hours. Parents need to spend time talking with their children, and not just a few minutes a day going over their schedules." Like many other observers, Kendrick deplores the growing trend among families of putting a TV in the kids' room (along with one in the parents' bedroom). "Everyone watching their own programs is not my idea of healthy family living," he says.

Take a Look at Your Own Viewing Habits. A dad who sits in front of the TV the entire day watching football may (or may not) have trouble criticizing his child's overindulgent viewing habits. Some parents criticize the shows their kids watch as stupid, while failing to notice that they themselves watch *Melrose Place* and other brainless fodder. Kendrick feels that kids should be able to watch stupid shows, too. "Cut them some mind candy slack," says Kendrick. "Life isn't one continuous PBS brainathon."

Make Sure Not to Overschedule Your Child. A child may retreat into the make-believe world of television if she's being pushed too hard in other aspects of her life. A child may be responsible to so many adults—parents, teachers, coaches—that she may just want to turn them all off. "It's a chance for a child to be mindless as opposed to mindful about everything," says Kendrick. "The TV acts like an IV numb drip. Nothing's being asked of her, and she can just veg out for a couple of hours." You may want to lighten your child's schedule if it seems like the load is getting too heavy for her.

Contact: The Family Education Company helps families become more involved in their children's education. Family Education Company, 20 Park Plaza, Suite 1215, Boston, MA 02116; 617-542-6500. Kendrick and others provide advice, TV and movie reviews, and other information on family issues at its www.familyeducation.com web site. Linked to this web site is KIDSNET, a national clearinghouse on the latest in children's television programs, radio, audio, and video programming. Kidsnet, 6856 Eastern Avenue NW, Suite 208, Washington, DC 20012; 202-291-1400.

LIVING IN A TV-FREE ZONE: ONE FATHER'S STORY

Jim Ewing, to borrow a line, has seen life from both sides now. When he was in college and early in married life, he didn't even own a TV. But after his daughter Sophie was born, he and his wife, Anne, bought one. Like so many other couples, they found that having a TV made life easier with a baby in the house. "We were stuck at home so much, it seemed like the thing to do," says Ewing, a software developer. "You put so much energy into entertaining the baby and caring for her, you need a break from dealing with her all the time. TV lets you take a break."

Only reluctantly did the Ewings commence the TV habit, buying a tiny four-inch diagonal black and white set that you almost had to press your nose up against the screen to see what was on. Gradually though, as Ewing says, their television watching took on "a life of its own." They bought a new, larger monitor that allowed them to actually see the faces of the people on the screen. They got cable and HBO. They bought a VCR. They had another child, Sam, and found that their children, like children everywhere, were happily content to sit and watch the same video over and over and over again.

Jim subscribed to Sports Channel and watched all the games on the weekends. On a dreary Thursday at work, he could look forward to watching *Seinfeld* that night. After putting the kids to bed, he and Anne could space out in front of the TV and unwind a little.

While there were benefits to having a TV, there were also drawbacks, and over time the minuses began to outnumber the pluses. The Ewings stopped listening to music so much, something they all loved to do. As Sophie and Sam got older, they became glued to the TV, flipping it on whenever they were home. But it wasn't just the kids. "We all spent too much time watching it," says Ewing.

Finally, the Ewings proposed a change: getting rid of the TV and replacing it with a piano. The kids agreed and perhaps surprisingly, they adapted almost immediately to living in a TV-free household. "At first you think, 'Oh your poor kids, how are they going to make it?'" recalls Ewing. "But they adjusted from the very beginning."

The parents, however, suffered from slight withdrawal pains at first. Ewing confessed to missing *Seinfeld* and some of the other shows he was following, as well as the excitement of a new TV season with its season premieres. There was no more Sports Channel or camping out on the couch over the weekend watching games. Then there was the larger issue of now having to spend more time with his kids.

"Not having a TV forces you to do stuff with your kids, which is a good thing," says Ewing. "You can't expect your kids to do nothing. TV's appeal is it keeps your kids busy so you can have free time." Without a TV to occupy her after school, Sophie now spends more time reading. Sam plays in his room with his Legos and flying toys. Everybody listens to music more, and the family spends more time doing things together on the weekends.

Restless and in need of entertainment, Sophie and Sam sometimes come up to their father and say, "I'm bored." But there are other times when they're reading or playing quietly by themselves in their room, and a blessed hush falls over the house. Learning to entertain yourself is a skill that must be developed like any other.

The Ewings tried for a while to monitor what their children watched as a way of restricting their TV time, but they found that very difficult to do. You (or your children) may turn on a good program, but the TV almost invariably stays on after that, and you can be sure that the next program represents a Grand Canyon–like drop in quality. "There's so much really stupid stuff that you end up watching," says Ewing.

As children get older, power struggles invariably erupt over what they can watch and for how long. Ewing advises against this. "You have to pick your battles with kids," he says. "They have incredible willpower. Do you really want to have a battle with them over watching some cartoon?" For the Ewings, it was easier and simpler just to get rid of the TV hookup.

They kept their monitor and VCR because they still like to watch movies on the weekends. They've found that it's easier to control videos because they're more of a special event. "You can't just plop down and watch a movie the way you do with TV," says Ewing. "You've got to go out and rent it. It's a bigger deal."

Ewing no longer follows his favorite TV shows, and his sports viewing habits have taken a serious beating. But a friend taped the U.S. Open for him, and he watched it even though he already knew what happened. He has also rediscovered the joys of listening to a game on the radio, and if he's in a really bad way, he can venture out to a neighborhood sports bar. "Once you get out of the mode of watching TV, it's not that difficult to adjust," he says. "And there's a lot to say for it."

Tip: For another look at this subject, you may want to read Breaking Your Child's TV Addiction, *by David Demers (Marquette Books).*

WARNING: WATCHING SPORTS ON TV MAY BE HAZARDOUS TO FAMILY LIFE

Though they may be unwilling to remove the television altogether, most fathers would probably agree that it's a good idea to place limits on their child's TV watching. Kevin Quirk, however, wants men to go one step further. The author of *Not Now Honey, I'm Watching the Game* (Fireside Books), Quirk is a former *Sports Illustrated* correspondent and sports reporter for the *Charlotte Observer*. Now the director of the Center for Gender Peacemaking in Charlottesville, Virginia, he conducts workshops and classes for couples. His premise, though a simple one, promises to cause a domestic earthquake. He believes that a man can create more time for his family and improve his relationship with his partner by cutting down on how much time he watches sports on TV.

Q: I love to watch sports on TV. But if you spend more time watching SportsCenter *than you do playing with your kids, I guess that's not so good.*
Quirk: If all you do when you get home is zone out in front of the TV, and you're not present for your wife or children in meaningful ways, you may want to take another look at things. I conducted a national survey on the sports viewing habits of men and women, and it's inter-

"Most of the programs are so bad that whenever I'm tempted to look at television I'm disappointed. Also, we have two little kids, and we have to be careful not to let them unconsciously become part of what I think of as a disenchanted culture."
—Thomas Moore, father and author

esting how different their perceptions are. Men feel great about it. But for women, it gets in the way of their relationship and intrudes in family life. For example, I once spoke to a couple who lived in a two-bedroom apartment and who were expecting their first child. The spare room was going to be turned into the baby's room, and the man was upset because that's where he kept all his sports memorabilia.

Q: Tell me more about your survey.
Quirk: Over 450 couples around the country participated. I asked them a range of questions. I asked the men how many hours of sports on TV they watched per week. Men who described themselves as "sportsaholics" watched about thirty hours a week. Most men said they watched sixteen hours a week. So the average for men was twenty-two hours a week—a solid part-time job.

Q: And this posed a problem for the wives who wanted their husbands to spend more time with them or their children.
Quirk: That's right. One survey question I asked women was: "When he's watching TV, what are you doing?" The two most common answers were household chores and parenting. While Dad's in front of the TV, Mom is watching the children or doing housework. Dad will take the kids, but his solution is to simply bring them into the TV zone with him. He's satisfying his addiction, not interacting with his kids.

Q: Some of the most pleasant sporting events I've ever watched on TV were with my daughter. Of course, I have to admit the games were on at night and she just wanted to stay up past her usual bedtime.
Quirk: Watching sports on TV is a way that fathers bond with their children, but it's one-dimensional. There has to be more. I remember one man I spoke to about this. He said that sports was the strongest bond between him and his father. He loved it when his dad took him to ballgames or they talked sports. But that's the only thing they could ever talk about. They couldn't talk about girls or school or anything else that was important in his life. So when his son was born he made a vow that he'd be involved in his life in more ways than just that.

Q: It's not a matter of wanting to shut your family out. Men work hard. When they come home from work, they want to flip on the game and relax.
Quirk: That's what men say, but relaxation is not really the point. It's stimulation. It's very common for men who are laid back in other aspects of their life to become very animated when they watch sports. They shout; they get angry; they get happy or sad. Men care deeply

about sports. They feel vital and more connected to life. They can connect with other people who feel as passionately as they do.

Q: I have a friend who tells me that his wife says to him, "You sit all day in front of that TV and you're perfectly content." For her it's a criticism. For him, it's the way it is. He can sit and watch a football game for hours and be perfectly content. Why can't she sit down and watch with him?

Quirk: It's an illusion of togetherness when you watch TV with your wife or family. Fifty-eight percent of the women I surveyed who watched TV said they only did it to join their husband in his world. All parents, not just fathers, use TV as a substitute baby-sitter. Children slip into a semicomatose state when they watch TV. What they really need from their parents is active involvement. Read to them; take them to the park; talk to them.

Q: Suppose a new dad who's a sports junkie wants to make the ultimate sacrifice and shut off the television. What do you recommend?

Quirk: First, get a clear picture. Keep a time log for a week. How much do you really watch TV? Many men don't even realize how much they do it. These habits are hard to break. Map out a game plan. Don't go cold turkey; ease down gradually. And then use the time that you've been spending watching TV by taking up a new hobby, or in activities with your kids and family. That's really important.

Q: I can see that. I'm trying to cut down on my coffee consumption. But it's impossible to not have anything in the morning. So I'm drinking tea.

Quirk: It's the same idea—hike, bowl, visit the zoo, play miniature golf, go to the movies. The idea is to shake up those old patterns and replace them with something new and fresh. I've found that when men start trying new things, women's anger toward them dissipates and the arguments tend to drop away.

Q: Speaking of which, is it just me or do women always pick the worst time during a game to ask you to do something?

Quirk: I hear that all the time from men. They say that women always seem to pick the most crucial part of a game to ask them for something.

Contact: Center for Gender Peacemaking, P.O. Box 4782, Charlottesville, VA 22905; 800–324–9373.

TOYS, PROJECTS, COMPUTERS

*W*hen little children receive a gift, they're more impressed with the package than its contents. They get this box, and they just love it. Maybe it has teddy bear wrapping and there's a big floppy bow on it. They gurgle and coo and they're just tickled pink to have it.

What's that? Oh, you're supposed to open it? What a concept!

It is, of course, the adults in the room—parents, grandparents, relatives, friends—who are most eager for the gift to be opened. They want to see what's inside, and they want to see the child's reaction. Then it's quickly onto the next gift . . . and the next . . . and the next after that.

Amidst all this hubbub the child remains a little baffled. Inside the box with teddy bear wrapping was an actual teddy bear that he just adores. He would love to cuddle it and play with it. But no, here's another brightly colored box being stuffed into his hands, and more voices shouting, "Open it! Open it!"

What's a child to do? He opens it (or a parent does it for him). It's only a matter of time before the child gets the message. At his gala third birthday celebration, he rips off the wrapping of a gift like it's not even there. He ignores the card indicating who it's from. Who cares anyway? After briefly inspecting the toy (or whatever) he issues a ritualistic "Thanks" before tossing it into a pile with all the other toys and discarded wrapping. Then, like a bloodthirsty lion ravaging a fallen deer, he tears open yet another package.

All this reminds me a little of when you start taking your toddler to the park. He fights the stroller, so you let him walk. But walking with him is like watching grass grow. He wants to look at everything. He stops to inspect what's in between the cracks in the sidewalk. Swept into the spell of a tiny potato bug, he calls for you to share his fascination. What is normally a five-minute walk becomes a half-hour long Euel Gibbons nature expedition.

All the while you're nagging at him to keep moving. He doesn't care if he's at the park or not; it's all the same to him, and he's having a good time. But you're fixed on your goal, and you're frustrated over how long it's taking to get there. Finally you just pick him up and carry him to the park.

Whether the subject is toys or television or money or nutrition or discipline or God, many parents wonder and worry if their children are developing the "right values." Well, right or wrong, they are developing the values being taught to them by their parents. Sobering thought, isn't it?

COMMON SENSE WISDOM ABOUT TOYS

Ruth B. Roufberg lives in Kendall Park, New Jersey. The author of *Your Child from Two to Five Years: A Comprehensive Guide to Toys* and a parent-child activity book, she is the toy editor for the Parents' Choice Foundation and has been a juror for the Parents' Choice annual Toy Awards every year since their inception in 1981. A graduate of Indiana University with two sons of her own, Roufberg reviews hundreds of toys every year to determine the best toys for children. Her annual "Toys of the Year" selections are featured in *Parenting* magazine, and she acts as a toy consultant for several toy companies and publications. Her answers to these basic toy questions are based on years of testing toys and watching children play with them.

Should Boys Play with Toy Guns? Playing with toy guns is a normal part of growing up for boys. When boys are given Legos or some other type of construction set, frequently the first things they build with it are guns. Boys who don't own toy guns will still crook their fingers and play "Bang, bang, you're dead." People who live in urban areas often have a different view of guns than those in rural areas. Urbanites associate guns with violence and crime. Many fathers in rural areas (and the suburbs and cities) hunt for recreation. But Roufberg draws a sharp distinction between harmless playing with toy guns and overaggressive or violent behavior. The latter should not be permitted. She also disapproves of buying a toy gun for a child, although she would tolerate his improvising one from materials at hand or from his imagination.

Should Boys Play with Dolls? "We want our sons to grow up to be good fathers and learn how to nurture," says Roufberg. "Dolls let boys practice being a daddy." She sees nothing wrong with boys playing dress-up either. Girls play pretend games, not always dressing up in sterotypically female costumes. There's no reason why boys have to be restricted to sterotypically male costumes. Stopping a boy from playing dress-up or with dolls is like stopping him from playing with toy guns. When a parent steps in, it raises the stakes and makes the issue bigger than it really is. "Anything you make an issue out of looms larger than it is," says Roufberg.

What's the Deal with Barbie Anyway? Barbie dolls are a cultural phenomenon and, like cavities in children, impossible to avoid. It is part of growing up for girls, and Roufberg would never deny a Barbie to a girl if she wants one. Not having Barbies could make her an outcast if all her friends have them, and no father wants that for his child. Roufberg draws the line, however, on what she calls Barbie's "sybaritic lifestyle." Dolls and clothes yes, but take it easy with sports cars, homes, and other toy consumer fantasies. Roufberg has noticed a kind of pecking order in how girls play with Barbies. Invariably the other girls go over to the house of the girl who owns the most Barbies and accessories. This girl tends to choose the role she wants to play in their games.

Can a Child Have Too Many Toys? Yes, says Roufberg. Parents, fathers especially, give toys to assuage their guilt over not being around during the day. So they buy things the child really doesn't need or even want. It's also sometimes easier for men to give a child a toy than to show their affection. Roufberg recommends getting away from store-bought toys and using real household items—empty boxes, pots and pans, wooden spoons—that allow children to engage their imagination. Or, if the child is old enough, many fathers enjoy making toys with them while teaching workshop skills.

Should a Toy Be Fun or Have Educational Value? It shouldn't be either/or. Toy manufacturers want to make fun toys that also encourage learning. If a learning and development toy isn't fun, the child isn't going to play with it. If he doesn't play with it, it's worthless.

Can a Toy Make a Child Smart? Less-educated parents think that electronic toys such as calculators can provide educational stimulus for their children and make up for what they can't give them intellectually or academically. But a toy can't make a child smart, says Roufberg, and there is no substitute for interacting with your child. These days children enter day care at such an early age, sometimes before their working parents have shown them how to do even simple things such as tying their shoelaces or cutting with scissors.

How Do Computers Rate as Toys? Nowadays any toy in which a child presses a button is called an "interactive" toy. But truly interactive computer programs respond to the child. Many programs force the child to conform to the computer, says Roufberg. For example, in one game a child was given five letters on a screen—*C D L O U*—and asked to form a word with them. There was a picture of a cloud on the screen, so it was obvious (at least to an adult) that the word the computer wanted was *cloud*. But the child typed in *could*, which also could be correctly formed using those letters. The computer sent back the message, "Wrong!" without a word of explanation. Now, with a parent standing nearby, he could explain that yes, *could* was a correct word but not what the computer wanted. But what if no adults were around? The computer told the child that he had made a mistake without explaining what the mistake was or why. But, in fact, it wasn't a mistake, it just wasn't what the computer wanted.

One problem with computer programs for children is they can't be personalized, says Roufberg. Math games, for instance, often combine problems that are overly simple or far too difficult. The simple problems are too easy for the advanced kids, and the tougher problems are too hard for the slower ones. Both sets of children lose interest.

The better computer games respond to the child. One game asks how many jelly beans are in a jar. When the child guesses one hundred (or any other number), the program shows what one hundred beans in the jar looks like. This allows him to change his answer and make a better estimate. A similar game shows a train entering a tunnel. The child is asked to estimate how long it will take the train to emerge from the tunnel based on its speed. The program then shows the train moving at whatever rate the child estimated. Again, the child can change his answer based on what he observes. (For more about computers, see "Computers and Kids" later in this chapter.)

Besides Sports Equipment, Are There Any Classic Gifts That Fathers Like to Give to Their Children? Dads love to give electric train sets. But a three-year-old simply can't sit still long enough to watch a train go round and round in a circle. He'd rather push the train on the track himself. Better to wait until they're nine or ten.

What If the Child Likes a Toy That His Father (or Mother) Doesn't Approve Of? Examples of this might be toy guns, Barbies, or electronic pets. Roufberg makes a comparison to chocolate eclairs. "You'd give your child a chocolate eclair occasionally, wouldn't you?" she asks. "There's nothing wrong with it as long as it's not obsessive."

Children eventually grow bored with novelty toys and move on. But again, if the parent makes a stink about it, he can turn a child's passing infatuation with a toy into a much bigger issue.

Tip: The Parents' Choice Foundation evaluates children's toys, videos, books, audios, computer programs, and other media. Its annual awards designate the best in children's media for the year. It publishes a quarterly journal and other publications. Parents' Choice Foundation, Box 185, Newton, MA 02618; 617-965-5913. The Oppenheim Toy Portfolio also publishes a highly regarded quarterly newsletter that reviews toys, books, and videos for children. Contact them at 40 East Ninth Street, New York, NY 10003; 212-598-0502 or 800-544-TOYS.

TOY SAFETY

- *Avoid toys with small parts that could be inhaled or swallowed.* Children under three like to put objects in their mouths. Infants and toddlers should play with toys with oversized pieces.

- *Give your child age-appropriate toys.* Most toy accidents occur when a child is playing with a toy that's too old for her, such as one with small parts. More toys to avoid with the under-three set: small balls, uninflated balloons, and toys with sharp points or rough edges.

- *Be sure that soft rattles, squeakers, and teething toys won't fit completely into your infant's mouth, so she can't swallow them.*

- *Pay attention to your child.* Parental supervision is a must, not only for safety reasons, but also for your own satisfaction: to see how she's developing and what toys she's ready for next.

- *Never hang or attach a toy or stuffed animal to a crib with string or ribbon.* It may appear harmless, but there's always a possibility the cord could get wrapped around the baby or an item of clothing and cause problems.

- *Be careful with balloons.* They represent a choking hazard for small children.

- *Check for sturdy, well-sewn seams on stuffed animals and cloth dolls.* Be certain that eyes, noses, and other decorations are securely fastened and cannot be pulled or bitten off.

- *Be sure that arrows and darts have blunt tips,* such as rubber or flexible plastic suction cups or other protective points.

TOY CATALOGS

Animal Town. Toys, games for "cooperative learning." P.O. Box 757, Greenland, NH 03840; 800-445-8642

Back in the Saddle. Horse stuff for girls and boys. 570 Turner Drive, Suite C, Durango, CO 81301; 800-865-2478

Back to Basics Toys. Classic toys and games. One Memory Lane, Ridgely, MD 21685; 800-356-5360

Bits & Pieces. Puzzles and gifts for older kids. One Puzzle Place, B8016, Stevens Point, WI 54481; 800-884-2637

Childcraft. Games, toys, and activities. 250 College Park, P.O. Box 1811, Peoria, IL 61656; 800-631-5657

Hand in Hand. Costumes. Genesis Direct, 100 Plaza Drive, Secausus, NJ 07094; 800-872-9745

HearthSong. Alternative toys, kits, books. 6519 N. Galena Road, P.O. Box 1773, Peoria, IL 61656; 800-325-2502

One Step Ahead. Useful baby products, toys. 75 Albrecht Drive, Lake Bluff, IL 60044; 800-274-8440

Pleasant Company. American Girls dolls. 8400 Fairway Place, P.O. Box 620190, Middleton, WI 53562; 800-845-0005; www.americangirl.com

Vtech. High-tech and electronic toys. 101 East Palatine Road, Wheeling, IL 60090; 800-521-2010; www.vtechkids.com

- *Check toys for minor damage.* Often tightening a bolt or applying some glue will prevent further damage and a possible accident. Get rid of toys that are rusted or beyond repair.

- *Discard all packaging before giving the toy to an infant or small child.*

- *Get a toy chest with a removable lid or one with spring-loaded support that allows the lid to remain securely open.* Watch for unfinished edges or improper clearances that can cause pinched fingers.

- *Look for cautionary labels on the toy*. Check to see if the manufacturer's address and phone are on the package or box, indicating that the manufacturer stands by its toy.

Source: American Toy Institute, a New York–based industry trade group. Its pamphlet, Toys and Play, *is available free through the Consumer Information Center 7-B, P.O. Box 100, Pueblo, CO 81002; 719-948-4000; www.pueblo.gsa.gov. The Juvenile Products Association publishes a free brochure,* Safe and Sound Baby, *for non-toy items such as cribs, strollers, and car seats. Send a* SASE *to* JPMA, *Two Greentree Centre, Suite 225, P.O. Box 955, Marlton, NJ 08053.*

WORK PROJECTS FOR FATHER AND CHILD

Bill Bekkedahl builds and renovates houses. A licensed general building contractor, he owns his own construction company specializing in home renovations. But he concedes that some of his most creative and challenging construction projects are done with his daughter, Jayce. He figures he started working on projects with her when she was about three. Before that, she was too young. Starting with the simplest jobs and working up to the more complicated ones, Bekkedahl reports on how fathers can work together with their children and enjoy it.

Painting. At about age three, Jayce approached her father while he was painting the house. "Can I help?" she asked. Bekkedahl gave her a brush, outfitted her in some old clothes, lay down a tarp for spills, and put her to work. He rolled the sides of the house while she painted the grooves in the plywood siding. How did it turn out? "Well," he says, "she got a lot of paint on herself." But Bekkedahl believes firmly in the benefits of painting for young children. It teaches them patience. They also quickly see the fruits of their labor. "There are two kinds of people," he says. "Those who can paint, and those who can't. Get your kids to use a paintbrush, and you've got them started on the right track."

Gardening. Painting is a simple, though sometimes messy, task. Another simple task is gardening. Depending, of course, on their size and age, children can learn to use hedge clippers and pruners. They can load a wheelbarrow with cuttings. They can rake the grass and sweep. Bekkedahl, who has a garage full of tools and machinery, is not keen on plastic tools. They're toys, not tools, which may be fine for infants, but when children get older, they will want to use what their father is using, not a plastic substitute.

Apprentice Helper. Bekkedahl thinks a good approach for children is to view them as apprentice helpers. Ask them for a tool and let them hand it to you. They can help carry things and paint. They can hand you a screw or a nail that you put in. They can catch the board that you've cut and possibly sweep up the sawdust. They grow familiar with tools and learn safety techniques, such as tying their long hair back.

Wrapping Gifts. Bekkedhal and Jayce have made Christmas presents together. But a gift isn't complete until it's wrapped. Let your child do the wrapping and feel even prouder about the finished product.

Going to the Junkyard. Undaunted by a heavy rain last winter, Bekkedahl and his daughter threw on rubber boots and rummaged around the auto parts yard to track down a part he needed for his truck. This wasn't a construction project, but Bekkedahl recommends it highly. "It's so different down there," he says. "There are all these characters. It's such a slice of Americana." Going to the auto parts yard and dump are unique experiences that fathers can provide for their children.

Changing the Oil. Bekkedahl does most of the work on this one, crawling under the truck and getting dirty. But he showed Jayce the drain plug, and when it was time to put the new oil in, she did the pouring. "Girls should know their way around a car just as boys should," says Bekkedahl. "I've known women who didn't even know how to pop the hood. Girls need to learn how to check the oil, water, and air and pump the gas." Now that Jayce's ten, her father wants her to get a feel for driving a stick shift. On a summer vacation in the mountains, he gave her her first driving lesson. She sat on his lap and held the steering wheel while trying to operate the clutch and stick shift. Bekkedahl gave advice and made sure they didn't run into any trees.

Mowing the Lawn. Kids need to be old enough to physically push a lawn mower around, but it's the type of job that Bekkedahl recommends for children. "You can't screw a lawn up too bad," he says. "They just have to be careful they don't run their toes over." Parents around the nation may be shocked to learn that Jayce, who likes working around the yard, recently asked her father if she could mow the lawn. He said, "Sure. No problem." He kept her company while she worked, sitting on the porch sipping a beer.

Building a Birdhouse. Bekkedahl admits he pushed the limits on this construction project, letting Jayce use a nailgun. He cut out the pieces: front, back, and bottom, and the two gabled roof pieces. Jayce used the hot glue gun, glueing and sticking the little shingles on the birdhouse. They both stained it with a clear redwood finish. The scariest part of the job was when he let her hold the nailgun and pull the trigger. "Obviously," says Bekkedahl, "you don't want to let your children do anything where they can get dismembered. Avoid the dismemberment stuff till they're teens."

Remodeling a Room. Their latest project together was a major one: renovating her bedroom. First they took out all the furniture and set her bedroom up temporarily in another room. Then they tore out the carpets and "demo'ed" the room. They resanded the wood floor, each using an orbital grinder, and painted and wallpapered. Bekkedahl would give Jayce a space to work on and then work on the space next to her, letting her make her own mistakes. "You have to let them do it themselves, even if it doesn't come out as good," says Bekkedahl. "You can go back later when they're not around and fix it up."

When he got frustrated, he'd go off to the garage to give himself some breathing room or ask Jayce to do something that would separate them for a while. Or if there was nothing for her to do, she'd go off and play.

A Good Investment. Bekkedahl says that his father taught him how to do these things, and now he's teaching his daughter. "My dad showed me how to weld and use a table saw. I sometimes got cut but we still did it. We built fences together. We changed engines. With my dad, after he showed me how to do something, it became mandatory. I had to do it. With kids, it's like putting money in the bank. Someone has to teach them. They don't know how to do it on their own."

Tip: For how-to information on science and nature experiments, mechanical and electrical projects, and arts and crafts you can do with young children, check out The Father's Almanac, Revised, *by S. Adams Sullivan (New York: Doubleday).*

COMPUTERS AND KIDS

Mard Naman is tuned in to both the computer and video game worlds. He's the managing editor for *Publish* magazine, a leading publication for computer design professionals. Before he joined the staff of *Publish*, Naman wrote game manuals for Nintendo, Atari, and Sega video-game systems. Like a lot of knowledgeable computer people,

Naman, whose son is Tyler, is not keen on starting kids on computers too early. Here, he explains why:

"My feeling is, Tyler is going to be playing on a computer all his life. Why push it? Why rush it? I want him to run around outside. I want him to get his hands dirty. I want him to pick up banana slugs and dig for worms and go down to the creek and do all that stuff. Part of it's personal, I admit," Naman adds. "I spend all day on a computer myself. I want to do other things with him. I want to kick a soccer ball around with him or hit a baseball. I don't want to raise a great indoorsman. I want to have a well-rounded kid."

He continues, "I know there are some parents who want their kids to get ahead and who think if they're not on the Internet already, they're going to fall behind. I don't buy any of that. Computers are the same as any other media. There have to be limits on it. Tyler likes to watch videos but if he starts to watch them one after another I have to pull him away and say 'Hey, let's go down to the park.' Kids have so much excess energy, they've got to burn it off. And developmentally, it's better if they learn through direct experience."

Naman set Tyler up with a computer at home around the age of six, though he'd of course played on them at schools and rec centers. Some people have expensive systems at home that they don't want their children to touch. In that case, it might be good to set your child up with a used or hand-me-down machine, one that you won't mind little fingers banging on. When a small child plays on your computer, get used to having your desktop rearranged. Strange things can happen when a child plays on a computer, things that you will be called upon to set straight.

Naman adds that when two or more kids are on a computer (or video game), playing time conflicts can arise. In the past, he has had to put a clock out to make sure each player gets an equal amount of computer time.

Naman concludes, "Computers are cool and kids can really get into them, but it's not where you start that's important, it's where you end up. You don't want them to burn out. It's okay if kids show interest in computers and you want to help them. But I wouldn't lead them or put pressure on them. If it's important to you and you start pushing them, they'll resist. You're better off if you let them grow into it naturally."

CHILDREN'S SOFTWARE

An infant can google and poke at a keyboard while seated on her father's lap, but she won't get much benefit out of a computer until about age three. A child must have a sense of connection between the clicker and what's happening on the screen. She must think, "I want to go there" and then be able to move the mouse to go there.

You'll know your child is old enough to use a computer when she can do so relatively independent of you. Getting her started and showing her how to use it should only last a few minutes. After that, she should be able to manage on her own. She may still be too young (or the program may be too advanced) if she can't function without you. But don't expect a young child to last too long at the keyboard at first; ten minutes may be the max before her attention wanders. Following is a list of recommended software titles for children ages three to six.

Pre-Kindergarten

Art/Creative Activities
Kid Cuts.* Broderbund
Kid Pix, Kid Pix2, Kid Pix Studio.* Broderbund

Language
Bailey's Book House.* Edmark
McGee Series. Lawrence
Zurk's Learning Safari. Soleil

Books
Just Grandma and Me. Broderbund
Harry and the Haunted House.* Broderbund

Numbers, Counting, Space, Time
Millie's Math House.* Edmark
The Playroom.* Broderbund

Science
Sammy's Science House.* Edmark

Music
Thinkin' Things 1.* Edmark

Appropriate for both kindergarten and pre-kindergarten children

Kindergarten Programs

Language

Stanley's Stickers. Edmark

Interactive Reading Journey. Learning Company

Numbers, Counting, Logical Development

James Discovers Math. Broderbund

Math Rabbit. Learning Company

Magic Bear's Masterpiece. KinderMagic

Music

MetroGnome's Music. Learning Company

Utilities

Kid Desk.* Edmark

COR-Pc/COR-Mac.* High/Scope

Source: Charles Hohmann, Ph.D., father of Tom and Susanna. For more information, consult Hohmann's book Young Children and Computers *or the* High/Scope Buyer's Guide to Children's Software, *both available from High/Scope Press, 800-40-PRESS. The High/Scope Educational Research Foundation publishes materials for parents and teachers on the use of computers in early childhood education. High/Scope, 600 North River Street, Ypsilanti, MI 48198; 313-485-2000; www.highscope.org. A good third-party source for software is Educational Resources in Elgin, Illinois; 800-624-2926.*

Children's Software Info on the Web

Children's Software Revue at
www.microweb.com/pepsite/Revue/revue.html

Newsweek's Parent's Guide to Children's Software at
www.newsweekparentsguide.com

School House Software Reviews at
www.worldvillage.com/wv/school/htmlscholrev.htm

Superkids Educational Software Review at www.superkids.com

Thunderbeam at www.thunderbeam.com

Some software publishers have created a site for girls' software titles.
Check it out at www.just4girls.com.

*Appropriate for both kindergarten and pre-kindergarten children

TRAVEL: BUSINESS AND FAMILY

For many fathers there are two types of travel: family or vacation travel and business travel. This chapter touches on both subjects. I'm lucky that I don't travel much in my occupation. I sit my butt in a chair for the most part, and that's my job. Most of the traveling I do is recreational travel with my family.

This spring, Annie, Jennifer, and I took a swing through the Southern California amusement parks—or, as Jennifer calls them, "abusement parks." At some point, all parents must take their child to a theme park such as Disneyland or Disney World. It's a law. You will be driven forever from the ranks of parenthood and your child will hang her head in shame if you don't take her at least once.

I've taken Annie twice to Disneyland. The first time, when she was three, she had an afternoon meltdown on a walkway near the Matterhorn ride. It was just too much; her little body couldn't take in all the noise and sights and excitement and junk food. She bawled like she had sat on a tack. Fortunately none of the other adults in the area noticed because all their children were having meltdowns, too. The best part of Annie's day was eating breakfast with Goofy, Mickey Mouse, and Donald Duck. The best part of my day was anytime I could sit down.

When we went back this spring, Annie was old enough to ride the adult rides and that was pretty cool. We went on the Matterhorn and Space Mountain and Indiana Jones rides and a bunch of others that she couldn't go on before. I still enjoyed sitting down quite a bit.

One of the benefits of being an old fogey is that you get to torture your children with memories of what you did as a kid. In the

Tomorrowland section, there was a charming, if anachronistic, piece of entertainment called Circlevision, which I had gone to as a mere lad of twelve. Walt Disney himself shot the footage for it—a travelog of the United States. The gimmick was that the film appeared on screens in a circle around the audience.

It was very popular in its time. Its time was long ago. Our Disney guide said it was soon to be shut down and replaced by something wilder, faster, and more in keeping with Tomorrowland's futuristic theme. Circlevision was more part of Yesterdayland than Tomorrowland.

Annie was bored to tears, of course. She wanted to go on a ride that was faster, wilder, and more futuristic. I couldn't argue with that. But at least she saw it. Together we witnessed a little piece of my past and for a brief few moments, my childhood merged with hers. I derived no small pleasure from that.

ONE DAD'S VIEW: PUT THOSE TRAVEL PLANS ON HOLD

Expectant fathers worry that after the baby comes, they won't be able to do all the things they used to do, such as travel. David Noland calls Mountainville, New York, home, but he's had his passport stamped in nearly as many countries as Phineas Fogg. A contributor to *Outside* and *Sports Illustrated*, he's traveled to Europe, Antarctica, Borneo, and New Zealand. He's trekked in the Himalayas and climbed Mt. Kilimanjaro in Africa. His book, *Travels Along the Edge* (Vintage Books), details adventure travel trips around the world. A new father himself, Noland says that yes, the worries of expectant dads are true. He is the father of Callie.

Q: How has becoming a father affected your freedom to travel?
Noland: Well, before Callie was born, I used to go on two or three major overseas trips every year, for two to four weeks at a time. But there was about a fifteen-month period where I didn't go anywhere. My travel window closed when Lisa was about six months pregnant. I had just gotten back from a trip to Oman in the Middle East, and we agreed it was a good idea for me to stick around for the last three months of the pregnancy. She needed my support and I wanted to be there to make sure everything went okay. Callie was born in March and

"The main thing is still for you to come into contact with new objects and new people. Go to places you have not yet seen, glean more from those you have seen; every place can yield the greatest treasures."

—Johann Wolfgang von Goethe, to his son, August

for the next year or so we were too busy figuring out how to be parents for me to do any serious traveling. Then a rafting trip to Chile came up that I really wanted to go on.

Q: Did you realize that having a baby would cause changes in your traveling?

Noland: Sure. It's one of the compromises you make when you have a child. Something has to give. We knew there'd be major changes for both of us. Travel writing is the major way I make a living. For that reason my wife is pretty understanding. When I get an article assignment where I have to go somewhere, I go. But traveling on my own, for pleasure, I've cut it back. It's also a self-correcting process. I can't afford to travel now unless I'm on assignment. My wife quit her job after Callie was born and she was the major breadwinner in the family. I'm a meager freelancer. You know how it goes. Our family income fell dramatically, and one of the first things to go is non-job-related travel.

Q: When you went to Chile, what was it like to leave your daughter for the first time?

Noland: Very interesting. I was a little concerned about it before I left. Callie was less than a year old at the time. I was going to be gone three weeks, and that's a long time for a little kid. I'm thinking, Gee, I hope she remembers me. During the flights down to Chile, I missed her a lot. Every time I'd see a baby in an airport, I'd get these pangs. The first night I was away from her, I dreamed about her. It was very strange. I'd never done that before. Then we went into the wilderness to this beautiful white water river called the Futaleufu, and it was very intense. I had to concentrate on staying alive in these gigantic Class 5 rapids, so I didn't think about her as much.

Q: What happened when you came back?

Noland: When I came home, Lisa and Callie met me in New York City at a restaurant we like. For the first couple of hours, she seemed a little puzzled. It was like, "Hey, remember me? You know, Dad?" I think part of it was that we were in New York with all these distractions. Once we got home, it was back to normal in a couple of days. That was very reassuring.

Q: Have you traveled with her yet?

Noland: We've flown to see her grandparents in Indiana. She took to it real well. We took along a baby backpack for getting her around the airport. I'd strongly recommend that if you're traveling with a baby. Some of these airports are so big, you can walk forever. Another time we flew out to California to a resort in San Diego, and Lisa and Callie came along. I was on assignment. And then we went on to a dude ranch in Arizona, for another assignment. That was definitely a learning experience. One thing I learned was that if you're traveling with a small child, you're better off going to one place and staying there. Traveling becomes something you have to plan much more carefully. Keep logistics as simple as possible. Dead simple. Go to one place and make that your home base. We went to three places in ten days. We were constantly transferring. It's a complex procedure traveling with a baby. There's all their gear, plus you have to coordinate everything around their nap times. That was tough. Also, the flights were much longer. Four hours is a long time for a kid in a plane. She did it, but it took constant toddling around with her and playing with her to keep her happy. I'd say a plane flight of one to two hours max, for a baby.

Q: You've traveled to Antarctica, climbed Mt. Kilimanjaro, rafted white water in Chile. But it sounds like traveling with a baby may be one of your biggest adventures yet. Any lingering resentments about traveling less?

Noland: I'm surprised how cheerfully I've accepted it. I'm not moping around. Partly my attention is diverted by Callie, of course. She's great. We have a good time. Sometimes she wakes up about five or six in the morning, so I get up and throw her in a jogger stroller and we play nine holes of golf at six in the morning. Callie has a great time, I have a great time, and Lisa has a great time because she's sleeping. No, I miss it less than I thought. I'm not sure why. It's definitely a trade-off. And as Callie gets older, I know I'll be able to resume traveling.

Tip: Outside *magazine's annual* Family Vacation Guide *is an excellent source for travel ideas, destinations, and equipment. Available at newsstands or call 800-688-7433 for more information.*

TRAVELING WITH A BABY

One of the hurdles in traveling with a baby is overcoming anxiety. Like David Noland, Alan Kesselheim combines adventure writing with fatherhood. A resident of Bozeman, Montana, he writes for parenting publications, such as *Parents* and *Mothering*, as well as *Backpacker* and *Canoe and Kayaking*, for which he is a contributing editor. His book, *Going Inside* (McClelland and Stewart), is the story of a fourteen-month paddling expedition across Canada that he took with his wife, Marypat Zitzer. She was eight months pregnant when they finished the trip.

Eli was the baby born after that trip. They have since added two more children, Sawyer and Ruby. Kesselheim gives these pointers to any new dads who still have an itch to go places and want to take their partner and children with them:

- *Go at a family pace*. When you were alone or traveling with your partner, you could expect to cover a certain amount of ground in a day. Bringing a child will slow you down. Expect to make more stops. Don't assume you're going to reach a certain spot, because you may not.

- *Create diversions along the way*. Children have mosquito-sized attention spans and need lots of breaks. They're not going to be able to sit in a car (or a canoe, Kesselheim's preferred mode of travel) for hours on end without squawking. Some parents report good luck traveling at night when the kid's asleep.

- *Have flexible goals*. Your trips need to be more open-ended than before, less deadline-driven. The kids will want to get out and play instead of always tromping on toward the goal. So build extra time for that into the schedule.

- *Be flexible*. Readjust your ambitions and expectations. The travel experience is different with children, and you have to realize that. They're going to cry and whine and cause a fuss sometimes. But remember: they could be just as whiny and fussy at home, so you're better off going.

- *Expect to do some work when you travel with your family*. "It's not always a pure vision of familyhood," says Kesselheim. "It's lots of work. You've got to stick a toothbrush in every mouth, tie every shoe, wash every dirty dish and pot." Trading chores with your partner will help in this regard.

- *Simplify*. Don't complicate your life unnecessarily. Who needs the stress? Make the day shorter, rather than taking it to the wall.

- *Leave plenty of time to enjoy where you are*. Kids like being there, wherever *there* is. They like to explore. They like to swim, meet other children, climb trees, play in the sand, run around. Adults are usually the ones who are hung up on getting to a certain place because they can't relax until they do.

- *Expect postponements and cancellations*. The Kesselheim family was set to canoe the White River in Colorado one summer when Ruby came down with a high fever. That's classic; something's always coming up with babies. They had to postpone their plans for two days and rearrange their itinerary. But they ended up making the trip and bringing Ruby along, and they all had a great time.

THE GRAND TOUR:
TRAVELING OVERSEAS WITH A FAMILY

You may not worry about traveling in the United States or Canada, but what about overseas or to more exotic destinations? Kevin Jeffrey and his wife, Nan, went to Jamaica when their twin sons, Tristan and Colin, were only six months old. The Jeffreys now have a daughter, Gwyneth, and they live on Prince Edward Island, one of the Canadian Maritime provinces off the coast of Nova Scotia. Nan is the author of three books distributed by Menasha Ridge Press (800-247-9437)—*Adventuring with Children, Best Places to Go* and *The Complete Buyer's Guide to the Best Outdoor and Recreational Equipment*—which cover the many issues of family travel. Kevin assists in the writing and acts as publisher for their own Avalon House imprint. Together they speak at informal travel seminars for families who want to go all the places the Jeffreys do.

The Jeffreys (like David Noland and Alan Kesselheim) are adventure travelers. Adventure travel consists of travel to exotic or unfamiliar locales, usually in foreign countries, with challenging outdoor activities as part of the experience. These activities may include hiking, camping, bicycling, sailing, and other pursuits. Now you may think this type of travel is all well and good, but not with a baby or small child. Kevin Jeffrey begs to differ and gives these reasons why:

Reason #1: The Baby Will Do Just Fine. Traveling with infants is in some ways easier than with older children. A nursing child's food supply is only as far away as Mom. He's portable, too. Before he learns to walk, he can travel fairly easily on Dad's back in a sturdy frame pack. New moms in particular worry about their child's health in a foreign country. What if something goes wrong? The Jeffreys have bicycled through Spain, Portugal, and Morocco. They have traveled in Africa, Latin America, and Asia, in dozens of countries around the world. They've always found an English-speaking doctor when they needed one. Jeffrey points out that the fears of parents for their children usually mask their own insecurities. "You can worry about your kids just crossing the street," he says. "Bad things can happen. But if you let those thoughts run your life, you won't ever do anything or go anywhere."

Reason #2: Children Are Very Resilient. Of course, you do need to adjust your schedule to accommodate their nap times. Kids need to feel comfortable. "We tried to create a kind of nest wherever we went," says Jeffrey, by carrying his children's sleep things, stuffed animal, sleeping pad, and bag with them. But most youngsters can and do nod

> "The main thing is not to hurry. Nothing good gets away."
>
> —John Steinbeck, to his son, John

off on buses, trains, airplanes, and ships—far more easily and quickly than adults. Jeffrey still remembers when his boys fell asleep on a pile of baggage waiting for a midnight ferry ride in Greece.

Reason #3: You Will Meet Wonderful People. Doors open for you when you travel with your family in a foreign country, doors that are not open to single travelers. Kids are an ice-breaker. Says Jeffrey, "Strangers approach you and ask, 'What can we do for you?' They're so happy to see a family. They love kids. People in Central America don't believe Americans have kids because they never see them."

Reason #4: Your Children Will Meet Wonderful People, Too. Another parental worry is that older children will feel left out in foreign lands and not feel comfortable socializing with other young people. Jeffrey finds that it's quite the opposite. His kids have played in pickup soccer games overseas with three or four languages being spoken on the field. When both parties are willing, people can overcome language barriers and communicate.

Reason #5: It's More Affordable than You Think. Many families do not travel to foreign countries or even out of state because of the expense. Jeffrey agrees that you need to make choices and establish priorities. Going to Disney World, staying in nice hotels, eating at restaurants, buying a bunch of trinkets—that's not the way the Jeffreys travel. Airfare is their single biggest budget item. Everything else, however, is a manageable expense. They travel in the off-season when they can get the best deals and there are fewer tourists. They stay away from big cities where housing costs more. They rent a villa or house, which provides inexpensive accommodations and allows them to get to know an area in depth. The house comes with cooking facilities. They cook their own meals (also a health consideration in some countries) and seldom go out to dinner. They camp frequently, minimizing their housing costs. Hiking and other outdoor activities are free. The Jeffreys took four children (their own plus one cousin) to the Yucatan Peninsula for six weeks, renting a car for one of those weeks. Total cost excluding airfare: $2,000.

Reason #6: You Don't Have to Rough It All the Time. Try one night of camping, followed by a night in a motel or inn. Get a room for a few nights if it's pouring rain and you're sick of slogging it out in a tent. There are ways to work it out if you're willing.

Reason #7: You Don't Need to Carry as Much Stuff as You Do at Home. One of the rules of travel is the more mobile you are, the better. At home, you carry tons of stuff when you travel with a baby. Packing up for a simple trip to Grandma's is like Hannibal crossing the

Alps. When you travel overseas with a child, you can't take all that stuff—and then you find you don't need it anyway. You carry a simple camping pad instead of a crib. The playpen and portable potty stay home. The eighty-nine outfits hanging in the closet are reduced to an essential one or two. (Jeffrey recommends lightweight cotton clothing for kids; always carry sun protection.)

Reason #8: It's Good for Your Relationship with Your Partner. Getting away from home can help rekindle a romance that may be flagging under the strain of night feedings and near-constant diaper changes. Jeffrey finds that dads initially bring a lot of enthusiasm to family travel—a gung-ho "Let's go!" attitude. Moms, who may be more involved in the day-to-day functioning of their children's lives, tend to be more cautious, concerned perhaps that the responsibility for pulling a trip together will land on their shoulders. You can help your partner share your enthusiasm by getting involved and following through on the details. Work it out together; make it a shared effort.

Reason #9: It Strengthens Family Ties. Travel promotes responsibility in children as they get older. They need to carry things and work even as they help decide where to eat and where to go. The typical (petty) child-parent hassles of regular life disappear in the shared excitement and adventure. Everybody has to pitch in to make it work. Then when your trip's over and you return home, says Jeffrey, bring some of those good feelings back with you. Incorporate the lessons you've learned from your trip into your everyday life.

BUSINESS TRAVEL:
STAYING IN TOUCH WITH YOUR FAMILY

Every father whose job requires a lot of travel must come to a decision. He must decide that family life has a high priority and that he is going to participate in it. Once he resolves this in his mind, everything flows naturally from that decision. This section and the one following discuss how men can stay in touch with their family while traveling on business.

Put Family Activities in the Schedule. Schedule family just as you do your work appointments. Your daughter has a dance recital at 5:00 P.M. Put it in your Daytimer, and that's where you are.

Don't Use All Your Vacation Time. Hold some vacation time in reserve for family commitments. You may need to take off from work to help with the baby. When the child enters school, you may want to go on a field trip with her. Hanging on to vacation time gives you that option.

Communicate with Your Family. Call the family on the cell phone in your car. When the bill comes write "mine" on the personal calls and charge the rest to the company.

Have a Voice Mail Number. You're probably hard to reach if you're on the road a lot. Your partner and child can call your voice mail number when they want to talk to you. As you check your calls during the day, call them back.

Tell Your Family Your Travel Plans. Tell them the hotel where you're staying and what time you expect to check in. Call and tell them your room number after you check in. Talk about where you went that day. You may have passed through several cities and towns in the course of a day. Let your family know. Give them a feel for what you do during the day. Your child may even want to follow your route on a map.

Talk to Your Child. Even a baby needs to hear the sound of your voice, even if she can't understand the words you're saying. Children can understand far more than they can express themselves. Be outgoing when you talk to your child. Lead the conversation. Make it more than a "How are you?" and "Goodbye" type of conversation. Tell her what town you're in, what it looks like, how the weather is, where you're going to eat dinner.

Talk About the Benefits of Your Travel. Explain how all your travel is building up frequent flyer points or rewards that will be used for their next family vacation. Perhaps plan the vacation ahead of time, so all of you can look forward to it. Maybe your partner can keep track of the points and mileage, helping to keep her involved and supportive of your travel.

Bring Back a Souvenir or Gift. Bring back something from the area where you've been if you've been gone for several days. In Florida for the week? Why not a stuffed manatee for your daughter? When in Atlanta, how about a Georgia Peach T-shirt for your partner? You can sometimes fall into a gift-giving trap, however. Kids come to expect a gift from Dad and grow bored over time. Surprise them and just bring back yourself.

Collect the Soaps and Lotions from the Hotels Where You Stay. Some children get a kick out of receiving the sample shampoos and lotions found in hotels. They mix them together and create their own potions. This may be a small thing in your eyes, but it is one more way to show your child that you've been thinking of her.

Stick to Your Guns. Do you get static from your company because of your commitment to your family? Is your work atmosphere hostile or indifferent to being an involved dad? If that's the case, your job may not be right for you over the long haul. As Gilbert Hart always told his son, you can always go back and make more money. But you can never re-raise your children.

Source: Matt Hart is son of Gilbert and father of Hayley. As a sales executive for an equipment and supply company, Matt logs 40,000 to 45,000 miles per year in his car.

MORE TIPS WHEN YOU HAVE TO TRAVEL ON BUSINESS

Travel Less or Not at All. Being away for long periods of time confuses young children. They need you to be there as much as you can. Talk it over with your boss. There may be some flexibility there. See if you can find a way to cut back on your travel in the first six months or year of your baby's life.

Take Shorter Trips, Rather than Longer. Shorter trips are harder on you and less convenient. But you won't be away from your child as long, and that's good.

Make Sure One Parent Is Always Home. Your partner may need to travel in her job, too. Coordinate your schedules. Make sure both of you aren't on the road at the same time.

Talk to Your Family Frequently, at Least Once a Day. We mentioned this in the earlier piece, but it bears repeating. Let your family hear the sound of your voice even if you're thousands of miles away. Postcards are nice, too. Kids love to receive mail.

Get Your Children Involved in Communicating with You. When you're moving around a lot, it may be hard for your family to reach you by phone. Teach your children how to use a fax machine when they get older. Ask them to E-mail you.

Take Your Family with You Occasionally. It's sometimes possible to build some family time into a business trip. Fly on Thursday, take care of business on Friday, then spend the weekend with your family.

Have a Drink on the Flight Home. One business traveler says he feels fine when he leaves on a trip. It's the flight home that gets him. He's less patient with delays, more anxious about turbulence in the air. If that sounds like you, relax. The trip's practically over. You've done

> "I have a big jar at home where I throw all my loose change and that becomes the kids' vacation money. It really adds up, too. One year it totalled over three hundred bucks. I was amazed."
>
> —Jeff Hicks, father of two

your job, and pretty soon you will see your family again. (However, be moderate in your celebration. You want to make it safely home from the airport.)

Turn Your Trip into a Geography Lesson. Bring your child a souvenir from the place where you've been. Afterward take out the atlas and show her where Daddy was.

Spend Some Time with Your Child After You Come Home. Be sure to touch her and hug her and show her how much you missed her. You may be exhausted after your trip, but try not to be grumpy. Bring a good mood into the room with you. Your child has moods too, and don't expect her to always gleefully run into your arms welcoming you home. Take a moment to get reacquainted with her.

Realize That Travel Is Hard on Family Life. It is an emotional drain to be away from your family for long periods of time. It is stressful. There's no getting around that. You may think things like, "What if the plane goes down? My kids won't even know me." But you're doing the best you can for them. Travel is part of your job, and your job puts food on the table and a roof over their heads. And they'll be there for you when you get home.

Source: David Nelson, father of Katie and Kristy. Nelson is a consultant and advisor for nonprofit organizations on the production and productivity of special events. Last year he traveled to more than sixty cities in thirty states in the United States and Canada.

EASY TRAVEL TO DISTANT WEB SITES

Children's travel, Klutz Press at www.klutz.com/treefort/travel.html

City.Net United States. Atlas, almanac at www.city.net/countries/united_states/

Forest Service Recreation at www.fs.fed.us/recreation/welcome.htm/

Gorp. Great Outdoor Recreation Pages at www.gorp.com/

Parknet. National Park Service at www.nps.gov/

Rec.Travel at www.remcan.ca/rec-travel/

Traveling with Kids at http://family.starwave.com/funstuff/pwhistle/pwtravel/pwttoc.html/

Source: Internet Kids and Family Yellow Pages, *2nd edition.*

VIDEO AND PHOTOGRAPHY

When Annie was a baby, we couldn't take enough pictures of her. "Oh look, isn't she adorable? Quick, get the camera. Look! She did it again. I don't believe it. She is so unbelievable. Did you get it? Get that. And that. What, we're out of film? Well, go get some more. Look at that smile. Isn't she amazing?"

If you're a new father, you know the drill. And if you don't, you will soon enough. We have boxes and boxes of pictures of Annie when she was a newborn. Every moment seems like a Kodak moment at that age.

But it's a very odd thing. As Annie has gotten older, we've taken fewer and fewer pictures of her. She's in the third grade now. She has her school pictures and her soccer team pictures. We take pictures or haul out the video camera on special occasions (Halloween, Christmas, school talent shows) or when we go on vacation, but that's pretty much it.

I don't think that's unusual. In fact I think it's pretty typical of most families. The kids don't change as rapidly as they did when they were younger. And the parents stop acting like paparazzi always sticking cameras in their children's faces.

The main thing is to be sure to take pictures. I know some people whose parents neglected to do even that. It's like a little bit of their childhood is missing because of it. When I was a kid, my mom and dad shot home movies that my mom later had transferred to videotape. This was very poignant for me because my dad died when I was young and I wanted to see pictures of him. We have a few black and white photos of him, but I thought the movies would give me a better sense of what he was really like.

The movies are herky-jerky and all over the place—my dad's camera style. They show my brother and me mugging badly for the cameras. They show us swimming. They show us playing Little League. They show Mom and us together. Sometimes my mom even took the camera and we get to see my dad.

My dad operated the camera almost all the time—in the tradition of dads everywhere. I know this is still true. Dads are still the main camera operators. But I wish my dad had turned the camera over to my mom more often. The mystery man in my life remains the mystery man in the movies—a man whose influence is always felt, yet whose presence is not seen. That's almost a perfect definition of the modern father.

The advice from this corner is this: let Mom operate the camera from time to time. Hell, let your kids do it when they get old enough. Because when they go back and look at these videos years from now, they will want to see pictures of you, too.

HOW TO SHOOT GREAT VIDEO

Doug Stevenson is a video whiz. He is a Tennessee-based video producer whose company shoots industrial and educational videos as well as an occasional music video. An expert in satellite television and camcorders, he writes for publications such as *Camcorder and Computer Video* magazine and *Satellite Entertainment Guide*. Additionally, as the father of Jody and Leah, he has hands-on experience in making videos of children. Here, he shares his insights on how to shoot great video:

Get Down on Your Child's Level. This is Stevenson's number one rule. When you shoot from your height, you're looking down on your baby. That's an adult's view of the world. Get down on your knees and shoot at her level. Capture her world as she sees it.

Fill the Frame Up with Faces. Television is a close-up medium. Wide shots are less effective. They do not contain the detail or resolution of close-ups. Focus on your baby and fill the frame with her chubby little fingers and face.

Get a Camcorder as Soon as You Know You're Going to Be a Dad. Don't wait until after the baby is born. Lots of changes occur during pregnancy. Your partner's body goes through an amazing transformation. Also, there's more time to practice and develop your skills.

"I love taking pictures of my kids. We have albums and albums of them. I never look at them, but I know they exist."

—Actor Martin Short, father of Katherine, Oliver, and Henry

Bring Your Camcorder into the Delivery Room. Stevenson, whose wife is a midwife and who just completed shooting an instructional birthing video called *Spiritual Midwifery*, thinks bringing the camcorder into the delivery room is a fine idea. (Check with the hospital before delivery, though, as some allow cameras but not camcorders.) The best approach is to set the camcorder on a tripod, allowing for a general view of what's going on. Dad, however, should not play director of photography; he needs to help Mom and support her. Better to let a friend of Mom's operate the camcorder. Stevenson jokes that a birthing video can be very valuable when your child becomes a teenager. It will teach her the importance of birth control.

Be Steady and Slow When You Shoot. Stevenson's rule on panning is to go as slowly as you can, then go slower. Lots of fast herky-jerky movements can ruin a video. Keep the zoom wide open; it's easier to keep the camcorder steady that way.

Get Close to Your Subjects. Don't be shy. Move in close rather than relying on the zoom. The zoom tends to magnify camcorder movement and increase unsteadiness.

Don't Stay on a Subject Forever. Hold a shot for five to ten seconds, twenty seconds at the absolute maximum, then move on to a different angle or subject. Stevenson's general advice is to imagine your shot, frame it in your camcorder, record, count to ten, stop, then look for the next shot.

Don't Just Shoot on Holidays or Special Occasions. Shooting during the holidays or on birthdays is what everybody does. Bring the camcorder out on a more regular basis. Adopt a reporter's view of your children's world. Interview them. Have them show you around their room as you film them. Record their daily world as it is.

Shoot the Little Things. "God," said Mies van der Rohe, "is in the details." So is great video. Let your children show you the treasures of their life—a stuffed animal, a special toy. Also, don't leave out the details of your life. A shot of the family car is a great way to evoke a time that is passing.

Try Your Hand at Editing. Stevenson suggests home methods of editing: Hook the camcorder to the family VCR. Press play on the camcorder; press record on the VCR. You're now viewing what you shot. Hit pause on the VCR, which stops the recorder as the camcorder keeps playing. When it's on pause you'll need to look inside the camcorder viewfinder to see and hear the video. Another approach is to use two TVs. The first TV needs to be a video monitor with video and audio in and out connectors. The video leaves the camcorder, passes through the monitor and then onto the recording VCR and second TV. Yet another way is to come out of the camcorder using an RF adapter. Connect the RF adapter to a signal splitter, sending one side to a TV that will show the picture from the camcorder while the other side of the splitter goes to the VCR's "antenna in" port. These techniques may not produce perfect results, but they can help you get rid of those sections of wasted tape when you thought you hit pause but, in fact, were shooting your feet.

Purchase a Wireless Mike. Children these days quickly become video-savvy. They know when the camera is on and they play to it. A wireless mike is an inexpensive way to capture your children in a more naturalistic way. Hide the mike where they're playing. Then stand off to one side, shooting (and recording) them without them knowing you're doing it.

Let Your Children Use the Camcorder. A camcorder is expensive, but as your children get older, let them use it, too. Set it up on a tripod (so they can't drop and break it), and leave the room. Kids are very imaginative. They'll know what to do, improvising skits, lip-synching songs, and acting silly. Give them their own videotapes and assure them of creative control. Tell them they can record whatever they want and that you won't look at what they do. Then years (or months) later, when they've forgotten about the tapes, you can plug one in and see what they did.

Contact: Doug Stevenson, Total Video Productions, P.O. Box 259, Summertown, TN 38483; 800-258-9336 or 615-964-2590; E-mail: totalvid@usit.net.

TIPS ON BUYING A CAMCORDER

Buying a camcorder is like buying anything else: buy what you can afford. It's better to have something than nothing.

You can get good value in a camcorder for $500 to $1,000. The more "bells and whistles" you want—titlers, digital effects, wipes—the higher the price. Considering all the expenses involved in having a baby, it might be wise to start with an introductory model. (It's useless to list specific camcorder models because they become obsolete rapidly.) As you develop your skills and interest, you can upgrade your equipment over time.

There are six camcorder formats: VHS, VHS-C, S-VHS, 8mm, Hi8, and digital. Leading manufacturers are Sony, Hitachi, Panasonic, JVC, and Canon. Like new cars, new camcorder models are released every year.

Each type of camcorder has pros and cons. The smaller, palm-sized 8mm and VHS-C (C for compact) camcorders are lightweight and easy to hold and operate. The Sony Handyman actually fits into a large pocket. Video veterans say that the smaller the camcorder, the more likely you are to take it with you and actually use it. No matter how wonderful it is, a camcorder will not take pictures when it sits in the closet.

Only VHS-C models use an adapter. The adapters allow you to play the VHS-C directly in your home VCR. Formats like 8mm and Hi8 won't play in a VCR any more than an audio cassesette will work in a CD player. Digital camcorders get the best picture but are still a bit expensive. Hi8 is second best, followed by S-VHS, which has virtually gone extinct as a consumer format.

One in five camcorders purchased today are full-sized VHS models. Although heavier and longer—one model is more than a foot long and weighs eight pounds—infrequent camcorder users find them more convenient and easy to use. They fit into any VHS VCR without an adapter. You can pop the tape you've shot into your family VCR and watch it with a minimum of bother.

Your local video store is an obvious place to start when looking for camcorders. Hold each model in your hand and feel what's comfortable. Another way to learn about camcorders is to ask your neighbor. What does he use and like? You may even want to view some of his home video to see how the quality measures up.

Source: Doug Stevenson. Stevenson cites Camcorder and Computer Video *magazine as a good video resource. It publishes an annual buying guide on camcorders and regular features on equipment and techniques.* Camcorder and Computer Video, *4880 Market Street, Ventura, CA 93003; 805-644-3824.*

PHOTOGRAPHY: HOW TO TAKE GREAT BABY PICTURES

1. *Keep your subjects out of the middle of the frame*. That makes for a visually stagnant composition. Studies have shown that the eye travels from left to right. Place your subjects off-center left or off-center right.

2. *Avoid mug shots*. Putting your subjects in the center of the frame and shooting their faces straight on will make your photographs resemble the one on your driver's license.

3. *Each side of a person's face looks different.* Hollywood stars have known this for years, restricting their close-ups to their more attractive profile. Check your subject out. Make a judgment on which side of a person's face looks more expressive.

4. *Change your camera angle.* You don't always have to shoot straight-on in the conventional way. Get down on your knees and shoot up. Get on a chair and shoot down. See what looks good and try it out. Experiment. Have fun. Be creative.

5. *Be careful of your background.* Make it as clean as possible. You don't want the background interfering with the main subjects. If an antenna or a plant is sticking up in the background, lower yourself and your camera angle so it doesn't appear in the frame. Or pick the object up and remove it physically. That's certainly allowed.

6. *Take your outdoor photos in the late afternoon, from about 3:00 P.M. to sunset.* That's when the light is warmer and most flattering to the skin. The light at this time even has a reddish tinge, much like the sunset.

7. *Avoid (if you can) noontime shots where the sunlight is bright and harsh and the shadows are strong.* The light at this time of day acts like an interrogation lamp in a bad detective movie. It adds twenty years to your subjects and shows all the bags under their eyes and their wrinkles.

8. *Make sure the sun is behind you (the photographer).* That's called "frontal lighting." Never have the sun in back of your subjects. That's "back lighting," and it's very difficult for the camera to read correctly. The camera is fooled by the sunlight in the background and casts the people in the foreground in shadow. Activate the fill flash feature of your camera and it will fill in the foreground shadows and brighten people's faces.

9. *Sometimes shoot indoors without a flash.* But you must have a camera with a large enough aperture to do this. A flash flattens the image. It makes everything one-dimensional and your pictures will tend to look like everybody else's. If your baby is sleeping contentedly in the late afternoon light, open up the f-stop of the lens and shoot it without a flash. You have a better chance of actually capturing what you see. Plus, without a flash, it won't wake or startle him.

10. *Be ready.* In a typical family shot, it is usually the baby who is least ready to comply with the photographer's wishes. Or, if he does comply, it is only for a fleeting instant. Try waving a stuffed animal or a brightly colored toy with one hand, to get the baby to look and smile and react to you.

11. *Sometimes Grandma (or someone else) doesn't want her picture taken.* Compliment her on her looks. More important, reassure her of her importance to the photograph. The picture is a historic family record, and she needs to be in it.

12. *Shoot film.* The only way you are going to get better is if you shoot lots of pictures. This is usually not a problem for enthusiastic moms and dads photographing their first child.

Source: Kenneth Lee is a professional photographer whose work has appeared in Sports Illustrated, Outside, Runner's World, *and Germany's* Bunte *magazine. He has traveled on assignment to Asia and Europe. His photographs have appeared in group shows for Amnesty International and other organizations.*

WHAT CAMERA SHOULD I BUY?

There are two main types of cameras: 35mm single lens reflex (SLR) and automatic, or "point-and-shoot," cameras. There are advantages and disadvantages to both.

The point-and-shoot camera usually comes with a built-in flash and automatic focus. Like the single lens reflex, it is a 35mm camera, but it is simpler and far less sophisticated than the SLR. You essentially put the film in and take pictures. An excellent point-and-shoot camera is the Yashica T-4. The Canon T-115 is also excellent, though more expensive.

Point-and-shoot cameras are lightweight and portable. You can carry them in a jacket pocket. They're easy to operate. If all you want is a photographic record of your beautiful baby, a point-and-shoot may be perfect for you. You may want to own both an inexpensive point-and-shoot and an SLR, and use them according to the situation and your mood.

One of the problems with point-and-shoot cameras is that the auto-focus only activates in the middle of the viewfinder. This is the cause of more out of focus pictures than anything else. Say you are shooting a group of people but the camera's center bullseye is focused on the wall behind them. Nothing in the foreground will be in focus, and your photograph will be a truly inspiring one of a wall with some blurry characters in front of it.

One way to avoid this is to press the shutter release halfway down prior to taking the picture. Set the bullseye on your baby's face. Put the shutter halfway down, which automatically locks the focus. Keep it pressed down and then compose your picture any way you want before pressing the release all the way down to take the picture. This will ensure that that beautiful baby who looks so much like his father always remains in focus.

Professional photographers use and recommend the SLR cameras. They are more expensive than point-and-shoots. They are somewhat more inconvenient and bulkier and heavier. But once you get used to an SLR and learn how to use it, it will give you much better results.

You will see the difference in quality the moment you compare pictures from a point-and-shoot and an SLR. Many point-and-shoots have soft lenses. The picture won't be sharp, the colors will be washed out, and the image will be grainy. The SLRs have sharper lenses and the pictures have better contrast with less distortion.

An SLR gives you more control over how your picture will look. You can lighten or darken the image. You can open up the aperture and shoot an indoor shot without a flash, capturing the softer light and the image as you truly see it. The flash is detachable on an SLR and mounted on the camera. An SLR flash will shoot much farther—thirty to forty feet. A point-and-shoot flash extends only ten feet.

When you look through the viewfinder of an SLR, you get exactly what you see because you are looking through the lens. For the point-and-shoot, you are looking through a viewfinder that is often inaccurate. And when the viewfinder is inaccurate, that throws the framing of your picture off. Many people get back photos with the heads of their subjects cut off. They swear they didn't shoot them that way, and they're right. The framing for their point-and-shoot was wrong.

An SLR provides faster shutter speed—a potentially important attribute when shooting fidgeting, ever-moving babies. A baby's eyes can be open when you snap the picture, but because there's a lag on a point-and-shoot between the time you press the shutter release and when the shutter actually opens and closes, her eyes can rapidly close and that is the moment you will have saved for posterity.

An SLR will shoot far superior action photos. It advances faster, shooting two frames per second (depending on the camera) or five frames per second with a motordrive. The point-and-shoot advances at one frame per second.

Point-and-shoots are relatively fragile, compared to the rough-and-tumble durability of a high-quality SLR. SLRS can take a pretty good licking and still keep ticking.

SLR lenses provide more versatility. You can switch lenses depending on what you want to shoot and where. You can go from a big-canvass, wide-angle lens to a close-up telephoto. For those who don't want to switch lenses back and forth or invest a lot of money into specialized gear, manufacturers offer a single zoom lens that covers a broad range of uses; two examples: the Canon 28mm–80mm lens and Tamron's 28mm–200mm lens.

Canon's "Rebel" series is an excellent line of SLRS, starting in the $350 range. Nikon makes excellent SLRS, as well. Nikon and Canon make the best and most lenses. Pentax, Minolta, and Olympus are also worth looking into.

The best source of information for camera equipment is your local camera store. Many amateur photographers belong to camera clubs where they exchange tips, organize outings, and hold contests. Community college and adult education classes on photography are often useful, as well.

Tip: Kenneth Lee recommends Popular Photography *magazine (800-876-6636) as an excellent resource for beginning photographers.*

BIBLIOGRAPHY

Amidon, Elias, and Elizabeth Roberts, editors. *Earth Prayers*. San Francisco: Harper San Francisco, 1991.

Bernard, Susan. *The Mommy Guide*. Lincolnwood, IL: NTC/Contemporary, 1994.

Blankenhorn, David. *Fatherless America*. New York: HarperCollins Publishers, 1995.

Bly, Robert. *Iron John*. Reading, MA: Addison-Wesley Publishing Company, 1990.

Brott, Armin. *The Expectant Father: Facts, Tips, and Advice for Dads-to-Be*. New York: Abbeville Press, 1995.

———. *The New Father: A Dad's Guide to the First Year*. New York: Abbeville Press, 1997.

Campbell, Jeff. *Talking Dirt*. New York: Bantam Doubleday Dell Publishing Group, 1997.

Corwin, Donna. *The Time-Out Prescription*. Lincolnwood, IL: NTC/Contemporary, 1996.

Corwin, Donna, and James Varni. *Time Out for Toddlers*. New York: Berkeley Publishing Group, 1994.

Cosby, Bill. *Fatherhood*. New York: Berkley Publishing Group, 1986.

Cuthbertson, Joanne, and Susie Schevill. *Helping Your Child Sleep Through the Night*. New York: Doubleday, 1985.

DeFrancis, Beth. *The Parents Resource Almanac*. Holbrook, MA: Bob Adams Inc., 1994.

Dominguez, Joe, and Vicki Robin. *Your Money or Your Life: Transforming Your Relationship with Money and Achieving Financial Independence*. New York: Penguin Books, 1992.

Donavin, Denise Perry. *American Library Association Best of the Best for Children*. New York: Random House, 1992.

Faber, Adele, and Elaine Mazlish. *How to Talk So Kids Will Listen and Listen So Kids Will Talk*. New York: Avon Books, 1980.

Hass, Aaron. *The Gift of Fatherhood*. New York: Fireside Books, 1994.

Hendrix, Harville. *Getting the Love You Want: A Guide for Couples*. New York: Henry Holt and Co., 1988.

———. *Giving the Love That Heals: A Guide for Parents*. New York: Henry Holt and Co., 1997.

Levine, James, and Todd Pitinsky. *Working Fathers: New Strategies for Balancing Work and Family*. Reading, MA: Addison-Wesley Publishing Company, 1997.

Maguire, Jack. *Hopscotch, Hangman, Hot Potato and Ha Ha Ha: Rulebook of Children's Games*. New York: Prentice Hall Press, 1990.

Nelson, Kevin. *Pickle, Pepper and Tip-In, Too: Over 250 Sports Games and Activities for Children*. New York: Fireside, 1994.

Nilsson, Lennart. *A Child Is Born*. New York: Dell Publishing, 1993.

Pipher, Mary. *Reviving Ophelia: Saving the Selves of Adolescent Girls*. New York: Ballantine Books, 1994.

Polly, Jean Armour. *Internet Kids and Family Yellow Pages*, 2nd ed. Berkeley: Osborne/McGraw-Hill, 1997.

Price, Tom, and Susan Crites Price. *The Working Parents Help Book*. Princeton, NJ: Peterson's, 1996.

Quirk, Kevin. *Not Now Honey, I'm Watching the Game*. New York: Fireside Books, 1997.

Ray, David, and Judy Ray. *Fathers: A Collection of Poems*. New York: St. Martin's Press, 1997.

Saavedra, Beth Wilson. *Restoring Balance to a Mother's Busy Life*. Lincolnwood, IL: NTC/Contemporary, 1996.

Shapiro, Jerrold Lee. *The Measure of a Man: Becoming the Father You Wish Your Father Had Been*. New York: Perigee Books, 1993.

———. *When Men Are Pregnant: Needs and Concerns of Expectant Fathers*. New York: Dell Publishing, 1987.

Sherline, Reid, editor. *Love Anyhow: Famous Fathers Write to Their Children*. New York: Timken Publishers, 1994.

Thornton, James. *Chore Wars: How Households Can Share the Work and Keep the Peace*. Berkeley: Conari Press, 1997.

Trelease, Jim. *The Read-Aloud Handbook,* 4th ed. New York: Penguin Books, 1996.

INDEX

Action for Children's Television, 270

Adult-to-child ratio at child-care facility, 44

Adventuring with Children (Jeffrey), 295

Affairs, 16, 166

Afterbirth, 27

Agent, life insurance, 158

Agreement between partners, 92, 97, 98, 164–65, 187

Air bags, 32, 37–38

Aleph, Alliance for Jewish Renewal, 244

Allowance, 193–94

American Academy of Family Physicians, 125

American Academy of Pediatrics, 125

American Cat Fanciers' Association, 208

American Council of Life Insurance, 157

American Heart Association, 131

American Kennel Club, 210

American Society of CLU and CHFC, 158

American Sportfishing Association, 59

American Toy Institute, 284

Amniocentesis, 266

Annual Directory of Placement Agencies, 48–49

Appalachian Mountain Club, 59, 61

At Home Dad, 18

Automobiles. *See* Cars

Baby Book: Everything You Need to Know About Your Baby—from Birth to Age Two, The (W. Sears and M. Sears), 125

Baby Stuff: A No-Nonsense Shopping Guide for Every Parent's Lifestyle (A. Lipper and J. Lipper), 128

Backpacker, 58

Barbie, 280, 281

Baseball, 252

Basketball, 247–48

Bedwetting, 120

Best Places to Go (Jeffrey), 295

Bicycling, 53–55

Birth coach, 21–29

Books/magazines for children, 213–23

Boot Camp for Dads (program), 28

Borrowing for College, 232

Bottle-feeding, 115

Bowel movements, babies', 116

Boy Scouts of America, 61–62

Breast-feeding, 115, 267

Budget, family, 187–89, 194

Burn prevention, 131–32

Burping a baby, 116

Camcorders, 303–6

Cameras, 306–10

Camp Fire Boys and Girls, 62

Camping, 57–58

Canoe and Kayak, 56

Canoeing, 55–56

Car seats, 32, 35, 36–37

Careers, fathers', 136–52

Cars, 30–38

Catalogs, toy, 283

Cats and babies, 207–8

Center for Gender Peacemaking, 275, 277

Center for Music and Young Children, 110

Cesarean section, 26

Checkups, baby, 114–15

Cheerleading, 253

Child care and preschool, 39–51, 103

Child Care Aware, 41, 43, 49

Child Care Resource and Referral Agency, 49

Childhood Emergencies: What to Do, A Quick-Reference Guide, 133

Childproofing, 93, 128

Choosing a Financial Advisor, 191

Choosing the Mortgage That's Right for You, 203

Christian Sportsmen's Fellowship International, 241

Cigar Aficionado Buying Guide, 174

Cigars, 173-74

Circumcision, 117, 122-26

Clubs and outdoor activities, 52-64

Colds, preventing babies', 116

Colic, 117

College, saving for, 19, 177, 190, 224-32

Complete Dog Book for Kids, The, 210

Computers, 281, 286-89

Consumer Federation of America, 187

Consumer Reports Cars: The Essential Guide, 38

Consumers Car Club, 38

Container, partner as (theory), 162-63

Cooking and food, 65-75

Coping skills for fathers, 5-7

Couvade, 13

CPR, infant, 130-31

Creating a Budget, 191

Credit cards, 183-84, 189

Crib death. *See* Sudden Infant Death Syndrome

Cribs, 126-28

Crying, babies', 117

C-section. *See* Cesarean section

Custodial savings account, 226

Dad to Dad (organization), 17, 18

Daddy track, 142-44

Danny Foundation, The, 126, 128

Daycare. *See* Child care and preschool

Debt, getting out of, 182-85

Diaper rash, 118

Diapers, 76-82, 267

Diarrhea, in babies, 116

Directory of Youth Organizations (Erickson), 64

Disaster preparedness, 134-35

Discipline of children, 88-99

    need for agreement between partners about, 92, 97, 98

Dividends, reinvesting, 229

Dog Buyer's Education Kit, 210

Dogs and babies, 208-10

Dolls, 280

Doula, 26-27

Doulas of North America, 26-27

Downsizing father's career, 147-49

Dr. Spock's Baby and Child Care (Spock and Rothenberg), 125

Ear infections, 118

Earmarked savings account, 226-27

Edmund's Auto Guides, 38

Emergencies, household/family, 129-35

Empathetic listening, 162-63

Epidural, 26

Episiotomy, 27

Fainting during delivery, 10, 14, 23

Faith, importance of in family, 236-39

Family and Medical Leave Act, 141-42

Family Education Company, 270, 273

Family Vacation Guide, 293

Fatherhood as social role, 3-4

Fatherhood as spiritual journey, 234-36

Father's Almanac, The, (Sullivan), 286

Father's role in child-rearing, 2-5, 100-112

Fears, fathers'

    about exclusion from child's life, 15

    about fainting during delivery, 10, 14, 23

    about loss of partner, 15, 164

    about own mortality, 15

    about partner giving birth in car, 23

    about paternity of child, 14

    about providing for family, 14

Federal Emergency Management Authority, 135

Federal National Mortgage Association (Fannie Mae), 203

Fever, baby's, 118

Field Guide to Sport Utility Vehicles, Pickups, and Vans, 38

Financial aid for college, 190, 228

Financial planning, 181-95. *See also* College, saving for

Fire prevention, 133-34

First trimester, supporting Mom during, 261-62

First-aid kit, 132-33

Fishing, 58-59, 241

Football, 253

4-H clubs, 62-63

401(k) accounts, 188, 192, 230

403(b) accounts, 230

Future Fisherman Foundation, 59

Gardening, 284

Get a Life: You Don't Need a Million to Retire Well (Warner), 193

Girl Scouts of the USA, 63
Golf, 248-49
Guide to Baby Products, 128
Guinea pigs as pets, 211
Gymnastics, 249-50

Hamsters as pets, 211
Having another child, 178-80
Health, infant, 113-28
Hey! Listen to This: Stories to Read Aloud (Trelease), 217
Hiking, 59-61
Hockey, 250-51
Home Buyers' Vocabulary, 203
Home Office Computing, 152
Home ownership, 196-205
Home-buying checklist, 202-3
"Hooked on Fishing Not on Drugs" (program), 59
Hospital, what to bring for childbirth, 29
Houses of worship, attending with family, 239-41
Housework, 82-85
    division of, 77, 78-80
How to Buy a Home with a Low Down Payment, 203
HUD Homebuying Guide, 203

Immunizations, 118, 121
Indian Guides/Princesses. *See* Y-Indian Guides/Princesses
Individual Retirement Account (IRA), 192, 226, 231
Infant CPR, 130-31
In-laws, 174-76
Institute for American Values, 2, 5
Institute for Imago Relationship Therapy, 160, 163
Insurance, life, 153-58
    term, 153, 155-57, 189
    universal, 156
    variable, 156
    whole life/permanent, 155-57, 189
International Nanny Association, 48-49
Internet, 18-19. *See also* World Wide Web sites
Involvement with children, father's, 100-112
Is Your Crib Safe?, 128

Jealousy
    of baby, father's, 159, 164, 165
    of father, baby's, 159
Jewish Renewal (movement), 242, 244
Job, father's, 136-52
Juvenile Products Manufacturer's Association, 128, 284

Kelley's Blue Book, 38
Kid's Guide to Fishing, A, 241
Kidsnet, 273

League of American Bicyclists, 53-55
Let's Go Fishing Ministries, 241
Life insurance. *See* Insurance, life
Life Underwriters Association, 158
Lindsay Wildlife Museum, 211-12
Listening to children, 110-12
Listening to partner, 162-63, 168
Little League baseball, 22
Lovers for Life: Creating Lasting Passion, Trust, and True Partnership (Ellenberg), 164

Magazines, children's, 223
Making love. *See* Sex
Manipulation of adults, babies', 92
Masturbation, 166
Media, depiction of fathers in, 9-11
Meditations for Mothers of Toddlers (Saavedra), 269
Meditations for New Mothers (Saavedra), 268
Men's Rights, Inc., 9, 11
Minivans, 33, 34-35
Mom, supporting, 259-68
Mom-dominated environments, 17-18
Money issues, 177, 181-95. *See also* College, saving for
Money market accounts, 189
Money-saving tips, 185-86, 189-90
Morning sickness, 261, 262
Mother-in-law/father-in-law, 174-76
Mothers of Supertwins (MOST), 178
Music, family enjoyment of, 109-10
Mutual funds, 227, 229
Mylicon brand drops, 117

Names, baby, 171-73
Nannies, 48-49
National Association for Family Child Care, 47
National Association for the Education of Young Children (NAEYC), 44, 51
National Association of Child Care Resource and Referral Agencies, 49
National Association of 401(k) Investors, 192
National Child Care Information Center, 49
National Fire Protection Association, 124
National Foundation for Consumer Credit, 182, 185
National 4-H Council, 63
National Organization of Circumcision Information Resource Centers, 124

National Organization of Mothers of Twins Clubs, 178
New Father: A Dad's Guide to the First Year, A, (Brott), 101
New Father: A Dad's Guide to the Toddler Years, A, (Brott), 101
Night/weekend shifts at work, 139–40
Nolo's Will Book (Clifford), 190
Nurturing
    child, 3, 102, 104–7
    Mom, 3–4, 7, 259–68. *See also* Birth coach

Object permanence, 102–3
Open Road, 35
Opening the Door to a Home of Your Own, 203
Oppenheim Toy Portfolio, 282

Pacifiers, 119
Parenting styles, different, 16
Parents' Choice Foundation, 279, 282
Paternity leave, 141
Paying for College, 232
Pediatrician referral service, American Academy of Pediatrics', 125
Pension plans, 156, 192
Permanent insurance, 155–57, 189
Pets, 206–12
Photography, 306–10
Placenta. *See* Afterbirth
Planning for College, 191
Play
    father's role in, 2, 104
    tips for father-child, 107–9. *See also* Clubs and outdoor activities; Sports
Play pens, 109
Play Tennis America for Kids (program), 257
Poetry, reading to children, 220–22
Pop Warner Little Scholars, Inc., 253
Popular Mechanics: Annual New Car and Truck Buyers Guide, 38
Potty training, 120
Pregnancy
    supporting Mom during, 261–64
    unplanned, 12
Prepaid tuition plans, 232
Preparing Your Child for College: A Resource Book for Parents, 232
Pretend Soup and Other Real Recipes (Katzen and Henderson), 75

Projects, father/child, 284–86
Promise Keepers (movement), 236–39
Proud Fathers (program), 137, 139

Quicken (software), 187, 189

Rabbits as pets, 210
Raising Spiritual Children in a Material World (Catalfo), 236
Rats as pets, 210
Read All About It! (Trelease), 217
Reading aloud, 213–23
Religion. *See* Spirituality
Relocating family for father's job, 146
Restaurants, taking babies/children to, 71
Retirement, 156, 188, 190, 191–92, 228, 230
Right and wrong, children knowing, 93
Risks, taking, 7–9
Road Test Annual, 35

Safe and Sound Baby, 284
Safety
    bicycle, 54, 55
    camping, 58
    canoeing, 56
    in cars, 30–32, 36–38
    childproofing, 93, 128
    cooking, 75
    outdoors, during play, 52
    of toys, 282–84. *See also* Emergencies, household/family; Health, infant
Sallie Mae (formerly Student Loan Marketing Association), 232
Salmonella, 113–14
Savings account, child's, 194, 226–27
Savings bonds, 228, 230
Say No to Circumcision (Ritter and Denniston), 124
Seat belts, using during pregnancy, 37
Second trimester, supporting Mom during, 262–63
Separating work and home life, 140
Sex, 159–69, 263–64, 267
Shots. *See* Immunizations
Siblings, 176–80
Siblings Without Rivalry (Faber and Mazlish), 180
SIDS. *See* Sudden infant death syndrome
Sleep schedules, babies', 119, 121–22
Small business, running, 149–50
Soccer, 254–55
Social Security, payments to retirees, 192

Software, children's, 288–89

Solid foods, for babies, 119

Solve Your Child's Sleep Problems (Ferber), 121

Sonogram. *See* Ultrasound

Spanking, 94–96

Spirituality, 233–44

Spitting up, 116

Sport utility vehicles, 32, 33–34

Sports, 245–58

    on television, 275–77. *See also* Clubs and outdoor
        activities

Station wagons, 32–33, 35–36

Sudden infant death syndrome, 125

Sudden Infant Death Syndrome Alliance, 125

Summer on Ice hockey camps, 250, 251

Support groups, 5, 18, 164–65, 167

Supporting Mom, 3–4, 7, 259–68. *See also* Birth Coach

Swimming, 255–56

Sympathy pains, 13, 261

Tantrums, 96

Television, 269–77

Temperature, taking baby's, 120

Tennis, 257–58

Term insurance, 153, 155–57, 189

Texas Tomorrow Fund, 232

Thermometers, 120

Third trimester, supporting Mom during, 263–64

Time off after birth of baby, for fathers, 141

Time-outs, 95, 96, 97

Toilet training, 120

TOUGHLOVE approach to discipline, 98–99

TOUGHLOVE International, Inc., 98–99

Toy guns, 279, 281

Toys, 278–84

Toys and Play, 284

Transporting the baby, 85–87

Travel, business, 143–44, 297–300

Travel, leisure, 290–97

Triplet Connection, 178

Truck and Van Buyer's Guide, 35

Twins, raising, 176–78

Ultrasound, 264–66

Umbilical cord, cutting, 27, 28

Uniform Transfer to Minors/Uniform Gift to Minors.
    See Custodial savings account

United States Golf Association, 248, 249

United States Tennis Association, 257–58

United States Youth Soccer Association, 254, 255

Universal life insurance, 156

U.S. Swimming (governing body), 256

Usa Gymnastics, 249, 250

Usta Junior Team Tennis, 257, 258

Usta/National Junior Tennis League, 257–58

Usta/National Tennis League, 257

Vacations. *See* Travel, leisure

Vaccinations, 118, 121

Values, transmitting to children, 161, 195, 241–44

Variable life insurance, 156

Video, home, 302–6

What Not to Name Your Baby (Meisler and Rey),
    172

What the Hell Do Women Really Want? (Clark),
    165

What to Expect the First Year (Eisenberg, Murkoff,
    and Hathaway), 125

Whole life/permanent insurance, 155, 157, 189

Wills, 189–90

Working at home, 150–52

World Wide Web sites

    for children's software information, 289

    for fathers/families, 20

    travel-related, 20

Y-Indian Guides/Princesses, 63–64

Y-Indian Papooses, 63–64

*Your Child from Two to Five Years: A Comprehensive
    Guide to Toys*, 279

*Your Next Fifty Years: A Completely New Way to Look
    at How, When, and If You Should Retire* (Wall and
    Collins), 193

Youth organizations and clubs, 61–64

ABOUT THE AUTHOR

KEVIN NELSON is a journalist and the author of twelve books. *The Daddy Guide* is his first book about being a father. He is the father of Annie and Leah and lives with his wife, Jennifer Kaiser, near San Francisco. They are expecting a baby.